FRENCH COMMUNISM

RONALD TIERSKY

FRENCH COMMUNISM, 1920 - 1972

Columbia University Press

New York & London   1974

*This book is sponsored by the Research Institute
on Communist Affairs, Columbia University*

LIBRARY OF CONGRESS CATALOGING IN PUBLICATION DATA

TIERSKY, RONALD, 1944–
    FRENCH COMMUNISM, 1920–1972.
    BIBLIOGRAPHY: P.
      1. PARTI COMMUNISTE FRANÇAIS—HISTORY.
I. TITLE. JN3007.C6T57   329.9'44   74-921
ISBN 0-231-03754-6

For Evelyne

"Qui t'a fait Comte?" demande Hugues Capet.

"Qui t'a fait roi?" lui répond Adalbert de Périgord.

(Probably Apocryphal)

PREFACE

This book is a somewhat revised version of a work that first was published in translation in France during a four-year residence there, 1969–73.[1] While most of the revisions have to do with editing and clarification, a few are corrections or additions of fact, and one section as a whole, which appeared previously in a conclusion relevant to the landmark general elections of March 1973, is now placed at the end of chapter 8.

It may be useful to note also that the English manuscript was almost completely prepared at the moment of the tragic events in Chile that began September 11, 1973. The connection between those events and this work will be readily apparent to those who have followed French and Italian politics in recent years. However, other than revising several remarks in the text and notes to take account of the coup d'état, I have made no new changes in the book. It is too soon to say what relation will obtain between the Chilean case and the French case regarding the strategy of Left-wing alliance and "peaceful transition to socialism."

The goal of the analysis of French communism in this book is double. On the broadest level I intend it as a study of how, and to what extent, both the legitimacy of public authority and the organization of society are still fundamentally problematic in France. To focus on the French Communist movement seems to me empirically the most fruitful perspective on this general question.

Given this perhaps unexpected statement of intent, it may be interesting to note that this book is one of a generation that had a genesis in the crisis events of 1968. I was a graduate student at Co-

[1] *Le mouvement communiste en France, 1920–1972* (Paris: Fayard, 1973).

lumbia University when the great conflicts over civil rights and, in a more immediate sense, the Vietnam War developed into a social explosion in April of that year. In the crystallization of political understandings and perspectives provoked ineluctably by crisis, surely I was not alone among my contemporaries—whose earliest political memories were etched during the Eisenhower years—to comprehend at that point, for the first time really, that the established order of government in America was not as a matter of course permanent and immutable. I and my generation were able then for the first time to understand viscerally the justification for distinguishing between government—in the curious American usage, the "Administration"—and regime. We all comprehended viscerally, no matter our opinions, what rebellion and even perhaps revolution might be like. One month later came the "events of May" in France, a country in which the specificity of the term "regime" is no more than self-evident. On its broadest level, then, the conception of this study was thus born out of a desire both to comprehend more deeply the problem of legitimacy in its most evocative Western setting and, therein, to gain perspective on my own society.

Yet the book is also a "case study" of a communist movement in opposition, and on a second level its goal is to provide a theoretical explanation of the phenomenon of French communism itself, and of its relation to French politics and society. The model is drawn explicitly in chapter 12. Between this page and that chapter the book is undoubtedly overly long, presenting first a political history of the movement and then an analysis of the four dominant roles the movement plays in French life. However, I was persuaded that the political history was valuable for two reasons. First, there is no history of French communism in English. Second, the French histories themselves are not adequate to scholarly purposes, in that they are either mainly anecdotal or polemical. In any case, all are now dated.

As any such exercise must be, the model presented in chapter 12 is an oversimplification. It does not adequately reflect the complex phenomena encountered in the pages which precede it. My intention was to conclude with a unified statement of the problem, to obtain comment and criticism, and to provoke others and myself to further understanding.

A first book is in a special sense a monument to one's teachers, and my debts are broad and deep.

Above all I wish to thank Professors Annie Kriegel and Raymond Aron. They alone will recognize the extent to which this work is a product of their criticism, collaboration, and example. Were Philip Mosely still alive, he would also, I may hope, have recognized the degree to which his concerns and his integrity have inspired my efforts, even where I have drawn different conclusions than he might have. And although the influence of Henry Simon Bloch on this book was quite indirect, I want to record here my gratitude for his counsel at a turning point in the development of my ideas. Finally, for their help, comments, and criticisms I wish to thank especially Mark Kesselman, Sidney Tarrow (in particular for his criticisms of chapter 12), Donald L. M. Blackmer, Georges Lavau, Jean Ranger, and Louis Bodin. Of course, the responsibility for errors and misinterpretations is my own. For their editorial help I would like to thank Mr. Leslie Bialler of Columbia University Press and M. André Chassigneux, my French translator.

AMHERST, MASSACHUSETTS
MARCH 28, 1974

CONTENTS

TABLES

FIGURES

FRENCH COMMUNISM

INTRODUCTION

The moment is both opportune and propitious for a general study of the French Communist Party.

The moment is opportune because various transformations of the national and international order indicate a decisive alteration in the conflict between communists and noncommunists that first ruptured the structure of previous political oppositions more than a half-century ago. The political effects of economic and social change, as well as the continuing realignment of political forces themselves in France—and between East, West, and the Third World—have created a new environment in which the traditional forms of French Communist thought and action have been constrained more than ever toward change and innovation. The problem posed to the political analyst is first to identify the points of departure and then to investigate the nature and limits of these transformations.

The moment is propitious because both the movement to de-Stalinization in the Soviet camp and the Sino-Soviet conflict have directly or indirectly given impetus to new research undertakings on the communist movement in France. Some of these have merely deepened our knowledge of previously explored terrains, while a few have branched off into previously dark areas of conception and data. Enough of these often striking and enriching investigations exist now to prompt an attempt, however modest, at a global view.

For the better part of fifty years after its bolshevization, the persistent solidarity and resilience of communism in France has been one of the major facts of French political life. To many of its opponents, the existence of a large communist party, flanked by a redoubtable communist-dominated labor union and other important ancillary organizations, has been a result of the "unfinished" Revolution of 1789 and its

tributary shocks since that time. To the communists themselves, however, this "success" is only a partial victory, for while the functioning
and legitimacy of the established order has been rendered perennially
problematic, the millenarian hope of replacing parliamentary democracy with proletarian democracy has not proved capable of fulfillment. The French Communist Party, unlike its Russian Bolshevik
model, has not found it possible to realize the "unity of theory and
practice" in a revolutionary situation.

Today, after more than fifty years, the PCF still claims to be pursuing a "socialist revolution." On June 27, 1972, the French Communist
leadership signed a "Common Program of Government" with the
French socialist leaders, the avowed goal of which is to "open the road
to socialism." Yet in May–June 1968, in the midst of the most widespread popular protest movement and general strike ever seen in
France, the PCF first opposed itself to the *gauchiste*-led student movement, which had touched off the explosion, and then refused to exploit the general strike which followed toward an insurrection. In
May–June 1968 the French Communist Party demonstrated emphat-
ically that, in the absence of some dramatic and unforseeable change
in the balance of political and military forces, a communist-led revolutionary *prise de pouvoir* would not be attempted.

On the following pages we shall examine the significance of this no
longer controversial assertion and the fundamental questions that
derive from it: Has the French Communist Party ceased completely to
challenge the established order? Has communism in France now been
integrated as a perennial protest movement—but nothing more—
within the status quo? Has the PCF "changed," or merely "shifted"
the nature of its relations with French politics and society? Have we
witnessed the transformation of French and West European communism, and, if so, what has the movement become? These interroga-
tions shall be a point of constant reference in this study of communism in France from the moment when the posing of the famous
"Twenty-One Conditions" first split communism from French social
democracy in December 1920.

On one level, this work is a study of the political "faces," or roles,
of the French Communist movement itself. Previous literature has not

generally attempted to deal with the entire history of the phenomenon. Instead, most writers have limited themselves to a particular
period, such as the Popular Front, or to a particular theme, such as
the relation of the Party and French intellectuals. While such works
have for the most part achieved their stated purposes, they have unfortunately tended to transform the particular into the general, while
overlooking one of the primary characteristics of Marxist-Leninist
movements: their great variety of forms and tactics at different places
and times. There exist, to be sure, a few general histories of the communist movement in France (the Bibliography lists them), written by
Frenchmen themselves; but on the whole these have respected somewhat too much the often obscure boundary between history and political science, and so have left insufficiently examined the subject of the
present volume, while on the other hand these have not respected
enough the line separating partisan from observer.[1] It should be added
immediately, however, that even in attempting to deal with all the
fifty-odd years of French communism, I do not make the exaggerated
claim that the following is a general comprehensive history of the
movement: too much of fundamental importance will not even be
touched on. I shall not, for example, be much concerned with the
social bases of the Party and its ancillaries: [2] nor shall I try to deal in
detail with the intra-Party controversies, or the disputes that have involved the Party and the intellectual corona surrounding it.[3] Likewise,
although the influence of the Soviet Communist Party on the PCF is a
theme which appears constantly throughout the analysis, a detailed
study of French Communism in relation to the international movement must be sought elsewhere.[4] And finally, those who may have a

[1] Jacques Fauvet, *Histoire du Parti communiste français* is in any case the most complete
and useful of these.

[2] A standard work for many years will undoubtedly be *Les communistes français* by Annie
Kriegel, translated as *The French Communists*. Also very helpful is Charles Micaud, *Communism and the French Left*.

[3] Three very readable studies giving much useful information on these subjects are
David Caute, *Communism and the French Intellectuals*; Raymond Aron, *L'opium des intellectuels*; and George Lichtheim *Marxism in Modern France*.

[4] A helpful compendium is François Fejtö, *The French Communist Party and the Crisis of
International Communism*. On the Italian Communist Party (PCI) see Donald Blackmer,
Unity in Diversity: Italian Communism and the Communist World.

particular interest in the foreign and colonial policies of the PCF will be undoubtedly disappointed by my preoccupations, above all in regard to the destinies of Indochina and Algeria.[5]

In an immediate sense the present work focuses specifically on the dominant political roles developed by the PCF in its search for power. A second and broader aim is to conceptualize and clarify the relationship between a communist movement of opposition and a liberal political regime. Because the rupture in world politics stemming from the Bolshevik Revolution is in the process of a new and apparently fundamental mutation, therefore, a priori, the French Communist Party provokes considerable interest and assumes new importance with reference both to the future of politics in the West European context—in particular as the European Economic Community expands and integrates more closely—and to the future of East-West relations in general. The point of departure for this aspect of the work is the assertion that the relationship between the French Communist movement and the established order has been characterized from the beginning by structural ambivalence. That is to say, it has been based on duality resulting not from tactical or temporal considerations, but rather from the fundamentally equivocal nature of Marxist-Leninist doctrine and strategy regarding presocialist and nonrevolutionary situations. In these "routine" times, the communist perspective both accepts and rejects the established order. In a liberal "bourgeois" regime and society, for example, a communist movement attempts, in Annie Kriegel's terms, to act simultaneously "within" and "without" the legitimized exercise of power and authority, in an attempt to make successful the apparently paradoxical roles of a reform-seeking and a revolutionary political force. This most fundamental aspect of communism in opposition, argued schematically in chapter 1, has underlain the frustration experienced by the noncommunist parties in their relations with the PCF, as well as much of the frustration of political analysts, who, in their search for an unambiguous interpreta-

---

[5] There is no published scholarly study of these questions. However one may usefully consult the collection of texts and the Trotskyite commentaries in Jacob Moneta, *Le PCF et la question coloniale, 1920–1965* (Paris: F. Maspero, 1972), 311 pp. On the PCF role in the French Indochina involvement, there is much information in Jacques Doyon, *Les soldats blancs de Ho Chi Minh* (Paris: Fayard, 1973), 521 pp.

tion, have often adopted a summary view, which amounts to an arbitrary conclusion that the PCF is either a revolutionary totalitarian party or a revolutionary party gone reformist. The evidence demands a more complex interpretation.

This last comment brings us to a third consideration of this study, the attempt to construct a model. For many years communist parties were viewed almost uniquely from the point of view of their opposition to liberal democracy, their strategy of revolution, and their espousal of the Soviet example as the form of society corresponding to the notion of proletarian socialist democracy. This was the conception formulated in Philip Selznick's classic study of *The Organizational Weapon* (1952), for example. The work of Maurice Duverger and Hadley Cantril in the 1950s began to bring out other aspects of communist movements, which had up to that point received but scant attention. In his seminal book on *Les partis politiques* (1951) Duverger insisted on the totalitarian party model, to be sure, but he also took pains to describe the broad range of nonrevolutionary practices tending to create a communist existence remarkably total and separate from the established society: a banal daily life within the communist movement, which had developed as a function of the Party's vanguard role itself. Through the use of an in-depth interview research program, Cantril's *The Politics of Despair* (1958) highlighted another aspect of communist opposition. This examination of the communist electorates in France and Italy, quite unusual at the time although now somewhat dated, concluded that a significant percentage of the communist vote is won from a group of electors seeking to "protest," even while they have little or no sympathy with communist goals or methods. This type of argument was particularly salutory in that it identified the failure of the "system" to satisfy mass needs as one of the root bases of communist support—a necessary balance to the simplistic view that postulated invidious infiltration and international conspiracy as cause of the otherwise unexplainable Marxist-Leninist electoral success.

Recent work by Annie Kriegel and Georges Lavau on the French communists and by Sidney Tarrow on the Italian communists has enabled us to progress still further in our comprehension of the diverse "faces"—sometimes quite unexpected—that Marxism-Leninism has assumed in Western Europe. Annie Kriegel has emphasized the dual and fundamentally ambiguous effect of communist opposition, and has developed her conception of the French communist "counter-society," which I think might better be called a "countercommunity." In another direction, Georges Lavau has reexamined the "protest" and other appeals of the communist movement to noncommunists, and has developed an analysis of what he has fruitfully termed the "tribune function" of communism in France. In regard to the PCI, Sidney Tarrow has underlined and deepened our understanding of the remarkable differences between urban and rural communism in Western Europe (in Italy essentially reflected in the North-South cleavage), and has demonstrated the very particular character of the way the PCI functions in the Mezzogiorno.[6]

And finally, recent and contemporary changes in doctrine and strategy by the nonruling communist parties themselves have provoked a general reconsideration of the vanguard party model, which until not long ago was the least controversial aspect of communist movements in that its position as the raison d'être of all communist activities was not disputed.

Doctrine, Strategy, and Tactics in French Communism

Part One of this study examines the historical development of the communist movement in France within a periodization corresponding to *les grands tournants:* each of the six periods are defined according to the particular tenor of the dominant political tactic pursued by the PCF at the time. Regarding the entire experience of French Communism as the subject of analysis permits one to place the tactical zigzags into a broad perspective. It is this perspective which leads to the conclusion that, however large or severe these tactical changes may have been, the characteristically dual and ambivalent nature of

---

[6] See Kriegel, *Communistes français*, and Michelle Perrot and Annie Kriegel, *Le socialisme français et le pouvoir;* Georges Lavau, "Le Parti communiste dans le système politique français," in Frédéric Bon et al., *Le communisme en France;* and Sidney Tarrow, *Peasant Communism in Southern Italy* and "Political Dualism and Italian Communism," *American Political Science Review* 61, no. 1 (March 1967): 39–53.

Marxist-Leninist opposition in a liberal parliamentary democracy has not been altered, and that the effect of French Communist activity—except in near-limiting cases such as 1939–41 (see chapter 4)—has been consistently ambiguous when evaluated as a whole.[7] The general argument of Part One is therefore that what has remained fundamental to the nature of communist opposition in France are its ambivalent strategic perspective and its ambiguous aggregate effect. What has been temporary are the ambivalent zigzags in tactics, however violent. This includes even the most radical zigzags: the Popular Front tactic of 1934–38 does not, for example, imply either a doctrinal or strategic denial of the increasingly sectarian tactics of 1924–32, just as the period of radical cleavage 1939–41 does not invalidate the Popular Front. Similarly, the Cold War tactics of 1947–62 do not contradict the second period of reintegration 1941–47, nor does the period of third reintegration after 1962 contradict its antecedent. All of these tremendous alterations in tactics have reflected temporary emphasis on one of the two poles of Marxist-Leninist strategy: cooperation and radical opposition. Or, to put it another way and anticipate the following pages somewhat, the grand tactical zigzags of the communist movement in France have reflected an emphasis on either the minimum or maximum program, determined by both the domestic political situation and, more importantly, the general interest of international communism, defined by the French Communists in the past as the interest of Soviet foreign policy.

Part Two of this study seeks to explain in another way in what sense the French Communist Party has evolved and in what sense it has altered. I have suggested a quadrapartite role model of the movement to demonstrate how the Communists have implemented the strategy of situating themselves simultaneously within and without the established order while waiting for the ever-elusive revolutionary situation. The classic role of *revolutionary vanguard* and its hard-line counterpart, the role of *countercommunity*, are apposed to the moderate and collaborative roles of *popular tribune* and *government party*. The

---

[7] The key terms "ambivalence" and "ambiguity" are used in the following senses in this analysis. Ambivalence is to be understood as contradictory or opposed attitudes or behaviors in an individual or structure (e.g. the PCF). Ambiguity is to be understood as the equivocation manifested by these attitudes or behaviors considered as a whole.

former two are located near the "hard" or radical opposition pole of strategy, while the latter two are placed near the "soft" or moderate strategic node. In chapter 12 the entire model is developed out of the historical and structural analysis presented previously, and the "contradictions" between the many faces of French Communism are developed conceptually and several lines of further research are indicated.

Finally, throughout the study, an attempt is made to weigh the continuing influence of the original Bolshevik example and the Soviet experience. Part Two (especially chapters 8 and 12) analyzes recent developments to address the question of whether, or more precisely, the extent to which the French Communist Party after a half century has repudiated its heritage.

At bottom, this study of communist opposition in a liberal Western-style polity becomes a study of the eternal problem of legitimacy —who rules who, and on what basis or by what right. The French state has endured many challenges to its nature in modern times, but few would contest that the French Communist Party has led the most persistent, organized, and focused movement of fundamental opposition to the status quo.

Both communists and noncommunists lay claim to one of the two major doctrines that purport to define democratic legitimacy. On the one hand, the liberal tradition, descending from Montesquieu and the English liberals of the eighteenth century, has emphasized a separation and balance of power in the state, based on the calculation that without structural opposition tyranny in some form or other is rendered almost inevitable. In a sense this may be said to be the underlying rationale and justification of the competitive party systems that developed in the nineteenth century in Europe and North America, and that have come to be identified with liberal democracy. On the other hand, the Jacobin tradition is founded not on the conception of internal structural opposition as a necessary counterweight to tyranny, but rather upon the idea of the will of the people as the basis of democratic government. From Robespierre on, it has been possible through invocation of the *volonté du peuple* to call dictatorship democracy, for if there is a single "will of the people" to be implemented, the representative of this unified will is justified in ruling against all opposition—that is, his dictatorship is on a purely logical level both democratic and legitimate.

The differences between liberal and Jacobin conceptions of democracy were manifested in historic divergences in the development of Marxism and its heritor movements. Marx considered that until the end of "prehistory," the time of the establishment of a communist society in which neither the state nor politics exist, political progress would be marked by the extension of democracy. Himself a heritor of the liberal tradition, and despite his condemnation of it as the ultimate solution, Marx wrote forcefully that bourgeois society was a revolutionary advance over the totally antidemocratic politics of feudal society. Nonetheless, he argued that, in bourgeois society, universal suffrage and representative institutions would never be able to overcome the class exploitation of the proletariat and peasantry inevitably characteristic of the capitalist mode of production. In short, as Raymond Aron has said, Marx did not want to eliminate bourgeois democracy, but rather to "surpass" it, fulfilling the promises of liberalism in a society without classes.

The development of a single-party dictatorship under Lenin and Stalin was not predictable from the tenets of classical Marxism. However this may be, in identifying the Marxist-Leninist parties alone with the authentic "will of the people," the Russian Bolsheviks consecrated the Jacobin notion of democratic dictatorship as the essence of what Marx had called the "dictatorship of the proletariat." Moreover, in developing the theory of the Soviet Communist Party as the "vanguard of the vanguards," the Jacobin conception was rendered essential to the Stalinist perspective on the level of the international communist movement as well.

The argument (if such a term may be permitted) between Communists and non-Communists, in France as elsewhere, has reflected the dual heritage of democratic doctrine and the profound disagreement as to the authentically legitimate form of the democratic state. Regarding France, where conflict between Communists, socialists, and liberals has been exceptionally intense, any study of the Communist movement must in the end reproduce this controversy. And one's interest in French communism is all the greater in that the electoral weight of the united French Left in 1967 and 1973, and the victory of the Popular Unity coalition in Chile in 1970 and 1973 (and now its demise in 1973 as well) have demonstrated that under certain conditions it is perfectly conceivable that a Marxist alliance including a strong communist party be chosen by a Western people in free elections. The coup d'état in Chile, ending that experiment in peaceful efforts to move from one structure of society to another, has moreover served to underscore both the difficulties and temptations in the strategy of the West European communist parties. In France, as late as the spring of 1972 few observers seemed to believe the Left parties would unite on a governmental program. The signature of the Communist-socialist Common Program on June 27 of that year, combined with controversial opinion polls and speculations on the franc, thereupon provoked vigorous reactions against this new alliance of liberal and Jacobin Marxists. And although the electoral system rendered improbable a victory of the French Left in the elections of March 1973, the hypothesis seems now to be one of the dominant conditions of French political life.

Would such an occurrence constitute a victory or a defeat for the French Communist revolutionary ambition? One of the purposes of this book will be to demonstrate the equivocation in the question itself.

Part One

LES GRANDS TOURNANTS

Chapter One

A MIXED HERITAGE: JAURÈS, MARX, LENIN, STALIN

As a consequence of its adherence to the Comintern, or Third International, the French Communist Party took up the difficult task of grafting Bolshevik theory and practice onto the several powerful and often contradictory traditions of indigenous French socialism. This complex branch of European socialist doctrine and practice, which under the influence of Jules Guesde and Jean Jaurès had become dominantly Marxist (Marx himself had drawn up the program of Guesde's *Parti ouvrier français* in 1880), had at the same time progressively developed an *attentiste* view of its own role in the hoped-for revolution. Drawn under the doctrinal umbrella of the German Social Democratic Party and its leading figure, Karl Kautsky, the "pope" of the Second International, the French socialists by the outbreak of World War I had turned away from a conception of the revolutionary situation as mass insurrection to an evolutionary and parliamentary—though not entirely gradualist—view of the socialist advent.

During the decade preceding the War, after the 1905 unification of various socialist groups into the *Section française de l'Internationale ouvrière* (SFIO), Jean Jaurès came increasingly to dominate socialist thought in France, particularly as the strong anarcho-syndicalist current in the *Confédération générale du travail* (CGT) began to weaken decisively during the first years of the twentieth century. While Jaurès did not exclude either violent methods or the general strike, he advocated a doctrine of "revolutionary evolution," in which universal suffrage, a "revolutionary legalism," would eventually press the capitalist class to the point at which it would be forced to violate its own legal structure to perpetuate its domination over the working class. Then, after an inevitable and decisive period of more or less aggravated mass struggle, the bourgeoisie would be constrained to cede effective economic and political power to the proletariat: "in the end, in capitalist society universal suffrage plays a revolutionary role. Because, in the first place, it is in absolute contradiction with the capitalist hierarchy. The salaried worker has no power to rule in the factory; yet he is admitted, with the same title and so the same degree as the large owner, to direct the affairs of the nation." [1]

As was the case of European socialism in general, the French socialists in the prewar period had taken little notice of Bolshevism, which at the time was merely a peripheral tributary of the Second International mainstream, and whose advocates were a small group of Russian exiles meeting in the cafés of Berlin, Paris, Vienna, and London. At the outbreak of World War I, the French socialists, like the European socialists at large, rallied to their separate national "bourgeois" regime, and Jules Guesde himself accepted the portfolio of Minister of State in the *Union sacrée* which went to war against the German Reich. In the process of taking up arms against their supposed brothers in the German socialist movement, the French socialists demonstrated that "international workers' solidarity" was little more than a myth. [2]

Flushed with victory at the War's end, both the leaders and the followers of French socialism wanted to believe that a revolution by parliamentary methods was near at hand. Yet in the elections of November 1919 the SFIO achieved only a limited success (more votes but a decline from 103 to 68 deputies), and in the spring of 1920 the utopian quality of anarcho-syndicalist conceptions was demonstrated in the failure of a broad strike wave to develop into mass insurrection. It was at this point that a majority of the SFIO delegates to the Con-

---

[1] Cited in Michelle Perrot and Annie Kriegel, *Le socialisme français et le pouvoir*, p. 62, from Jaurès, "Le socialisme français," *Cosmopolis*, January 25, 1898, p. 118. See also Jaurès, *L'armée nouvelle* (1910), for his most complete statement of doctrine, and the very worthwhile biography by Harvey Goldberg, *The Life of Jean Jaurès*, which, in tracing the evolution of Jauressian thought, points up its incomplete character and lack of what might be termed Marxian "rigor."

[2] Only a few French anarcho-syndicalists made their way to the Zimmerwald Conference of September 1915, at which a small group of unflagging internationalists—Lenin, Trotsky and 36 others—issued the Zimmerwald Manifesto condemning both the war and the Social Democrat betrayal of the Second International principles. Jean Jaurès was assassinated by a Right-wing fanatic just before hostilities broke out, and by the War's end Léon Blum had taken his place as the leading figure in the SFIO.

gress of Tours in December 1920—disillusioned by the bankruptcy of both the Jauressian and anarcho-syndicalist strategies—decided to opt for adhesion to the Third International, therein creating the *Section française de l'Internationale communiste* (SFIC), which took the name *Parti communiste français* (PCF) in October 1921 to conform with Comintern instructions.[3]

Before we analyze the bolshevization of French Communism, let us examine briefly the dual core of the model that appeared to confront Jauressian socialism: the doctrine and practice of prerevolutionary Bolshevism, and the "dictatorship of the proletariat" as it was presented for the first time in history in the figure of the Soviet regime.

The Model of a Communist Movement as Opposition

One of the most fundamental characteristics of Marxist-Leninist doctrine and strategy concerning the prerevolutionary phase is duality and ambivalence; and although this assertion may at first seem surprising, a brief reflection reveals that this was implicit from the very beginning.

Let us consider Marx's theory of history. Writing at a time when industrial capitalism was only in the process of emerging as the dominant form of economic organization in Europe and when liberal or "bourgeois" democracy (which Marx saw as the most likely political system of a developed industrial capitalist state) had not yet established itself either, Marx called for a socialist revolution based on the proletariat. Marx pictured this call to revolution as the second step in the unfolding of the historical epoch, the first step of which had still to be consolidated. In other words, the Marxists, like nearly all nineteenth-century European socialists, believed that a bourgeois revolution would have to be undertaken and completed before the proletarian revolution could become possible.

The Marxist historical perspective was thus permeated with a dual and equivocal view of the value or justification of bourgeois capitalist

---

[3] See Annie Kriegel, *Aux origines du communisme français*, esp. pp. 426–39.

society and the parliamentary republic. The liberal bourgeois stage
was taken to be a necessary prerequisite to "higher" forms of human
organization, yet this was not a statement of its legitimacy in the tradition of classical political philosophy. In contrast to the latter, Marx
did not pose the question of what was the most legitimate polity.
He merely affirmed that the bourgeois regime, like all regimes, was
necessary and inevitable at a given moment in order for the course of
history, activated by the dialectical pressure of the class struggle, to
pursue its end. Nor was the Marxist view in this regard compatible
with the work of Max Weber, from whom the present conception of
legitimacy is largely derived. While Weber also avoided asking *in ab-
stracto* what was the nature of the most legitimate regime, he nonetheless affirmed that legitimacy was a fundamental characteristic of the
state and went on to define its ideal-type forms and sources. To a
Marxist, who believes that the foundation of the nonsocialist state is
naked force, the posing of such a question in all societies before the
classless society on a theoretical level is banal, or worse, an ideological
"mystification" of the class struggle.[4] In the Marxist view, then, all
regimes are justified (or "legitimate") insofar as they exist in fact or
will be necessary at a later time to serve toward the end of establishing
a classless society. An established order finds its partial and temporary
justification precisely in the impossibility of immediate revolution,
and in another sense in the historically inevitable contribution which
it brings to the fomentation of revolutionary conditions. The Marxist
attitude toward the existing order was thus compatible with two conceptions of socialist action: a first based on a judgment that the revolution was not imminent or that it would come only gradually (this
became the dominant Social Democratic view), and a second based on
a more immediate and brutal view of the revolutionary transformation
(this was the view of the extreme wing of the Social Democratic
movement, in particular of the Bolsheviks). Both the evolutionary and
insurrectionary conceptions of the socialist revolution, however, re-

[4] Nonetheless, Marx and Lenin spoke in another sense of the "legitimacy" of the
workers' struggle, at times in a moralizing departure from their "scientific" theory, at
times in the sense of historical "necessity." Moreover, when General de Gaulle invoked
the "destiny of France" or of his historical role to legitimize his action during the war
and again in 1958, the French Communists sometimes sought to use the vocabulary of
legitimacy as a tactical weapon. See pp. 229–231 below.

tained the dual theoretical perspective as to the justification of the existing order. The difference between them referred to the strategy necessary to "resolve the contradiction," that is, to when and how the revolution would occur or be made.

In strategic terms, this equivocal attitude toward the status quo was translated into what became known as the minimum and maximum programs: a program of immediate reforms and a revolutionary program. The programs were to be pursued by the Marxists simultaneously. The establishment of this dual mini-maxi strategy was crucial to the inheritence of twentieth-century socialist and communist parties, for, in effect, it condemned them to a perpetually equivocal position tactically as well as vis-à-vis any nonsocialist regime: they were to struggle at once for "partial gains" and for the "success" of the regime (in the Marxist sense of creating the conditions for its own revolution), and also for the revolution itself. Condemned to being neither totally revolutionary nor totally nonrevolutionary, the Marxist mentality was rendered permanently schizophrenic toward nonsocialist societies.

Leninism, while transforming classical Marxism in important ways, retained the dual perspective toward presocialist regimes, in particular toward "bourgeois" capitalism and liberal parliamentary politics. Operating in the "prebourgeois" context of Czarist Russia, Lenin retained, until the Revolution itself, the conviction that a period of capitalist expansion would necessarily have to precede a socialist revolution. Thus, the Bolsheviks, still keeping in mind the long-range goal of socialism, saw themselves in a more immediate sense as seeking to lead a bourgeois revolution, since the Russian bourgeoisie was thought incapable of achieving the task. Added to this dualistic doctrinal perspective was a version of the mini-maxi strategy: on the one hand, the Leninist conception assigned the trade unions the role of winning immediate gains to rally the working class and to act therein as a conveyor belt into the revolutionary movement, while the Party would seek to develop revolutionary consciousness and to prepare for a revolutionary situation. Yet, on the other hand, even the Party itself was to engage in some forms of partial collaboration with the established order, such as making the greatest possible use of parliamentary and other legal channels. This was the lesson of the 1907 controversy in

which, after the Czarist regime had decimated the socialist groups following the failure of the 1905 revolt, the latter split into two opinions: the so-called "liquidators"—who wanted to abandon the clandestine struggle in favor of legal tactics alone—and the "boycotters"—
who proposed that the socialists operate only from the underground.
Lenin, reaffirming the legacy of previous Marxism in this regard, succeeded in making prevalent the point of view that *both* forms of activity were necessary to the long-term revolutionary struggle.[5]

The "dual power" situation that existed between February and October 1917 was the practical result of the ambivalent attitude that
continued to prevail among the Bolsheviks until the slogan "All Power to
the Soviets!" came to express their immediate plan of action. It was on
the basis of the two-stage view of the coming Russian transformation that
Lenin could write, as late as 1917, in *State and Revolution:* "We are in favor
of a democratic republic as the best form of state for the proletariat under
capitalism; but we have no right to forget that wage-slavery is the lot of
the people even in the most democratic bourgeois republic." [6] Until
Lenin adopted Trotsky's thesis of "permanent revolution" (at least for
the Russian setting) the manner in which the "dual power" situation was
to be resolved remained a point of extreme controversy among the
Bolshevik leaders, most of whom argued, one may note in passing,
against an attempted proletarian uprising on the doctrinal basis that the
bourgeois revolution had first to come to fruition.

In finally opting for "permanent revolution," Lenin decisively influenced an issue that was to have tremendous significance for later
communist movements in similar prebourgeois settings, by rendering
it doctrinally acceptable for them to seek an immediate socialist revolution and to bypass the bourgeois stage. For the communist parties
established in the parliamentary democracies of bourgeois Europe,

[5] See, e.g., Isaac Deutscher, *The Prophet Armed*, pp. 175–76. In *Left-Wing Communism*
(1920) Lenin recalled: "Bolshevism . . . went through fifteen years of practical history
(1903–1917) unequalled anywhere in the world in its wealth of experience. During those
fifteen years, no other country knew anything even approximating that revolutionary
experience, that rapid and varied succession of different forms of the movement—legal
and illegal, peaceful and stormy, underground and open, local circles and mass movements, and parliamentary and terrorist forms" (*Selected Works*, p. 520).

[6] *Selected Works*, p. 276.

however, the problem was not essentially altered: until the advent of a revolutionary situation, the existing regime enjoyed a temporary and partial legitimacy based on the doctrine that it was a historically necessary step toward socialism.

Marked by a penury of exploitable revolutionary situations, the history of the Western European communist movements has been in one sense but a continuous attempt to preserve this dual doctrinal and strategic perspective: to gain demands of the minimum program without allowing themselves thereby to be assimilated into the established order. Communist movements in liberal democracies have been movements of *fundamental* opposition but not *total* opposition, which is to say that the communist parties have advocated revolution of the established order but have not rejected partial and limited cooperation within it. Moreover, in this regard, one should not confuse *fundamental opposition* and *revolutionary action* because, for example, the lack of an attempted takeover of power by the French Communist Party in the past does not necessarily imply either that it has renounced fundamental opposition to the established order or that it has forsworn an attempt at revolution at some future date. A final goal of this study will be to estimate whether and in what sense the French Communist Party has been able to retain the potential for revolution after a half century of political struggle within and without the Establishment.

In attempting to retain the dual perspective, the model of prerevolutionary Bolshevism has played heavily on the French Communist psychology, as has allegiance to the maximum program on an international scale (i.e., the chimera of "world revolution"), the pursuance of which the French Communists have in the past translated as allegiance to the Soviet interest and Soviet leadership. The French Communist movement provides, with the Italian movement, one of the two most interesting examples of the the struggle to remain revolutionary in the absence of a revolutionary context, because it has the longest nearly continuous history of any of the European movements, and because it has developed a split revolutionary-nonrevolutionary role structure of extreme depth and resilience (see Part Two). Furthermore, while the PCI was living an underground existence during the Mussolini dictatorship, the French Party had to deal with the decline of a "progressive" parliamentary democracy and with the "retrograde" Vichy regime; finally, it had to participate actively in the reestablishment of a "bourgeois" regime during the Liberation and Tripartite periods. Thus, more than any other single case, that of the PCF provides the richest materials for comprehending the historical development of the various "faces" of communism as opposition in a western liberal democratic context. Finally, it is by situating French Communism in the perspective of its generically dualistic doctrine and strategy that one may most fruitfully comprehend the persistently and fundamentally ambiguous nature of the historical relationship between the French Communist Party and the French polity as a whole during the last half century. It is from this vantage point that one may most profitably consider the classic problem of whether or not the PCF "changed" as a result of its adoption of apparently contradictory tactics so often in the past, not to mention the infinitely controversial and discutable question of the loyalty or treason of Communist actions.

The Prototype "Dictatorship of the Proletariat"

For the first time in history, after October 1917 a regime existed that claimed to be the incarnation of the Marxist dictatorship of the proletariat. One of the results of the Bolshevik ascendancy was to split the world of European Marxism from top to bottom, based on a division between those who accepted the Bolshevik claim and those who rejected it. The abortive Russian revolution of 1905 had first posed an alternative to parliament as the most advanced form of democratic political regime with the invention of the *soviets*. Because that revolution failed, however, the issue of parliament vs. soviet did not then become a point of contention not subject to compromise, and between 1905 and 1917 the leading theoreticians of the Second International continued in a majority to assume that proletarian democracy would be bourgeois parliamentary democracy made honest through a social and economic transformation. The year 1917 marked the point of unavoidable choice, however, because the Bolshevik success was a fact, and it placed into question the doctrine and tactics of the Second International in an unmistakable manner.

Leaving aside the role of terror, two aspects of the Bolshevik model as it was developed in the early years interest us most in this context: these two are the adoption of the soviet form over the parliamentary form of government as implied by the dissolution of the Constituent Assembly and the gradual development of the single-party dictatorship between 1917 and 1921.

The key to both series of events was the Bolsheviks' increasing willingness to believe that their own party, alone and through the force of circumstances, was being compelled into a monopoly of authentic representation of the proletariat, and that, because the proletariat was the fundamental revolutionary force, the Bolshevik Party was justified (indeed "forced") to make of itself the sole legal and legitimate political force. The one-party regime had not been part of the often vague and equivocal social democratic doctrines before the Russian Revolution, and it was only gradually over the years 1917–20 that the "necessity" of a political monopoly became a fundamental tenet even of Bolshevism, although one may argue that this result had been implied even as early as the publication of *What Is to Be Done* (1902). In any case, the homogeneous Bolshevik government, in conjunction with the Left Social Revolutionaries, issued the famous order dissolving the Constituent Assembly in January 1918. Nonetheless other parties continued to exist in the soviets until 1920. However, by the end of 1920, widespread economic difficulties, the failure of "war communism," and deep peasant resistance had turned the bulk of the population against the Bolsheviks, who would likely have been voted out of office had free elections to the soviets been permitted.[7] Because they had come to identify the fate of the regime with their own, the success of the revolution with their own, they felt themselves impelled and justified in eliminating all opposition. At that point, convinced of their uniqueness, they argued that all opposition to their party would inevitably become a source of counterrevolution. Later justified on the basis of other formulas, not of central concern here, the one-party dictatorship soon became, through the vehicle of the Comintern, the

[7] Isaac Deutscher, *The Prophet Armed*, p. 504.

unquestioned model of the revolutionary regime for those factions of the European socialist movement which joined the Third International.[8]

While there remained perhaps a chance of a renewed democratic evolution of the new regime for some years after the non-Bolshevik parties were banned, the rise to power of Stalin and the somber transformations that ensued placed an irremovable block between the French Communists and not only the "bourgeois" parties but also their "brothers" in the SFIO. The Soviet example obliged the PCF to acknowledge that their political strategy implied the eventual seeking of total power, and that, in consequence, the relations of the PCF and the other French parties had no future. Over the past half century, this disagreement over what is to be done has in large measure caused both the failure of French socialism and the structural fragility of French politics as a whole.

[8] The original justification for the one-party regime was based on the supposed dangers of failure in the revolution and of counterrevolution. Speaking to the 11th Comintern Congress, Zinoviev remarked: "We have taken away political freedom from our opponents . . . we could not have acted otherwise. . . . The dictatorship of the proletariat, Comrade Lenin says, is a very terrible undertaking. It is not possible to ensure the victory of the dictatorship of the proletariat without breaking the backbone of all opponents." (Quoted in David Shub, *Lenin*, pp. 375–76.) Neither the Soviet Constitution of 1918 or 1924 mention the Communist Party however; the first intimation of the Party monopoly in the official text of the regime occurs only in the third Constitution, promulgated in 1936: Article 126 states that "The most active and politically conscious citizens from the ranks of the working class and other strata of the toilers unite in the All-Union Communist Party of Bolsheviks, which is the advanced detachment of the toilers . . . and the directing nucleus of all the workers' organizations, both social and state." Aside from this discreet reference, the 1936 document resembles a liberal constitution in the theoretical rights and liberties it specifies. Later, other justifications for a one-party regime were added: one was the argument that social classes no longer existed, and that more than one party was therefore unnecessary. This however, according to Marx, might also have meant that *no* party was necessary. Thus it was further asserted that the former exploiting classes might revive and that "capitalist encirclement" still existed, both of which necessitated the retention of the Party and its monopoly.

Chapter Two

THE MIXED HERITAGE
"BOLSHEVIZED" (1920–1934)

In early 1923, when the French Communist Party was already over two years old, two communist syndicalist leaders, Pierre Semard and Gaston Monmousseau, found themselves called to Moscow. Lenin bluntly told them, in effect: "There is at present no communist party in France. Do you want to build one?"

Lenin's meaning might have seemed paradoxical to an outsider, but Semard and Monmousseau—though probably ignorant still of much of what Bolshevism implied—nonetheless must have felt the French Communists quite vulnerable to the reproach. The fact of achieving a split in the SFIO at the December 1920 Tours Congress had not in itself assured that the resulting communist movement would develop into an "authentic" Bolshevik-style party. And events during the two years since the split in the French Left had not gone far toward resolving the genetic contradictions inherent in the birth of the French Communist movement. In these first months of 1923 the French Communist Party was Bolshevik neither in its organization nor its leadership. Rather, it presented the spectacle of a supposedly redoubtable and tightly disciplined revolutionary vanguard in fact hardly capable of controlling its own energies, let alone of mastering a revolutionary situation which was in any case nonexistent in France.

From a position of hindsight, one quickly perceives that the early years in the history of communism in France were above all else a period of homogenizing a mixed and contradictory heritage, of resolving fundamental conflicts over organization, method, and purpose resulting from three distinguishable generic oppositions. This time of internal conflict and struggle for dominance in effect ended first of all in the triumph of Leninist Bolshevism over Jauressian Social Democracy; secondly, in the transference of the major revolutionary impulse in France from the anarcho-syndicalist currents to the Communist Party; thirdly in a purge of Trotskyite Bolsheviks and assimilation of the emergent Soviet example to the point where by 1934 the French communist leadership had become unequivocally Stalinist. The early years of French Communism thus appear to the observer as a second period of gestation, complementary to the first period, which began with the controversial socialist rally to the Great War in 1914 and ended with the schism at the city of Tours. It is true that as the Party developed in the 1920s there occurred a pattern of increasing militancy, sectarianism, and isolation on a tactical level, but one is more inclined to characterize these developments as a prelude to the second birth of French Communism than as examples of revolutionary maneuvering along the pre-1917 Bolshevik model. Half-hearted, confused, and at most only very marginally successful in its first battles, the PCF and its syndicalist ancillary, the *Confédération générale du travail unitaire* (CGTU),[1] influenced the internal balance of forces on the French Left much more than government policy, not to speak of a French or world revolution. Moreover, insofar as membership figures are a significant measure of success at this time, the struggle between Bolshevism and Social Democracy on the French Left before 1934 evolved decidedly against the former. As we shall see, however, both the Soviet leadership and those who were eventually to emerge at the head of a Bolshevized communist movement in France were prepared to sacrifice numbers for organizational efficacy and ideological purity.

The "problem" of the false start in French Communism had greatly preoccupied the Soviet Bolshevik leaders following the creation of the Third International, or Comintern, in March 1919. In March 1922, for example, Lenin had written in typically direct form that "The transformation of a party of the old parliamentary type . . . into a party of a new type, a truly revolutionary party, truly communist, is

[1] Founded in 1922 as a section of the Profintern, the "Red" syndicalist international, the CGTU continued to exist until reunification with its parent, the *Confédération générale du travail* (CGT) in 1936 (see below). Outside of the Soviet syndicates it was the only relatively significant branch of the Profintern.

an extremely difficult thing. The French case demonstrates this difficulty in perhaps the most evident manner." [2] In putting the matter once again to Semard and Monmousseau in 1923, Lenin was adumbrating a process of radicalization that would begin the next year in the PCF and continue for ten more before it was complete.

Bolshevization of the PCF organizational structure may be dated during the period 1924–26. Transformation of the leadership cadre was a much more difficult task, however, and it is not an exaggeration to say that until the final consolidation of power by Maurice Thorez and his allies, culminating with Stalin's anointment of Thorez rather than Jacques Doriot in 1934, the French Party did not experience unified and disciplined leadership in the Bolshevik sense. However, the time sequence, continuity, and thoroughness of Bolshevization in the French case resulted in the most rigidly Stalinist party in the West.

Once the Soviet leadership decided to organize the Comintern on the principles of democratic centralism (meaning that the member leaderships were to be entirely subordinated to the Soviet leadership), it became vital, if the French Party was to become "authentically communist," that it submit to this discipline. [3] The visible expression of this fundamental alteration of former socialist and communist practice was to be the rise of Maurice Thorez, ambitious and strongly Comintern-oriented, to a predominant position in the PCF, and the identification of the French Communist interest with that indicated by the Soviet Party leadership.

Bukharin once remarked that the sequence of events which perverted the Revolution of 1917 was traceable to a "single mistake": the

---

[2] Lenin in the *Internationale communiste*, cited in Gérard Walter, *Histoire du Parti communiste français*, p. 8n.

[3] During the first years after 1919, the Bolshevik leadership did not explicitly seek to subordinate the other communist leaderships to itself. The Russian leaders expected a revolution in Germany, after which, it was assumed, the center of the revolutionary movement would no doubt shift to Berlin, since according to Marx the world revolution would be led by the most advanced countries. It is still a point of controversy among specialists as to whether the transformation of the Comintern should be imputed the Leninist or Stalinist inspiration, this being part of the broader controversy over the connection between Leninism and Stalinism as a whole.

identification of party with state. Insofar as this is true, one may likewise assert that the perversion of French Communism was assured by its identification with the Stalinist example.

The Process of Bolshevization

Despite the fact that Lenin's desire to split European socialism over the question of adhesion to the Third International had obtained the required result in France, the victory in that country was ambiguous. For whereas he had hoped to split off only a small and dedicated revolutionary vanguard from the loose and heterogeneous mass of those calling themselves socialists, in the French Socialist Party a broad and undisciplined majority, in a moment of millenarian fervor and severe disappointment with recent events, opted for bolshevism.[4] It is significant in this regard that at the Tours Congress the famous "Twenty-One Conditions" posed by Lenin for admission to the Comintern were not officially voted by the delegations. The Cachin-Frossard motion proposing adhesion to the International (without mentioning the Conditions) received 3,208 votes to 1,022 for the Longuet-Faure motion against. In effect, until 1924 two factions battled internally for control of the Party: a "center" faction headed by the first Secretary-General of the PCF—Ludovic-Oscar Frossard—and Marcel Cachin, and a "left" faction, in which the leading figures were Boris Souvarine, Pierre Monatte, Alfred Rosmer, and Fernand Loriot. After the Frossard-directed leadership had been rebuked several times by the Comintern executive,[5] the original uneasy alliance of centrists and leftists became intolerable, with Frossard and a number of others who had attempted obliquely to reconstruct the pre-Tours situation leaving

[4] The two fundamental works on the split in French socialism are Annie Kriegel, *Aux origines du communisme français* and Robert Wohl, *French Communism in the Making*. Kriegel argues that the size of the majority at Tours was a matter of circumstance: disillusionment with the rally of the socialist parties to the wartime governments, disappointment with the results of the strikes of Spring 1920, and overly optimistic enthusiasm for the success in Russia, which the 1919 and 1920 setbacks had not yet dimmed.

[5] See, for example, the reference in footnote 2, which is only one of several open and formal condemnations of the PCF leadership in the 1920s by Comintern leaders or the Comintern executive.

the Party.[6] Soon the most uncompromising of the leftist group within the leadership was also purged,[7] and with the contending "deviationist" elements thus eliminated, bolshevization of the Party was continued at other levels.

Bolshevization at the structural level meant application in the PCF of the organizational principles enunciated at the 5th Comintern Congress (June 1924).[8] These principles implied that the Comintern members were to execute a self-imposed organizational revolution, a revolution in three parts all of which revised not only the practice of the ancestor SFIO but also the entire previous experience of socialism in France.

First, bolshevization meant bringing to the fore the proletarian character of the Comintern parties by transforming the basis of party structure, and therein the focus of organizational efforts. Because Leninist doctrine rested its justification of the vanguard party upon the claim that the "new type parties" were now the most authentic representatives of the rising revolutionary proletariat, it was obvious that were the communist parties not to be thoroughly working class in aspect and membership, the special claim of Leninism among the competing Marxian socialist tendencies would be rendered vulnerable. And in France, where the PCF has the task of overcoming a traditionally strong Social Democratic tendency, the problem was all the

[6] The "confession" Frossard later wrote, in which he justified his decision to return to the SFIO, is interesting for what it implies about much of the PCF membership, 1920–24: "I had been able to remain in the Party only by living an equivocation. I could not come to take the Twenty-One Conditions seriously. . . . I had dreamed of associating the vast humanitarianism of Jaurès and the revolutionary audacity of Lenin in a harmonious synthesis. . . . In the shipwreck of my hopes, I could only save my honor as a socialist" (*De Jaurès à Lénine, Notes et souvenirs*, p. 229). This attitude was no doubt characteristic of many others, as the debate over the Twenty-One Conditions was carried on largely among the leadership factions alone, leaving the mass of militants to simply ignore them and to carry on as they had in the SFIO. For Léon Blum, leader of the SFIO, departure of the "reconstructionist" faction in the PCF was but the inevitable consequence of an alliance between unlikes, and he saw the continuing disagreements within the PCF and between the latter and the Comintern as a possible prelude to "a new Tours." This would not be the last time that Léon Blum's optimism led him to illusory conclusions regarding the implantation of communism in France.

[7] Souvarine was excluded in July 1924; Monatte and Rosmer before December of that year. They were in sympathy with Trotsky, and their fortune declined with his.

[8] See Kriegel, *Les communistes français*, pp. 120–21 ff., upon which the following section is based.

more pressing and particularly visible since the membership balance between the two parties, favorable to the PCF claim in 1921, had by 1924 come to mitigate against it:

Table 1: PCF and SFIO Memberships: 1921–1924

	PCF	SFIO
1921	110,000	50,000
1922	79,000	49,000
1923	55,000	50,000
1924	60,000	73,000

The PCF before 1924 had conserved the organizational structure of the SFIO, basing itself on the *commune*, the primary administrative and electoral unit, of which there were approximately 36,000 in metropolitan France. Thus, whereas Marxist-Leninist doctrine exalted the factory as a focus of agitation and propaganda, the French Party had continued to organize its adherents not where they worked but rather where they lived. Apart from making the local party apparatus almost impossible to survey and control, the commune-based organizational structure tended also to diminish the extent to which the Party took its nourishment at the focal point of the "contradiction between capital and labor." Furthermore, to base the limits of the party federations upon the departmental division of France and the cell structure upon the commune was symbolically to attach the organization to the administrative and electoral map of the established regime, whereas to make credible the Leninist challenge to this prevailing legitimacy implied that the PCF had to differentiate itself as much as possible from the old society, and—perhaps even more important from a strategic point of view—from the ancestor socialist organizations. Instead of this structure, therefore, the bolshevized PCF was to be constructed on a foundation of party cells created in the "individual capitalist enterprise," and the grouping of cells into sections and federations was to be based upon the needs of the Party rather than upon the administrative structure of the established regime. For example, in large enterprises a number of cells were grouped into a single section, whereas in a rural area an entire department might constitute a section.

A further gain hoped for in this implantation of the Party in the factory would be to capture the traditional French revolutionary mystique, whose impulse had been co-opted by the anarcho-syndicalist movement during the first years of the century, at a time when the socialist parties had been embroiled with the "Millerand affair." [9] The socialists had not thereafter reestablished a vigorous and unequivocal revolutionary élan, and their pretensions were all but liquidated by the general European social democratic rally to the wartime governments of "National union." For the French Communists, effective takeover of political agitation in the factories would thus facilitate a dual goal: to center national revolutionary activity in the vanguard party rather than in the syndicalist movement, and to assimilate the anarcho-syndicalist militants into the Communist Party.

The second aspect of bolshevization was its elimination of autonomy in the lower party echelons, which the SFIO had permitted, and its substitution by the organizational principle of democratic centralism, which meant the absolutely binding authority of all higher levels on all lower levels. Combined with the reorientation of the structural basis of the Party, this would imply tight control of the entire organization by the Central Committee and the different levels of the Secretariat.

The third aspect of bolshevization, closely related to the second, was to create a disciplined and ideologically "pure" leadership cadre, one that would exclude such left and right "deviationists" as Souvarine and Frossard. Their substitutes would be capable and pragmatic tacticians able to execute the political line decided by the Comintern executive. Whereas the first two steps in the process of bolshevization were begun with some success during the period 1924–26,[10] it was not until 1932–34 that the leadership weaknesses

[9] Millerand was a socialist who, breaking a tradition of refusal to take part in "bourgeois" governments, accepted the portfolio of Minister of Commerce in the 1899 government of the Radical Waldeck-Rousseau, after an election in which the Socialists and Radicals had cooperated in the *Bloc des gauches* on the understanding the former would not participate in a government.

[10] See Jedermann (pseud.), *La "bolchevisation" du PCF*. It should be noted that while the factory cells became of dominant importance because of the number of members, the number of factory cells was always much fewer than local or neighborhood cells, organized on a geographical basis.

were finally resolved in the PCF and the process of bolshevization definitively completed.

In the pre-World War I development of French socialism, unified and disciplined leadership, like centralized authority, had never been characteristic of the SFIO, which did not even possess a continuous central organizational apparatus. The SFIO relied upon a "Permanent Administrative Commission" to provide that measure of organizational continuity deemed necessary to the tasks of the party. Parallel to its structural foundation in the commune, with the degree of autonomy and simple lack of commununication implied therein, the SFIO had permitted local and individual initiative full sway in party politics and policy, and had never attempted to mold an effective "organizational weapon." French socialist doctrine implied a party closer to the conception of Marx (in which the party is not much differentiated from the working class) than to the conception of Lenin.[11]

One may note that while this was evidence of the socialist self-image of radical liberalism, it was also a measure of the ineffectiveness of the SFIO as a political organization.

It was a sign not merely of the changing orientation of the Communist Party toward leaders from working-class backgrounds (Pierre Semard, named Secretary-General at the 4th Congress in January 1925, was the first of working-class origin) but also of his particular talents that Maurice Thorez, at the time Secretary of the *Fédération du Nord*, was promoted in 1924—when he was only twenty-four—to the Central Committee. In July 1925 Thorez was named Organizational Secretary and was admitted to the Politburo. He spent much time during the following four years (especially 1927–29) living a furtive

[11] This organizational perspective reflected the dominant view in the SFIO of how the revolution would occur. As opposed to those who argued that a political revolution could create the conditions for a social and economic revolution (the Leninist position), the prevalent view in the SFIO, shared by Jaurès and Blum, was that the latter must of necessity precede the former and be completed by it. For that reason they were reluctant to think in terms of taking power. They supposed they would be propelled into assuming power, in some unspecified manner, once the more basic social and economic transformation from capitalism to socialism was undertaken "by the workers themselves." After 1917 the socialist doctrine was decisively weakened by the Russian Revolution, despite socialist objections that it was not an authentic proletarian revolution. The successful assumption of power by the Bolsheviks, whatever its consequences, pointed up the vagueness and, ultimately, the lack of strategic direction in social democratic revolutionary theory.

and often fugitive existence because his Party activities made him the object of arrests and warrants many times over. In the spring of 1929, while Secretary-General Semard was in jail, Thorez joined the syndicalist leader Benoît Frachon and two former leaders of the Young Communists, Henri Barbé and Pierre Célor, in a collective general secretariat set up on the Comintern's instructions to seek a regeneration of the party.[12] In June 1929, however, Thorez was arrested by the police and spent the next year in jail. Frachon was arrested in August, and thus Barbé and Célor—supported in the Politburo by François Billoux, Raymond Guyot, André Ferrat, and Henri Lozeray—became the effective leaders of the Party. Thorez was released from prison on April 24, 1930, and began to criticize the Barbé-Célor leadership, at first only by implication but then more openly. Thorez was elected Secretary-General of the Central Committee in July 1930, and successfully maneuvered in October to have himself elected to a new and specially created position, "Secretary of the Politburo." He had urged such a position because "The Politburo is unwieldy and slow to act. . . . We need a single comrade to be politically responsible." [13] This was probably, as Jacques Fauvet has commented, "truly the great turning point for himself and for the Party. The Party had had leaders; from that point it had a chief." [14] The consolidation of this power came only over the next few years however. The "Barbé-Célor group," accused of sectarianism, a refusal to apply Comintern directives thoroughly, and failure to make a success of the "united front" tactic (see below), was gradually removed in 1931–32.

[12] In terms of the problem of finding capable leadership, one may note that by the time of the "Barbé-Célor group" the PCF already had had three Secretary-Generals. Frossard, the first, resigned in January 1923. Albert Treint was removed in January 1924, after a year in office, for reasons of incompetence and a general *manque de sérieux*. He was later excluded in 1928. Pierre Semard held office during 1924–28, but the former anarcho-syndicalist had little success in transforming the declining fortunes of the Party, nor was he always the most powerful figure in the complex interplay of individuals and groups which characterized the PCF leadership before 1934.

[13] Fauvet, *Histoire du Parti communiste français*, 1:91. Of the Barbé-Célor period Thorez wrote in his autobiography, *Fils du peuple:* "The Party had been weakened . . . the membership had declined. Arbitrary decisions from above, passive discipline demanded at all echelons . . . a barracks atmosphere. . . . It was really a caricature of the Party, reduced to impotence, condemned to vegetate miserably." (1949 edition, p. 70. See also Walter, Histoire du Parti communiste français, p. 213.)

[14] Fauvet, *ibid.*

From the end of 1931 on, Thorez was schooled and supported by a team of "advisors" sent by the Comintern Executive Committee. But despite this, the internal power situation retained a certain fluidity and Stalin had not yet definitely settled on Thorez as the man to lead the French Communist Party. One serious rival to Thorez remained, a rather skillful but ultimately undisciplined member of the Politburo, Jacques Doriot. From 1927 on, Doriot had challenged Thorez in numerous ways, generally being identified with an "opportunist" current whereas Thorez consistently accepted the Comintern's directives. Nonetheless, through adroit maneuvering Doriot had retained both his Politburo seat and his seat in the Comintern Executive Committee. Finally, Thorez and Doriot were called to Moscow by the Comintern in April 1934, to settle the leadership question. However, Doriot refused to make the voyage, no doubt conceding what would have proved to be in any case a *fait accompli*. In May, Doriot was censured by the Comintern, and in June he was excluded from the PCF Central Committee. The superficial character of his attachment to Bolshevism, though not to dictatorial politics, was evident two years later when he organized the protofascist *Parti populaire français* (PPF).

In sum, one may consider that with the accession of Maurice Thorez to undisputed dominance in the French Communist Party in Spring 1934, the bolshevization of French Communism was completed. The structural transformation and the "proletarianization" of the 1920s had been secured with a structural and ideological transformation of the top leadership. Thorez, seconded above all by Jacques Duclos (primarily responsible for parliamentary affairs) and Benoît Frachon (responsible for communist syndicalism) from this time forward was the center of a unified, pragmatic, diligent, and bureaucratic leadership core. Around this core could be found the various concentric circles of membership and participation in the movement, the psychology of which had now been irrevocably conditioned to Comintern patterns of thought, that is to say, permeated with the Stalinist conception of proletarian internationalism.

The Development of a Specifically Marxist-Leninist Goal Structure and the First Attempts to Practice Leninist-Style Strategy

The first period of French communist history considered in this chapter (1920–34) was predominantly a time of organizational and ideological assimilation of the Leninist model, as progressively modified by Stalin after Lenin's death. These years may also be studied as a period of apprenticeship in the application of Leninist-style strategy and tactics; or, to be more precise, in the application of the "correct Marxist-Leninist line" as defined by the Comintern. Despite the very limited success of almost all Party undertakings before 1934, it is probable that failure at this time may have been important in aiding the construction of a Leninist-style movement: for example, a nearly fatal decline in membership permitted closer control over what remained; the blunders of weak or uncommitted leaders incited their purge; the failure to seriously threaten the regime precluded unmitigated governmental repression and perhaps even dissolution of the organization; and, finally, its lack of political influence prevented the posing of certain questions—such as governmental participation, with which the Party was not yet equipped to deal. Had the PCF, for example, been constrained by circumstances into a Popular Front before the emergence of a "democratic centralist" authority structure and a bolshevized leadership, the history of Marxism-Leninism in France might have developed much differently.

In defining the goal structure of the French Communist movement—that is, the simultaneous pursuance of the minimum and maximum programs—it should first be said about the 1920–34 period that at no time was it possible to consider that the much-sought "revolutionary situation" was near. Whatever fears of revolutionary insurrection the formation of the PCF might have engendered at first,[15] the French Party (unlike the German and Hungarian movements, which

---

[15] Kriegel and Wohl (see Bibliography) both indicate that the birth of the French Section of the Communist International was not generally perceived as necessarily an irrevocable split in French socialism, nor unreservedly dangerous or imminently revolutionary.

each were involved in significant, if short-lived, rebellions in 1919) before 1934 neither faced a revolutionary situation nor would have been capable of exploiting one.

Thus, while preserving the millenarian image of a Bolshevik-style revolution, during these first years the French Communists learned to live partly in the future and partly in the present, with the necessity of dealing with a nonrevolutionary situation coming to dominate the choice of tactics.

If the PCF can be said to have pursued any immediately revolutionary goals during this period, they concerned only the prospect of revolution abroad, and even this second-hand form of revolution was short-lived. In essence, the Party was to prevent, by means of propaganda and agitation, any intervention by the government of France in the proletarian revolution in Germany, which was anxiously awaited during the first postwar years.[16] However, even the hope of success in Germany was dimmed by the failure of the *Marzaktion* in 1921, and it was then extinguished completely for the time being with the insurrectionary fiasco of the Hamburg communists under the leadership of Ernst Thälmann at the end of 1923. A second task of the Comintern members, conceived by the Soviet leadership upon the realization that a worldwide revolution was not going to occur and camouflaged with the thesis that international capitalism had entered a phase of "temporary stabilization," was to attempt to solidify the international position of the USSR by aiding the establishment of diplomatic relations between their own countries and the Soviet Union, the point of which was to break through the *cordon sanitaire*. In 1922, the Bolsheviks, having announced the NEP, scored a diplomatic breakthrough with the ratification of the Rappallo Treaty with Germany,[17] and in the next few years they succeeded in establishing further diplomatic and commercial relations, as the rivalries that would eventually lead to a second European civil war tempted several governments into hesitant agreements with the USSR. The French gov-

---

[16] See Kriegel, *Les communistes français*, p. 309.

[17] The Weimar government, though not sympathetic to Bolshevism, accepted an alliance with the Soviet Union against the system of alliances being constructed against Germany by France. The KPD made tremendous propaganda out of the alliance, of course.

ernment itself recognized the Soviet Union on October 29, 1924. Relations between the two regimes never warmed, however, and until the rise of Nazism, Stalin continued to designate France as the most "imperialist" and "warmongering" of the European powers.[18]

The strategy attempted by the French Communist Party in the period 1924–34 directly manifested the strong ambivalence of non-Russian European Bolshevism as opposition: always seeking to combine elements of sectarianism with elements of conciliation and elements of militancy with elements of collaboration, all the while avowing its revolutionary intentions. At the same time, and despite a lack of system and continuity in strategic execution, if one views the period from a global perspective, one will perceive a gradual predominance of sectarianism and radical militancy over conciliation and collaboration, with a tremendous leap in this direction in the key year of 1928.

The broad themes of communist activity in France during this period can be summarized under three headings: the *united front;* the struggle against *militarism* and *colonialism* after the Treaty of Versailles; the relation of French communism and *bourgeois legality.*

The history of the PCF's attempts to implement the united front tactic up to 1934 illustrates well both the confusion of the first years and the gradually more disciplined yet still unsuccessful pursuance of Bolshevik-style behavior that characterized the implantation of a Marxist-Leninist movement in France. Essentially, the united front meant some sort of joint action and unity with the socialists and other "democratic" forces. This apparently straightforward policy of alliance was nonetheless capable of numerous and radical variations. The overall design was indicated in the slogan enunciated at the 5th Comintern Congress (1924): "United front only at the top, never. At the top and at the bottom, sometimes. At the bottom, always." [19] "At the top" meant an alliance among party leaderships, in particular in France

---

[18] In general, the Soviet attempt to treat with the rest of Europe, 1923–28, ended in failure. After the occupation of the Ruhr by the French in 1923, the German government was obliged to conciliate the Allies, and its signature on the Locarno Pact (1925) emphasized the isolation of the Soviet Union once again.

[19] Fauvet, *Histoire du Parti*, 1:89. For a general discussion see Jane Degras, "United Front Tactics in the Comintern: 1921–1928," in Footman (ed.), *International Communism*, pp. 9–22, and Franz Borkenau, *World Communism*, pp. 221–238.

with the SFIO and in Germany with the SPD, whereas "at the bottom" referred to the socialist rank and file and the explicit goal of weaning the lower echelons from their leadership by means of "Committees for Proletarian Unity." And in any case, the united front was always to be guided toward the ultimate exclusive gain of the communists, despite the use of whatever concessions might prove necessary along the way. Quickly acquainted with the dangerous ambivalence in the united front policy, the SFIO leaders, and in particular Léon Blum and Paul Faure, sought to make certain that the *frère ennemi* character of communist-socialist relations after the split would not be resolved at the expense of the socialists.[20]

First adopted by the Comintern in December 1921, as a respite after the defeated revolutionary attempts in Germany and Hungary, the original united front was to be sought both "at the top" and "at the bottom." The basis of this Left-Wing rapprochement was to be a temporary sublimation of the revolutionary impulse on the part of the communists, in order to ally with the socialists on a reform platform of economic and social demands, such as defending the eight-hour working day and seeking higher wages and a lower cost of living.[21] However, the *Comité Directeur* of the PCF,[22] and in particular Secretary General Frossard, argued that it was morally indefensible for the

---

[20] Paul Faure tended to be much more openly anti-communist and anti-united-front than Blum, although the latter was as little likely to concede anything vital to the PCF as the former. The SFIO was in a difficult position during the first years of the split, however, having been flanked doctrinally on the Left and decimated organizationally. Not wanting to ally on the Right if possible, and seeking always to reinvigorate the revolutionary credentials of the SFIO, Blum saw the necessity of extreme diplomacy regarding the communists, and during the 1920s pursued a strategy of refusing the united front while attempting to appear as little anti-communist as possible. The trends in membership figures illustrate that the Blum policy was rewarded, at least in terms of a reversal in the 1921 balance of forces:

Membership	SFIO	PCF
1921	35,000	110,000
1924	72,000	60,000
1925	111,000	60,000
1932	138,000	30,000

[21] An obvious parallel exists between the united front abroad and the NEP in Russia.
[22] The *Comité Directeur* was the prebolshevization ancestor of the Politburo.

Party to seek collaboration with those whom the leadership had for more than a year been castigating as "objective allies of the bourgeoisie" and "traitors to the working class." A resolution of January 17, 1922, stated that "The *Comité Directeur* believes it impossible to apply the united front tactic in our country, insofar as it concerns agreement between the dissident leadership, [i.e., the SFIO] and the confederal majority" [i.e., the PCF].[23] On January 22, 46 federations voted against the united front, while only 12 were in favor of it; with this vote the entire Party placed itself in opposition to the Comintern Executive.[24] At a Comintern conference at the end of February 1922, after arguing against the united front policy, the French delegation nonetheless voted its approval "for reasons of discipline," yet insisted on presenting a minority declaration in common with the Italian and Spanish delegations.

During the next year, opposition to the Comintern line persisted, led by Frossard and the "center" faction grouped around him. The Second PCF Congress (Paris, October 1922) brought the issue to a head when, over the question of whether to accept the "arbitration" of the Comintern Executive in choosing the *Comité directeur*, or to retain autonomy of choice, a "left" motion in favor of "internationalism" and inspired by Boris Souvarine was defeated 1,698–1,516 by Frossard's "center" motion in favor of the latter alternative. The weak victory over the rigidly internationalist faction, demonstrating the extent to which the Party was divided as a whole over fundamental problems, did not prove durable for the center faction, however. On December

[23] Cited in Walter, *Histoire du Parti*, p. 83. Frossard's position, in particular its moral justification, demonstrates his noncomprehension of Leninism.

[24] Still, numerous Party leaders (e.g., Dunois and Treint) argued publicly in favor of the united front in the weeks that followed. The openness of the discussion and the moral tone of the opposition to the Comintern were of course a proof of the extent to which the PCF was not yet bolshevized, and most of all the extent to which obedience to the Comintern, to "proletarian internationalism," was not yet a characteristic of the French Communist leadership. Maurice Thorez, the man who more than anyone else would later typify the loyal "proletarian internationalist," wrote of the reactions of the Pas-de-Calais federation: "The communist militants in the Pas-de-Calais did not understand the united front tactic; they saw in it a capitulation to the reformist leaders, almost treason. I struggled . . . for the united front." Maurice Thorez, *Fils du peuple*, in *Oeuvres choisies*, 3:361.

6, the Comintern Executive formally censured the French leadership,[25] and on January 1, 1923, Frossard resigned with a small group of allies, an event followed during the next year by the resignation or exclusion of most of the other centrists. This departure of the centrists signalled a transformation in the PCF attitude toward the Comintern line on the united front, although from the communist point of view much precious time had been lost. For by 1924 the Socialist Party had regained enough organizational strength and confidence to adopt a more aggressive demeanor toward the PCF, and to appear less easily embarrassed by the ironical communist offers of a united front.

The communist tactic in the cantonal elections of May 1922—the only national elections before the beginning of bolshevization—had been a blanket refusal to agree to mutual withdrawals on the second ballot, despite socialist overtures in this direction. Then, as the balance of organizational momentum between the two parties changed over the years 1921–23, the SFIO leadership calculated the party could resist the electoral pressure of the PCF on its left flank. This rendered sterile the communist efforts at a united front "at the top" in 1923, after the defeat of the center faction. Moreover, upon repression of the Hamburg communist insurrection by the Weimar government (which included the socialists) at the end of October, the PCF (as were Comintern sections elsewhere) was obliged to take a harder line toward the social democrats. The PCF, to be sure, had already suffered a steep decline in its powers of attraction, but nonetheless refused to step down in favor of socialist candidates in isolated local elections, and communist militants harassed and often disrupted socialist electoral meetings. In response, socialist propaganda increasingly adopted the open hostility of Paul Faure as its keynote, and when the latter wrote in November 1923 that any sort of unity with the communists was unthinkable, his vehemence expressed a feeling shared increas-

---

[25] Manouilski, the Comintern delegate to the October PCF Congress, had written to the *Comité directeur* before leaving Paris in the following terms: "Before the entire Party, the delegation of the Executive and the representatives of the fraternal parties are unanimous in finding that the entire responsibility for the present situation is incumbent upon the center faction. It is this impartial witness that the Executive delegate will carry before the Fourth [Comintern] Congress . . ." Cited in Walter, *Histoire du Parti,* p. 111, from the *Bulletin communiste,* October 19–26, 1922, p. 804.

ingly even by those who earlier had favored the cautious diplomacy of Léon Blum.[26]

For the legislative elections of May 1924, the first general election in which Marxism-Leninism tested its potential in the parliamentary situation of France, the PCF on the surface opted for the united front "at the top" by proposing the constitution of a *Bloc ouvrier et paysan* (BOP) with the socialists, who themselves were simultaneously negotiating with the Radicals. The communist offer was hardly negotiable, however, since it demanded conditions which the SFIO obviously would not accept: an unconditional electoral alliance on a national scale, irrespective of local situations, and the exclusion of all Radicals and Freemasons. Not wishing to appear in alliance with the bourgeoisie against the working class, the SFIO replied nonetheless, but with an offer of selective coalitions—an offer which the communists refused out of hand. Thus the PCF had no allies in the 1924 elections, facing both the *Cartel des gauches* (SFIO and Radicals) and the Right-wing *Bloc National*. Using the electoral campaign primarily as a propaganda tribune, as they would their seats in the Chamber of Deputies, the PCF leadership nonetheless hoped to win a sizable number of seats.

[26] Although in this context one cannot be much concerned with internal debates in the SFIO, a brief description of the various forces opposed to alliance with the communists may interest the reader: The Guesdist element in the SFIO—particularly strong in the Nord federation (led by Delory, mayor of Roubaix, Brache, and Salengro), also strong in the Massif Central (in particular the Haute-Vienne federation led by Paul Faure), and in Narbonne and the Gard (dominated by Compere-Morel)—was by nature dogmatically anti-Leninist. Guesde himself had died in 1922. The Jaurèssian element— strong in the federations south of the Loire, the Haute-Garonne, the Tarn, the Var, the Gironde and the Bas-Rhin—was more openly reformist (it emphasized municipal government as one possible step to a gradual socialist transformation) and a protagonist of a "union of the Left" on the basis of a liberal and heterogeneous socialist doctrine, making room even for the middle classes within it. Finally, the large number of SFIO leaders who were also Freemasons had still another reason to refuse an alliance with the communists. Léon Blum may be taken as most representative of the Jaurèssian tendency in the SFIO, while Paul Faure was perhaps the most influential Guesdist. Both were perhaps also Masons. In the CGT, both the traditions of reformist syndicalism (one may mention in particular Keuffer, Secretary General of the *Fédération du livre* and his successor Liochon, who together held the top position in this federation from 1884 to 1940) and of revolutionary syndicalism (expressed in the famous Amiens Charter of 1906, the banner of the CGT leader Léon Jouhaux) mitigated against acceptance of the Leninist point of view. (This classification of tendencies in French socialism was suggested to this writer by Georges Lefranc.)

In fact, they won 26 seats, 17 more than were left them after the split of 1920. Yet, withal, this was but a localized success, for of the 26, fully 16 were returned from the Paris region alone. In the provinces, only 10 communists were elected, and then in only six departments.[27]

Because of the Cartel's tactics, the SFIO went from 67 to 104 seats, while the Radicals jumped from 106 to 162 (including allied groups), all on the basis of a very minor increase in the percentage of votes won. With but nine percent of the total votes cast, five percent of the seats in the Chamber, and no allies, the Communist Party could thus hope to use Parliament only for propaganda purposes, while the socialists, still struggling with the implications of the "affaire Millerand" and the rally of 1914, had all they could do to restrain themselves from abandoning the principle of nonparticipation and joining the government, which was widely expected of them.[28]

With the SFIO linked electorally to the Radical Party through the Cartel, from 1924 through 1928 the united front tactic was practicable by the communists only "at the bottom," where little was achieved in any case because of bitter feelings on both sides and the inconsistencies of communist behavior. The municipal elections of 1924 and the cantonal elections of 1925 showed no significant gains, and the PCF failed to elect even a single senator in the elections of 1926 (an indirect

[27] Three each from the Seine-et-Oise and the Nord; one each from the Seine-Inférieure, Cher, Lot-et-Garonne, and Bas-Rhin. Thirty-four percent of the PCF vote came from the Paris region alone, yet this was in another sense a victory, for it demonstrated that the Party had began to capture the crucial Parisian suburbs from the socialists. The latter, however, retained their hold on the industrial Nord and Pas-de-Calais departments. The PCF won less than five percent of the vote in 40 of the departments, but in the largely peasant Cher and Lot-et-Garonne, the communist vote topped twenty percent. Thus, as Jacques Fauvet asserts, the 1924 elections revealed the dual electoral basis of French communism: the industrial Paris region (plus a sizable representation in the Northeast) and the rural Massif Central, to which would gradually be added a third bastion in the South and in particular the Southeast of France. For a summary of the relevant trends, see François Goguel, *Géographie des élections françaises sous la 3e et 4e Républiques.*

[28] Ultimately they did not participate, and a Radical-dominated cabinet was formed. Within two years, despite the victory of the *Cartel des gauches*, the government was in the firm control of a Rightist majority. This was an example of the famous "shift to the right" in French parliamentary politics of the Third and Fourth Republics: despite a left-oriented electoral result, after an early ministerial crisis a conservative cabinet would take power.

and conservative suffrage to be sure). Party membership figures continued to shift in favor of the SFIO, and the CGTU remained but a small challenge in its syndicalist struggle with the CGT. Because of the lack of communist gains, as late as 1927 Léon Blum apparently continued to hope for a reunification of the *vieille maison* of French socialism, a union in which the liberal socialist perspectives of the SFIO would be combined with the revolutionary fervor of the PCF apparatus. For him the PCF could play a useful role as the "shock troop" of the socialist advance, but it was not the authentic socialist revolutionary party in France. Nonetheless, he considered that both organizations had something positive to contribute to that eventual transformation of society in which he continued to believe with a certain naive confidence.[29]

In any case, by the end of 1927 the PCF use of united front tactics had proved ineffective both "at the top" and "at the bottom." Having finally accepted the Comintern line, the French Communists had learned a vital lesson from their lack of success: in the absence of an outside force pushing communists and socialists to cooperate, the aspects common to Bolshevism and Social Democracy were not of sufficient strength to surmount the differences. Successful bolshevization of the extreme left wing of the French Left had, as the Twenty-One Conditions originally intended, made definitive the split at Tours.

The French Communists first undertook vigorous radical opposition to the established regime in adopting antimilitarist and anticolonialist actions as the keystones of the minimum program in the 1920s. The two major events in this regard were the communist actions against the French occupation of the Ruhr (January 1923)—which helped divert attention from the resignation of Frossard and his followers ten days earlier—and against the colonial war in the Rif (1924-25).

The policy of the French government at the end of the First World War had led to rather voracious efforts to draw from the German government the broad reparations indicated in the Versailles Treaty. Success proved difficult, however, and after a year's futile efforts following his election as Premier in January 1922, the conservative leader Raymond Poincaré invoked a sanction clause in the Treaty (the pre-

---

[29] See Blum's *Bolchevisme et socialisme*, 3d. edition (Paris, 1927).

text was a failure to deliver telegraph poles in sufficient quantity!) and sent two French army divisions to occupy the Ruhr. The Weimar Prime Minister, Cuno, proclaimed a policy of passive resistance and refusal to accept contact with the occupation forces. A tense situation, which strained Franco-British relations almost to the breaking point, lasted until the end of September, when Poincaré accepted the failure of the occupation tactic. An international conference beginning in November 1923 produced the compromise Dawes Plan, whose principles the French government accepted in the spring of 1924.

The occupation of the Ruhr gave the French Communist Party its first opportunity to demonstrate some tactical vigor in pursuit of Bolshevik-style goals, in particular as the application of proletarian internationalism—manifested in cooperative actions between the PCF and the KPD—contradicted the policy of the national government, and, in a deeper sense, its very sovereignty. (Before the Ruhr campaign the PCF had, to be sure, denounced the Versailles Treaty and had demanded self-determination for the Alsace and Lorraine populations, rather than French annexation. Under the centrist leadership in 1921–22, however, little mass action of significance had occurred, although communist deputies consistently voted against military credits.)

In late December 1922, an Action Committee had been created, which grouped together the PCF, the CGTU, and the Young Communists. This Committee directed a campaign of "Tracts, posters, and meetings. . . . Hundreds of thousands of tracts were given out in the factories. Dozens of meetings were held." [30] More importantly, in terms of demonstrating a capacity for radical actions (especially in relation to traditional French socialist behavior), the Communist Party openly called for fraternization between French soldiers and German workers (some of its militants actually did so and were arrested), while French Communist leaders spoke at mass meetings organized by the KPD at Essen, Duisburg, Frankfurt, Stuttgart and Cologne.

The same types of action were used to protest the Rif War, which was an intervention by the French government in an uprising in the north of Morocco (the Rif area, as it was called, was under the con-

---

[30] *Histoire du Parti . . . (Manuel)*, p. 137.

trol of Spain), in order to protect its own share of Morocco, the south, and its interests in the rest of North Africa as a whole. And soon afterward the communists began a protest campaign again against the French government's repression of a rebellion which broke out in Syria in July 1925. Moreover, whereas the PCF called for fraternization and the recognition of an independent republic under the rebel leader Abd el-Krim in the Rif, the SFIO took a vague and equivocal position. This permitted the communists to appear as the only group favoring outright self-determination of peoples, a position described in the official Party history in the following terms: "The SFIO abandoned the traditions of Jaurès and Guesde and openly supported an adventure of colonialist brigandage. . . . The Party, on the contrary, took upon itself the anticolonialist heritage." [31]

These antimilitarist and anticolonialist campaigns were not generally effective, despite such occasional successes as the 24-hour general strike of October 12, 1925, which the Party claimed attracted 900,000 participants. In terms of affecting government policy, the results were negligible.[32] Nonetheless, the PCF had been able to separate itself quite markedly from the SFIO on the important question of anticolonialism. Reinforcing the PCF claims in this regard was the fact that the provocative and radical appeals for fraternization and complicity with a foreign communist party against the policy of the national government resulted in the arrest, trial, and conviction of several hundred communist militants, a large number of the Party leadership, and even a number of communist deputies—in particular the well-known former socialist Marcel Cachin, who had cosponsored the Tours motion to join the Comintern.[33]

The imprisonment of communist deputies was particularly signifi-

[31] *Ibid.*, p. 160. It is worth noting that in July 1925, the young Maurice Thorez was named president of the Action Committee, now called Central Action Committee.

[32] Even the *Histoire . . .* (*ibid.*, p. 169) makes only the following laconic claim: "The avant-garde of the French proletariat, at the appeal of the Communist Party, broke with the chauvinist and colonialist ideology. The Party was able to extend its propaganda campaigns to the organization of effective action."

[33] On December 18, 1923, the Chamber voted 374–143 to lift the parliamentary immunity of Cachin, and two days later he was imprisoned, accused of having participated in the creation of a "Committee Against War and Imperialism" whose members were foreign nationals belonging to other communist parties. See Fauvet, *Histoire du Parti* 1:60–62.

cant because it required a suspension of parliamentary immunity. Such action was normally taken only in isolated and extreme cases, and therefore the extraordinary number of requests by the government and favorable votes in the Chamber demonstrated that the communist parliamentary group as a whole had already been placed outside the normal rules of parliamentary deference. Moreover, in order to emphasize their separation, the communists did all they could to sustain it. On one occasion Jacques Doriot even announced pontifically from the Chamber rostrum that he did not consider himself "linked through any engagement whatsoever to the Prime Minister and the French State." [34] At the end of 1925 the third Secretary-General of the Party, Pierre Semard, claimed that 165 communist militants were imprisoned and 263 had charges pending, and that 320 years of prison terms had been imposed, along with 45 years of exile, and 26,833 francs worth of fines. [35] This enumeration of the clash between the nascent communist movement and the legal and political Establishment, while demonstrating the extent to which communists were then prepared to carry their opposition to the regime, at the same time was a rather pathetic effort to demonstrate the force of communism by counting its casualties. Moreover, once arrested or convicted, the communists often tended to behave anomalously in comparison with the Russian Bolshevik example. As Jacques Fauvet has remarked: "One saw militants, and even leaders, complacently allowing themselves to be arrested, or supplying their own transportation to prison, suitcase in hand." [36] Thus, despite the evident progress in radicalizing the French Communist mentality, the process was far from completed at this time.

Continuing bolshevization of the Party began to further harden communist behavior, however, and during the first part of 1928 the Central Committee formally debated the question of whether or not to continue to submit more or less obsequiously to "bourgeois legality." In particular, the leadership discussed whether or not to accept searches and "verifications" by the police, whether or not to allow themselves to be arrested, whether or not to demonstrate only as authorized by the prefecture, and so forth. Here was probably a moment of consequence in the trans-

[34] *Ibid.*, pp. 63–64.   [35] *Ibid.*, p. 65.   [36] *Ibid.*, pp. 76–77.

formation of Jaurèssian socialists and anarcho-syndicalists into Bolshevik-style militants in that, characteristic of the Bolshevik perspective, the PCF attitude toward the established legality was discussed not as a matter of principle but rather of tactics: the policy adopted would be a reflection not of any moral rule, but rather of the means most likely to achieve a given goal. In other words, the "cooperative" attitude of the Party before 1928, expressed in submission to the police and judicial apparatus once a violation had occurred, had manifested a certain reluctance to accept all the implications of Bolshevism in the attempt to transfer it to the context of French parliamentary politics and the liberal regime.

In consequence, the Central Committee of the PCF pronounced a "solemn" rejection of "bourgeois" legal structures, and when Parliament convened in 1928, three of the five communist deputies sentenced to prison terms at that time were in hiding (Doriot, Duclos, and Marty) and the other two (Cachin and Vaillant-Couturier) were incarcerated after brazenly attempting to propagandize the new communist position before the Chamber, and, through the media, to the country as whole.[37] Maurice Thorez, demonstrating a sixth sense insofar as predicting the "correct" position was concerned, had at that time been evading the police for a year, and would do so for another year before being caught and imprisoned.[38]

The refusal to accept "bourgeois" legality in the name of revolutionary Bolshevism synthesized a mentality of increasingly radical militancy which had been progressively imposed in the French Communist Party leadership. The Russian Bolsheviks, given the nature of the Czarist regime, did not find it difficult to develop a mentality amenable to permanent illegality and clandestine existence. Among the French Communists, on the other hand, such a mentality, one of the essential aspects of bolshevization, was of necessity a more conscious fabrication.

This hardening of the nature of communist behavior in France was

[37] *Ibid.*, p. 77.

[38] "In June, 1927 . . . I began an errant life which was to continue for two years, living and sleeping with comrades and changing addresses often. In not allowing myself to be arrested . . . I had brutally broken with certain 'legalist' and opportunist habits, practiced at the time even by the leaders of the Party" (*Fils du peuple*, in *Oeuvres choisies*, 3:372).

accompanied by a new, extreme sectarian version of the united front, itself a reflection and consequence of the changes about to shake the Soviet Union and the CPSU in 1928.

At the time of its introduction in 1921–22, the united front had been intended to be a broadly conciliatory line, motivated by the weakness of both the new Soviet regime and the national communist parties, and the ebbing of revolutionary impulses in Europe generally. In 1924, Stalin had rationalized these policies with the argument that international capitalism had entered a period of relative stabilization, thus making necessary, and justifying, his policy of "socialism in one country." Now, in 1928, to justify his plans to terminate the NEP and to begin the forced peasant collectivizations, Stalin suddenly announced that the period of "capitalist stabilization" had come to an end. The desire (or "necessity") to achieve a homogeneous worldwide communist policy obliged him to introduce the new radical turn into the Comintern as well. The result was the extreme sectarian tactic of "class against class."

In a sense explainable as simply a more militant version of the united front "at the bottom," the tactic of class against class no longer advocated alliance with the socialist rank and file but went further to assert that the time had come for the European working classes as a whole to unite under the sole leadership of the communist parties. As was true in Germany, in France the Comintern and the PCF thereupon took an implacably hostile attitude toward social democracy, vilified more openly than ever in choosing to ally with the Center (in France the Radicals) rather than with the communists. The SFIO leadership, in particular the most prominent anti-Leninists such as Léon Blum and Paul Faure, became at this time the object of malicious abuse, reminiscent of Lenin's most violent polemical style. The odd maledictions of "social patriotism" (referring to the 1914–18 rally) and even "social fascism" were now common currency in communist propaganda. In effect, despite the seriousness of its recent membership losses and its dim electoral prospects, the PCF, in applying class-against-class tactics, and in rejecting the established legality, had set out on a road that was to lead it ever more completely into isolation from the French nation and into contact with the international Bolshevik community centered around the Soviet Communist Party.

To accept these class-against-class tactics was a radical and dangerous gamble, and the Comintern directive provoked tremendous dissension within the French leadership, especially from "parliamentarist" and "opportunist" elements still unpurged or unbolshevized. Renaud Jean, for example, termed the class-against-class position a "tactic of catastrophe and folly," while Jacques Doriot and others who still refused to abandon totally the idea of an alliance with the SFIO tried to make it a selective tactic.[39] Maurice Thorez, again revealing his fundamental concerns, declared himself in solidarity with the Comintern executive.

The acceptance of class-against-class tactics by the PCF, even considering the internal opposition, must be seen as a measure of the degree of the Party's bolshevization and internationalization. For the benefits (assuming the Soviet leadership actually thought there would be some) were not expected in France, at least immediately. At this time the Comintern still considered Germany as the next site of revolution. The prominent position of the SPD in Weimar politics had compromised its revolutionary pretensions, in a manner broadly similar to the French SFIO. And the Comintern's reason for ordering an amputation of all ties with the social democrat leadership was the doctrinally logical but practically erroneous deduction that at the decisive moment the working classes would rally to the KPD position as the only authentic revolutionary party in Germany. Indeed, the KPD position at this point seemed relatively stronger than that of the PCF, and the French Communists' decision to adopt the Comintern line was therefore an unmistakable demonstration of its increasing willingness to weigh gains and losses on an international scale. Ironically, the catastrophe that class-against-class tactics proved to be was infinitely more damaging to the KPD than the PCF. Whereas the tactics merely accelerated the French Party's previous decline, the split on the left in

---

[39] See Walter, *Histoire du Parti*, pp. 190ff. and *Classe contre classe: La question française au IXe exécutif et au VIe Congrès de l'I. C.*, where one finds justifications by Jean and Doriot and two rather typical Thorez statements. In one of them (p. 64) he makes the reproach that "until recently the problem was that we remained very strongly linked to democracy, that we were not able to disengage ourselves, that we were not able to loosen the constraints which weigh on our party. Our party is developing in a country that has been infested with democracy for 57 years; this party has not yet undertaken revolutionary battles, serious struggles."

Germany was one of the decisive factors in Hitler's rise to power and the annihilation of the KPD in 1933.

The French Communists employed class-against-class tactics for the first time in the 1928 general elections. During the campaign, they had attempted to place the onus of division onto the SFIO leadership once again by offering an alliance whose conditions were such that the latter could only flatly refuse them. This and public dissatisfaction with the SFIO role in the Cartel probably had some effect, for on the first ballot the PCF gained 184,500 votes over its 1924 total (1,066,000 in 1928). Nonetheless, the number of communist deputies dropped from 26 to 14 because of the antialliance tactic and a change in the electoral law. Precisely in order to weaken communist representation in the Chamber, the prewar system of *scrutin d'arrondissement* in two ballots, a single-member constituency system favoring alliance and mutual withdrawals, had been readopted in July 1927, with even a majority of socialists (traditionally in favor of a proportional representation system) voting with the Center and Right. In the second ballot in 1928, about forty percent of the first-ballot communist voters involved in runoff elections apparently deserted the Party.[40] They seem to have voted communist on the first ballot as a protest against government policies, against the system as a whole, or against SFIO participation in the Cartel; or else they simply did not want to waste their second-ballot votes where communists had no chance of being elected. In any case, this was the first indication that large numbers of electors might vote for the PCF without either joining the Party or accepting its strategy and maximum goals (see chapter 10). Moreover, the second-ballot result, in revealing that the PCF was unable to mount sustained electoral pressure against the socialists, ensured the failure of class-against-class tactics as a whole over the next five years. To be sure, the SFIO also suffered in 1928. It lost approximately 100,000 votes on the first ballot and ended up with 99 deputies (it had returned 104 in 1924) only because of its second-ballot cartel with the Radicals *à contre coeur*. The Left split was epitomized when, in a bitter

[40] Walter, *Histoire du Parti*, pp. 191–192. The PCF *Histoire* gives a figure of one-third second-ballot desertions, while Jacques Fauvet suggests the percentage was as high as two-thirds (*Histoire du Parti*, 1:81).

contest symbolic of the trend in the Paris region at least, Léon Blum himself was beaten in a runoff by Jacques Duclos in Charonne.

Continued in the cantonal elections of 1928 and 1931 as well as in the municipal elections of 1929, the PCF class-against-class tactics prevented an expansion of communist representation in the institutions of government while they held SFIO gains to a minimum. It is difficult to present a meaningful global statistic on the municipal elections, but a compilation of statistics on the cantonal elections reveals that in the 1925–28 renewal (one-half at each vote) the PCF had 42 of 3,106 total seats (one percent) and in 1928–31 had 39 of 3,107 total seats (one percent). In 1925–28 the SFIO won 284 of 3,106 seats (nine percent) and in 1928–31 it had 302 of 3,107 seats (ten percent).[41] By 1932, therefore, radical tactical sectarianism had shown itself to be, if anything, less fruitful than the partially equivocal 1922–28 communist alliance posture. The 1932 general elections appeared to indicate that, even given the now worldwide Depression, the struggle between the PCF and the SFIO for dominance on the French Left had taken a decisive turn against the communists: from 1,066,000 first-ballot votes in 1928 the PCF dropped to about 785,000 votes (despite a slight increase in the number of persons casting valid ballots), while from 1,708,000 votes in 1928 the SFIO rose to 1,964,000 votes. Moreover, the pattern of alliances developed by the SFIO on its right flank, as well as the increased number of second-ballot votes it received from first-ballot communist electors, increased the number of deputies it elected.[42] Whereas the PCF declined from 14 to 12 deputies, the SFIO rose from 99 to 129.[43]

[41] Figures compiled from J. L. L. D'Artrey, *Conseils généraux: Elections juillet 1925–octobre 1928*, and *Conseils généraux: Elections 18–25 octobre, 1931*.

[42] Walter calculates that 45 percent of the first ballot voters deserted the PCF on the second ballot in 1932. (*Histoire du Parti*, p. 241).

[43] Even Stalin is said to have been taken aback by the possible consequences of the class-against-class tactic for the French movement. Between the first and second ballots in 1932 he is said to have snapped that "the Soviet government cannot tolerate the absence of Communist deputies in the French parliament!" Nonetheless, given his mechanical obstinacy in pursuing this line in Germany, where the KPD had launched the slogan *Nach Hitler kommen wir!* the PCF was obliged to pursue a tactic unsuited to its own position. The SFIO leaders even claimed that key informal withdrawals on their part made possible the election of eight Communists in 1932, without which the PCF would have had only four deputies.

In terms of membership, the trend continued increasingly in favor of the SFIO as well. The PCF (110,000 in 1921; 79,000 in 1922; 50,000 in 1928; 30,000 in 1932) had increasingly taken on the character of a sect, while the SFIO (50,000 in 1921; 73,000 in 1924; 110,000 in 1928; 138,000 in 1932) seemed once again to be the great mass party of the working class, its revolutionary character being another matter. By 1933, which one may take as the moment when the final consolidation of effective authority by Maurice Thorez had become almost irreversible, the Party membership had dropped to around 28,000, perhaps even less. And although the well-known description in *What Is to Be Done?* (a "small compact core, consisting of reliable, experienced and hardened workers, with responsible agents in the principal districts and connected by all the rules of strict secrecy") was therein more closely approximated by the French Party, this was not the conscious or primary intention.[44] The PCF, born as a mass party in a liberal parliamentary setting that offered a legal existence and regular, popularly legitimated elections, seemed on the point of being extinguished by the contradiction inherent in the importation of an organizational and strategic doctrine that had proved itself only in a context of extreme political repression, economic breakdown, and defeat in war. Not only was the party itself on the wane in France, but the CGTU, having come under total control of the communists through the purge or "reeducation" of the anarchist element (the CGT leaders Frachon and Monmousseau were themselves former anarcho-syndicalists), had simply never become very significant in its struggle for power with the CGT. This was due in part to the development of the clerically oriented *Confédération française des travailleurs chrétiens* (CFTC) after its creation in March 1919, and the vigorous anticommunism and anti-Marxism of the Church in general. More importantly, however, the avowed CGTU goal of seeking to "constitute syndicalist revolutionary committees in every enterprise, at once factional groups and future soviets," [45] was not embraced by the rank and file. The CGT, which for 20 years had been the sole French national syndicate, continued to be seen as the central organization defending working-class

[44] On the eve of the February Revolution the Bolshevik Party claimed 26,500 members, according to E. H. Carr, *The Bolshevik Revolution*, 1:211.

[45] J-D Reynaud, *Les syndicats en France*, p. 70.

interests against the *Patronat*. Thus, while the small CGTU membership remained relatively stable until it merged with the CGT during the Popular Front, the latter made some significant gains between 1922 and 1930. In both cases, however, membership figures would have been better had not many workers simply deserted syndicalist activity completely during the 1922–34 period (all the more indicative of the general weakness of French syndicalism was that less than fifteen percent of the workers in the prewar CGT were unionized.)

In sum, the strategy and tactics pursued by the French communist movement between 1920 and 1934 had been but slightly successful. Due first to the internal chaos out of which the bolshevized movement progressively took shape, afterward the failure to mark French society decisively was a function of the degree to which the Comintern perspective, based above all on the needs of the Soviet Union and focused outward primarily on the situation in Germany, proved counterproductive in France. Bolshevism seemed to find little fertile ground in the context of a politically liberal and socially conservative regime which, unlike the situation in Germany, had been victorious in the Great War. Not even the onset of economic depression had reversed the French Communist decline.

However, once its ideological purity had been obtained, the PCF leaders decided to determine the interest of French Communism first of all in relation to the international movement. Although the class-against-class period was not the last time cooperation with Stalin would sabotage the PCF national stake, the Party had now deeply internalized the Comintern's internationalist and millenarian vision of world revolution based upon the Stalinist version of Leninism.

As Thomas Thornton has characterized the post–1921 situation in Europe, in France "the possibilities for revolution . . . were . . . negligible due to the changed situation in the area and the extreme weakness of the communists. . . . On all counts, the prospects for any sort of revolutionary activity based on mass urban uprisings were dim." [46] In effect, during this first period the PCF in the context of French politics, as was true of the Soviet Union in the context of world politics, used only limited leverage with regard to a situation it

---

[46] In Black and Thornton (eds), *Communism and Revolution*, pp. 57–58.

nonetheless sought to comprehend, manipulate, and finally control. The united front in France—at the top, at the bottom, and in the class-against-class version—had produced only two apparently durable successes: consolidation of the schism in the French Left and completion of the Bolshevik apprenticeship of the communist movement in France. Thereby the Party made credible its pretensions to a radical, militant, and exterior position with regard to the established order, even while the PCF participated in elections, in parliament, and administered many local governments. French Communist militancy in the 1920s, while often spectacular and provocative of political repression and inflammatory rhetoric from the government,[47] never succeeded tactically in becoming more than a surface pattern of radical action against the regime. Furthermore, although the crucial implantation of the movement in the Paris region and in the rural center of France at this time was to be rendered of permanent consequence in later years, in the immediate arenas of political decision making the communists were more or less powerless.[48]

The 7th PCF Party Congress in 1932 was the last before the Popular Front Congress of January 1936. In the proceedings of the 1932 meeting one finds the expression of that mentality toward which the bolshevization and growing militancy of the 1920s had been building. Stalin's 1928 announcement of a new and more critical stage in the "general crisis of capitalism" had sounded the call for the extreme tactics of the 1928–33 period. By 1932, despite the general decline of the communist movement in France, the economic depression provided an opportunity for Maurice Thorez to speak boldly and threateningly with some effect, and he did not fail to claim the communists had cor-

---

[47] Albert Sarraut, Minister of the Interior, was to declare flamboyantly on May 27, 1927: *"Le communisme, voilà l'ennemi!"* The phrase became a sort of battle cry.

[48] Given the almost immediate failure of the class-against-class policy, in 1928–29, why did Stalin pursue it? Deutscher gives a reasonable response: "It is doubtful, to say the least, whether Stalin believed in the imminent eruption of all the revolutionary volcanoes. . . . With even greater emphasis than hitherto . . . he made 'socialism in one country' the supreme article of faith. . . . There was an undeniable contradiction between his two lines of policy, the one he pursued in Russia and the one he inspired in the Comintern. It is easy to guess which of the two policies had the greater weight. The Comintern was now indeed engaged in a mock fight. . . . Stalin, in all probability, countenanced it only because he attributed very little practical significance to whatever the Comintern did in those years" (*Stalin*, p. 400).

rectly predicted the crisis in the capitalist world, therein validating the scientific character of Marxism-Leninism and promising a renaissance of the revolutionary impulse in Europe:

Capitalist stabilization is coming to an end. . . . The capitalist regime is condemned. The proletariat must execute it. . . . There is no bourgeois solution to the general crisis of the capitalist system. . . . [We] are once again at a turning point in history. . . . Two worlds oppose each other . . . that of a rotting capitalism . . . and that of a triumphant socialism. . . . The war is begun, rendering imminent the attack against the Soviet Union. We are moving toward grand battles. The bourgeoisie will not spare us. It will strike at us. It is necessary . . . to prepare oneself for systematic attacks against our Party, against our militants. It is necessary to assure resistance and counterattack.[49]

Whether or not the French Communist leadership really expected such events to occur is unknowable and not of considerable importance to us. As a symbolic expression of the evolution of French Communism during the years 1920–34, however, this scenario of Thorez reflects at once the successful bolshevization of the communist movement in France and its achievement of a radically exterior and militant position vis-a-vis the established order.

The Comintern line of the early 1930s predicted an increasingly radicalized political context in Europe. But when the decisive shift in polarities occurred in Germany in 1933–34, communist perception of the changed balance of forces was realistic enough to recognize that an Armageddon opposing the "forces of progress" and the "forces of reaction" would most likely result in the total destruction of European communism and certainly threaten the Soviet Union itself. By 1934 the common enemy on the Right had forced the dominant immediate concerns of not only the French Communists and Socialists but also the Radicals into accord for the first time since Marxism-Leninism had captured a part of the French Left in December 1920. In a word, the rise of fascism created the conditions for the Popular Front, and in doing so probably rescued the French Communist Party from increasing and perhaps permanent impotence.

[49] Thorez report, PCF-7, pp. 18–19. (Abbreviations such as PCF-7 indicate the 7th PCF Congress, and so on. See the Bibliography for complete references.)

Chapter Three

THE POPULAR FRONT (1934–1938): COLLABORATION IN A "BOURGEOIS" REGIME

If one views the situation from today's vantage point, one is tempted to interpret the Popular Front in France primarily as a first attempt to remake the unity of the split in the French Left at Tours. Yet at the moment of its birth, it was not at all a planned and agreed upon movement of compromise, but rather, as Léon Blum wrote later, a "grouping of forces rather than of parties . . . a defensive coalition, formed spontaneously after February 6, 1934, by a sort of survival instinct for the defense of democratic principles." [1] In other words, without the pressure of European fascism it is unlikely that communists and socialists would have allied in 1934. And if one may say that the growth of Nazism provided the general conditions for a reconciliation of the French Left, it is equally correct that a series of unconsidered actions of the antiparliamentary and sometimes fascist Right in France itself—culminating in the famous clash of February 6—supplied the immediate occasion when, again in the words of Léon Blum, "A spontaneous and irresistible instinct of the masses imposed the rapprochement." [2]

On February 6, 1934, after a year of increasingly more aggressive antiparliamentary agitation, the Stavisky Affair exploded, providing a pretext for a concerted Right-wing demonstration of antirepublican feeling. [3] In a demonstration at the Place de la Concorde, the *Ligue d'Action*

---

[1] *A l'échelle humaine*, p. 69.   [2] *Ibid.*, pp. 103–04.

[3] The financier Stavisky, with the aid of several friends in parliament, had embezzled dozens of millions of francs. Most of them were Radicals, and the Radical Premier Chautemps was accused of seeking to cover up the scandal. As a result, Chautemps resigned on January 27.

Française, the *Jeunesses Patriotes*, the *Solidarité Française*, and several extreme Right wing veterans organizations such as the *Croix de Feu* and the *Union Nationale des Combattants* sought to pressure the deputies across the Seine in the Palais Bourbon into rejecting the newly presented government of the Radical Edouard Daladier. As the hours wore on, many parliamentarians even began to fear an outright attempt at a coup d'état; and indeed, this fear, ultimately unfounded, was reinforced at one point when the fascist leagues attempted to cross the Pont de la Concorde to reach the Chamber of Deputies. In the skirmish, the police fired on the crowds of demonstrators. The violence resulted in seventeen deaths and injuries to over two thousand. In the midst of all this, the Daladier government was nonetheless invested by a vote of 343–237; the solid majority was more a product of circumstances than of fundamental agreement.

The demonstration of Feburary 6, although not so politically dangerous as it then seemed, appeared to be an overwhelming show of antiparliamentary strength, and besides inflating somewhat the Daladier majority in the Chamber, the event was more importantly a catalyst for the union of the Left after fourteen years of bitter division.

On February 9, Benoît Frachon announced that the Communist-dominated CGTU would join Léon Jouhaux and the CGT in an order for a general strike on February 12 as a counter show of strength. Then, on February 11, Maurice Thorez announced that the PCF would support a demonstration proposed by the SFIO, also planned for the 12th. These events of the week of February 6–12, 1934, were crucial: "A large step was thus taken; the communist union engaged itself in an action for which the initiative came from its rival; the Communist Party relegated the 'united front' [at the bottom] to the accessory boutique, contenting itself with bringing a stone to the building of [joint action]. This was a radical change in orientation." [4]

On the 12th, separately organized communist and socialist demonstrators met at Place de la Nation. Hesitant about what would happen, the leaders on both sides held back. However, the rank and file of both delegations, taking the initiative, rushed together chanting repetitively "Unity! Unity! Unity!" Quickly, Léon Blum, Paul Faure,

[4] Louis Bodin, "Le Parti communiste dans le Front Populaire," *Esprit*, October, 1966, p. 438.

Marcel Cachin, and Jacques Duclos were hoisted onto improvised platforms to speak. Swept past the obstacles of the past fourteen years by a tremendous popular current, the SFIO and PCF leaders were more or less forced into accepting the principle of "unity of action" on the spot.

But in any case, the polarization of French politics since the 1932 elections had already rendered such a development probable for many months. The PCF leaders, for their part, had been moving toward a reversal of alliance posture tentatively and intermittently since the end of 1932. Hitler's rise to power and the repression of the KPD in 1933 had moved them farther along the road to the *grand tournant* of 1934, and had also forced the Comintern leadership to recognize that the class-against-class tactics had been a disaster. During the last two weeks of February 1934, moreover, the Austrian Social Democrats were crushed by Chancellor Dollfuss, and an authoritarian regime was installed.[5]

Only a short time later, on July 15, a special session of the SFIO National Council formally accepted the principle of common action with the PCF. On July 27, a "Pact of Unity of Action" was signed. Throughout the rest of 1934 and into 1935 joint meetings and declarations indicated an increasing willingness on the part of both to unite against a common danger, and finally, in the huge demonstration of July 14, 1935—which included a delegation from the Radical Party as well—the move toward a Popular Front was ratified in the streets. The *Comité National de Rassemblement Populaire*, created to organize the July 14 demonstration, was transformed into an electoral committee that united socialists, communists, and Radicals with a number of smaller organizations. The purpose of the *Comité* was to prepare for the 1936 general elections, and after a period of discussions marked above all by a desire to come to an agreement, a joint electoral program was made public in January 1936.[6] The general elections of

---

[5] Later that year, Dollfuss was to be assassinated in an attempted coup by Austrian Nazis.

[6] The "Unity of Action" agreement of July 27, 1935, a PCF-SFIO "Common Platform" of September 23, and the Popular Front Program are reproduced in Jacques Delpierrié de Bayac, *Histoire du Front populaire*, pp. 500–512.

April 26–May 3, 1936 brought the Popular Front coalition to power in a government headed by Léon Blum.

The course of events during the Popular Front is known so well that here one need only provide the essentials in order to supply a background for this analysis of what the Front meant for communist activity in France.

By stretching a point, one may consider that five Popular Front governments were formed during the period 1936–38: the first Blum government (June 1936–June 1937), two successive governments headed by the Radical Camille Chautemps (June 1937–March 1938); the second Blum government (March–April 1938); and the government of Edouard Daladier (April 1938–March 1940). The Communist Party helped to invest all of these governments, but participated in none of them. While all five governments thus were supported to some degree by the original 1936 partnership, the first Blum government was *the* Popular Front; and although it is true that the dislocation of the alliance did not become definitive until late 1938, the failure of Blum in the winter and spring of 1936–37 was the determining factor.

Although not generally realized, the parties composing the 1936 Popular Front had already held a majority in the Chamber of 1932. The dominant parliamentary force in 1932 was the Radical Party, but of course the PCF class-against-class tactic disposed neither the Radicals nor the Socialists to consider them as coalition partners. Radicals and Socialists, as in 1924, had once again formed a *Cartel des Gauches* in 1932. The SFIO stood by its policy of support without participation in the government, and during 1932–34 the classic parliamentary "shift to the right" occurred once more (this time essentially over economic and financial policy in the Depression) as the conservative Radicals gained dominance over the socialist-oriented Radicals, as symbolized in the list of successive premiers: Herriot, Daladier, Doumergue, Laval.

The adoption of Popular-Front tactics by the communists in 1934 and the announcement by the Socialists of their willingness to lead a government resulted not only in a renewed majority from the Radicals leftward, but, more importantly, also in a tremendous internal shift in the balance of this majority. Theoretically numbering 322 in 1932, the

Left majority elected in 1936 rose to 370 (of 615 and 618 total seats), and the gains of the SFIO and PCF were quite extraordinary, because of the practice of mutual withdrawals and a shift in the electorate toward the extremes of the political spectrum. The following table gives figures for votes, percentage of valid ballots, and seats obtained from the Radicals leftward in the elections of 1932 and 1936:

Table 2: Leftist Representation, 1932, 1936

	1932			1936		
	Votes	*% Ballots*	*Seats*	*Votes*	*% Ballots*	*Seats*
PCF	796,630	8%	12	1,504,404	15%	72
SFIO	1,964,384	21%	129	1,955,306	20%	149
Various left *	78,412	1%	11	748,600	10%	56
Radical-Socialist	1,836,991	19%	157	1,422,611	14%	109

Source: Maurice Duverger, *Constitutions et documents politiques* (Paris: Presses universitaires de France, 1968), 5th ed., pp. 280–81. The statistics for total vote and % of valid ballots refer to the first ballot; the statistics for seats refer to the final result.

* Groups various minor parties such as Socialistes-communistes; Union Socialiste Républicaine, Gauche Indépendante, Parti Camille Pelletan, etc.

Despite a slight decline in its electoral base, the SFIO in 1936 became the largest single force both in the majority and in the Chamber as a whole, because of mutual withdrawals in its favor by both PCF and Radical candidates. On the extreme Left, the Communist Party nearly doubled its electoral base, and because of the mutual withdrawals it increased its parliamentary representation by over 500 percent.[7] In addition, various minor Left-wing parties, some to the Left and some to the Right of the SFIO, had also made considerable gains. The only Popular Front loss was, therefore, the decline in the Radical fortunes, both in terms of votes and seats. Explainable largely by the defection of conservative Radicals from the Popular Front co-

[7] The PCF was particularly successful in the industrial centers: in the Paris region 43 deputies were elected, of which 32 were from Paris and its immediate suburbs; 6 deputies were elected in the Nord, 3 in the Bouches-du-Rhône, 2 in the Gard. Some considerable degree of success was also obtained in the rural Massif Central as well as in the Southeast, due to the support of small merchants and shopkeepers: two deputies each were elected in the Lot-et-Garonne, the Var, the Dordogne, and the Alpes-Maritimes.

alition, this put the party led by Herriot and Daladier in a difficult position, and the internal differences among the Radicals would later have considerable repercussions.

Immediately after the elections were terminated, Léon Blum proposed that he be called to head the government; he announced that since the situation could not be considered revolutionary, his government would "exercise bourgeois power" in order to defeat fascism but would not attempt to institute socialism. Between the May 3 ballot and the investiture of the Popular Front government on June 4, however, a series of strikes and occupations of enterprises broke out all over France, stemming largely from the rank and file, and took the syndicalist leadership by surprise. This mass action quickly became so widespread that it began to appear that the working class was actually taking power. By the beginning of June, approximately 1,000 establishments had been occupied, 12,000 were struck, and over 2 million workers were participating in what had become virtually a general strike. Moreover, the extreme left wing of the SFIO, led by Marceau Pivert, incited popular fervor for a "revolutionary" decision from the Popular Front government, promoting the incendiary slogan *"Tout est possible!"*

The majority of strikers apparently desired a bloc settlement of outstanding grievances with the *Patronat*. The general atmosphere was one of *fête*, and newsreel films of the day depict more dancing in between the assembly lines than revolutionary consciousness. Nonetheless, by June 1, the situation had become extremely volatile, and the *Patronat* and the conservative parliamentarians were obviously fearful of a continued rise in popular pressure on the ruling structures in the economy.

On June 5, one day after taking office, Léon Blum invited representatives of the *Patronat* (the association of business) and the syndicates to a conference at the Hôtel Matignon, where, as Alfred Cobban has well put it, in a brief negotiation "alarm at what seemed a revolutionary situation extracted revolutionary concessions from the employers." [8] On June 9, the famous "Matignon Agreement" was signed, and the basis was laid for the implementation in a few months'

[8] Alfred Cobban, *A History of Modern France*, 3:152.

time of the most serious social reforms in France since the birth of the
Third Republic. The major gains were a pay raise averaging 12 percent for salaried workers; nationalization of the armaments industry;
an agreement in principle to impose government control on the pri-
vately owned and run Bank of France; the introduction of a forty-hour
week; agreement on the principle of collective bargaining; formal recognition by the *Patronat* of the right of unions to represent the workers; and, probably the most popular of all, introduction of two weeks'
paid vacation. (In fact, this provision allowed many workers to take
their first vacations over.) [9]

After the Matignon conference, the problems of how to get the
workers back on the job remained, because they continued their occupations and strikes even after the Agreement had been signed. The
workers were perhaps somewhat drunk with the quick and sudden effectiveness of their power and also somewhat unconvinced that the
Patronat would actually implement the accord. At this point, the communists undertook their most controversial act of the Popular Front
period: on June 11, Maurice Thorez announced that

the workers should not allow themselves the illusion that "all is possible," as
the irresponsible formula of Marceau Pivert would have it. No, all is not possible. To pose the question of the socialist revolution at this stage would signify a division of the working class and a break in the alliance realized with
large sectors of the laboring peasantry and the working classes on the basis of
the Popular Front program. . . . If the present goal is to obtain satisfaction
of demands of an economic character . . . then one has to know how to stop
once satisfaction has been obtained. It is necessary even to know how to consent to compromise when all demands have not yet been accepted, but when
one has obtained victory on the most essential and most important demands. [10]

Within a few weeks after the communists called for an end to the general strike, factory workers were back at their jobs. By the end of

[9] Nationalization of the armaments industry, never efficiently implemented, was to
have permitted a more active defense policy against German belligerence, such as was
being advocated by the young Colonel de Gaulle. Government control of the Bank of
France, not achieved definitively until its nationalization in 1945, was to have extended control by the government of its own finances. The shareholders of the Bank
were represented in the General Council of Two Hundred, and it "was in both form
and substance an oligarchy of the Third Republic." (David Thomson, *Democracy in
France Since 1870*, pp. 69–71). The General Council of Two Hundred was symbolized
in communist propaganda as the "200 families who control France," which provided a
specific target for popular grievances.

[10] Cited in *Histoire du Parti communiste français (manuel)*, pp. 318–19.

June, the salaried masses were no longer endangering domestic stability or embarrassing the PCF posture of moderation.

Having taken over the reins of government in a period of critical uncertainty, the coalition partners recognized that the possibility of implementing the Popular Front program depended upon renewed economic prosperity and a relatively stable political situation: for the communists and Radicals—motivated first of all by the struggle against fascism—and for the socialists—whose primary focus at this point was economic and social reform—the achievement of the goals that had led them into the Front required that they be able to control the domestic crises. In general, the lack of a coherent and forceful economic and monetary policy was the key failure, but more specifically, a series of four factors combined to prevent the Blum cabinet from achieving this control: first, an angered and frightened industrial and propertied class sent its money out of the country, and this flight of capital drained the financial resources upon which Blum had hoped to rebuild; second, the general strike, combined with the immediate introduction of a forty-hour week in many industries, had debilitated present production; third, the unwillingness of Blum himself to demand stricter fiscal and monetary controls from the parliament at a time when they might have been passed condemned the Popular Front program in the long run; and fourth, foreign-policy disagreements among the three major coalition factions weakened the united-front position in parliament and among the masses.

Thus, the Matigon Agreement can be considered the high point of the Popular Front successes, for almost immediately thereafter the situation, Blum's enemies, and (unwittingly) he himself, acted together to destroy the *élan* of early June. Because of his failure to stabilize the economy Blum was forced to jettison one of the fundamental policies of the Front—the promise not to devalue the franc. (The conservative Poincaré had accepted devaluation in 1928.) On October 1, 1936, the franc was devalued, with even the communists voting approval.[11] With the huge reform momentum having been broken within a few weeks after Blum had taken office, however, this compromise of principle had no chance of conciliating the resurgent conservatives. The

[11] This was a bitter pill for the Communist and socialist rank-and-file to swallow, for they had been made to understand that the Popular Front would "tax the rich" as a solution to financial crisis rather than follow the traditional pattern.

situation deteriorated continually through the fall and winter, and Blum was obliged to declare a "pause" in the implementation of the Popular Front program in February 1937. In reality, this declaration signaled both the end of the reform (it had lasted but a few months) and the death of hope in Blum's government.

During the summer of 1936, foreign policy questions, in the form of the Spanish Civil War which broke out on July 19, presented another crisis requiring Blum's immediate attention. Essentially, the debate within the French government concerned whether and in what way to intervene on the side of the Spanish Republicans. Moreover, the public appeal to the French government by the Spanish Prime Minister Giral aggravated Blum's personal dilemma. His pacifist sentiments and his fear of provoking Hitler conflicted with his republican and humanitarian principles. Within the French government as a whole, opinions were bitterly divided, and the coalition nearly split apart at that early point. The Radicals, who also refused to provoke Hitler, were generally against intervention. At the same time, within the Radical Party and the SFIO both, an interventionist left wing led by Pierre Cot (himself a Radical) pressed for shipments of arms, while in the SFIO an important current of opinion led by Paul Faure argued for complete nonintervention largely on pacifist grounds. Lastly, the communists, while calling for military aid to the Spanish Republicans, nonetheless remained prudent. Stalin also feared the possible consequences of placing the Comintern, albeit indirectly, into opposition to Hitler. And this was an interest that dovetailed with Blum's arguments that such action by the French might provoke both an external and civil war.[12] Furthermore, until the Germans and Italians themselves intervened, Stalin's policy was also to avoid abusing the pacifism of the English, in order to conserve his eventual chances of allying with them against the Germans.[13] After the Ger-

---

[12] Thorez indicated the Communist acceptance of this line of argument as early as July 25, 1936: "One must consider what would become of our country if the fascist bands in the service of capital succeeded in provoking disorder and civil war here as well. . . . Everyone understands that a France weakened by civil war would be soon the prey of Hitler." (Fauvet, *Histoire du Parti Communiste français*, 1:203). There would be no French equivalent of the KPD slogan *"Nach Hitler Kommen wir!"*

[13] For these reasons, Stalin instructed the Spanish Communist Party to restrict somewhat its role in the Republican government. The PCE could have played a stronger hand, had they seen it in their interest.

mans intervened, however, the French Communists moved to a more open policy of aid to the Spanish Republicans, probably based upon Stalin's calculation that a victory by General Franco would encircle France and thus render a Franco-Soviet alliance all the more unlikely in case of war.

Left alone, Blum himself would very probably have opted for nonintervention in almost any case, both because of his pacifist leanings and because of his more realistic fear of the consequences of a war for France. Publicly, however, he put his decision in terms which indicated that France was following the British lead, following the implicit foreign policy of previous interwar French governments, which consisted in seeking to shift responsibility for the post-Versailles European situation onto the English. Moreover, whereas before 1936 the French armies could have faced the Germans alone if necessary, after that time the changed military balance made an alliance with England a *sine qua non* in case of war on the Continent.[14]

Because of these various considerations, when in August Blum finally announced his support for the British position of nonintervention, the French Communists did not consider leaving the Popular Front. In their eyes, and those of Stalin, the broader stakes at issue justified a policy symbolized by the slogan "unity at any price." Over the next two years, they would demonstrate this priority more than once in even worse circumstances.[15]

With the Popular Front domestic program blocked in a completely mortgaged economic and financial situation, and with foreign policy questions dividing the coalition and threatening the security of France itself, the cohesion of the three major partners had been fundamentally shaken within their first months in office. Perceiving this break-

[14] See Raymond Aron, *Peace and War* (New York: Praeger, 1967), pp. 41–42.

[15] The PCF nonetheless aided the Spanish Republicans on their own. Thorez was apparently one of the most important in getting Stalin to accept the idea of the International Brigades, in which many PCF leaders and militants actively participated. Furthermore, the French Communists provided or acted as conduits for considerable amounts of money and materiel. In essence, the PCF policy was to go as far as possible (Thorez himself went to the war zone in February 1937) without comprising the preeminent goals of national defense and a Franco-Soviet alliance. Some of the details of these events can be found in Hugh Thomas, *The Spanish Civil War* (New York: Harper and Row, 1961) 721 pp., passim.

down of momentum, the opponents of the Popular Front became more aggressive, and the Radical Party was already reconsidering a change in its alliance policy. Given this, the *attentiste* position of Blum in foreign policy could not help but be transferred into domestic affairs. Several times during the winter and spring Blum announced the imminent implementation of those measures in the Popular Front program not yet put into effect. A renewal of the original *élan* was not forthcoming, however, and while the government sometimes deposited a text which was voted by the Chamber and allowed to die in the conservative-dominated Senate, more often the weak financial situation dissuaded Blum from attempting to realize the rest of the coalition program at all. Only in one area, implementation of the forty-hour week, was the reform continued, and this by a series of executive decrees (rather than parliamentary bills) that instituted the law industry by industry.[16] Blum's official declaration of the "pause" on February 13, 1937, thus only consecrated a *situation de fait*.

As early as March 1937, Blum seriously considered resigning his government. After the March 16 riot of opposing Rightists and Leftists (during which the police clashed several times with communist and socialist militants, resulting in five deaths and injuries to 200) he resolved nonetheless to end the pause and make one more attempt to recoup. On June 10, he requested emergency plenary financial powers in order to get the Popular Front moving once again. The Chamber granted him the powers by a 346–247 vote.[17] The bill was voted down in the Senate, however. After several weak and dispirited attempts to sway the upper chamber had failed, Blum publicly admitted the bankruptcy of his efforts and submitted his resignation on June 22, 1937.

The same day a new government was formed by the Radical Camille Chautemps. The speed of its constitution indicated that it had been in preparation beforehand and its accession signaled a definitive

[16] The use of decree laws by Blum was a further admission of failure, as it implied a lack of parliamentary support. A major SFIO and PCF critique of previous governments had been the lack of "authentic" use of parliament, the only governmental institution based on universal suffrage. Of course, Blum's problem was the Senate, where conservative Radicals dominated, rather than the Chamber, and the Senate was only indirectly based on universal suffrage.

[17] All the Communists and almost all the Radicals were still supporting the government.

rightward shift of the spirit as well as the practice of the Popular Front.[18] After a morose half-year, during which Chautemps "contented himself with expedients to temporize the monetary and financial problems which had been the occasion for the fall of the Blum ministry. . . . [executing] without saying it the pause which Léon Blum had envisaged in the spring," [19] the second Popular Front government resigned in March 1938, without even having been placed in minority.[20] A sensitive historian of the period, François Goguel, has described the increasingly desolate situation:

> Never had the divisions of public sentiment been so profound: they paralyzed the state almost completely at the exact moment when the rising tension in relations between Hitler and Chancellor Schuschnigg made likely new threats to peace in Europe. Chautemps understood that the parliamentary base of his cabinet was too narrow to assure the government the authority necessary in such circumstances. Also perhaps, he wished to escape the responsibilities which the imminence of the Anschluss threatened to place upon him.[21]

Upon the resignation of Chautemps, President Lebrun recalled Léon Blum, for despite the fact that Chautemps had alienated the socialists from participation in the cabinet, nevertheless the majority in the Chamber was still theoretically based on the SFIO. Furthermore, Lebrun appeared to believe that only a reinvigoration and perhaps an extension of the Popular Front had even a slim chance of avoiding war, which was his first concern.

Because of the events since his first resignation, Blum agreed that the threat of war demanded a radical compromise among the competing forces in parliament. He therefore proposed the formation of what he called a "government of national unanimity," whose overriding purpose would be to defend the security of the nation. Essentially the plan implied the reconstruction of the "national union" government of

---

[18] Chautemps had been Premier in Center-Right governments twice before: once for four days (1930) and once for two months (1934).

[19] François Goguel, *La politique des partis sous la IIIe République,* pp. 521–22.

[20] Chautemps had originally constituted a Radical and SFIO cabinet: in January 1938, after a dispute over financial policy in which the SFIO proposed a return to the controls envisioned by Blum in 1937, Chautemps formed a second cabinet entirely of Radicals. He would no doubt have liked to return the Radicals to a Rightward alliance, but the situation was not ripe for such a move.

[21] Goguel, *Politique des partis,* pp. 523–24.

1914–18, even to the point of including the communists as ministers this time around.

Never before had the initiative for a national unity government been taken by the socialist Left, and Blum's proposal indicated a final attempt to resolve his personal contradictions, to conciliate socialism, pacifism, and national defense at a time when indecision was unacceptable. However, two factors precluded the Blum project from the beginning; first, by now the progressive Radicals could no longer raise a majority within the party willing to accept communist participation, and the Moderates were *a priori* against such an idea; second, the personal animosity of the conservative, clerical, and diehard capitalist Right toward Blum himself was virulent to the point of ferocity.[22]

Frustrated once again, Blum "resigned himself to the constitution of a government in which he did not believe," [23] and whatever he might have hoped in the beginning, the second Blum ministry resembled his first on all counts.[24] Including neither the conservatives nor the communists, Blum's cabinet this time lasted less than one month—from March 13 to April 10, 1938. And once again, it was the conservative Senate that put the government into minority over financial policy. The occasion was a new and vigorous (in principle) financial and economic plan, in which Blum wanted to "mobilize all the means of production and all the wealth of the nation in order to raise our defense to the very highest degree of efficiency." [25] Yet, some eighteen months before the Nazi-Soviet Pact, the French Right still hoped above all to avoid war and was ready, if necessary, to appease Hitler with concessions. Thus, the second Blum government program was quickly blocked and was followed by his second resignation. A few months later, another government would attempt to mollify Hitler at the Munich conference. Oscillating without firmness, French foreign policy during these last prewar years was nothing if not indecisive and ineffective. Its dominant goal was to avoid a war with the Nazi *Reichswehr*, although no one seemed to know how, or acted to do so.

By the time the conservative Radical Édouard Daladier succeeded

[22] On this, see, for example, *ibid.* pp. 525–27.

[23] Lefranc, *Le mouvement syndical sous la Troisième République*, p. 109

[24] See Goguel, *Politique des partis*, p. 527.

[25] The phrase is that of Pierre Mendès-France, who helped Blum in the drafting of this plan and held his first high office in the second Blum cabinet. See his *The Pursuit of Freedom*, a translation of *Liberté, Liberté chérie* (New York, 1943), p. 5.

Blum as head of government in April 1938, the Popular Front was all but officially dissolved. Since the SFIO leadership refused to participate, the Daladier cabinet itself was made up of Moderates (conservatives) and Radicals. Nonetheless, both the SFIO and PCF voted for the investiture, hoping to preserve at least the appearance of the Front at a moment when unity in the face of German belligerence and the desire not to abandon the regime to the antiparliamentarian, fascist-oriented groups dominated the goal structure of the socialist Left. However, this last prewar French government, which closed the Franco-Spanish border to arms shipments, signed the Munich agreement, and was in office when the Nazi-Soviet Pact was concluded, in fact incarnated an end of hope for some sort of national *rassemblement*.

During the Daladier ministry the SFIO was indecisive and divided, and its leadership was politically impotent; Léon Blum, Paul Faure, and the other foremost socialists were simply unable to formulate a coherent view of the events that were, by this time, out of the control of the French government in any case. After the Versailles settlement, France had been considered the pillar of the European security structure; the seeds sown by the failure of French leadership in the interwar period—a failure imputable in no small degree to the indecisiveness of the socialist leaders—had now matured into bitter fruits.

When Daladier brought the Munich Pact to the Chamber for ratification, only the Communists did not split over the issue; they voted unanimously against it. They charged that the French and British governments, in order to avoid war with Germany, were in effect attempting to make a sacrifice of the Soviet Union, rendering the maxim "Better Hitler than Stalin" the watchword of Western European foreign policy. Furthermore, the PCF leaders undoubtedly concluded also that by accommodating Hitler, those governments had indicated they were prepared to follow a policy that by implication threw into question the Communist movement in France as well. While other parties and groups thus debated alternatives in a vain search for a possible and positive policy, the Communist position was rather obvious.[26]

---

[26] Isaac Deutscher has written, "The unwritten maxim of Munich was to keep Russia out of Europe." (Deutscher, *Stalin*, p. 419). This, at best, is but a half-truth. Here is not the place to enter into a discussion of the Munich controversy. Rather I limit myself intentionally to an explanation of the PCF position.

After the Munich vote had saddled them with the appearance of "warmongers," the Communists moved into total opposition to the government, officially dissolving the Popular Front. The socialists, disunited over the question of whether or not appeasement was a viable policy,[27] finally joined the PCF in declared opposition in December 1938. From that point on, the situation was irretrievable as far as the French Communists were concerned. The Popular Front was dead and all attempts at a united front strategy "at the top" were now purely symbolic.

From this brief sketch of the Popular Front experience emerge a number of key problems to investigate concerning this first period of French Communist governmental collaboration in a "bourgeois" regime. We want to isolate the dominant and latent aspects of communist participation in the Front. We want to analyze the manner in which the Party conceived and presented its role, and how the role was played in fact. Finally, we want to determine what consequences PCF participation in the Front and in the governmental coalition had upon its position of fundamental opposition to the regime and to the society.

The Doctrinal Justification

A first approach to an understanding of the developments of communist strategy and tactics during the Popular Front is to examine doctrinal justifications.[28]

---

[27] This debate was further confused by the pacifist considerations posed by many leading socialist figures, sometimes including Blum himself. Paul Faure, Secretary General of the SFIO and recognized leader of the pacifist wing in the party, wrote articles against resistance to the Nazis in *Le Populaire*. When Daladier returned from Munich expecting violent opposition, he was undoubtedly astonished to read Léon Blum writing in *Le Populaire* that "every man and woman in France would pay their just tribute of gratitude to Chamberlain and Daladier." See Cobban, *Modern France*, 3:170–171.

[28] This, of course, can tell us only how the Communist leadership sought to present its actions. The question of whether or not the Communist leadership "really" believed its public justifications is impossible to answer definitively. As Deutscher writes of Stalin: "Did Stalin sincerely seek alliance with the bourgeois democracies of the West? If not anti-fascist virtue, then the demands of self-preservation drove (him) to seek security in a solid system of alliances" (*Stalin*, p. 412).

The essence of the Popular Front as conceived in the Marxist-Leninist perspective was to move the French Communists tactically from a position of hard-line and sectarian opposition to the established order to a position of general collaboration in the national government, while at the same time preserving their fundamental rejection of the political regime and socioeconomic order. In other words, the communist leadership attempted to maintain the movement strategically at once within and without the established order, while switching its tactical emphasis from sectarian to alliance politics.[29]

The origin of the Popular Front tactic in France has not been definitively established, and is in any case not of first-magnitude importance.[30] The key to understanding the tactical blend fashioned by the French Communists throughout the Popular Front period is on the other hand quite clear. Party policy from 1934 onward was based on the "struggle against fascism." This was translated into the policies of containing the French antiparliamentary and pro-Hitler groups, defending France against German aggression, and therein defending both the French Communist movement itself and the frontiers of the Soviet Union. Until 1938, these goals were on the whole immediately reconcilable; the French Communists became the leading advocates of a firm policy of national defense, which had the double merit of emphasizing the common interest of France and the Soviet Union (and thus pointing up the need for a viable Franco-Soviet alliance) and of reconciling communism and patriotism for the first time.

The major doctrinal statement of the French Communist attitude toward the Popular Front is the 8th Party Congress (January 1936), the first Congress since the preunity gathering of 1932. It is there that Maurice Thorez, having solidly implanted his authority and his personality in the Party hierarchy and having been officially annointed

---

[29] For a similar conception, see Perrot and Kriegel, *Socialisme français*, pp. 111ff.

[30] Logic and some considerable evidence indicate that probably the first move and at least the final sanction came from Moscow, given the constitution of Popular Fronts in other countries (e.g., Spain, Belgium). (See, eg., Albert and Célie Vassart, "The Moscow Origin of the French 'Popular Front,' " in Milorad M. Drachkonitch and Branko Lazitch [eds.] *The Comintern: Historical Highlights* (New York: Praeger, 1966), pp. 234–52. (A. Vassart was the PCF delegate to the Comintern in 1934–35). PCF historiography implies the opposite, e.g. Thorez, *Fils du peuple*, pp. 400–401; as does Bodin, *"Parti communiste,"* pp. 440–41.

leader by the Comintern, made the report that consecrated the strategy
developed during the preceding two years.

The Secretary General, in line with the tradition of communist
congresses generally, opened his keynote speech with a summary of the
historical juncture, the "correct" definition of which indicates the
proper Party line. For Thorez "At the present moment, fascism constitutes the principal danger. . . . Fascism is, in effect, 'the open terrorist dictatorship of the most reactionary, most chauvinist, most imperialist elements of finance capital.' " [31] Thus, whereas in a situation
not directly threatening "retrograde" movement in the class struggle,
the main dangers to a communist party are usually said to be the internal dangers of "opportunism" and "sectarianism," the main danger
in the 1934–36 period, with its tendency toward "reaction," was said
to be the "exterior" menace of fascism. And while the Comintern's
conception of fascism was swallowed whole only among the faithful,
Thorez's prescription of how to react received much wider currency:

It is possible for France to avoid the shame and the barbarianism of fascism.
Fascism was able to win in Germany because the working class, which could
have taken the road of the proletarian revolution, was detoured from it by
Social Democracy, because the working class was divided by the policy of
collaboration of classes. [32]

Translated into noncommunist vocabulary, Thorez's remarks blamed
the split between the SPD and KPD for the lack of working-class resistance to Hitler, which according to the Comintern line had been the
decisive factor in permitting Nazism's rise to power. Of course, few outside the communist movement placed the onus entirely on the SPD, particularly since the KPD, like the PCF, continued to practice class-
against-class tactics during Hitler's ascension, although this policy was
so misguided that, if it had any effect at all, it helped rather than restrained Hitler. [33] Nonetheless the proposal of unity of the Left as a
bulwark against a fascist coup in France possessed an evident political

[31] PCF–8, Thorez report, pp. 76, 108. The definition of fascism (in single quotes)
used by Thorez here is the Comintern definition verbatim.

[32] *Ibid.*, p. 114.

[33] Some even went so far as to accuse Stalin of allowing the German Communists to
be annihilated as a gesture to Hitler.

logic, and events were to demonstrate that in certain situations socialists and Radicals were willing to apply the classic strategy of "the enemy of my enemy is my friend" even to Communists. For the PCF, defense of "the republican order" against fascism—that is, preservation of the most favorable possible regime—became the dominant *mot d'ordre:*

The situation appeared clear. . . . The condemnation of democracy by the elite cliques . . . dictated our policy for us: it was necessary to defend democracy, to incite the *petite bourgeoisie* to struggle for the safeguard of its threatened liberties, to call the proletariat to support, along with its own interests, those of the middle strata. . . . In defending the Republic, we were defending the working class and we were preparing the future.[34]

It was here that the Communist analysis joined that of the socialist and Radical groups; whatever might be the differences between partners in the proposed Popular Front coalition, the extent of immediate dangers to all provided a justification for temporary common action. In a word, the Popular Front partners perceived it worthwhile to save the Third Republic in order to be able to dispute it at a later date.

The uniqueness of the Popular Front in terms of parliamentary coalition-building was of course that it included the communists in a governmental majority for the first time.[35] For the communists this event was obviously a doctrinal problem of considerable proportions, and the expected charges of revisionism came from three principal sources: the Trotskyites, the revolutionary syndicalists, and the Left-

[34] *Fils du Peuple*, p. 392. In his report to the 8th Congress, Thorez underlined the importance of the Republic: "without question Marx showed that 'the bourgeois republic cannot be other than the most advanced form of the domination of the entire bourgeois class,' But he underlined at the same time that the republic 'was the most likely terrain of the struggle for the revolutionary emancipation of the proletariat, but not that emancipation itself.' " (PCF-8, Thorez report, p. 104. Thorez is citing *The Class Struggles in France.*)

[35] Previous unions of the French Left had occurred in 1899–1904, the *Bloc des Gauches*, in which Radicals and socialists supported a series of governments, the first of which had seen the "Millerand affair" over the question of socialist ministerial participation; in 1924 and 1932 the same two forces had allied in the *Cartel des Gauches*, neither of which saw socialist participation. Whereas the *Bloc* slogan had been "no enemies on the left," the *Cartel* was in effect only slightly left of center, and in both instances the socialists returned to opposition after a short time.

wing socialists (led by Pivert). To deflect this sort of attack, Thorez attempted to impose a definition of the Popular Front in terms of the dual Marxist legitimacies:

One sometimes hears . . . that the [coalition] of the Popular Front appears to be a copy of the governments of the Cartel. Others . . . seem to believe that our Party would be disposed to participate in governments such as those which one has seen at work in Germany and in Austria, of which one knows the results. Let us repeat once again that for us, in the condition of aggravated crisis, of a general paralysis of the *bourgeoisie* and of the revolutionary development of the masses, the government of the Popular Front will be a government that will end the fascist menace . . . a government *that will make the rich pay* . . . a government that, to realize this double task, will rely on the extraparliamentary activity of the masses, on the organization of the Popular Front committees . . . a government permitting the preparation of the total assumption of power by the working class; in short, a government that would be the preface to armed insurrection for the dictatorship of the proletariat.[36]

In short, the Popular Front was to be no more than a tactic, undertaken by the PCF and the other European parties, "without ever losing sight of . . . fundamental goals," in a logic similar to both the "united front at the top" tactics of the 1920s and the class-against-class tactic of 1928–34. Yet at the same time Thorez did not link the Popular Front in a *necessary* causal schema to armed revolution. He intimated only that, should the situation develop as the communists hoped, revolution *might* result from the Popular Front. Dimitrov, Secretary-General of the Comintern, had stated the Soviet consecration of this line a few months earlier at the 7th Comintern Congress.[37]

Despite the always optimistic Party line, however, the Communist hope for an actual revolutionary possibility was relegated to some future time. The PCF slogan "All for the Popular Front!" indicated the real Communist concern of the moment, as manifested in the controversial action taken by the Party leadership during the general strike of late May and early June 1936. Caught by surprise when the wildcat strikes and occupations burst out, leaving even the syndicalist leadership hanging at the gate, on June 5 the PCF suddenly found itself part of the governmental majority assuming office in the midst of

---

[36] PCF–8, Thorez report, pp. 133–34.

[37] *L'Internationale communiste*, September 17–18, 1935, cited in Perrot and Kriegel, *Socialisme français*, pp. 123–25.

a profound, possibly even revolutionary, upheaval. Furthermore, the CGT—led by the reformist Léon Jouhaux and now representing both communist and socialist tendencies after the unions voted to reunify in March—had been completely unprepared for such a turn of events, and could not regain control of the situation for the government.[38] With revolutionary syndicalists, Trotskyites, and the Left-wing socialists proclaiming "All is possible!" the general strike threatened to compromise the immediately reformist and defensive mission of the Popular Front. With the SFIO leadership and the majority of its rank and file committed to maintaining the established regime, the attitude of the Communist leadership was to be crucial in determining in which direction the situation would turn.

At this moment Thorez made manifest the Communist intention to play it safe, that is to retain the "defense of democracy" rather than insurrection as the operative goal of Communist action. The communist *mot d'ordre* resulting in the quick conclusion of the general strike was justified as necessary in order "not to cut off the working class from its newfound allies, a situation which might easily result in the victory of the principal danger to the long-range revolutionary movement, fascist reaction." The Communist perspective was summed up in a single remark of Thorez: "There is no possibility of taking power at the present time." [39] In short, this meant that while the ultimate intention of revolution was not in question, it was necessary, given the context, to support the most favorable nonrevolutionary situation, that is the "bourgeois" republic, until some decisive change would permit a reevaluation of the strategic mix of minimum-and maximum-oriented actions. Moreover, while this policy was justified on the basis of the balance of forces in France and in Germany (the effect of Hitler's action against the KPD is not to be underestimated), it is also

[38] The Communist-dominated CGTU was reabsorbed into the socialist-oriented CGT, a move permitted by the Communist leadership to further the Popular Front in an immediate sense, and to attempt a takeover of the parent syndicate in the long term. Once again, the dual strategy logic is apparent: Communist infiltration of key positions in the CGT hierarchy had begun by the time the Popular Front was dislocated, and the outbreak of war ended the experience for the moment. The process was begun again in 1944–45, and by early 1946 the Communists had effectively won the CGT. (See chapter 6.)

[39] Thorez on June 11, 1936, cited in *Fils du peuple*, p. 420.

true that the PCF action served the Soviet policy toward Germany and Europe in general at this time.

While the general strike of May–June 1936 was therefore not perceived as indicative of a revolutionary situation, the classic Leninist focus on "the movement of the masses" as the signpost of the revolutionary conjuncture remained the basic definitional criterion by which the Party leadership justified its conclusions, and during 1936–37 the role of alliance "at the bottom" came increasingly to be emphasized as the coalition "at the top" disintegrated.

At the 1937 Congress, held in a mood of increasing pessimism after the fall of the first Blum cabinet, Thorez went far toward a reformulation of the Communist focus in the Popular Front, in order to prepare an eventual disengagement if, as seemed likely, the new government led by Chautemps moved away from the Communist interest: "The Popular Front is not a parliamentary coalition. It is the movement of the masses, with its legal expression on the parliamentary and governmental level." [40]

The Soviet interest did not permit the Communists to disengage themselves from the coalition for another year, however. Even after Chautemps, and still more Daladier, came to treat them with disdain and often outright hostility, the PCF leadership attempted to maintain its policy of support without participation, hoping that a turn of events would permit them to successfully promote a Franco-Soviet alliance. While the Party continued to woo the mass base of the Popular Front to the extent possible, and to issue sanguine statements about the ultimately revolutionary content of this action, it became clear through the clinging-vine attitude of the PFC during 1937–39 that they were committed, above all else, to influencing French policy at the top.

The dominant Communist concern as the Popular Front tactic seriously degenerated in 1937 was reiterated by Thorez at the 9th Congress: "The fundamental problem of the moment, which has determined all the policy of our Communist Party, [is] . . . who will be victorious: the working class and democratic solidarity, or fascism." [41]

---

[40] PCF–9, Thorez report, p. 69.   [41] *Ibid.*, p. 71.

There is little reason to doubt that this was an honest statement of PFC perception, as expressed succinctly in the slogan "vanquish fascism; save the working class by saving democracy and peace." [42]

Nonetheless, even at this point of rapidly disintegrating prospects, the communists attempted to retain their mortgage on the revolutionary dictatorship of the proletariat against the charges of revisionism:

> For our people, for our working class, the struggle for liberty and for peace is joined *for the time being* with the struggle for the independence and the security of France. Such a struggle does not have a strictly national character. *For the time being*, as during other glorious periods in the history of our people, it takes on a universal character. . . .
>
> Those who refuse to understand this *real* and *new* form of the proletarian struggle . . . those who would oppose it after the example of the . . . Trotskyites and other agents of the Gestapo . . . those people may give out with cute revolutionary phrases; they are in fact the worst enemies of the revolution, the shameful accomplices of fascism. [43]

In sum, a vigorous and involved manipulation of revolutionary symbols was a first way in which the French Communist leadership sought to neutralize the dominant aspect of Communist activity during the Popular Front period, one of large and deep collaboration with "bourgeois" forces. Besides such doctrinal justifications one may point to several practical, and therein more significant, ways in which the Party attempted to preserve its exterior position, and even to prepare the way for a renunciation of this collaboration if possible.

---

[42] *Ibid.*, p. 85. In a passage obviously designed to elicit sympathy for PCF and Soviet intentions from the British and American governments, Thorez added: "What French diplomat has explained . . . that the presence of communists in the governmental majority constitutes an element of force for French democracy, attesting to the real and profound unity of the French people, revealing the existence of a generalized French community capable of defending the independence of France. . . . The essential force of France resides in the union of the people around a government which it recognizes as its government." (*ibid.*, p. 47).

[43] *Ibid.*, p. 59. Emphasis textual.

The Question of Ministerial Participation and the SFIO Dilemma

In his volume on the Popular Front, Daniel Brower has demonstrated that the key partner as far as immediate communist goals were concerned was the Radical Party. This was because the Radical leaders who joined the coalition were, besides the communists themselves, more favorable than any other party leadership to a policy of alliance with the Soviet Union.[44] Despite the fact that the conservative government of Pierre Laval had earlier signed the Franco-Soviet Mutual Assistance Treaty of May 2, 1935, "Laval made no mystery of his low opinion of the Soviet alliance and of his desire for a reconciliation with Italy and Germany,"[45] and the French Right was in general ferociously against enlarged Franco-Soviet cooperation for self-evident motives. In the negotiations concerning the Front, the Radical leader Herriot had been one of the most important of those favorable, and as far as the Soviet leadership was concerned, "a French government under the direction of the Radical party presented much greater hope for the application of the newly signed treaty than one headed by conservatives, particularly of Pierre Laval's sort."[46]

The SFIO leaders, on the other hand, continued to hold fast to their previous policy of antimilitarism. (It was somewhat ironic that only the Communists, who had been voting with the socialists against defense credits for fifteen years, reversed their 1920–34 policy of antimilitarism, the pretexts being the Franco-Soviet Treaty, and Stalin's famous statement to Laval expressing "sympathetic understanding" of French defense preparations.) The socialists, who hoped to defeat domestic fascist tendencies mainly by economic and social reforms (an approach consonant with the strong current of pacifist and *attentiste* attitudes in the leadership with regard both to foreign policy and revolution), thus often found themselves opposed by a coalition of Radicals and Communists in discussions on the Front program of January

---

[44] Brower, *The New Jacobins*, pp. 93, 117–18, 138 ff.
[45] *Ibid.*, p. 93.   [46] *Ibid.*

1936. Indeed, as evidence of their emphasis on foreign policy, communists took a rather moderate stance as far as social and economic reforms were concerned, and in particular did not press for "structural" reforms. The PCF-Radical coalition on this question was expressed in the Prologue to the program, which noted that the Front policy would be "intentionally limited to immediately applicable measures."

Before the elections of April–May 1936, the Radicals had been the largest party in the Chamber, and the PFC had won only twelve seats in the 1932 elections. When the 1936 elections returned a quite restructured balance among Radicals, socialists, and Communists, the result was an unexpected and not entirely pleasant surprise as far as the latter were concerned. The Communist predicament at this time has been described by Brower: "For the first time in the history of France, a Socialist would be Premier. But the Communist leaders had struggled for almost a year for a *Radical* cabinet, one whose foreign policy would reflect support of the Franco-Soviet alliance. The elections had deprived them of that objective." [47] Many Communists shared the apprehension of the Secretary-General of the Comintern, Dimitrov, who suggested the elections had perhaps been *too* successful.

During the electoral campaign of Spring 1936, a Popular Front victory was more or less generally assumed by everyone, and in this context the Communists and socialists had often debated the question of participation in government. For the SFIO, the question of participation had long been one of principle, given that the Socialist International, following the "Millerand affair," had formally voted against the practice at the 1904 Amsterdam congress. Outside of the rally to the "national union" governments during World War I, the socialist parties had contributed no ministers to government since Millerand, despite the possibilities in 1924 and 1932. Moreover, in addition to the matter of doctrine, SFIO decisions against participation were influenced by the relative weakness in parliament of the SFIO vis-à-vis the Radicals and, more important perhaps, fears that participation

[47] *Ibid.*, p. 138.

would be tantamount to abandonment of the working class to communist monopoly.[48]

During the late 1920s and early 1930s, Léon Blum became convinced that the SFIO might soon be constrained by unwelcome events to participate in a nonrevolutionary government. Because of the SFIO's theory of revolution—based on the doctrine that capitalism could only rot from within, and that the revolution could neither be organized nor controlled—this conviction implied for Blum that some revision of prerevolutionary justifications of socialist action would be necessary.[49]

Thus motivated, Blum developed a new doctrine regarding the socialists' excercise of power in bourgeois society. Essentially, he distinguished the *exercise* of power from the *seizure* of power by the working class. His point was that in certain situations a socialist might be constrained to participate in the exercise of state power without giving up the ultimate goal of its seizure. Later, he temporarily added a third distinction, that of the *preventive occupation* of bourgeois state power, which referred explicitly to the assumption of power to block fascism. This became the doctrinal justification of the SFIO leadership in the Popular Front despite its overtones of Leninist-style tactics.[50]

Ministerial participation by the SFIO did not come as much of a surprise in 1936. For the Communists, however, the matter was dif-

---

[48] In fact, the debate on the question of participation was complicated within the SFIO. From 1924 on, a number of the SFIO parliamentary group had been willing to participate in "Left-wing" governments, meaning essentially a government of the SFIO and the Radicals (some would have permitted Communist participation as well). It was the Party executive that continually forbade such a practice, as in 1924, and in 1929, when a majority of the SFIO deputies had voted for a favorable reply to an offer of participation from the Radical Daladier. Disputes over this problem often set the socialist parliamentary group against the party executive, even as late as 1954 when the leadership (under Guy Mollet) vetoed an offer of participation from Mendès-France. Essentially, the parliamentary members argued they had a mandate direct from their constituents, while the leadership argued the deputy was subordinate to the Party leadership.

[49] At bottom, Blum had little to say of how "the revolution" would come outside of the vague idea that the social and economic revolution would have to start before a socialist *prise de pouvoir* would become possible. If power were taken before the revolutionary base was secured, Blum argued the result would be state capitalism rather than socialism.

[50] See *L'oeuvre de Léon Blum* (7 vols.), esp. vols. 4 and 5. The latter includes his 1936–37 speeches, entitled *L'exercice du pouvoir*.

ferent, as they had made no pledge to Blum, who could well understand the PCF desire to protect both its left flank and its intentions toward his own party.

Three days after the second ballot, on May 6, a Central Committee communiqué announced that the PCF would not participate, in opposition both to the entreaties of Blum and the broad trend of mass opinion. Instead, the PCF leadership opted for the old SFIO tactic of loyal support without participation, which the latter had used toward governments of the *Cartel des Gauches*. The communists argued that by not joining the government they would reduce hostility to the Blum cabinet and avoid frightening the Right into violent opposition, which could create social disorder or possibly civil war. This explanation received little credence at the time, however, and one writer, well acquainted with internal Party developments, has demonstrated that "this argument was produced a posteriori and for external consumption. What is more, the Communists knew well that their refusal to associate themselves with the responsibilities of governmental power, while perhaps tranquilizing the petits-bourgeois milieux, would on the contrary worry the socialists terribly: did not Léon Blum fear becoming another Kerensky?" [51]

To what can one attribute Communist reluctance? First of all, it is necessary to restate that the question of participation for the Communists was not, as it had been for the socialists, a matter of principle. As early as 1935, Maurice Thorez had made known that the PCF would consider ministerial participation in the context of a French Popular Front: "The momentum of the movement of the masses can impose the necessity of a Popular Front government, which our Party would support and in which it might, in certain cases, participate." [52] The 7th Comintern Congress, in August 1935, had issued the following resolution indicating the general Communist line internationally:

Insofar as a [Popular Front] government takes effective and decisive measures against the counterrevolutionary financial magnates and their fascist agents, and does not in any way disturb the activity of the Communist Party and the struggle of the working class, the Communist Party will support with all means such a government, the participation of communists in a united front

---

[51] Perrot and Kriegel, *Socialisme français*, p. 122.   [52] Cited in *ibid*.

government being decided in each particular case, taking account of the concrete situation.[53]

Moreover it seems established that at least Thorez, and possibly also Duclos and Frachon, spoke in favor of participation in the Politburo discussions, but if so, they did not insist upon it against a strong majority that favored nonparticipation.[54]

In his speech to the 8th PCF Congress (January 1936), Thorez had posed the following hint to the later Communist decision in a passage that splits doctrinal hairs to the point of becoming a riddle:

To those who find that the Popular Front tactic will lead us into a vulgar policy of collaboration, we reply quite briefly: . . . as long as conditions will not permit the constitution of a Popular Front government such as we conceive it, we have decided to support with our votes a government of the Left realizing a program conforming with the interests and the will of the French people.[55]

The relevant point was the distinction drawn by Thorez between a "Popular Front government such as we conceive it" and "a government of the Left." In essence he defined two alternatives: a government with Communist participation or a government of Radicals and socialists. The difference between the two was simply whether or not the Communists chose to participate. In other words, the constitution of a "Popular Front" government (when the question was first raised in 1936) was a self-defining proposition as far as the Communists were concerned: if the Party chose to participate, the government would be a "true" Popular Front; if it did not, the result would be only a "government of the Left." The conditions that affected this choice (if one relegates to a secondary position the desire to avoid "frightening the bourgeoisie) and the question whether the Communist decision not to participate in the Blum cabinet can be related to more fundamental concerns of the leadership, approach the center of the argument.

Léon Blum was not an ardent enthusiast of an alliance with the Soviet Union. There had been too much substance and emotion in the

[53] Cited in Fauvet, *Histoire du Parti*, 1:194.
[54] See Perrot and Kriegel, *Socialisme français*, pp. 130–31; Brower, *Jacobins*, p. 141; and Fauvet, *Histoire du Parti*, 1:195–97.
[55] PCF–8, Thorez report, p. 134.

divergence of Bolshevism and Social Democracy for the antipathy to be overridden by any but the direst of circumstances. And despite the growing threat of German aggression against France, the European situation in the middle of 1936 was not such that it compelled Blum to abandon his policy of avoiding war at all costs and to replace it with an unambiguous position of alliance with Stalin against Hitler.[56] Indeed, Blum continued to waver even as late as the end of 1938. Thus, the communists probably reasoned that, with regard to their fundamental objective, the mere fact of occupying ministerial positions was no guarantee of greater influence. Furthermore, they could hardly expect to receive any of the most important ministries, as this would have been unacceptable to the Radicals and a provocation of Hitler that Blum wished to avoid.

This being the case, it was good tactics that the Communists should seek to turn the matter of participation or nonparticipation to their advantage in another way. First of all, by refusing to participate, and therein casting doubt on the authenticity of the SFIO-led government insofar as the PCF doctrine of the Popular Front was concerned, the Communist leadership hoped to reaffirm its position vis-à-vis the Socialist Party—to demonstrate that the French Communist Party, while bowing to the pressure of circumstances insofar as the fight against fascism was concerned, was more than ever the sole authentic exponent of the maximum program of revolution. With the SFIO having taken a definitive step in agreeing not simply to participate but even to lead the government in a nonsocialist society, the PCF leaders undoubtedly saw a chance to deal the former a decisive blow in their struggle to incarnate the revolutionary impulses of the French working class. Moreover, because such action would not directly jeopardize the immediate, or minimum, Communist objectives, it would be, if successful, a victory on the cheap. Finally, independent of the socialists, the Communists had also to worry about their own credibility. Having linked themselves to the national government, however ten-

[56] Moreover, as Raymond Aron has argued, there was considerable doubt as to whether the Soviet Union would have honored the military aspects of its commitment to France, since there was at this time no common border between the *Reichswehr* and the Red Army.

uously, they did not underestimate their need simultaneously to cover their left flank as fully as possible.[57]

A second benefit of nonparticipation was its signal that the Communist leadership did not believe very strongly that the Popular Front might lead to a revolutionary situation. Thus a doctrinal escape hatch would be created once the Front had served its purpose. The Comintern line was that the Popular Front was a *possible* revolutionary instrument, but one that was neither necessary nor adequate to effect a revolutionary change. (That would have been to deny the model of 1917.) In 1935, Dimitrov had defined the position of a Popular Front in a revolutionary scenario as follows:

The united proletarian front and antifascist Popular Front movement [is] capable of overthrowing or crushing fascism without passing directly to the liquidation of the dictatorship of the bourgeoisie. . . . [It occurs] *on the eve* of the victory of the socialist revolution and *before* that victory.[58]

By refusing to participate, by suggesting that the Blum cabinet would not be what Thorez referred to as an "authentic" Popular Front government but rather merely a "government of the Left," the Communists were in effect signalling that the "conditions. . . . [permitting] the constitution of a Popular Front government such as we conceive it" had not been fulfilled. Had Stalin considered that a Communist revolution in France might have succeeded without provoking a combined British-German intervention the PCF perhaps would have been instructed to join the government and attempt to reproduce the "dual power" tactic of 1917 in a new form. Surely there were some in the PCF leadership who agreed with Pivert that all was possible in the general strike of June 1936; however, that the estimation of the international situation as nonrevolutionary and the determination to seek a Franco-Soviet alliance within the context of a "bourgeois" government remained the dominant guideposts of Communist tactics was revealed when Thorez exhorted the strikers back to work on June 11. From

[57] Not surprisingly, during the Popular Front period, the Trotskyite movement blossomed briefly, as it would in 1945–47 and after May 1968.

[58] Cited in Perrot and Kriegel, *Socialisme français*, pp. 123–25, from Dimitrov's speech at the 7th Comintern Congress, August 1935. Kriegel notes that the insertion of the Popular Front into a revolutionary schema caused a certain excitement in the Comintern, for it was the first explicit reference to a form of peaceful action leading to revolution since some of Lenin's writings during the "dual power" period.

that point on, there was little reason to suspect the Communists were playing for immediate revolution.

In sum, the decision not to participate was another attempt to serve both ends of the dual Communist program: by coming out clearly for the minimum goals (alliance with the Soviet Union abroad and defeat of fascism at home) through an acknowledgment that the situation was not revolutionary, the Party hoped, paradoxically, to strengthen its credibility as vanguard strategist of the long-term revolutionary struggle.

Other forms of the Communists' exterior position

The Communist doctrinal attitude toward ministerial participation in May–June 1936 was paralleled by ambivalent behavior within the governmental majority in general. In both cases the goal was to prevent the organization and its mass image from permanent contamination. That this was the major intent of the doctrinal justification of nonparticipation is further evidenced by its practical implementation: the famous "ministry of the masses," an imaginary ministerial portfolio claimed by the PCF leadership. Announced by Paul Vaillant-Couturier in *L'Humanité* on May 14, 1936 (one week after the elections and four days after the Communists announced their decision against participation), it was a reanimation of the Roman institution of tribune in the context of class-struggle politics in modern France.[59] Vaillant-Couturier wrote that: "At the side of the government of the Left, supporting it, assuring its stability, [the Communists] will exercise from outside a sort of ministry of the masses, with the participation of the most ardent and most disciplined elements of the Popular Front." [60] Thus, in a bit of conceptual acrobatics, the Communists defined their position in relation to the reformist government to be formed by Blum: "within" the governing majority, "at the side . . . supporting . . . and assuring the stability" of the government itself, ("without

[59] In the Roman Empire, a tribune was a magistrate appointed by the government to protect the rights of the plebians.
[60] *L'Humanité*, May 12, 1936, p. 1.

reserve" and "without eclipse," Thorez said), yet at the same time
"outside" the actual "exercise" of power. This partially "without"
position was to enable them to speak for and agitate among the
masses, whose élan and political education would be guaranteed by
"the most ardent and most disciplined elements of the Popular Front"
(an obvious reference to the Communist rank and file). Léon Blum
might have been given to ask indignantly: "Does not a socialist-led
government speak for the People?" Thorez might have answered:
"No, for the pre-1914 social democratic mandate to represent the People
has been given over by History to the communist parties." Quite
clearly, in fabricating the Ministry of the Masses out of thin air, the
Communists were seeking to play on their self-assigned role of
vanguard; in this case they used it to justify keeping the tribune role
even while they entered the governmental majority. In other words,
the proclamation of this imaginary ministry was to recall and underscore the temporarily latent but nonetheless still demanded Communist revolutionary "chain of legitimacies," supposedly linking the
masses, the working class, the proletariat, and the Party in the fulfillment of an ineluctable Destiny.

The Communists' intention to set themselves off from the exercise
of "bourgeois" power, implemented with the decision against ministerial participation and the unilateral announcement of the ministry of
the masses, had been foreshadowed by Dimitrov as early as the 1935
Comintern Congress: "The communists will support united front governments with all means, to the extent that the latter will truly combat the enemies of the people, and *will permit liberty of action by the
Communist Party* and the working class." [61]

Later that year, Maurice Thorez had emphasized this matter once
again, when he asserted that "The Popular Front government will be
a government giving every possibility of agitation, propaganda, organization, and action to the working class and its Communist Party.
. . ." [62] In other words, in the maximum perspective should it have
come to fruition the ministry of the masses was to be a variation of
the dual-power Bolshevik tactic of 1917.

Application of the ministry of the masses in one direction took the

[61] Cited in Perrot and Kriegel, *Socialisme français*, p. 133.   [62] *Ibid.*

form of a continual critique of the Blum government, a critique tending to subsume even the apparently extraordinary gains of the first months within thinly veiled harangues on what remained to be done. This was evident bad faith, however, in that the Communists continued to press Blum toward more vigorous action when the latter had a delicate situation to preserve and when the PCF analysis itself had declared the situation was not only nonrevolutionary but above all potentially reactionary. The Communist plan, to be sure, was to cooperate with Blum only as much as was necessary to obtain the minimum goals, but at the same time to discredit the SFIO revolutionary claims if possible. The Communist attacks on Blum were all the more ironic in light of the parliamentary behavior of the PCF group. As one observer has noted: "The Communists voted for all the government bills. They respected as well the unwritten rule that no member of the [coalition] demand discussion in the Chamber of his bills without the consent of the other members. For novices in parliamentary ways, they performed rather well." [63] Yet this was hardly the entire story, and French socialists even today speak with some bitterness of the "double game" and "treachery" of the Communists toward Blum.

As early as June 13, 1936,—only a few days after the Matignon Agreement—the Communists signaled their intention to take the role of the ministry of the masses quite seriously. On that occasion, Jacques Duclos, president of the PCF parliamentary group, mounted the podium to caution Blum: "We are going to give you our votes, *but* outside the walls of this chamber, there is an entire people which wants to see its legally expressed will respected." [64] Throughout the summer of 1936, the Communists continued a running critique of Blum's activities in all the Party publications, complemented by similar attacks published in the *Correspondance internationale*, the Comintern organ. The indecisive attitude of Blum toward the question of aid to the Spanish Republicans, for example, left him an open target for Communist propaganda, despite the PCF's determination never to go so far in demanding "Guns for Spain!" as to bring the Popular Front coalition itself into question. Nevertheless, the other SFIO leaders

---

[63] Brower, *Jacobins*, p. 157.
[64] Cited in Perrot and Kriegel, *Socialisme français*, p. 135.

—particularly those inclined to pacifism and noninterventionism such as Paul Faure and Jean Lebas—became extremely concerned with the ambivalence of Communist support of the cabinet. Vigorous, and probably somewhat desperate, discussions of this matter were held often in the Hotel Matignon during the latter months of 1936. As Premier, however, Blum could not permit himself the luxury of an open counterattack; nor, because he needed the Communist votes, could he face them with an ultimatum in private.

The question of the Communist critique of the government's action came out into the open late in August, upon the visit to Paris of Hjalmar Schacht, German Reichsminister of the Economy and President of the Reichsbank. Upon learning that Blum had agreed to receive Hitler's emissary, Maurice Thorez released a public protest which appeared at first to be a Communist declaration of war on the government.[65] Then, on September 2, Thorez made a speech in Paris in which he gave implicit support to the calling of strikes in the metallurgy industries over the issue of aid to Spain; rather large sit-down strikes occurred on September 5, 6, and 7, while lesser strikes continued throughout the month. This seemed to contradict the PCF's attitude of June, when Thorez had come out for an end to political strikes, and the Schacht incident thus appeared as a likely pretext for a coming break between the PCF and the SFIO.

On November 30, 1936, Thorez for the first time publicly indicated a Communist desire to seek a change in the leadership of the Front, announcing that "the fate of the Popular Front is not restricted to the survival of one cabinet." [66] Soon thereafter rumors were circulating to the effect that Léon Jouhaux, head of the CGT, "would be acceptable" to the communists as a replacement. On December 4, Blum posed a question of confidence with respect to foreign policy, in particular on policy toward Spain. As expected, Jacques Duclos criticized the policy of nonintervention with vehemence, but after remarking that the Communists ought to vote against the government, he announced that they would merely abstain. The Communists were not getting what they wanted from Blum, above all regarding the key area of foreign

---

[65] Schacht was received by Blum, but only "unofficially."
[66] Quoted in Brower, *Jacobins*, p. 173.

policy and the question of a Franco-Soviet alliance, but nonetheless they were reluctant to break openly with him and opt for a new Premier because the original Popular Front élan had been so much associated with his person. In a word, while the Communists had probably decided that Blum was not the man to serve their purpose, they judged the probable consequences of a sudden cabinet crisis too dangerous to allow themselves an easy and complete opposition.

Despite the PCF hesitancy to force a break, a Central Committee pamphlet, published December 12 and entitled "Blum and the Action for Peace," nonetheless indicated a continuing progressive disengagement:

We are not tied to a ministerial formation because of the men who compose it or because of the intentions they may have, but only as a function of the resolute accomplishment of electoral promises made in common. . . . The destiny of the cabinet is one thing; the forceful movement of the Popular Front another.[67]

The further events leading to the resignation of Blum in June 1937 have been evoked above. Despite their never-abated critique, the Communists remained in support of the government between January and June 1937, and if anything they tended to forget the ministry of the masses and the other attempts to demonstrate an external position as political momentum swung back to the Right. As long as the locus of power had been lodged in the SFIO and leaned farther Left, the communists could push toward a more extreme situation; once the momentum began to move in the other direction, however, they were obliged to moderate their tactics.

The downfall of the first Popular Front government incited a change in the PCF attitude toward participation. Thus, when the Radical Chautemps, whose hostility toward the PCF was well known, was in the process of forming his cabinet in June 1937, the Communist leadership nevertheless offered to participate in his government. This was the farthest they had ever gone in the direction of "bourgeois" power. So long as Communist attempts to preserve revolutionary credentials did not endanger the primary goal of combating fascism, the policy of nonparticipation and the ministry of the masses

[67] Quoted in Perrot and Kriegel, *Socialisme français*, p. 135.

had been gains made on the cheap. Between June 1936 and June 1937, however, these tactics had become counterproductive, and the Communist offer to participate in the Chautemps cabinet can be seen quite simply as a recognition of the growing danger from the fascist Right which accompanied the failure of the French Popular Front and the failure to form an antifascist alliance internationally. Later, the Communists were to offer their participation to the second Chautemps cabinet, to the second Blum ministry, and finally, even to Daladier in May 1938. In each case, the Communist action can be explained by a desperate resolve to push for a Franco-Soviet alliance and to prevent a slide toward the extreme Right within France itself. Often during these two years, *L'Humanité* carried headlines such as "The Country Demands a Government of the Popular Front and None Other!", and the Comintern leadership spoke and wrote favorably of the French Communist efforts to save the Front, on the reasoning that cabinets such as that of Chautemps "would inevitably form a transition to a reactionary Right-wing government [unless] the political and organic cohesion of the Popular Front is preserved." [68] Checked by the conservative Radicals and the Moderates who had by 1937 regained the initiative from the united front on the Left, the Communist efforts became increasingly pathetic during the period 1937–39, an indication of both their declining influence on the French situation and of the failure of Stalin's bids for alliance with the Western democracies. However, there was an important difference: whereas Stalin could at the same time negotiate with the latter and with Hitler, the French Communists were completely blocked, for under no condition would the extreme Right deal either with them or with the Soviets. Thus, the Communists were by 1939 finally reduced to issuing rather hopeless appeals for a "French Front," the traditional wartime proposal for a government of national unity. There was little reason to believe, however, that they would succeed where Blum had failed in March 1938.

Before leaving the Popular Front period, one may point to one additional area in which the French Communists attempted to preserve and further a long-term revolutionary perspective while at the same time emphasizing the minimum program and its aspects of collabo-

---

[68] *Correspondance internationale*, September 1937, p. 810.

ration in the exercise of "bourgeois" power. This was the Communist attempt to advance the one-party model at the rank-and-file level and in the party system, actions linked to the tactic of discrediting the SFIO as a revolutionary party through the tactics of nonparticipation and the ministry of the masses.

Three different approaches were tried in pursuit of this goal. In 1935, the communist leadership announced that the basis of success of the Popular Front would be the creation of "Popular Front committees" throughout France, whose purposes would be to organize the working classes and to support the Front with "nonparliamentary mass action." Moreover, as the Communist line went, the Popular Front committees could become the basis of the future soviets, should a revolutionary situation come to pass. From the beginning, however, the SFIO and Radical leaderships, afraid of seeing their rank and file infiltrated and absorbed by the Communist militants, refused to allow participation in these committees. The committees never became widespread, and later the Communists would argue that the Popular Front failed because it had remained merely an alliance "at the top" and had never based its strength sufficiently on the masses.

A second tactic was the merger of the Communist and socialist unions, the CGT and CGTU. This was accomplished in March 1936, in what at the time appeared as an absorption of the much smaller CGTU by the non-Communist CGT. Despite fewer members, however, the Communists used syndicalist reunification to make considerable headway in terms of an eventual takeover of power within the labor movement.[69] The events of 1939 interrupted the Communist infiltration of the reunified CGT, however. On September 25, one month after the signature of the Nazi-Soviet Pact, and one day before the dissolution of the Communist Party, the socialist leadership excluded the Communists from leadership positions, and shortly thereafter a decree of the Daladier governement dissolved all the Communist syndicalist organizations.

The third attempt to advance the goal of unipolarity is probably the

---

[69] See, e.g., Antoine Prost, *La C.G.T. à l'époque du Front Populaire, 1934–39. Essai de description numérique.* (Paris, 1964) chapter 6. Despite being normally less strong numerically than their socialist counterparts, within the terms of reunification the Communists often obtained parity in the leadership of the unified federations, as, for example, in the Seine-Maritime.

most interesting, while probably also the least known. This was the plan to achieve a merger of the SFIO and PCF themselves, referred to as "organic unity." [70]

The French Communists since 1922 had continuously called for unity on the Left, but, as we have seen, the approach to unity was quite variable. The formula of "unity of action" had both included and excluded the socialist leadership during the 1920s, and its class-against-class variant of 1928–33 had been no less than virulent in its hostility to cooperation with the SFIO. The Communist goal was eventually to capture all of the working classes under its influence, but it was by no means clear how this could be accomplished.

During the original discussions on Popular Front unity in 1934, Communist proposals had first been couched merely in terms of "unity of action" alone. Léon Blum, however, had replied by offering "organic unity" to the Communists, which given that the SFIO was at that time by far the larger party would have meant a certain risk for the PCF. [71] By 1935, however, the Communists had made serious gains toward closing this gap, [72] and a "unification commission" was set up to discuss the problems involved in "organic unity." During 1936, a startling development occurred: for the first time since 1924, the size of the PCF had come to exceed that of the SFIO. [73]

It is on the basis of this shift in numbers that one may understand

[70] The most useful study focusing directly on this crucial event is an article by Georges Lefranc, "La tentative de réunification entre le Parti socialiste et le Parti communiste de 1935 à 1937," *L' information historique*, February 1967, pp. 19–27. It has been analyzed further in polemical terms by several Communists and socialists, and is discussed briefly in Perrot and Kriegel, *Socialisme français*, pp. 138–43, and de Bayac, *Front Populaire, passim*. While the Lefranc article gives much space to the SFIO position, a concise synthesis of the PCF bias is contained in Jacques Duclos' report to the 10th PCF Congress (1945), "Vive l'unité de la classe ouvrière," 40 pp. In light of the continuity of this theme on the French Left, as expressed in the reunification discussions of 1921–22, 1944–46, and the renewed Communist-Socialist dialogue of recent years, the events of 1936–37 deserve greater attention.

[71] Whereas the PCF membership was less than 40,000 in 1934, the SFIO was approximately 125,000 strong. In fourteen years, the original figures after the split of Tours had been thus almost exactly reversed.

[72] In one year, the PCF had climbed to about 85,000 members, whereas the SFIO membership level had remained approximately stable.

[73] In December 1936, the PCF numbered about 280,000 adherents, the SFIO approximately 250,000.

the two phases of the 1935–37 negotiations. During the first, the SFIO took the initiative and appeared to be most inclined to make concessions because it was most interested in reunification. This period lasted from March 1935 until July and August 1936, at which point appeared the turnaround in memberships and the great difficulties of the SFIO leadership in government. The swing of momentum away from the SFIO then began to look irreversible. During the second stage, which lasted from the end of 1936 until the rupture of the negotiations in December 1937, it was rather the Communists who were eager.

The first exchange of unity proposals found the socialists offering an exact reproduction of the 1905 unity charter, which had bound the Guesdist and Jauressian tendencies into the SFIO. The Communists, on the other hand, introduced a "Charter for the Unification of the Working Class of France," which had the following to say about the organization, methods, and goals of the proposed unified party:

> We consider that the unified party must proclaim its absolute independence vis-à-vis the bourgeoisie and its parties, and admit no compromise, in peacetime as well as in time of war, with imperialism; that it must recognize the necessity of the violent overthrow of the power of the bourgeoisie and of the installation of the dictatorship of the proletariat *through the means of soviets;* and that it must be organized on the model of the Grand Party of Lenin and Stalin.[74]

Of course, neither party would accept the other's conditions. The Communists argued that the socialist proposal of the 1905 charter ignored the gains of the previous thirty years, during which time "the road traced by the builders of a new society in the Soviet Union, guided by Stalin, has brought socialism out of the realm of [mere] hopes."[75] The socialists countered that the Communists advocated a model of revolution which was foreign to both the traditions and aspirations of Frenchmen.[76] Nonetheless, because of their greater interest in unification at that point, it was the SFIO that proposed a compromise first, on November 21, 1935.[77] On that day also, Léon Blum

---

[74] PCF–8, Thorez report, p. 128, paraphrasing the Charter, which was published in *L'Humanité* of June 8, 1935.

[75] From the preamble of the Charter, *L'Humanité, ibid.* p. 1.

[76] See Lefranc, "La tentative," p. 20. [77] See *Ibid.*, pp. 20–21.

wrote in *Le Populaire* in a manner that indicated unmistakably his eagerness to strike a bargain while the socialists still had the upper hand: "Here is the decisive step [that of "organic unity"] that we must vow to take within the coming year." [78] The Communist leadership refused to accept dilutions of Marxism-Leninism, however, and insisted on their own conception of the three major points of ideological cleavage: 1) the relation of class and party; 2) the nature of the passage from capitalism to socialism; 3) the nature of the dictatorship of the proletariat. Finally, before the February 1936 congress of the SFIO, Blum struck at the heart of the matter:

I do not consider that the [Communist] proposal is serviceable as a basis for unification. A unification is a fusion between parties and not the absorption of one party by another. . . . [The Communist] unity Charter of May 29 is the charter of a Communist Party and not the charter of a unified Proletarian Party. [79]

The Communists thereafter continued to stall the negotiations with their refusal to consider compromises. By May 1936, however, the PCF membership had surpassed that of the SFIO, and, after the setbacks of the Popular Front during July and August for which the SFIO leadership received the bulk of the blame, it was the Communists who produced a compromise proposal in November. By this time, on the other hand, the socialist leaders had no desire to isolate themselves with the Communists. Moreover, Blum calculated that a serious attempt at unification at this time would surely alienate the Radicals from the government coalition. [80]

In December 1936, the Communists once again made public a compromise document, vaguely worded and offering the possibility of negotiations on vital issues. The socialists, having had to put up with the "ministry of the masses" and the progressively stronger indications that the Communists were considering an abandonment of their support for the Blum ministry, [81] not surprisingly refused to rise to the

---

[78] Quoted in Perrot and Kriegel, *Socialisme français*, p. 141.

[79] Lefranc, "La tentative," p. 21.

[80] *Ibid.*, p. 22. In July, when Blum was still considering unification favorably, he was outvoted in the 33-member executive of the SFIO as to whether an SFIO compromise, drafted by Séverac, should be offered the Communists.

[81] E.g., the Communist abstention on the December 4 question of confidence.

bait. Preoccupied with the problems of trying to save the Blum cabinet and rekindle the Popular Front flame and, at bottom, simply no longer seriously interested in the question of "organic unity," the SFIO leadership did not reply until July 10, 1937, after the Blum ministry had been resigned. At that point, they sought to save face by posing what they considered would be unacceptable conditions for the Communists: 1) the social democratic conception of democracy at all organizational levels; 2) the sovereignty of national and international congresses; 3) independence of the unified party vis-à-vis all governments.[82]

Much to the astonishment of the socialists, however, on July 23 the PCF Central Committee issued a manifesto accepting these conditions. The socialists then had little choice but to draw attention to the fact that the Communist conceptions of democracy, sovereignty, and independence did not coincide with their own, despite their hopes of avoiding any open ideological confrontations for the sake of Popular Front goals. After stalling for most of the fall of 1937, the SFIO executive finally broke off the negotiations on November 24, perhaps because, in the rank and file's disillusionment with Blum, the Communists had begun to have some success in promoting "organic unity" among lower structures and local committees in defiance of the decision of SFIO leadership.

In sum, as Brower had concluded, "The Popular Front never became a movement of the masses . . . [and] Communist efforts to build up a mass political movement," whose eventual purpose might be revolutionary, "were denied fruition."[83] To the defeat of the first Blum government had been added a second, the defeat of reunification of the French Left: the Communist attempt to further the single-party idea had been repulsed, but not without hammering more nails into the coffin of the Popular Front.

Many observers believe that adoption of the Popular Front strategy by the French Communists marked their finish as a revolutionary element. Georges Lavau, for example, has asserted flatly that "Between February 11, 1934 . . . and Summer 1936, the Communist Party . . . progressively ceased to be a revolutionary party and to act like

---

[82] See PCF–10, Duclos report, p. 18. [83] Brower, *Jacobins*, p. 111, 114.

one. One may consider that the transformation accomplished at this time was definitive." [84] Taking as evidence of the 1920–34 revolutionary tendency of the PCF the illegal actions and "provocations of the bourgeois order" that were committed,[85] Lavau concludes that "the Popular Front of 1935–37 constituted the decisive moment in the change in the nature of the PCF." [86]

Moreover, with regard to the ministry of the masses, syndicalist unity, and "organic" party unity, Lefranc has justly commented:

[The] Communist Party considered that the last word had been uttered by the installation of the Soviet regime; implicitly, it affirmed the [doctrine of the] "single road" to socialism. . . . [Yet] It manifested a singular divorce between what it proposed and what it did, between doctrine and action, between the ideology of the class struggle and the practice of the Popular Front. . . . The principles invoked, far from justifying the acts, seemed to condemn them, or rather the acts seemed to contradict the principles.[87]

Did, in fact, the contradiction between long-range principles and short-term tactics bear out the argument of those who saw in it a capitulation to a nonrevolutionary future? Perhaps. Yet on the other hand this seeming paradox of doctrine and tactics might also support the contrary hypothesis: that the Popular Front was a further and variant stage in the continuing unresolved ambivalence of the relationship of communism to French "bourgeois" democracy—of a potentially revolutionary opposition movement acting to gain the greatest possible advantage in a nonrevolutionary situation. To carry this hypothesis further: If the conditions within France and Europe had developed according to the most optimistic Communist plans, we might today conclude that Communist participation in the governmental majority was from the beginning the first step in a Western European variation of the "dual power" tactic.

The situation in France in 1936 was not revolutionary however, or at least the Communist leadership did not perceive it as such. And since Leninist strategy depends ultimately on the advent of a revolutionary situation, the argument that the PCF ceased to be revolutionary must rest upon the assumption that the French Communist

---

[84] Lavau, "Le Parti communiste dans le système politique français," in Frédéric Bon, et al., *Le communisme en France*, p. 19.

[85] *Ibid.*, pp. 19–20.   [86] *Ibid.*, p. 20.   • [87] Lefranc, "La tentative," p. 27.

leaders failed to perceive or to act upon a situation that was in fact capable of a revolutionary outcome, a contention that cannot be either verified or refuted.

For the purpose here, the relevant conclusion is rather that throughout the period of Popular Front alliance politics, the French Communists attempted to preserve and maintain fundamental opposition to the system in which they were obliged to participate ever more deeply, and to safeguard both their actual revolutionary mentality and their radical popular image. Communist behavior toward the socialists, and their reactions to the Communists, were perhaps the most obvious pieces of evidence in support of this conclusion. This evidence is all the more indicative when one considers that it was the socialists who understood the dangerous ambiguities of Leninist alliance strategy better than anyone.

Still, a proof of this interpretation of French communism during the Popular Front could have come only a posteriori: It was impossible to judge whether the PCF had compromised itself irrevocably until a test situation arose. The signature of the Nazi-Soviet Pact provided a test of the most relevant sort.

Chapter Four

LE PARTI NATIONALISTE
ÉTRANGER (1939–1941)

It was in *A l'échelle humaine,* written by Léon Blum in a German prison during the winter of 1941, that the leader of the Popular Front first spoke of the PCF as "not an internationalist party, but in fact a *parti nationaliste étranger.*" [1] Since then, the French Communist Party has often been stigmatized as *le parti étranger,* but during the years 1939–41 this epithet came closer to characterizing a totality than at any other time in its history.

Le parti étranger is an image of profound cleavage, stressing first of all the perennial and voluntary allegiance bestowed by the French Communists upon a political leadership and national myth not their own. In June 1940, it implied as well that at the time of the fall of France they were more isolated from the rest of the nation than ever before.

The conclusion of the Munich Pact had engendered repercussions far beyond the narrow vision of those who believed, or at least hoped, that war had been avoided by that confused and controversial act. In terms of domestic French politics, its effect was to destroy any remaining possibility of reconstituting a Popular Front government with strong Communist participation, the only potential coalition that might likely have acted differently during the sad, almost suicidal, days between August 1938 and June 1940. After ratification of the Munich Pact by the French Chamber, Stalin must have concluded that there was no longer any hope of an effective Franco-Soviet alliance and that the 1935 treaty signed with Laval would rest mute against the "better Hitler than Stalin" attitude of the most powerful

[1] Pp. 105 ff.

elements in French politics. The Soviet dictator had played a double game for several years, courting the future Allied and Axis partners at once, just as the latter had been playing double games with the Soviet Union and each other. One may say that the fundamental goal of all the governments shadowboxing with Nazi expansionism was simply to avoid war, and that, moreover, they would not have been averse to achieving this aim at the price of a conflict between others. In the event of a war between fascism and Bolshevism, the British, French, and Americans would have been relieved of a double dilemma, while the Soviets would no doubt have rejoiced over the prospects of picking up the pieces after a struggle between France, Britain, and Germany. Carrying on his part in the series of double games as long as he dared, after failing to obtain a definite commitment from the Western powers, Stalin finally made his move in August 1939, when he arranged a mutual pact of nonaggression with Hitler's representative in Moscow, von Ribbentrop.

Between the Munich Pact and the Nazi-Soviet agreement—a period of almost exactly twelve months—the options of the French Communist Party had been rather barren. The Party had backed some minor strikes during September and October to protest Daladier's retreat from the Popular Front program, but otherwise it had accomplished little. In the Chamber, the Communist parliamentary group was excluded from influence; the failure of a CGT-called general strike on November 30, 1938, epitomized the weakness of both the CGT and the trade-union movement in general. And the mass of Frenchmen—at once confused, disappointed, and afraid—were hardly disposed to the policy of active preparations for "antifascist collective security" and the alliance with the Soviet Union proposed by the PCF. Thus, the Communist leadership had to content itself during these months with largely symbolic actions, such as a series of ill-received proclamations calling for the creation of a "national front" against fascism, a policy which the dominant political mood, the spirit of Munich, rejected out of hand. While a few individuals of some influence (de Gaulle among them) spoke out for a policy of armament and mobilization, on the whole French political elites clung to the twin delusions of appeasement and the Maginot Line. Only the Communists, whose ultimate motives were by nature suspect, appeared to stand unified in their opposition to fascism. This was the great shame of the leaders who presided over the last decade of the Third Republic.

The Immediate Effect of the Nazi-Soviet Pact in France: Dissolution of the PCF and its Ancillaries

While the PCF remained largely paralyzed by the lack of a situation capable of manipulation between August 1938 and August 1939, the conclusion of the Nazi-Soviet Pact permitted a return to offensive tactics, built upon the change in Soviet foreign policy.[2]

The Nonaggression Pact was signed on August 22. The French Communist leaders were then on vacation, which indicated that Stalin had not informed them beforehand. In the midst of this great shock, complicated by the absence of the top leaders, the PCF did not react immediately. Thorez and Duclos returned to Paris on August 24, and on August 25 the first public PCF commentary was issued by the Communist parliamentary group, which released a statement by Thorez. This document, while supporting the German-Soviet alliance, was evidence of the French Communist reluctance to believe the former antifascist posture was relaxed, and that the Comintern line was to be somersaulted in a way that left France directly in the path of German expansionism:

We find ourselves once again, one year after Munich, in the presence of a situation in which the people might be dragged into war at any moment. Hitler's fascism . . . is a constant menace for the security of the [European] peoples. What can one do to prevent any new aggression? The Soviet Union, loyal to its policy of peace, has undertaken a policy of dislocation of the aggressor bloc. . . . The German-Soviet Pact . . . has checked the Munich Plan. . . .

But if, despite all, Hitler begins war, let him understand well that he will find before him the united people of France, the communists in the front line,

---

[2] As Isaac Deutscher has written: "No sooner had Molotov and Ribbentrop put their signatures to the pact of August, 1939 than the Comintern called off the anti-Hitler crusade. . . . The European shadows of the Russian Secretary-General adopted an ambiguous pose of neutrality. Both belligerent camps, it was now said, pursued imperialist aims, and there was nothing to choose between them." (*Stalin: A Political Biography*, pp. 448–49.)

defending the security of the country. . . . It is because we are desirous of peace and of French security that we seek the conclusion of a French-Anglo-Soviet alliance, which remains perfectly possible and necessary. Such an alliance would complete . . . the Franco-Soviet Pact of Mutual Assistance still in vigor.[3]

In taking such a position, Thorez was either misinformed of Stalin's intentions or had chosen to challenge the Comintern line, as an extract from a further paragraph from the above statement, "supporting the measures taken by the Government to guarantee our borders," would indicate. The same day, Gabriel Péri, Florimond Bonte, and Félix Brun spoke for the Communist parliamentary group in the session of the Chamber Commission on Foreign Affairs, with Péri declaring that "the French Communists will collaborate without reticence toward national defense." [4] The new Comintern policy, on the other hand, would have indicated a policy of "revolutionary defeatism."

Despite the partial contradiction of French Communist and Comintern policies, the PCF turnabout of August 22–24, 1939, was seen in France as a treasonous action.[5] It was also quite nearly a suicidal action: the Communists could hardly have expected that their "fraternal" support of the Nazi-Soviet agreement would change either the dominant sentiment of French public opinion or the policy of the French government toward the USSR, for it was clear that the document signed by Molotov and von Ribbentrop almost certainly meant

[3] The entire text is reproduced in Rossi, *Les Communistes français pendant la drôle de guerre*, p. 24, plate 1. The "Franco-Soviet Pact" is the 1935 treaty.

[4] Cited in Rossi-Landi, *La drôle de guerre*, p. 136. Even as early as the first part of 1940, a clandestine brochure entitled *Le Parti Communiste à vingt ans* had already begun to present a rewritten history of the events of Fall 1939: "The French Communist Party was not disoriented by the events of August and September; it perceived the imperialist character of the war; it recognized, from the first day, the soundness of Soviet policy." Cited in Auguste Lecoeur, *Le Parti Communiste français et la Résistance, Août 1939–Juin 1941*, pp. 56–57.

[5] Rossi-Landi points out that "In the official historiography of the Party, Munich is presented as a case of treason *par excellence.* . . . It is also demonstrated that the German-Soviet Pact was an almost unavoidable consequence of it." (*Drôle de guerre*, p. 134). It is evidently difficult to deal with the French Communist movement in terms of a simple "loyalty-treason" dichotomy (see Chapter 12), and most non-Communist analyses of the immediate prewar period do not attempt to deny the element of truth contained in the Communist version of the events: needless to say, one element of truth does not add up necessarily to a whole, from either point of view.

war in Western Europe. Moreover the Daladier government, led by
mediocre men trapped in a difficult situation, was above all in the
market for a scapegoat.

Thus began a campaign of vigorous repression against the PCF. On
August 25, the government seized the two Communist daily newspapers, *L'Humanité* and *Ce Soir*, and a transparent decree of August 26
banned "any newspaper, periodical, or other writing whose publication is of a nature as to undermine national defense." [6] *L'Humanité*
thereafter was not to appear legally again until August 1944. These
first acts of repression, of dubious legality, were merely the beginning, however. Soon, the government had banned all Communist
meetings and publications, quite explicitly separating the Communists
from the national community and throwing away, for the price of a
scapegoat, any chance of obtaining a wholesale rally of the Communists to national defense, as the great majority of socialists had rallied
in 1914. [7]

Somewhat surprisingly, despite both the apparent contradiction
with Stalin's foreign policy and the anti-Communist actions of the
Daladier government, the PCF leadership nonetheless continued to
support an antifascist policy of national defense for almost one month
after August 22. For example, on September 2, the day following the
Nazi invasion of Poland, they voted unanimously for national defense
credits, and the Communist parliamentary group actually stood and
applauded Daladier's speech to the Chamber! On September 3,

---

[6] *Ibid.*, p. 137. Rossi-Landi notes that the headline of *L'Humanité* of August
26—never permitted to circulate—was "Union of the French Nation against the Aggressor Hitler!" Such an exhortation can hardly be construed as contrary to the defense
of France, implying that Daladier and Sarraut had decided to repress the Communists
no matter what.

[7] At the same time, Rossi-Landi's argument that "nothing justified this suspension" is
undoubtedly too presumptuous. "It was the beginning of a repression which pushed the
Communists, little by little and despite themselves, outside the nation. . . . It was to
impose upon them, through persecution, one fatherland instead of another" (*ibid.*).
There is at least some evidence that even without the repressive campaign waged by the
government, the Communists would eventually have taken up the Soviet line in any
case. One is inclined to believe that at least a majority of the top and middle leadership
of the Party would have chosen "internationalism," based upon the Leninist precedent
in World War I. The rank and file, most of whom had joined only a few years before,
would have been less certain to do so.

Maurice Thorez himself rejoined his military unit, as did numerous other Communist leaders.[8]

This "national" and "patriotic" attitude remained the Party line until the latter half of September, when, once the Soviet Union had associated itself with German aggression by sending the Red Army across the eastern Polish border on September 17, the Central Committee issued a protest against the fact that the French government had declared war on Germany without the agreement of parliament, and called for an examination of the "peace" proposals of the Soviet Union. This, in effect, meant that the PCF had decided to embrace the Soviet line entirely.[9]

Presented with an opportunity he had long sought, Daladier quickly acted, and on September 26 the Council of Ministers voted unanimously to dissolve "of all legality the Communist Party, all associations, organizations or groups attached to it, and all those who, affiliated or not to this party, conform, in the exercise of their activity, to orders issuing from the Third International." A further decree authorized the government to suspend Communist mayors and local counselors from their function, "from motives of public order and the general interest, until the cessation of hostilities."[10]

Thus, after almost twenty years of a complicated and stormy existence, the communist movement in France had become illegal. One was to learn shortly to what extent its leadership had heeded the

[8] Thorez's unit was stationed in the small town of Chauny, in the Aisne, and his willingness to leave Paris was perhaps meant to indicate the purity of Communist intentions by the fact that the chief had left the central operational headquarters. Also, as we shall see, this move had the advantage of putting him only 100 kilometers from the Belgian border.

[9] Fauvet notes that between August 23 and September 17, the Comintern leadership and its delegate to the French Party (a Czech named Fried, known as Clément) had pressured the PCF leadership considerably. This, combined with the attitude of the French government, was probably the major factor in resolving the partially non-Comintern PCF policy. Nonetheless, many important leaders and large numbers of the rank and file refused to accept this completion of the *volte-face*. (See below.)

[10] For example (among many others) on October 6, all the Communist municipalities of the Seine (27) and Seine-et-Oise (37), the heart of the Paris suburbs and Communist strength, were suspended. All in all, more than 300 Communist municipalities were disbanded in the country, and 2,500 municipal councilors and 87 general councilors were disbarred. See Fauvet, *Histoire du Parti communiste français*, 2:21–22.

Comintern instructions to "prepare and operate an illegal organization at all times." On October 4, Maurice Thorez deserted his military unit. He fled probably through Belgium and Switzerland, and arrived eventually in the Soviet Union. More than five years would pass before he was to set foot once again on French soil, and during this time the Party was directed by Jacques Duclos and Benoît Frachon, the leading Communist parliamentarian and syndicalist leaders.[11]

To evade the dissolution order, the Communist deputies reorganized briefly during the winter of 1939–40 under the title *Groupe Ouvrier et Paysan* (Workers' and Peasants Group). The group immediately became a spokesman for the Comintern's new line, denouncing the war as a simple battle of imperialists and calling for an immediate peace on the basis of the Nazi-Soviet Pact.[12]

The incipient adoption of a policy of "revolutionary defeatism" was further signaled in a famous letter of October 1939, sent by Florimond Bonte and Arthur Ramette, as leaders of the *Groupe*, to Edouard Herriot, President of the Chamber of Deputies. This letter, also calling for an immediate armistice, referred obliquely to peace propositions that would be made by Hitler only later on October 6, thus indicating some sort of intelligence or complicity with the Nazis, and, furthermore, through its evocation of pacifism, an acceptance of the dismemberment of Poland.[13] This first expression of pacifism, suggesting a

[11] The two men were to spend the entire Resistance period hidden in Paris itself, from which point they directed the communist resistance organizations. They were in radio contact only sporadically with Thorez and the Soviet leadership. During the early part of the war, a more secure line of communication was through the Soviet embassies in Paris and Vichy. After November 1942, Soviet couriers occasionally reached France via Switzerland, but detailed instructions were minimized because of the security danger involved. The clandestine PCF leadership thus improvised its strategy and tactics within the general line of the Soviet press and radio. See Alfred Rieber, *Stalin and the French Communist Party: 1941–1947*, p. 361. For other details on the clandestine PCF leadership, as well as on Thorez's situation see the recent memoir by Giulio Ceretti, *A l'ombre des deux T: 40 ans avec Palmiro Togliatti et Maurice Thorez* (Paris: Julliard, 1973) 407 pp, passim.

[12] The *Journal Officiel* published a list of the Group on September 29, explicitly giving the new organization legal status. Of 75 former PCF deputies, 43 joined at first, and new memberships on October 4 and 6 brought the number to 51. Disillusioned with the Party, the Comintern, and the Soviet Union, 21 deputies and one of two senators (Clamamus resigned, Cachin remained) left the movement.

[13] Rossi-Landi, *Drôle de guerre*, p. 143.

return to the pre-Popular-Front policy of strict antimilitarism, was nonetheless not yet an open condemnation of the war. By October 14, however, in a clandestine appeal to "the French people," the Party leadership finally mimicked the Stalinist line completely, condemning at once the "imperialist war" and the idea of a "national union" government to prosecute it: "The war which has been imposed on the people of France is a war of capitalists, a war which pits English imperialism against German imperialism, with the French people reserved the mission of executing the orders of the London bankers." [14] From this point on, the break with the regime was complete. The French Communist movement, minus those who had defected, was embarked upon a policy of "revolutionary defeatism," which placed into question its very existence. [15]

On September 30, 1939, an investigation of the *Groupe ouvrier et paysan* was begun by the Military Tribunal of Paris, and on October 5 a sudden governmental decree ended the parliamentary session, thus suspending the immunity of deputies. This was quite obviously aimed at the Communists, and during the night and early morning of October 7–8, fourteen *Groupe* members were arrested. A few days later a total of 39 Communist deputies had been sent to *La Santé* prison. Astonishingly, as Jacques Fauvet observed, "None offered resistance, and one is amazed that a party for whom illegality is like second nature was so little prepared for a clandestine existence." [16]

During the next few months the liquidation of Communist means of action continued: for example, in January 1940, the government proposed and obtained the vote of a law dissolving completely the par-

[14] From the clandestine manifesto of October 16, cited in Fauvet, *Histoire du Parti*, 2:17.

[15] It would be interesting to be able to establish figures for the number of rank and file militants who deserted. However, given the general disorder of the Party and the lack of liaison between the bottom and top of the hierarchy during the clandestine period, such a task is impossible, even had such records been made, which is unlikely. Lecoeur (*Le Parti communiste français et la Résistance*, pp. 57–58) estimates that the rank and file and middle leadership cadres, "despite being literally stunned with surprise and disoriented at the announcement of the Pact," remained in the Party in a majority.

[16] Fauvet, *Histoire du Parti*, 2:20. See also, Lecoeur, *Le Parti et la Résistance* pp. 97–98, and Charles Tillon, *Les FTP*, pp. 63 ff., for a discussion of the lack of caution exercised (even as late as 1941–42) by Jacques Duclos and other leaders during the early clandestine period.

liamentary mandates of those Communist deputies who had not repudiated the Party and the Comintern publicly before October 26, 1939.[17] This retroactive law was a prelude though unnecessary juridically) to the trial of 44 Communist deputies, which took place from March 20 to April 30, 1940. At its end, the deputies were convicted of having reconstituted the Communist parliamentary group under the name of *Groupe ouvrier et paysan*,[18] and penalties of four or five years in prison, fines of 4,000 or 5,000 francs, and deprivation of civil rights for five years were pronounced.[19]

With its leadership either in jail or in flight, its organizational base officially dissolved, and its ideological and structural unity weakened by the open and immediate conflict of national and proletarian internationalist imperatives, it is easy to accept that what one of the (since purged) leaders of the Party, Auguste Lecoeur, has called "The political and organizational mess which existed in the Party during 1939–40," was indeed a fact.[20]

In effect, the activities of the Party and the movement in general during this period were at best sporadic and rather confused, and at

[17] Both Rossi and Rossi-Landi, neither of whom can be said to be overly sympathetic to the Communist point of view, judge this forfeiture law rather harshly, on the basis of both its juridical and practical ramifications (See Rossi, *pendant la drôle de guerre*, p. 125 ff., and Rossi-Landi, *La drôle de guerre* p. 152 ff.). In effect, the most eager anticommunists were, not surprisingly, also the most ardent supporters of Munich and of compromise and, later, collaboration with Hitler. Léon Blum was one of the first to say that this overzealous repression of the PCF would tend to martyrize it rather than aid its dismemberment.

[18] In other words, under the provisions of the decree of September 26, dissolving the Party and all organizations "attached to it." There are three detailed accounts of this trial, all written by Communists: Jean Fonteyne, *Le Procès des 44*, (Anvers: Ed. Regenboog, 1940), 238 pp.; André Marty, *The Trial of the French Communist Deputies*, (London: Lawrence and Wishart Ltd., 1941), 126 pp.; and the account in Florimond Bonte, *Le chemin de l'honneur*.

[19] As a summary of the other sanctions against the communists, one may cite the balance sheet drawn by Albert Sarraut. Minister of the Interior, in a speech to the Senate, March 19, 1940: besides *L'Humanité* and *Ce Soir*, 159 communist newspapers and revues had been seized; 11,000 perquisitions had been carried out; 620 Communist syndicates had been dissolved as well as 675 political organizations; 3,400 militants had been arrested, with 1,500 convictions already pronounced. From the *Journal Officiel, Débats Parlementaires, Sénat*, 1940, pp. 265–66, cited in Rossi-Landi, *La drôle de guerre*, pp. 156–57.

[20] Lecoeur, *Le Parti et la Résistance*, p. 35.

worst self-contradicting and completely futile. The organizational structure of "democratic centralism" broke down more or less completely, and the difficulty in converting to clandestine activities indicated that the Party had been rather unprepared for illegal operations.[21] In this sense, it might be said that the "bolshevization" had been incomplete, although this assertion loses much of its impact when one takes into account that no more than one-tenth of the 1939 membership (somewhat more than 350,000) had joined before 1934. Moreover, the extraordinary growth of the PCF between 1934–38 had diluted the extent to which the French Communists were able to incarnate the ideal Bolshevik party. In particular, a small, tightly knit organization has a broader potential for strategic and tactical maneuver than a mass party, in which the group's ideological cohesion is likely weaker. The latter was especially true of the PCF in 1939, since the 1934 cadres had had only four years, at the most, to transform the Popular Front adherents into committed Communists and experienced militants.

The Policy of the PCF, October 1939 to June 1941

PCF historiography of the Resistance period attempts to prove that the French Communists never wavered in their policy of antifascism. In the process it rests silent about, seeks to explain away, or interprets falsely the words and deeds of the Party before it entered into the Resistance upon the Nazi invasion of the Soviet Union in June 1941.[22] As the authors of *Le Parti communiste français dans la Résistance* put it:

[21] This unpreparedness was probably more a psychological phenomenon, a result of the confusion and indecision in Party ranks, than a lack of material provision. Lecoeur notes, for example, that, "From one day to the next, the Party . . . could enter into illegal operations. In each region, and most of all in the Paris region, "hideouts" had been prepared, [with] machines, paper and money, carefully placed in reserve, utilizable at once" (*Ibid.*, p. 85). It is interesting that Lecoeur does not note a presence of weapons.

[22] The major PCF documents in this regard are *Le Parti communiste français dans la Résistance* (the official Party history of the period); Florimond Bonte, *Le chemin de l'honneur;* Jacques Duclos, *Mémoires,* vol. 3 (*Dans la bataille clandestine*); and the report of Maurice Thorez to the 10th PCF Congress (1945). The major works to consult on the

The French Communist Party was in the front ranks of the Resistance combat. . . . The Resistance and collaboration were . . . the result and the
prolongation of struggles begun years before. . . . The resolutely antifascist
policy of the working class was continued in the Resistance, and it is precisely
because the Communist Party *never ceased* to direct this policy that it was to be
the determining force in the liberative struggle.[23]

Yet, while no one can deny the eventually crucial role played by the
Communists in the Resistance, the evidence demonstrates as well that
despite the acts of some individual militants, the PCF did not join the
movement until Hitler ruptured the Nazi-Soviet alliance.

In reality, once the partial contradiction with Stalinist foreign policy (i.e., the PCF tendency to rally to defense of the country) had
been resolved, the French Communists were viciously attacked within
the Comintern for the "grave errors" committed during this time.
Consequently, after a round of public self-criticism, which appeared
in the clandestine issue of *Cahiers du Bolchévisme* published in January 1940,[24] the underground Party press adopted an outright pose of
neutrality and even conciliation with the Germans. The first issue of
L'Humanité circulated secretly *after* the Germans invaded France in

---

PCF during this period by non-PCF sources are above all: A. Rossi, *pendant la drôle de
guerre, A Communist Party in Action, La guerre des papillons;* Lecoeur, *Le Parti et la résistance;* Rossi-Landi, *La drôle de guerre,* (pp. 133–166); and Fauvet, *Histoire du Parti,*
2:11–85. Rossi, whose real name is Angelo Tasca, is a former Italian Communist and
leading figure in the Comintern until 1928; Lecoeur is a former PCF leader. Both
sources, while clearly written expressly to discredit the PCF official viewpoint, are
nonetheless well documented, and include photostats of clandestine editions of *L'Humanité* not available anywhere else. Lecoeur writes that he is perhaps the only person to
have the full set of *L'Humanité* during the clandestine period. (For example, during
the Liberation, the PCF militants systematically "borrowed" (permanently) sources
from the Bibliothèque Nationale.)

[23] Op. cit., pp. 14 and 35, emphasis mine.

[24] This issue, condemning the war as "imperialist" and explaining the errors of
August and September as the result of the Party, "in the aura of its former policy maintaining itself in the old ways and repeating the old formulas, . . ." nonetheless did not
condemn Nazism. Rather, the militants were called upon to mobilize in order to "destroy the legend of the supposed anti-fascist character of the war." Furthermore, "by
proceeding to a serious, Leninist self-criticism of the errors and mistakes, the Party and
its leadership will render still more comprehensible to the workers the reasons which
determined the change in Communist Party policy." (Cited in Lecoeur, *Le Parti et la
Résistance,* pp. 63–64). The result was the rewriting of history suggested in footnote 4.

May 1940 had this to say: "When two gangsters fight among them-selves, the honest people have no obligation to aid one of them, on the pretext that the other had dealt an unfair blow." [25] The clandes-tine publications of the Party, in particular *L'Humanité*, developed this theme continually over the next year, and the last issue of *L'Humanité* before the German invasion of the Soviet Union, dated June 20, 1941, still bore the headline: "Down With the Imperialist War!" [26]

On June 22, 1940, the Franco-German armistice was signed, and from that point on government in France was carried out only with the agreement of the Nazi occupying forces. During the year between the French defeat and the German attack on the USSR, the clandes-tine Communist leadership participated in what was in effect a tacit understanding with the Germans. The Communists did not disturb to any extent the Germans' intentions in France, but instead even pro-posed active collaboration with them in certain respects. For ex-ample, *L'Humanité* of July 13, 1940, headlined "Franco-German Friendship," carried the suggestion: "The friendly conversations be-tween Parisian workers and German soldiers are multiplying. . . . We are very happy about this. Let us get to know each other." [27] Also in July, on instructions from Moscow, the editor-in-chief of the clan-destine *L'Humanité* (none other than Jacques Duclos) wrote to the Ger-man authorities requesting permission for the paper to appear legally once more:

L'Humanité published by us would fix as its task to denounce the activities of the agents of British imperialism. . . . *L'Humanité* published by us would fix as its task to pursue a policy of European pacification and to support the conclusion of a Franco-Soviet friendship treaty, which would be the comple-ment to the German-Soviet Pact, thus creating the conditions of a lasting peace.[28]

Such initiatives were taken by other communist parties as well, and while *L'Humanité* never appeared legally, the Danish Communist

---

[25] *L'Humanité*, underground edition of May 15, 1940, cited in Lecoeur, *ibid.*, p. 65. Altogether, about 50 editions of *L'Humanité* appeared from October 26, 1939 to June 20, 1941.

[26] *Ibid.*, p. 66.   [27] Cited in *Ibid.*, p. 89.

[28] Cited in *Ibid.*, pp. 76–77, and Fauvet, *Histoire du Parti*, 2:56–57.

Party newspaper did so for a brief time under German occupation. In France, however, "Neither Vichy nor Berlin wanted to have *L'Humanité* [appear] in Paris." [29]

During the six weeks between the Nazi blitz across the French border and the armistice, the PCF had, it is true, circulated several leaflets protesting certain aspects of the German actions and had called a number of times for a government that would include the Communists.[30] Probably the appeals for an immediate peace and Communist participation in the government reflected a vague "revolutionary defeatist" hope that somehow the Leninist model of Brest-Litovsk could be repeated out of the French catastrophe.[31] Nonetheless, given the weakened condition of the movement as a whole and the turn of events since August 1939, this all was little more than self-delusion. The 1940 Chamber was certainly not likely to legalize the Communists and include them in the government, nor were the Germans likely to aid the establishment of a Bolshevik regime in France, the Hitler-Stalin Pact notwithstanding.

After the Armistice, while the underground Communist publications of 1940–41 continued to criticize details of the German occupation, the French Communist Party faithfully carried out the Stalinist and Comintern pose of neutrality. This had proved utterly counterproductive for itself, but it was a course of action the remaining French Communists were willing to justify on the basis of a stubborn and unrelenting faith in the Russian Bolshevik revolutionary myth. As for the Soviet leader himself, "It would be naive to suppose that Stalin was not aware of [such] results of his 'friendship' with Hitler. But he almost certainly thought them of little importance in comparison with the tangible advantages he had obtained." [32]

During the rest of 1940 and early 1941 the Communist movement in France was in limbo, and the Party's decision to rally completely behind the Nazi-Soviet Pact had been demonstrated to be one of nearly suicidal consequences. Had the French regime been in a posi-

---

[29] *Ibid.*, p. 57.

[30] "Only one party is capable of governing France. Only one party opposed the war. . . . That party is the Communist Party." A PCF clandestine tract, cited in Rossi, *A Communist Party*, p. 67.

[31] Rossi, *A Communist Party*, chap. II, esp. p. 12.   [32] Deutscher, *Stalin*, p. 449.

tion to withstand the Nazi offensive, it is likely that the PCF would have been either completely exterminated or permanently reduced once again to its pre-Popular Front proportions. Extremism on the Right had, for better or for worse, saved the movement from attrition in 1934. Nazism performed the same service, but in a manner incomparably more tragic, in 1940–41.

As for PCF attempts to justify its behavior during the "phony war" period, the leadership is reduced to but a few documents, mainly debatable, and a few incidents, of little consequence. The most important of the documents is a tract, allegedly dated July 10, 1940, and supposed to prove the "patriotism" of the Communists at that moment. However, even if one ignores the fact that the PCF rewrote its contents *post facto*, this one partial exception does little to challenge the overall conclusion demanded by any reading of Party publications.[33] The most significant incident cited by the Communists before June 22, 1941, was a strike of miners against occupying forces in the Nord and Pas-de-Calais during late May and early June 1941. This event, which might be given some significance as it occurred before the German invasion of the Soviet Union, was directed by Auguste Lecoeur who, after his exclusion from the Party, wrote demonstrating that it had taken place not only primarily at the instigation of local militants, but also against the wishes and formal orders of the central Party leadership.[34]

The antinational character of the period 1939–41 in the history of

---

[33] Lecoeur dates the document at September 1940, and charges that the original text, in his possession, was later altered by the Party, in an attempt to make it coincide with the July 10 vote of 80 deputies against full powers for the Vichy government. See *Le Parti et la Résistance*, pp. 20–22.

[34] "Before June 1941, direct actions against the Germans . . . were due to the initiative of local militants. At the national level, the leadership considered such actions provocations, anti-German slogans included" (*ibid.*, p. 82). On the miners strike, see pp. 78–80 and 61–62, and his separate volume, *Croix de Guerre pour une grève: 100,000 mineurs contre l'occupant, 27 mai–10 juin 1941* (Paris, 1971).

Lecoeur attributes his later rise to leadership in the PCF in large part to his role in this strike, which is crucial to the Party claim to have been in the Resistance before June 1941: "Thanks to the miners strike, which I had prepared and directed in May 1941, I was, in the Party leadership, the living proof that the action against the Germans had begun before and not after the German aggression against the Soviet Union" (pp. 61–62). His documentation decries the charge that his revelations are false accusations based on a desire for revenge.

the communist movement in France is thus not subject to doubt. Yet, can one say for certain who betrayed France during those dark years? Can one say for certain who or what represented the nation at this time? Perhaps the most impartial conclusion is simply that the legitimacy forfeited by the Third Republic during 1939–40 went into hibernation until it was refashioned in the wake of military victory half a decade later. At the time General de Gaulle made his first appeal from London on June 18, 1940, he was more or less a lone wolf, and the future Vichy politicians, no heroes, could see no alternative but to accommodate themselves and France to the "Thousand-Year Reich." In this light, Thorez's justificatory statement at the 10th PCF Congress (1945)—in effect arguing that if it is true only limited numbers of Communists joined the Resistance from the beginning, was this not true of all groups?—must be accorded a degree of pertinence.[35] It is far from irrelevant to the discussion that most of those politicians who considered the Communists to be traitors were at one time or another considered so themselves—either as Vichyites or as Gaullists.

The somewhat arbitrary question of treason is thus of necessity placed on the periphery of analysis. For this study the most important implication of Communist behavior in France during the *drôle de guerre* is rather that, precisely because of the antinational actions it now seeks to paper over, the Party was led to a reaffirmation of the radical nature of the movement, of its extremist capacity. In other words, the PCF decision to support Stalin's policy totally was nothing less than an empirical verification of its willingness to act toward a fundamentally radical ideal which, to its mind, was to be pursued through the vehicle of Soviet foreign policy. In this sense, the *volte-face* of 1939 demonstrated that the Popular Front years had not worked a change at least in the orientation of the Communist movement toward French politics and society. As Lecoeur, whose authority on the matter must weigh heavily, has written: "The Communist Party conducted its action . . . as a function of its fundamental objectives, with the single concern of the interests of communism to the exclusion of all others.[36] More specifically, because of the Stalinist character of the proletarian

---

[35] PCF–10, Thorez report, p. 15.   [36] *Ibid.*, p. 30.

internationalist vision, "the internal and external policy of the Communist Party . . . could be determined only as a function of the foreign policy of the Soviet Union." [37] The events of June 1941, provide still further proof of the unabated French Communist potential for radical zigzag tactics.

[37] *Ibid.*, p. 43.

Chapter Five

THE RESISTANCE, THE LIBERATION, TRIPARTISM (1941–1947)

During the years 1941–1947, the wartime alliance between the Soviet Union and the liberal democracies permitted the French Communists to pursue the united front successfully for the second time. Moreover, they collaborated with non-Communist political forces so successfully that whereas the movement had never been more isolated from the nation than it was in 1939–40, from 1944 to 1947 the PCF participated in the national government itself. This startling turnabout in itself would be worth a detailed analysis, for to all appearances it made final the French Communist contradiction of pre-revolutionary Bolshevism. However, if the general argument regarding the nature of Marxism-Leninism presented in this study has been successful, it will not be impossible to demonstrate that appearances in 1941–47, as in 1934–38, were misleading.

At the same time, the dilemmas of PCF governmental participation during these years should not blind one to the other questions of doctrine, strategy, and tactics for which the Resistance and Liberation periods constitute an important reference. For one thing, the possibility of a Communist insurrection came to the fore in 1943–44, and the relation of forces explaining why no mass uprising was attempted during the Liberation has proved to be a *situation de fait* of enduring consequence. Secondly, once it was established that a new French republic would be created by the victorious Resistance forces, the Communists were an integral part of all the structures concerned with what Gordon Wright has termed "the reshaping of French democracy." And having elected to help create a renewed "bourgeois" democracy, they were obliged as well to spell out more clearly than ever before their relation to the possible forms of prerevolutionary society. Communist positions in the constitutional debate and in the drafting of the documents themselves are thus of considerable interest for our purpose here. Finally, with the weapon of insurrection discarded (at least temporarily), the "struggle for unity"—i.e., the tactics of unity of action, the popular front and the merger-infiltration-takeover pattern—became once again the typical cudgels with which the French Communist leadership hoped to clear a path forward. But toward what goal? That is, toward what goal possible of attainment, which in its very achievement would not compromise the fundamental exterior position of the Communist mentality to "bourgeois" conceptions and end in the movement's co-optation into the status quo?

The Resistance: Toward the Provisional Government

When the Communists joined the Resistance after Germany's attack on the Soviet Union in June 1941, they were the only political group dating from the Third Republic to have done so wholeheartedly and unanimously—a fact consequent, to be sure, of the organizational nature of the movement. Moreover, despite the badly damaged organizational base from which they began, in the course of the next three years the Communist leaders were able to remold the party into the single most unified and powerful force among all the metropolitan Resistance groups. By both military success and efficient propaganda, recruiting was raised to previously unmatched numbers such that the Communist Party in 1945 was not only bigger than ever before but also the largest in France. The paradoxical result of this was that precisely in reestablishing French Communism as a mass movement and leading the Party victoriously into participation in the Liberation government, all of the inherent tensions between the minimum-maximum Communist perspective were exacerbated to the extreme.

The military exploits of the *maquis* after June 1941, are not our main interest here. We must rather limit ourselves to following the political developments (based upon military success to be sure) that led to the emergence of the French Communist Party as one of the dominant partners in the Liberation coalition under General de Gaulle.

After the Nazi invasion of Soviet territory on June 22, 1941, Stalin immediately called upon the Comintern to reorganize the European "united front against fascism." On French soil, this took the form first of a rehabilitation by the PCF of the "national front" proposal, which had first appeared from time to time during the period 1937–39 and which now became their slogan for unity in the resistance to Nazism and to the Vichy regime.

The basis of the National Front was to be an eight-point program of action: a restriction of industrial production through slowdown and sabotage; continual demands on the Vichy and occupation authorities; agitation against Vichy's Labor Charter; restriction of agricultural production combined with a refusal to deliver produce; exploitation of the food shortage as a weapon against German requisitioning; agitation among young people; agitation to win the intellectuals and middle classes; finally, "direct action," to include (illegal) patriotic demonstrations, outright terrorism, and defense against repression.[1] Because the Communists now were advocates of active resistance, as contrasted with isolated acts of sabotage and more discreet forms of protest, they were able almost immediately to focus much of the Resistance movement upon themselves, as no other group had yet been able either to organize extensively or to take such a hard line.[2] Moreover, the Communist battle to regain popular legitimacy and to recruit extensively received unwitting aid from the Vichy government and the German occupation forces, who themselves sought to identify the *Résistants* with the *Communistes* in order to discredit the former. In fact, this produced the result of making effective propaganda for the PCF among those Frenchmen who leaned toward the anti-Vichy and anti-Nazi struggle.[3] In short, combining its increasingly reorganized clandestine organization, its now uncompromising attitude toward the enemy, and useful propaganda from both their own and enemy outlets, the French Communists increased their dominance among the

[1] A. Rossi, *A Communist Party in Action*, p. 106.
[2] Raymond L. Garthoff, "The Advanced Countries", in Black and Thornton (eds.), *Communism and Revolution*, p. 392.
[3] Alfred Rieber, *Stalin and the French Communist Party, 1941–47*, pp. 84–85.

metropolitan Resistance forces and came to occupy a decisive political role with which they later were able to pressure the Gaullist resistance in London and Algiers. Within the developing Resistance structures, it was completely within the now-established character of Communist activity that they attempt to predominate: The Marxist-Leninist tactic of collaboration, once it has become the dominant expression of strategy, is in effect to occupy as much "terrain" as possible, deciding "how far to go" with the leverage gained as a matter of circumstances. Eventually, although de Gaulle and the Western Allied leaders never discounted a possible Communist attempt at revolutionary insurrection in France as a product of the Resistance, the PCF was denied this alternative.

The political arm of the Communist Resistance effort was called the National Front (FN); the military adjunct of the FN was named the *Franc-Tireurs et Partisans* (FTP). The PCF leaders originally hoped to make the FN the basis of unification of all the different strands of the Resistance. Although they failed early in this goal, through their influence in the FN and by participating actively in other organizations, in particular the *Mouvements unis de la Résistance* (MUR), the Communists gained a strong position in the *Conseil National de la Résistance* (CNR), the organization created in late May 1943, which finally unified the metropolitan Resistance forces.

The impetus to organize the CNR had come from the Gaullists in London, who, in addition to purely military considerations, wanted to demonstrate to the American and British governments that the French underground was firm in its support of General de Gaulle rather than his unfortunate rival, General Henri Giraud. It was thus vitally important from the beginning to de Gaulle that he obtain Communist cooperation, at the same time as he suspected its possible consequences. Having failed in their original plans for the FN, the Communist leaders at this point probably wanted to make of the CNR the government of liberated France, and, if possible, to be in a position to oppose it to the external (first in London and then in Algiers) Resistance organization of de Gaulle.[4] During the sad days of 1940–41, the Communists had described General de Gaulle's activity in London

---

[4] See Jacques Fauvet, *La IVe République*, p. 28.

quite viciously: In the context of their policy of neutralism and revolutionary defeatism in the "capitalist war," de Gaulle was vilified as an
"imperialist agent" of the "London bankers." The PCF somersault of
June 1941 had perhaps camouflaged but never bridged the chasm
separating Gaullists and Communists. This initial and violent enmity
was responsible for the fact that, before the agreement to establish the
CNR, "Fighting France" and the "National Front" kept their distance
for a year and one-half. The first PCF-deGaulle contacts probably
took place in May 1942 through the intermediary of "Colonel Rémy,"
but it was not until January 8, 1943, that the first PCF representative
(Fernand Grenier) arrived in London to join de Gaulle. And even at
that point, the sentiments of the new partners were rather transparent: for de Gaulle, the Communist Party and the FN were a means by
which to create as large a Gaullist movement as possible, a basis to
permit him to argue in the Allied councils that he represented all of
France. For the Communists, alliance with de Gaulle meant first of all
that their patriotism had received an "official" sanction.[5] (Another
sign of the transformation in Communist–non-Communist relations
was release of the 27 PCF deputies condemned during the "phony
war." Transferred to Algiers in 1940, they were released February 3,
1943, on orders of General Giraud.) Moreover, in exchange for a part
of their independence the Communists had opened new possibilities
for the united front, the consequences of which were yet to be defined. Thus, while neither was particularly enamored of the other,
both Gaullists and Communists had a vital interest in the partnership.
Its exact conditions—and, of equal importance, its duration—were, as
both might have said, matters to be decided by "History."

   The first meeting of the CNR took place in France on May 27 under
the presidency of de Gaulle's personal delegate, the legendary Jean Mou-

   [5] Fauvet, *Histoire du Parti*, 2:116. De Gaulle's concern to represent all of France cannot be underestimated. This desire created serious and lasting conflicts even with the
non-Communist Resistants. In a recent personal recollection, Henri Freney—who
organized the first Resistance movement in the South (*Combat*) and remained one of the
Resistance leaders throughout—asserts that de Gaulle foresaw the possibility of a postwar confrontation, concluding: "Then, Charvet (Freney's pseudonym), France will
choose between you and I." *La nuit finira* (Paris: Robert Laffont, 1973), p. 257 and passim.

lin.[6] The Communists Villon and Gillot were elected to the five-man executive committee as representatives of the FN and the PCF respectively. A third member, a socialist representing the *Fédération républicaine*, Louis Saillant, often supported Communist positions in situations of conflict. Yet, while very strong in the CNR apparatus, the Communists did not dominate it, although this was more evident in the COMAC, the military adjunct of the CNR.[7]

On June 3, 1943, the *Comité français de libération nationale* (CFLN) was established at Algiers, with two chiefs, de Gaulle and Giraud, but no Communists, despite the fact that many of the latter had already arrived in Algiers by this time to join the 27 recently released PCF deputies. In any case, one of the CFLN's first acts was to declare null and void the 1939 dissolution of the Communist Party.

On October 1, de Gaulle succeeded in "resolving" the dual leadership of the CFLN, and in succeeding weeks he went on to eliminate General Giraud from political power. From that point forward, the Communist leadership must have realized that in addition to whatever parties were reorganized upon the Liberation (the SFIO and Radical parties had been accepted into the CNR without having been officially reconstituted), General de Gaulle had imposed himself as an independent force. Nonetheless, like both Churchill and Roosevelt, they could not have guessed at that point how powerful and prestigious de Gaulle would actually become.

On September 17, 1943, a Consultative Assembly was created in Algiers, the purpose of which was to deliberate in parliamentary fashion the future reconstitution of French government while the CFLN expedited present affairs. Of the 102 members of this body, 27 were Communists, among them André Marty, Fernand Grenier, Etienne Fajon, Waldeck Rochet, Florimond Bonte, and François Billoux.[8] Nonetheless, acceptance of Communists in the CFLN itself, the executive organ of the Algiers movement, continued to remain problem-

---

[6] Stalin had dissolved the Comintern on May 23.

[7] Fauvet, *La IVe.* . . , p. 29m.

[8] The top leaders, Thorez, Duclos and Frachon, did not seek to join the Algiers Assembly. Maurice Thorez, still considered a deserter, remained in Moscow, and the latter two continued to direct the metropolitan Communist forces from a hiding place in Paris.

atic. It was not until April 4, 1944, that General de Gaulle and the PCF agreed on the conditions of participation.[9] On that day, Grenier and François Billoux joined the unified executive organ of the Liberation movement, the former as Minister of Air, the latter as Minister of State. Given the exceptional circumstances, few stopped to measure the implications of such an event in terms of Bolshevik revolutionary doctrine and practice.

On April 21, an ordinance on "The Organization of the Public Authorities in France" was issued at Algiers. This document was to be the basis of the future provisional government. Envisioned was a network of Military Governors and Departmental Liberation Committees (which began to be effectively organized after September 1943) under the global jurisdiction of the CFLN. Finally, on June 3, 1944, the CFLN assumed officially the title of Provisional Government of the French Republic (GPRF), and after the Liberation it was to be the GPRF which governed France for two and one-half years, until the Constitution of the Fourth Republic came into effect.

The military dimension of the metropolitan Resistance movement was consolidated February 1, 1944, with the creation of the FFI, or *Forces Françaises de l'Interieur*. The FTP, the military adjunct of the Communist-organized National Front, was merged into the FFI and was particularly involved in *maquis* action in the southwest of France during the summer of 1944. Somewhat in contradiction to this move to stabilize and homogenize military jurisdictions and plans, during June of that year the PCF set about establishing the famous Patriotic Militias, essentially a parapolice institution whose immediate task concerned reprisals against collaborators, but whose ultimate task—at least as seen by de Gaulle and the Allied leaderships—could have been of an insurrectional nature.[10] The Communists in general were

[9] Disagreements had centered, not surprisingly, on Communist demands for greater influence than de Gaulle was willing to give them. For details, see Rieber, *Stalin*, pp. 55–59.

[10] Moreover, in the Southwest of France (including Bordeaux, Toulouse, Limoges, and Montpellier) the Communist military chiefs dominated the COMAC, unlike elsewhere, because the area was outside Allied operations. They have sometimes been accused of having planned at the time to proclaim a soviet republic, though probably wrongly. This is suggested in Billoux, *Quand nous étions ministres:* "It would certainly have been possible to establish [socialist] "islands" on a temporary basis. But what

more severe than were even the Gaullists in demanding and, where they were dominant, in executing a purge of collaborators and traitors. This was no doubt in part a matter of outright vengeance against the Vichyites and fascists, but it also may have been part of an attempt to vacate sensitive positions of authority, and thus open them to Communists. In any case, the scope of the purge eventually carried out fell far short of their demands. In the Departmental Liberation Committees as well, put into operation progressively as France was retaken during 1944, the Communists also sought maximum possible participation, thus establishing power positions in all the structures of government in liberated France from their inception.

Despite this success, however, the Gaullist and other non-Communist groups were able to restrain the degree to which the PCF was able to penetrate and control the Provisional Government apparatus. First, the FFI, and thus the old FTP as well, were integrated in a new French Army after August 1944; and in any case the presence of the American and British armies after the Normandy invasion nullified the position of strength the Communist paramilitary forces enjoyed relative to Gaullist and other metropolitan French forces. Secondly, the PCF leaders had presented a list of Communist candidates for the posts of prefect and Military Governor to the GPRF, but were accorded only two prefectures (in the Haute-Vienne and Loire) and no military governorships, although three men known to be sympathetic to the PCF were named Military Governor in Lyon, Toulouse, and Marseilles, an action taken by de Gaulle possibly to smooth over possible trouble spots.[11] Thirdly, as far as the Departmental Liberation Committees were concerned, the Communists did not approach dominating a majority of the 71 that had been established at the time of

---

would have happened then? First, a clash from one city to another, from one region to another. Thereupon, the American troops would not long have tolerated such a situation" (p. 60).

[11] See Rieber, *Stalin*, p. 64. Alexander Parodi and Michel Debré selected the candidates for de Gaulle, adhering to an unwritten rule that there would be no communist prefects or governors in maritime or border areas. In July 1944, de Gaulle asked Parodi to take steps to reaffirm the authority of the GPRF vis-à-vis that of the CNR and the Departmental Committees, which meant mainly to limit communist influence in the emerging state. See Fauvet, *La IVe. . .* , p. 30, and René Hostache, *Le Conseil National de la Résistance*, pp. 200–01.

the Liberation.[12] In late 1943 and early 1944, the Party had proposed that these Departmental Committees should become the basis of the provisional government on a local level, and already in Eastern Europe the creation of such local Resistance committees was becoming a standard partisan device, serving to guarantee Communist power in the countryside. While the ultimate use of this tactic in the French case could not be foreseen, it was obviously in de Gaulle's interest to limit the scope of their power a priori. This he did with the Ordinance of April 1944, which established a highly centralized governmental structure, and placed regional and local powers under the control of the military governors, who were themselves immediately responsible to the national executive, the GPRF.

A last and decisive problem in circumscribing Communist possibilities arising in the last months of 1944 was de Gaulle's order to disband the popular militias. Although not very powerful in purely military terms, they might have provided a rallying point in an attempted insurrection. During the summer and fall they had operated as a combined parapolice and judicial organ, even going so far as to execute a number of collaborators in summary circumstances. Once the FFI-FTP complex had been quickly merged into the new French army after the Normandy landing, the militias implied a last and potentially dangerous question in terms of whether or not the Communists would agree to integrate completely with the Gaullist Provisional Government.

On October 28, the GPRF Council of Ministers decided upon the dissolution of the Patriotic Guards, as they had come to be called. The Communists at first protested violently and for a month this controversy raged within the Provisional Government. Then, on November 27, 1944, Secretary-General Maurice Thorez returned from Moscow, and on November 30—in his first public speech to Frenchmen in over four years—it became apparent that dissolution of the militias was no longer a barrier between the Party and the new legality. The controversy died quietly over the next two months. Finally, in a long report to the Central Committee on January 21, 1945, Thorez remarked upon this originally heated debate in a passing reference:

---

[12] *Ibid.*, p. 62 ff.

These armed groups had their raison d'être before and during the insurrection against the Hitlerite occupation and its Vichy accomplices. But the situation is now different. Public security is to be guaranteed by regular police forces constituted for this purpose. The civic guards, and *all* irregular armed groups in general, should not be maintained any longer.[13]

What had happened? Although discussions among the top Communist leadership at this time have remained secret, the Thorez statement, taken in a general perspective, was no more than a final admission of the limits of the Communist position in liberated France. In effect, since the Big Three wartime conferences of 1943–44, acceptance of the *de facto* division of spheres of influence in Europe had been an implicit condition of continued alliance. To risk upsetting the balance in France was therefore not permitted the PCF, given that it accepted to be first of all an appendage to an international strategy, which is to say the French Communists agreed to forego any plans for a revolutionary takeover of power in France in favor of facilitating the more certain Soviet-sponsored plan to create a socialist bloc of states in Eastern Europe.[14] And in any case, had the balance of purely French military forces been susceptible to Communist insurrection in 1944 (and there persists a vigorous if minor debate on this point) the presence of American and British troops voided a priori any such plan. As Alfred Rieber has concisely and brutally put it: "The French and Soviet Communists were well aware that the Americans had the dominant military power, and it was obvious that no army could have tolerated a civil war in its rear." [15] The Soviet position vis-à-vis the Provisional Government had been based on this consideration, reinforced by de Gaulle's already clearly apparent tendencies toward independent attitudes often at odds with those taken by Roosevelt and Churchill. Given the implicit agreement over spheres of

[13] Thorez, "S'unir, combattre, travailler," Report to the Central Committee, Jan. 21–23, 1945, p. 18. See also Rieber, *Stalin*, pp. 189 ff. and Fauvet, *Histoire du Parti*, 2:147 ff.

[14] This is true even though at the founding meeting of the Cominform three years later the French Communists were attacked for having pursued too soft a policy at the Liberation. Although the relation of military potentials was no doubt the dominant reason for the Communist acceptance of the dissolution order, it has also been argued that Maurice Thorez, his position in the Party weakened by his years of absence, had wanted to remove the power base of possible rivals—the Resistance or "military" leaders, who reproached him for the position of safety he had accepted.

[15] Rieber, *Stalin*, p. 157 n.

influence, Stalin's major goal with regard to France became to encourage its independence from American influence, insofar as was possible. Franco-Soviet diplomatic negotiations had been going on at the time of the conflict over the militias, and it might not be too much to say that the Treaty of Alliance and Mutual Assistance signed on December 10 was in part an immediate *quid pro quo* from de Gaulle to Stalin for the indifference shown by Thorez to the demise of the last possibly insurrectionary tool that the PCF had developed during the Liberation.

It is in the light of Stalin's interest in adhering to his bargain with Roosevelt and Churchill (at least at this point) that one may comprehend why the PCF preoccupied itself with the CNR program and the problems of reinvigorating production in 1945, as opposed to attempting to save the militias or the Departmental Liberation Committees—both of which died a quiet, slow, and efficacious death. The least convoluted explanation is in this case the most powerful; having no chance of seizing power, the Communist leadership realized that attainment of the minimum primary objectives—diplomatic support of emerging Soviet power in Eastern Europe and French independence in the West—implied maximum effectiveness of the PCF in the institutions of provisional government. Thus, as in Italy and Belgium, the Soviet foreign policy interest rendered possible a reproduction of the international alliance in national contexts in Western Europe. Moreover, the Italian case (where there was no counterpart to the figure of General de Gaulle and thus less indigenous resistance to eventual Communist designs) tends to confirm this evaluation of Communist strategy and motives. While Stalin was later to encourage tests of Allied resolve at the periphery of the Western sphere of influence (i.e., Greece and Turkey), the behavior of the French, Italian, and Belgian Communist parties remained under limits in place as early as 1943.

The Legal Pursuit of Hegemony: "Unité! Unité! Unité!"

The tactical expression of these limits was that all the French Communist goals were to be pursued through a nonviolent application of the Janus-like strategy of "unity." In earlier chapters, we have seen that the different possible forms of the unity aspect of Bolshevik strategy were often in evidence. In 1945–46, the PCF leadership sought to use the unity strategy in its most varied forms, so that by the time the first postwar elections were held, French politicians, and in particular the socialists, were denouncing a communist attempt to "stack the deck" of the future regime, so to speak, through a plan of common actions and mergers designed to gain hegemony in the party system, in the syndicalist structure, and among the most important mass organizations of political significance.[16]

Since the Congress of Tours, Communists and socialists had disputed without cease their mutual claims to authenticity as representatives of the French working class and the socialist struggle. In 1934, however, the rise of Nazism and incipient French fascism had caused a halt in this open vendetta and during the period 1935–36, as we have seen above, the renewal of dialogue on the French Left went so far as to envision a total reunification of the two parties. Separated once again as the Popular Front and the Munich policy failed with such tragic effect, the Resistance had once again made partners of them. In 1944–45, there were many who felt the Resistance élan was profound enough and intense enough for the two Left parties to accommodate their differences within it. Such individuals naively underestimated both the superficiality of the *maquis* alliance, and, equally significant, the depth of the chasm that separated Bolshevism from Social Democracy.

With Léon Blum still imprisoned at Buchenwald, the reemergent SFIO in 1943–44 was led by a group of younger men who, having taken an active and often dangerous role in the Resistance, and exhilarated by the vision of a new France, had very early begun to seek a new era of relations with the communists. Daniel Mayer, the acting Secretary General, and Jules Moch were among the most optimistic socialists in this regard.

Toward the end of 1943 the SFIO first proposed the establishment of a Communist-socialist committee to discuss the possibility of reunification, and on December 11, 1943, the SFIO proposed a radical common program, calling for considerable nationalization of industry,

[16] Municipal elections were held April 25–May 13, 1945, cantonal elections on September 23–30, and the first Constituent Assembly was elected October 21.

at a time when the Communists were more in agreement with the Radicals (but for expedient reasons) on the question of leaving out "structural reforms" from the CNR program.[17] One cannot be certain of all the reasons underlying these socialist initiatives during the clandestine period, but it would appear that in addition to patriotic and radical reformist intentions the SFIO leaders either had also envisioned a dangerous strategy, in which the social democrats were to act within a reunified party to dominate the Communists, or had overestimated the significance of Stalin's dissolution of the Comintern May 23, 1943.

The Communists, perhaps suspecting a trap and in any case reluctant to limit their alliance options at a point when the situation was still extremely fluid and one could not know whether it would be possible to do better than a constricting alliance with the SFIO (especially in terms of influencing policy toward the Soviet Union) stalled throughout most of 1944. Then, at the first post-Liberation SFIO congress in November 1944, the socialist leadership renewed the offer to discuss "organic unity," and, though reticent, the PCF leaders now agreed to meet separately with the socialists.[18]

A delegation from each party met on December 4, the result of which was the creation of a *Comité permanent d'entente*, which itself met on December 19. Three subcommittees were established:[19] the first to plan common actions, the second to pursue "organic unity," and the third to resolve conflicts and litigations between the parties. The subcommittee on common actions produced a few significant results, one of the most important being a resolution of January 8, 1945, concerning the principles to be applied in the punishment of traitors and in the purges, and another being a manifesto of March 2 concerning the nationalization of banks, natural resources, energy sources, some key industries, and transport and insurance companies.[20] Yet at the

[17] See Roger Quillot, *La SFIO et l'exercice du pouvoir, 1944–1958*, p. 201.

[18] Probably the Communists had drawn the implications from the difficulties their *maquis* had experienced in obtaining arms from the allied and Gaullist forces and from the reemergence of open anti-Communist maneuvers during the Liberation.

[19] See Duclos, "Vive l'unité de la classe ouvrière de France," report to the 10th Congress, June 1945, 40 pp.

[20] These were published in *L'Humanité* and *Le Populaire* of January 9 and March 3, 1945.

same time, the Communist delegates to the Economic Commission of the CNR attempted to dilute the program of nationalizations in question there.[21]

The key aspect of the *Comité d'entente,* however, was to be the Subcommittee on Organic Unity. Nonetheless, after deciding, at the end of negotiations, to draw up two separate documents to avoid a decisive split at the preliminary stage, this Subcommittee never even met in a working session. By mutual agreement, it was allowed to sit dormant during the first months of 1945. The SFIO was occupied with internal reorganization and conflicting opinions in the leadership, and the Communists were not yet sure of their own strength and likely bargaining leverage and, therefore, the "correct" line to take toward reunification. Moreover, a new factor had been added to the political configuration with the creation and rapid growth of the Christian Democratic *Mouvement Républicain Populaire* (MRP), which had begun in the early part of 1944 in Lyons. Combined with the decline of the Radicals and the Right in general, the MRP—which had been built largely around Georges Bidault, now President of the CNR—was to emerge quickly as the third wing of the new tripartite system. The municipal elections of April–May, 1945, the first in liberated France, were to confirm this political trichotomy and to open what appeared then to be a new era in French republican politics.

For the municipal elections, the Communists sought (as the *Comité d'entente* and the anticommunism of the MRP implied) an exclusive alliance with the socialists, but the SFIO leaders refused the idea of common lists. Rather, they preferred to exercise their options to ally with both the MRP and the PCF. In seeking to take maximum advantage of its tactical position, the SFIO was aided by the use of a PR electoral law, which de Gaulle had somewhat grudgingly accepted. PR was useful to the socialists in that it provided them with a pretext to go into the first round of the electoral battle alone, thus permitting them to escape being swayed by arguments of efficacy to enter into a first-ballot coalition with the PCF, an alliance choice which they feared would alienate them irrevocably from the MRP.[22] In any case, the municipal elections were a tremendous Communist success, and

[21] Quillot, *La SFIO,* p. 204.
[22] See Philip Williams, *Crisis and Compromise,* p. 23.

while the exact figures are a matter of some disagreement, it appears that PCF lists won approximately 25 percent of the total vote and more or less tripled their control of medium and large local governments as compared with the 1935 totals.

After this success, and understanding the implication of the socialist electoral maneuver, on June 12 the Communist leadership suddenly and unilaterally made public a "Project for a Unity Charter of the Working Class of France," which Jacques Duclos presented to the 10th Party Congress on June 26–30.[23] Rather than demonstrating a new desire for reunification, the Charter was a blatant attempt to play to what the Communists considered their ultimate strength: the link with the mystique of the Russian Revolution and the organizational methods and determination that produced it. For rather than being a compromise document (and, in this regard, the rules of the unity committee indicated that any document was to be examined by it before being made public) the Charter contained a set of familiar statutes basing the proposed united working class party on "the dialectical materialism of Marx and Engels, enriched by Lenin and Stalin," on the organizational principle of "democratic centralism," and citing as the expression of its hopes "the grandiose socialist victories achieved by the Bolshevik Communist Party of the Soviet Union." [24] In sum, this was but a rehash of the Communist proposal of 1935–37, although, as before, some attempts were made to conciliate the sensibilities of socialist militants, the most important of which was to avoid the bogey term "dictatorship of the proletariat," replacing it with the following doctrinal irony: "The *Parti ouvrier français* [will be] therefore the Party seeking the disappearance of the *dictatorship of capital* and the establishment of a State assuring the exercise of power to the working class." [25]

In the 1935–37 unity dialogue as well, the PCF had at one point tried to finesse the problem of the dictatorship of the proletariat model by calling it something else, but the ruse was too obviously transparent to have any chance of success. As André Philip, a leading socialist, was later to write, the PCF proposal for reunification "was evidently unacceptable" to the SFIO.[26]

[23] *L'Humanité*, June 12, 1945, and Duclos, *"Vive l'unité,"* pp. 36–40.
[24] Duclos, *ibid.*, p. 38.   [25] *Ibid.*, p. 37.   [26] Philip, *Les socialistes*, p. 113.

Moreover, the problem in 1945 was the same as in 1935, which in turn had been the same as in 1920: a refusal of the social democrats to accept the Bolsheviks as the incarnation of what Marx had meant by "dictatorship of the proletariat." It was the argument between Kautsky and Lenin all over again, with Léon Blum (returned from Germany in May 1945) assuming the former's role in a series of 18 articles entitled *Le problème de l'unité* that appeared in the July 5–August 7 issues of *Le Populaire*. As in 1936 the Communist leadership now openly insisted that its refusal to disavow the Soviet model's applicability to France must be a precondition of Left-wing unity. In consequence, the unity movement in the SFIO, which had flourished for a year under Daniel Mayer, was quickly dissipated by the Communist proposition. In 1941, Blum had written that two changes might permit a reintegration of the French Communists into the national community: "It will be necessary that French communism disengage itself from Soviet Russia, or that Soviet Russia engage itself toward Europe; perhaps even the first and the second. . . . [Thereby] Soviet Russia would lose the character of a power foreign to Europe, and French communism would lose the character of a sect foreign to the nation." [27]

In 1941–42 Blum had written with guarded optimism of the chances for such an evolution, based on the beginning of the alliance against Germany. In 1945, he was prepared to conclude that nothing had occurred to change the status quo ante of the French and Soviet Communist attitudes, including the Comintern's dissolution. Thus, under his influence, by the end of the summer of 1945 the Subcommittee on Organic Unity had been placed in limbo. What had taken over a year to occur in 1935–36 was accomplished in 1944–45 with much less fuss and in much less time: a reaffirmation of the schism at Tours. [28]

[27] Blum, *A l'échelle humaine*, pp. 109–10.

[28] For the SFIO Congress of August 1945, the party executive sent to its section leaders a memorandum drafted by Vincent Auriol which contradicted the PCF Unity Charter in detail (see Quilliot, *La SFIO*, pp. 785–803 for the complete text). The SFIO executive finally terminated formally the existence of the entire *Comité d'entente* on September 3, 1946, after it had been moribund since its last meeting, January 18. Moreover, in the spring and summer of 1945 the SFIO executive had already issued instructions prohibiting local SFIO organizations from setting up PCF-SFIO unity committees

During the time it was becoming clear that the SFIO and PCF were not going to surmount the doctrinal and practical conflicts between Bolshevism and Social Democracy, two other conceptions for realigning the party structure were in the air as well. One of them concerned a possible alliance or even fusion between the SFIO and the newly emerged MRP. Although not a party in its original design (or rather not *only* a party), the MRP had done very respectably in the Spring 1945 municipal elections, the first test of party strengths in postwar France. And this was true in particular where it had formed alliances with the socialists. Moreover, the MRP was directed by a progressive leadership apparently geared toward broad social and economic reforms. The difficulty in fomenting such an alliance was twofold: for one thing, the clerical question still had not been erased as a significant political issue. The PCF, seeking to impede a Center-Left alliance of SFIO and MRP, consistently made the question of *laïcité* an issue in 1945, and in particular during constitutional debates. The communists thereby succeeded in maintaining a wedge between them. Their efforts were helped considerably by the SFIO militant rank and file, who, having emerged from the Resistance more *pur et dur* than at any time since Tours, agitated against an alliance with the MRP, reviving the sentimental *Bloc des gauches* slogan of "no enemies on the Left!" The attitude of the militant SFIO rank and file also prevented the second idea for party reform from coming to fruition: This was an idea—endorsed by Léon Blum and Daniel Mayer, among others—to remodel the SFIO into a sort of *Union travailliste*, based on the British Labour Party model. The aim was to broaden the party's base by assimilating the young and vigorous elements of the Resistance, and eventually to absorb all the prewar splinter movements dedicated to political and social reform into a hopefully majority party of workers and other democratic elements. The militants, preferring doctrinal fidelity to coalition politics, would have none of this however; furthermore they presented the not illogical argument that if the SFIO opened its back door to "bourgeois" elements, the front entrance

---

and had prohibited SFIO militants from becoming members of Communist *amicales*. The aim was to prevent the militants, generally more radical than the leadership, from moving toward reunification at the local level in contradiction to the increasing divisions at the national level.

would become a much-used passage of the old members into Communist ranks.[29]

The somewhat uncertain tergiversations of the SFIO leadership at
this time were to affect profoundly not only the incipient tripartite
period, but also the destiny of French social democracy for a quarter-
century. In 1944, it was not at all sure which political party (if any)
would emerge dominant in the postwar regime, but a great many observers assumed that with the prewar conservative forces stigmatized
with collaboration and with the MRP just beginning the SFIO was in
the most powerful position.[30] Because of its inability to make decisive
choices, however, all the SFIO's fusion projects failed to materialize.
The lack of a potent strategic orientation was symbolized in the preoccupations of Léon Blum: the aged former Premier considered of fundamental importance the new "Declaration of Principles" that he
wanted the party to adopt.[31]

At bottom, Blum was still traumatized by the power successes of
Bolshevism and by the bankruptcy of social democracy in the interwar years. His failure at this time to offer a decisive new perspective in ideological or strategic terms and the rank and file's refusal to
transform the nature of the organization no doubt cost the SFIO its
chance of becoming the largest party, and, moreover, condemned it to
gradual decline in the long run.[32] Its role in the immediate future
would consist mainly of acting as the swing party of the tripartite coalition. It would attempt to juggle its difficult alliances with the MRP
and PCF on the one hand, and the conflict between the parties as a
whole and General de Gaulle on the other. Adding to this the other
fundamental questions of drafting a constitution and reacting to the
widening gap between the wartime allies on an international level, the
SFIO had arrived once again at a set of positions internally contradictory and externally equivocal, which made success impossible.

[29] Gordon Wright, *The Reshaping of French Democracy*, p. 71.

[30] Implicit in this view was the added assumption, soon to be invalidated, that the
French electorate would not vote more strongly Communist than socialist.

[31] Philip, *Les Socialistes*, p. 114.

[32] Wright, *Reshaping*, p. 72. The disappointment in militant ranks was vented at the
August 1946 Congress, when the Mayer leadership was ousted by a new *pur et dur* team
headed by Guy Mollet. Caught in the beginnings of the Cold War, Mollet was soon led
to adopt the outlook of the former leadership.

The failure of the Communists to force a fusion with the socialists was matched by failure to unify the still-existing Resistance organizations under their own standard. In essence, the project envisioned was a merger of the *Mouvements de Libération Nationale* (the MLN was the former MUR enlarged) and the *Front National*, to create what Thorez called a unity "from Communists to Catholics." However, at the January 1949 National Congress of the MLN, only a minority of the delegates voted for plans that would have resulted either in a federal union with the FN or in a much more vague and more impractical union of MLN, FN, SFIO, PCF, and CGT. The rest, by a majority of 250–119, voted for the simpler formula of unity of action. In May, Communist elements provoked a split in the organization: they succeeded in passing a motion at the Lyons MLN Departmental Congress calling for fusion with the FN, and the MLN national executive expelled all those who had voted for it. With this action, the refusal of the non-Communist elements in the MLN to permit an alliance with the FN had been shown to be firmly in the majority. The Communist-leaning minority thereupon seceded from the MLN and fused separately with the FN on June 21, to form the *Mouvements Unifiés de la Résistance Française* (MURF). In May, the MLN majority had itself fused, in the opposite direction, with *Libération-Nord* and the *Organisation Civile et Militaire*, the result of which was the UDSR, or *Union Démocratique et Socialiste de la Résistance*.

These events not only broke the hopes of continuing the Resistance union of Communists and non-Communists into the postwar period, but they also ended whatever prospects may have existed that the Resistance would continue as a strong and independent force in French politics. The MURF, completely in sympathy with the Communists, soon disappeared as a separate organization. The UDSR would exist until it was absorbed into the *Convention des Institutions Républicaines* in 1966, and during the first postwar years generally identified itself with the SFIO. One of the reasons for its continued independent existence was to challenge General de Gaulle's attempt to identify the non-Communist resistance forces completely with his own person.[33] Thus, when on July 14, 1945, the PCF-inspired *Etats-*

---

[33] On the above, see Rieber, *Stalin*, pp. 215–17.

Généraux de la Renaissance Française met in what was supposed to have been the culmination of Resistance unity to prepare a single list of candidates for the elections to the Constituent Assembly, the Resistance leadership was already deeply rent with prewar and some new ideological cleavages. And popular opinion was already drifting away from its earlier esteem of the Resistance as the foundation of a new regime.

Despite the failures to fuse with the SFIO and the Resistance, the Communist movement as a whole did have one great, if temporary, success in its campaign for organizational mergers during the Liberation. This was the reunification of the Communist- and socialist-oriented syndicalists, reenacting the "vertical mirror effect" of 1920–22, 1934–36, and 1939–40. Even this fusion was not pure, however, because of the fact that the CGT had not really split in 1939; rather, the Communist leaders had simply been evicted, leaving the organization itself a single entity.

On April 17, 1943, a set of accords signed clandestinely at Le Perreux by representatives of the two factions reintegrated the Communists into the ranks. And when the reconstituted Federal Bureau began to operate openly upon the liberation of Paris, they had already obtained a strong position. The 1936–39 executive had normally contained a six-to-three ratio of former *confédérés* (CGT) to *unitaires* (CGTU). In the new executive, however, most often a position of equality existed.[34] Moreover, the local dynamism of communist militants, plus their effectiveness both in recruiting new followers out of the Resistance and in purging the opposition (great numbers of whom had had suspect associations with Vichy to be sure) helped to extend Communist infiltration of important positions in the hierarchy all the way down to the lowest levels of the "base."

In March 1945, the newly elected National Central Committee of the CGT voted to reconstitute the federal executive, the result of which was that the Communist syndicalists were given official parity; five secretaries each represented the two factions. Moreover, even the

---

[34] Léon Jouhaux was still a prisoner in Germany, and Louis Saillant generally voted here also with the Communist positions, as in the CNR executive. The new CGT executive was thus usually divided with the socialists Bothereau, Buisson, Neumayer, and Gazier opposing Frachon, Racamond, Raynaud, and Saillant. Rieber, *Stalin*, p. 220.

return of Léon Jouhaux from Germany in May 1945 did not change things because, unlike Léon Blum, he was initially reluctant to risk open conflict by taking a hard-line position against the Communists.

The situation of parity within the CGT was symbolically reaffirmed in the first week of September, when the Central Committee created a dual Secretary Generalship, filled by the most eminent representatives of the allied factions, Jouhaux and Frachon. The faction led by Jouhaux was soon weakened by fate, however: First with the death of Buisson and then with the election of Gazier as a deputy to the Constituent Assembly in October, the Communist faction became dominant.[35]

The National Congress of April 1946 was the point at which it became clear that the infiltration process begun in 1936–39 had now been completed. The Communist syndicalists had elected most of the delegates, and by a vote of 21,238 to 4,862 the former *unitaires* changed the statutes, and created a method of voting in which the seven largest federations, all controlled by Communists, would in the future be assured of a perpetual majority.[36] To soften the shock of their victory, the Communists elected fifteen *confédérés* to the 35-man administrative commission, and the dual Secretary Generalship was retained.[37] But this attempt to mask the takeover was utterly transparent. By the middle of 1946, moreover, the other Communist initiatives toward unification among parties and Resistance groups had ended in failure, the first draft Constitution (written by the PCF and SFIO) had been rejected, and the reemergence of a *régime des partis* torn by profound ideological conflict had been symbolized by de Gaulle's resignation in January 1946. At the same time, during 1946 the Soviet Union and the United States moved toward an open break. All of these events rendered the French Communist position difficult, as they brought to the fore anti-Communist feelings vehement enough so that even at this early point in the postwar period the legitimacy of Communist activities had become once again a matter of debate.

[35] *Ibid.*, p. 222.

[36] These seven were Engineers, Textile Workers, Railwaymen, Miners, Building-Trade Workers, Agricultural Workers, and Food-Trade Workers. Moreover, whereas in 1939 the *unitaires* controlled 10 of the 30 largest federations, in 1945–46 they controlled 21. See Dorothy Pickles, *French Politics*, p. 270.

[37] Rieber, *Stalin*, p. 223.

In any case, with a Communist as Minister of Labor and the primary PCF objective being reconstruction of the country quickly enough to avoid dependence and eventual subordination of France to American influence, the Communist leadership of the CGT did not pursue a policy of political strikes and demands that would have been insupportable for the *confédérés*. Nonetheless during the period 1945–46 the CGT was gradually given a progressively more political posture in other ways, which tended to repudiate the traditional apoliticism of *confédéré* syndicalist doctrine. For example, the CGT participated in the determination of electoral lists in the municipal campaign of April–May 1945. A further sign of Communist aggressiveness in the syndicalist movement was a proposal to merge with the CFTC, the Christian Democrat union. The CFTC rejected this offer in September 1945, but at the April 1946 National Congress, nonetheless, Frachon announced that the CGT policy would be to achieve this unity in any case, by winning over the Catholic workers "at the bottom." Thus, in effect, having infiltrated and increasingly politicized the CGT itself, the Communist leadership seemed intent on seeking broad domination of the labor movement.[38]

Most probably, even at this time the Soviet and French leadership foresaw the limits of the Communist movement in postwar France, and in particular the limits of the Party itself. The defeat of the first Constitution and the increasing friction between the Tripartite partners (see below) had made clear that possibilities for influence within the parliamentary setup were becoming increasingly more constricted. As a result, the preservation of Communist political options would likely be increasingly vested in the CGT. It was surely this sort of calculation that lay behind Jacques Duclos's statement of December 9, 1946, that "The principal task of Communist parties in each capitalist country is to do all in their power to assure the unity of the syndicalist movement." [39]

However, the Communists were unable to prevent a renaissance of

---

[38] The Italian syndicates also united at end of World War II. In contrast to the French case, in Italy the Christian Democratic syndicate joined as well. However, although it attempted the same tactic, the Communist-oriented CGIL was unable to dominate the labor movement.

[39] Speech to the Central Committee at Saint-Denis (32 pp.), p. 23.

factionalism during the latter part of 1946. In addition to the *confédérés*, who organized a *Force ouvrière* group within the CGT itself before the split of December 1947, there also occurred a rebirth of anarchist, Trotskyite, and revolutionary syndicalist tendencies. Thus, the global PCF strategy of 1944–46—even in the one case where it was temporarily successful—could not avoid the characteristic reaction against Communist methods, which in the end amounted to an ethical rejection of the Bolshevik concept itself.[40]

Coalitions, Constitutions, and de Gaulle: A Communist Movement in the Heart of "Bourgeois" Democracy

The Provisional Government of the French Republic took its seat in Paris on the day that ancient and cherished city was liberated, August 25, 1944. The GPRF and the Consultative Assembly were to exist until the referendum of October 21, 1945, at which time a Constituent Assembly would be elected to draft a new constitution out of which also would be named a new government.

How much time would be allowed to pass before the election of a Constituent Assembly had been a matter of considerable debate throughout the latter part of 1944 and the first months of 1945. De Gaulle's original plan, which envisioned a period of presidential government to last approximately two years, had been accepted by socialists and the future MRP leaders at Algiers. However a minority of Radicals and the Communists, who did not want to allow the General an opportunity to render an executive-dominated regime a *fait accompli*, contested the plan. The Communist group had offered a counterproposal limiting the period of "irresponsible" government to six months, but had made little headway.[41] For some reason, however, perhaps to answer fears that he was planning to establish an authoritarian regime or perhaps, as he said, simply to allow the people back into politics as soon as possible, De Gaulle himself decided to cut the

---

[40] The following chapter will deal with the growth of dissension in the CGT and its split in December 1947.

[41] Wright, *Reshaping*, p. 49.

interim period short, and the Constituent Assembly was indeed elected just six months after the Germans had been entirely beaten back across the Rhine.[42]

During the fourteen months between the liberation of Paris and the opening session of the First Constituent Assembly, the government of France was more or less a consensual dictatorship. Although de Gaulle was perhaps in his own mind responsible to the people, there were no formal limitations on his powers. Moreover, it was he who chose the ministers, and because of the unique position he had acquired over the preceding four years the informal counterweight of party and faction was less a factor than it might have been. Given the relation of communist goals and available methods, the PCF leadership was obliged to accept this situation and its ministers at first gave the General little trouble, fulfilled the relatively minor roles he offered them, and scrupulously avoided direct criticism of his actions.[43] Even after the PCF success in the municipal elections of April–May 1945, when a cabinet reshuffle failed to increase Communist participation sufficiently to reflect their electoral strength, the Communists did not defect, although, to be sure, the always latent tension between themselves and de Gaulle was increased. Rather, they continued to seek power through mergers within the vitals of the polity, as described above. In addition they took an active part in the campaign to reactivate the economy by reorganizing and rechanneling production efforts.

[42] In his *War Memoirs*, de Gaulle wrote only this ambiguous phrase: "Public safety was now a *fait accompli*, and I had no desire to maintain the momentary dictatorship which I had exercised in the course of the storm and which I would not fail to prolong or resume if the nation were in danger. Therefore, as I had promised, I would let the people make their choice in a general election" (p. 939). That a fundamental PCF goal at this time was to avoid presidential government becoming permanent is indicated by Jacques Duclos's statement to the Consultative Assembly on July 29, 1945: "In sum, it is a question of a union of republicans, above all on the problem of ministerial responsibility. Then, after we have thus reestablished the Republic, that is to say popular sovereignty, in all its rights, the constitutional problems may be resolved . . . in the serene confrontation of opposing conceptions. On the other hand, if we allow the principle of popular sovereignty itself to be placed in question . . . one would have to fear for the future of the Republic." (Cited in Georges Cogniot, "Le peuple est souverain" Paris, 1946, p. 25). This in effect also intimated that the Communists would make concessions as far as the Constitution itself was concerned (see below).

[43] Thus it was not until some months later that the fact de Gaulle was the first to bring Communists into a French government began to take on a certain bite.

The 10th Party Congress (June 1945) can be described as the "production" congress in this regard. In the "Manifesto to the French People" issued by the delegates, the key slogan was "Produce! . . . the first and most imperious duty proclaimed by the 10th Congress." [44] Thorez explained further that "It is a question of refashioning the grandeur of France, it is a question of assuring other than in words the material conditions of French independence." [45] In support of the production program, Thorez toured the country, making speeches at factories and coal mines and urging increased output and smooth labor relations. [46] This last became increasingly difficult for the Communists to support as the gap between wage and price rises grew significantly during the latter half of 1945, but for the moment the Communist part in the production effort was considerable, [47] and based on an endorsement of the CNR program rather than on any specifically Communist platform. In fact, the PCF attempt to identify the Communist movement with the CNR was quite logical, reflecting the strategic calculation that the greatest chance to influence relations between France and the Soviet Union lay in a posture of moderation and strict cooperation:

We must develop in the masses the idea that nothing serious can be accomplished without the Communists, at the same time proclaiming that on the day when the people give us a mandate to apply our communist program, we will respond with acts. . . . But today, the problems are posed differently. What is necessary is to apply the program of the National Resistance Council. . . . It is understood that we will go to the elections with the CNR program as our own. [48]

Charles de Gaulle later wrote of the Communist attitude:

[44] PCF–10, Document no. 2, p. 12.   [45] *Ibid.*, p. 5.

[46] Thorez's most important speech on this subject was delivered July 22, 1945, at Waziers. He later commented upon it: "Without coal. . . . the economy would be paralyzed. I did not hide from the miners that. . . . they would have to redouble their efforts. . . . I appealed to [their] pride, to their class sentiment, to their patriotism." (Thorez, *Fils du peuple*, [*Oeuvres choisies*], pp. 488–89.

[47] An analysis of the problems of economic recovery is beyond the scope of this study. A summary of the problems and figures can be found in Raymond Aron, *Le grand schisme*, pp. 201–23.

[48] Jacques Duclos, "Union des forces démocratiques," speech to the Central Committee on September 1, 1945, pp. 13–14.

The Communists multiplied their intrigues and their invectives, though they attempted no insurrectional movement. Better still, so long as I was in office not a single strike occurred. . . . As for Thorez, while making every effort to advance the interests of Communism, he was to serve public interests on several occasions. . . . Was this out of patriotic instinct or political opportunism? It was not my job to unravel his motives. It sufficed that France was served.[49]

The electoral campaign of Fall 1945 for the first Constituent Assembly was in a sense a campaign to see whether the Assembly would be constituent at all, that is to say, one of the possible choices in the October 21 referendum was to vote a return to the Third Republic's constitutional system. This alternative never really had a chance however.[50] The real battle was fought over whether or not the Constituent Assembly would be "limited" or "fully sovereign," the limits being the imposition of a maximum session of seven months and the specification beforehand of the form of government during the interim. De Gaulle wanted both limits, the Communists wanted none, and the socialists and MRP sought a compromise. When de Gaulle agreed to make the Provisional President responsible to the Assembly, the latter endorsed his plan, and in the election itself, in addition to the rejection of a return to the Third Republic by 96 percent of the electorate, about two-thirds voted to constrain the Constituent Assembly, limiting its duration and denying it the right to fix an interim regime. Only the Communists had campaigned for a fully sovereign body, and they had not been able to attract the support of more than one-third of the socialists.[51] The Communists' interest in an unlimited Constituent Assembly was clear: their constitutional program was moderate compared to their ultimate goals, but was still very radical compared to prevalent ideas. An unlimited Constituent Assembly would have allowed them to resist compromise based on the pressure of time (which did eventually indeed become an important factor in drafting the sec-

[49] Charles de Gaulle, *The Complete War Memoirs*, pp. 782–83.

[50] All the same, the Radicals and most of the discredited splinter Right parties called for a return to the constitutional acts of 1871–75.

[51] De Gaulle's proposal demanded a "oui-oui" vote on the two questions; the Communists called for a "oui-non" vote. On the events of the electoral campaign see Wright, *Reshaping*, pp. 78–98.

ond Constitution) and would have avoided an interim executive-
dominated government that might have influenced the process of con-
stitution-making itself. De Gaulle's switch was also understandable, as
he saw in the alliance of the SFIO and MRP the only feasible non-
communist majority, and thus the only desirable long-term basis for
parliamentary politics.[52] Finally, vigorous and sometimes rather vicious attacks by the PCF on the SFIO leadership during the campaign
(in contradiction to the rules of the *Comité d'entente*), charging that the
socialists were leaning rightward and also raising the bogey of the
MRP position on the clerical issue, had exacerbated relations between
the two parties, placing the SFIO leadership in a difficult position
once the election returns were known.

   The October 21 ballot confirmed the relation of political forces already established in the Consultative Assembly, namely that tripo-
larity had come to dominate the national electorate as well as the party
structure. Three parties—the PCF, the SFIO, and the MRP—had
won three-fourths of the votes and four-fifths of the seats. Moreover,
the Communist Party had become the largest party, having received
5,024,174 votes to 4,580,220 for the MRP and 4,491,152 for the
SFIO. In terms of seats (including allied Resistance deputies), the
PCF had 159, the SFIO 139, and the MRP 150.[53] The biggest surprise of the election was the meteoric rise of the MRP, whose most optimistic leaders had earlier predicted only 100 seats. The MRP success
re-created the classic post-1920 problem for the SFIO: it could gain
power by allying either with the Right or the Left, but only by risk-
ing grave dangers in either case. With the MRP they would have had
a clear majority, and with the PCF the majority would have been even
larger. Complicated by the predominantly Right-leaning tendencies of
the leadership and the more Left-leaning sympathies of the militants,
the socialist choice finally was to ally with both. Trapped without a
real alternative (since the first goal was to remain in the government to

---

[52] Despite his hostility to political parties as a matter of experience, by this time de
Gaulle realized that his plans could be realized only with their help. At this point he
still wished to work with them. During all the time he worked with Communist support, he never expected the arrangement could or would be durable.

[53] The size of the electorate was more than double that of the pre-war period. In
1945 women were first given the vote, as were all the overseas French possessions except Indochina.

influence the development of the postwar situation), the Communists were obliged to accept the tripartite coalition demanded by the action of the SFIO.[54]

The Communists decided not to put forth their own candidate for President of the new government, as they realized that the SFIO would not support a PCF candidate. The socialists did not support a candidate either, and the MRP proposal of a renewed de Gaulle Presidency was immediately acknowledged to be the only solution likely to avoid a political crisis. The Communists did, however, demand increased representation in the Cabinet, and wanted in particular one of the three key ministries—National Defense, Foreign Affairs, and Interior—for which Thorez suggested respectively General Malleret-Joinville, Florimond Bonte, and Laurent Casanova.[55] De Gaulle, however, adamantly refused to consider a Communist for any of these delicate positions, and after an involved period of negotiations a compromise was worked out. The Defense Ministry was separated into two sections, and divided between a Minister of Armaments and a Minister of Armies. Thereby, the communist Charles Tillon was named Minister of Armaments, but had no forces under his control. As a further consolation prize, Thorez was named Minister of State and given charge of reform of the civil service. Lastly, François Billoux, Marcel Paul, and Ambroise Croizat were named respectively Ministers of National Economy, Industrial Production, and Labor, and the Communists were given two undersecretaryships, one of them being the crucial department of coal production. This job went to August Lecoeur, who had organized the miner's strike of May 1941.[56]

At this point, the long-term weakness of the Communist position

[54] "Because . . . a communist and socialist coalition government . . . was shown to be impossible because of the socialist refusal, we were forced to rally to the tripartite government formula." Thorez, *Fils du peuple (Oeuvres choisies)*, p. 491.

[55] Rieber, *Stalin*, p. 279.

[56] The policies of Communist ministers were in general within the norms of the other Provisional Government ministries, and shall not be examined in detail here. For a very useful case study one may see François Pommerolle, "Etude de la gestion communiste du Ministère de la Reconstruction et de l'Urbanisme" (unpublished thesis, Reims, 1969, 177 pp.). The PCF ministries were, however, extraordinary in the extent to which they were "packed" with party militants. For a separate analysis of this question see chapter 12.

had become an open secret. Despite its immediate electoral success, despite its emergence as the largest party in France, the PCF could do little without an alliance with the SFIO. (Given, of course, that Communist strategy temporarily stressed coalition parliamentary politics and rejected a foredoomed attempt at revolution.) Their policy had been partially defeated in the referendum, and they had not been able to avoid an unwelcome compromise over their claim to a larger share of the important positions of government. The SFIO, having rejected the idea of reunification with the PCF and having become concerned on the contrary with the Communist attempts to gain control of the CGT and the Resistance organizations, had demonstrated that while it was not yet ready to give up an alliance on the Left, neither was it prepared to abandon the MRP. The Communists could not afford to quit the government, for they did not have enough votes to defeat it or to act successfully alone in opposition. Thus, they were obliged to accept Tripartism, and (for only a few months more as it turned out), General de Gaulle. The dual Communist goal of increasing the movement's political influence while promoting a rapid return to normality and self-sufficiency in order to promote national independence had become a self-contradiction: to increase their influence they needed time to maneuver before the situation became hardened in political and constitutional terms, whereas to promote a policy of nonalignment demanded a rapid assertion of economic independence and a lack of crisis between the Communists and their somewhat unwilling partners. Concomitantly, the disintegration of the East-West alliance made the question of time still more pressing. Thus, on all sides, the PCF appeared to be locked in by an increasingly constraining set of conditions.

In the Constituent committee appointed to draft the constitution there existed either a PCF–SFIO or MRP–SFIO majority of one, again placing the socialists in the key position. During the life of the commission, which met for the last time on April 26, 1946, the socialists here too attempted to maintain a three-party alliance, a goal made difficult by vigorous disagreements with each of the other two parties and between the latter themselves.[57]

[57] A useful history of the socialist predicament can be found in B. D. Graham, *The French Socialists and Tripartisme, 1944–1947*.

Before the war, the Communist position on a reorganization of the French Republic had never been stated, for it had never been a question of anything other than the existing parliamentary regime or revolution, out of which was to emerge a "republic of soviets." The advent of Vichy, a "retrograde" regime in the dialectically linear Marxist-Leninist perspective of political change, had now obliged them to develop a position on the creation of a regime "more advanced" than the Third Republic, but still not a revolutionary system.[58]

Essentially, the Communists proposed a *régime d'assemblée*, a unicameral regime in which the legislature would be elected on the basis of proportional representation calculated on a national scale,[59] and which in turn alone would elect the President, and to which the Council of Ministers was to be responsible collectively. Furthermore, to remedy the "lack of responsibility" of prewar deputies, the Communists proposed that the right of recall, the possibility for an electorate to revoke its mandate at any time by petition, would be the continuing link between the Assembly and the people during the interval between elections. The system of prefects was to be abolished and its powers given over to the Departmental and Municipal Councils. Lastly, the armed forces were to be placed under the direct authority of the Assembly.

Despite some equivocation in the Communist proposal,[60] it did not require a professor of constitutional law to realize that such a regime resembled in its broad outlines the classic revolutionary formula of 1793 and 1871. Moreover, a unicameral legislature with all but unlimited powers would open the way to dictatorship by any single group that achieved a majority. In short, the original Communist proposal was drafted to contain the possibility of an evolution into "popular" or

[58] The first PCF statement on the future constitution was apparently the article in *Cahiers du communisme* (clandestine) of January 1944, by Georges Cogniot (see Wright, *Reshaping*, pp. 38–40). The entire formal PCF constitutional proposal is "Texte intégral de la proposition de loi constitutionelle déposée par le groupe des députés communistes à l'Assemblée nationale constituante" (Algiers; Editions Liberté, 1944), 24 pp.

[59] The PR law accepted by de Gaulle in 1945 worked on a departmental basis, which tended to hold down the somewhat localized Communist voting strength.

[60] For example, Article 42 stated that "Property, the fruit of personal labor, is inviolable," while Article 43 foresaw the nationalization of all "monopolistic" enterprises. Discrimination among the two was to be the object of later specific laws.

"people's" democracy, as this new transformation of the Soviet model was being developed in the countries of Eastern Europe.[61]

The PCF leadership was surely not so naive as to hope for the immediate appearance of a French people's democracy. On the contrary, the fact that the Communist representatives began to compromise almost immediately in the constitutional debates demonstrated they were willing to moderate their demands in exchange for at least some of their "advanced" program.[62]

The negotiations went on for many months, and the document that finally was reported out of the committee reflected to a great extent the Communist point of view, a development made possible by a socialist willingness to be bold in matters of constitutional reform, despite this inconsistency with other SFIO positions toward the Communists.

The draft constitution proposed a unicameral legislative structure, with the President of the Republic reduced to mainly ceremonial functions. The SFIO, even more than the PCF, had a score to settle with the upper chamber (the Senate, dominated by conservatives, had led the battle against both Popular Front governments of Léon Blum), and together the two parties rebuffed the MRP proposal for a second house. Moreover, a similar coalition turned down the proposal that the President be elected both by the Assembly *and* the proposed Council of French Union, as well as denying him the prerogative of presiding over either the Council of National Defense or the Council of Ministers.[63] Though the Communists did not get all they sought from the committee deliberations, the MRP had gotten almost nothing, and the proposal was therefore (and somewhat incorrectly) seen by the public as a "Marxist" constitution in that it was almost entirely the product of SFIO and PCF conceptions. The Communists, on the

[61] See the translation of an article by the Hungarian Communist theorist Joseph Revai which explains the "People's Democracy" strategy, "The Character of a 'People's Democracy," *Foreign Affairs* 28, no. 1 (October 1949): 143–53.

[62] For example, one of the first ideas to go was that of permanent right of recall, the basis of the revolutionary conception of representation. The MRP pointed out that recall was incompatible with a PR electoral system. The Communists wanted a PR system. To insist on the recall principle before the Party was in power would have thus been premature from the communist point of view. See Rieber, *Stalin*, p. 286n.

[63] *Ibid.*, pp. 284–85.

contrary, argued that it was neither a "Communist" nor a "socialist" constitution, but rather a "democratic" proposal.[64] The reason for this was twofold: First, in terms of doctrine, no political regime could be called socialist in the absence of a collectivized economy, and the PCF was promoting the CNR program rather than their version of socialism in the latter regard. Secondly, the Communists wanted to avoid the possible crisis that might result from "frightening the bourgeoisie," in the 1936 phrase, and to this end much Marxist-sounding phraseology was cut from the draft on their initiative.

During the height of the constitutional negotiations, on January 20, 1946, General de Gaulle had abruptly resigned as President of the Provisional Government. His departure had created a void in the provisional regime. There was no longer either a strong President acting outside the party framework or a possible successor of equal weight in this central role. The Communists had first pushed the candidacy of Thorez, but in the face of an adamant MRP refusal, the SFIO leaders cut short a burgeoning rank-and-file sentiment to accept this idea, and a *faute de mieux* situation brought Félix Gouin, the unassuming President of the Constituent Assembly, to the position of head of government on January 23. His more-or-less caretaker cabinet of 20 included 6 MRP, 7 SFIO, 6 PCF, and 1 "apolitical" technocrat.[65] The new Communist minister was Laurent Casanova, who took over the Ministry of War Veterans and War Victims. In addition, Thorez moved from Minister of State without Portfolio to the position of Vice-President of the Council and François Billoux moved from Ministry of the National Economy to the Ministry of Reconstruction and Urbanism.

With this background of de Gaulle's resignation and the political weakness felt to be inherent in the position of Félix Gouin, in May 1946, the first draft constitution was submitted to a referendum. The MRP campaigned against it vociferously, as did the Radicals and the Right of course. The MRP slogan, "Block the threat of one-party dic-

[64] See e.g., Jacques Duclos, "Notre politique," *Cahiers du communisme*, April 1946, p. 318.

[65] Despite its caretaker status politically, the Gouin government presided over the passage of much of the legislation prepared furing the previous year. The degree of social and economic reform contained in these bills inspired Gordon Wright to call this "revolution in a spare moment." *Ibid.*, pp. 168–76.

tatorship!", was opposed to the PCF slogan, "Bar the way to reaction!" The SFIO (like the PCF) was certain that the proposal would be adopted, as the French people had never voted no in a referendum or plebiscite. Looking to the future, the socialists decided to reject a Communist offer to campaign together on the premise that this would leave open a chance to renew an alliance with the MRP after the vote. They let the Communists take the initiative, preferring to key their own campaign on the idea that "any constitution is better than none" and the lukewarm reasoning of *il faut sortir du provisoire*.[66] At bottom, they had simply acquired a case of cold feet, a not incomprehensible reaction to the Communist takeover in the CGT at the April 1946 congress and the implications of the new PCF suggestion that Thorez be made head of the Provisional Government.

Public opinion shook the elite at this point, when, in contradiction to the general assumption, the first draft constitution was rejected by the French people on May 5 by a margin of 53 percent to 47 percent. The Communist decision, at the last moment, to publicize the slogan *Thorez au pouvoir!* resulted in a ballot that became for many Left voters a plebiscite for or against the idea of a PCF-dominated government. Moreover, in addition to these political defections, generally from socialist ranks, a considerable number of people also voted "no" to protest the continuing shortage of food and consumer goods. This, combined with the opposition of all the parties from the MRP to the Right-wing PRL, had unexpectedly crystallized a majority against the PCF-SFIO constitution.[67]

Thus, in a few days' time the rather promising Communist position on the new regime had disintegrated, and the Party's victories in the constitutional committee had been voided. The SFIO leadership, drawing the electoral conclusion, switched its alliance, and conducted the campaign for the June 2 election of a second Constituent Assembly on a platform of increasing resistance to the PCF and to Communist conceptions in general. The Communist tactic of collaboration in the drawing of a constitution was thus sapped of its momentum, and from this point on the PCF leadership found the possibilities for pur-

---

[66] See Wright, *Reshaping*, pp. 176–78.   [67] *Ibid.*, pp. 178–79.

suing an active and aggressive policy in the tripartite coalition more limited than ever.

The Gouin government lasted only five and one-half months, until the elections of June 2. Like the first constitutional referendum, the elections of the Second Constituent Assembly were disappointing for the PCF in that the Party lost two seats despite gaining 115,000 votes, and was displaced by the MRP as the largest party: the MRP had won close to 5.6 million votes while the Communists had garnered about 5.12 million. Given the new position of his party, the MRP leader Georges Bidault formed a second interim government to succeed Gouin's. As before, Bidault divided his ministries on a tripartite basis. The Communist leaders, fearful of a move to exclude them from the government, decided both to accept the Bidault candidacy (by abstaining in the investiture vote) and to avoid raising once again the question of claiming one of the three key ministries. For their gesture, they were rewarded with still another ministry (René Arthaud became Minister of Public Health), giving them a total of seven altogether. This conciliatory behavior was no doubt influenced as well by the fact that in middle and late June General de Gaulle had finally spoken on the constitutional question at Bayeux and then at Epinal. His proposal for an executive-oriented regime as well as his vigorous anti-Communist polemics both emphasized that the PCF was being pushed progressively closer to the wall, and that its most optimistic constitutional strategy was now simply to achieve the most favorable possible constitution in the least possible time. At that point, not even the MRP leaders could be certain of how far de Gaulle was prepared to act against the emerging parliamentary regime, or how much popular support he could raise. Thus, Bidault accepted Communist participation and Party leaders such as Jacques Duclos began to hint of the Communist willingness to compromise yet further on the constitutional question in order to "discourage any tendency to slide toward dictatorship." [68]

The three-month-long negotiations over the second draft constitution demonstrated the continuingly weakened Communist position in

[68] Rieber, *Stalin*, p. 297.

that the SFIO and MRP leaders drew up a constitution in much the same manner as the earlier draft had been a product of an SFIO–PCF coalition. The Communist representatives were obliged to swallow one concession after another. First, the crucial unicameral formula was jettisoned, and an upper chamber, the Council of the Republic, was added to the legislative branch. Moreover, the President of the Republic was to be elected by both houses, effectively cutting off the possibility of one party dominating the Assembly and electing its "own" President. The President's effective powers were increased somewhat, and the original Communist plan to make the judiciary closely responsible to the single-house legislature through a far-reaching reform [69] was completely forgotten.

After first beginning a campaign against the new constitutional proposal on the assumption it would be passed in any case, the Communists were almost immediately forced to shift gears when General de Gaulle attacked this second proposal on the basis that it did not go far enough in equalizing executive power with legislative power. Had they continued to attack the credibility of the new proposal from the Left with de Gaulle and an embryonic movement, the Gaullist Union, doing the same from the Right, it might have become necessary to elect a third Constituent Assembly, at which point the momentum would be still more potent against the Communist conceptions than it was at that time. The leader of the ephemeral Gaullist Union of 1946, René Capitant, even spoke speculatively of the "period of uncertainty which would follow a second constitutional rejection," upon which the situation would become amenable to a third constitutional draft based on the principles espoused by de Gaulle at Bayeux. [70]

Thus, in the second referendum campaign, the PCF found itself in the embarrassing position of asking its supporters to vote the MRP–SFIO proposal, which was at the same time the expression of its own defeat. Added to this anomaly was the SFIO's constitutional zigzag, no mark of consistency to say the least. The socialist turnabout, combined with the positions of the Gaullists and Radicals, created a situation in which the general public was at once disappointed by the lack

---

[69] See "Texte intégral . . ." (reference in note 58).   [70] Rieber, *Stalin*, p. 298.

of united leadership from the Constituent Assembly, confused by the plethora of arguments presented, or simply fed up with the quite classic machinations over the drafting of a constitution—a document that might have been an expression of new civic purpose. The result was that the referendum became a tragic demonstration of all that had been lost since the united Resistance movements had reestablished a free and peaceful regime. On October 13, 1946, the MRP-SFIO second draft constitution was approved by a weak majority of 53 percent to 47 percent, a victory whose significance was further discredited by the fact that some 5 million Frenchmen had abstained from either approving or rejecting the regime under which they were now going to live.

Despite its unconvincing genesis, the Constitution of the Fourth French Republic now existed, and was to be implemented first by the election of a National Assembly, scheduled for November 10. In the brief electoral campaign, the Communists adopted a moderate posture. Basically they wanted to avoid forcing the SFIO into an untenable position, for the mood of 1945 was now transformed and it seemed that the socialists—should a choice become necessary—would be more disposed to an MRP alliance than one with the PCF. The thrust of the Communist electoral platform was thus the simple pledge to retain the tripartite *status quo*. The MRP, on the other hand, was seeking to force the issue, making its electoral slogan a government of "Bidault without Thorez!" The SFIO, eternally caught with its heart on the Left and a political context forcing it to the Right, adopted the position of continuing tripartism, yet, even as Maurice Duverger wrote at the time, "The position of the socialists is untenable in the long run; it amounts to refusing a Right-wing as well as a Left-wing alliance and taking refuge in a tripartism in which [the SFIO] remains the ham in the sandwich, becoming thinner all the time." [71] In addition, the shadow of General de Gaulle, despite the failure of the Gaullist Union to rouse much support for the idea of a third Constituent Assembly, continued to darken the political situation by injecting overtones of an-

[71] *Le Monde*, October 22, 1946, cited in Graham, *Socialists and Tripartisme*, p. 229. The SFIO, for example, had lost almost 400,000 votes and 19 seats in the elections to the Second Constituent Assembly. They had 115 seats to 146 for the PCF and 160 for the MRP.

tiparliamentarism, Bonapartism, and the perhaps undeserved reputation of an interest in a possible coup d'état.

The seeming indecisiveness of the socialists and the surprisingly open anticommunism of the MRP leaders led to still another reshuffle of party strength in the November 10 election of the First Assembly of the Fourth Republic. The moderation of the Communist campaign had served them well, since the Party won twenty new seats (146 in June, 166 in November) and almost 400,000 new votes (5.12 million in June, 5.49 million in November). The SFIO continued its nose-dive, losing 44 seats (from 134 in October 1945, the total dropped to 115 in June 1946, and to 90 in November 1946) and almost 750,000 of its electors. The MRP retained its seats (160 in June, 158 in November) but lost over 500,000 electors despite this. Surprisingly, besides the PCF, the other big gain was made by the Radicals, who increased their total from 32 to 43 seats. Apparently, the failure of the Resistance parties to construct successfully and efficiently a new institutional framework had provided an opening through which the once-discredited Radicals (and even the Conservatives to a certain extent) were maneuvering an increasingly large place in postwar political life.

Also in November, the SFIO suffered a further setback in elections to the first Council of the Republic. This occasion emboldened the PCF leadership to try once again for an exclusive Communist-socialist alliance, the keystone of which would be mutual support of Maurice Thorez as a candidate for President of the Provisional Government. The Presidency had become vacant because, in recognition of the result of the November 10 election, Bidault resigned his cabinet on November 28, and the PCF immediately proposed a two-party government to the SFIO.[72]

It was in the context of his candidacy for the Presidency that on November 17, 1946, Maurice Thorez accorded an interview of unusual interest to the *London Times*, in which he went to great lengths to stress the moderation of Communist actions and the possibilities for long-continuing cooperation between Communists and other "progressive" forces. In part, he sought to demonstrate that the PCF foreign policy was a "peace" policy, because the Communists were against a

---

[72] "Résolution du Comité Central à Puteaux, 27 novembre, 1946," *Cahiers du communisme*, November, 1946, p. 1011.

division of Europe into two hostile blocs. This argument was unconvincing, however, because it was generally taken to mean merely that France should remain independent of the United States. No one doubted that Thorez was in favor of as "cooperative" a Franco-Soviet alliance as possible! More importantly, however, Thorez tried to reassure the public about Communist intentions in France. For the first time a French Communist spoke of a "French" or "national" road to socialism in a serious manner:

We have expressly repeated, in the course of our electoral campaign, that we do not ask of the people a mandate to implement a strictly communist program, which is based on a radical transformation of the present regime of property and of the relations of production which result from it. We have proposed a program of democracy and national reconstruction, acceptable to all republicans. . . . It is evident that the Communist Party in its governmental activity and within the cadre of the parliamentary system which it helped to reestablish, will constrain itself strictly to the democratic program which has won it the confidence of the popular masses.

The progress of democracy across the world, in spite of rare exceptions that confirm the rule, enables one to consider other roads to socialism than that followed by the Russian communists. In any case, the road is necessarily different for each country. We have always believed and declared that the French people, rich in a glorious tradition, would find its own way toward greater democracy, progress, and social justice.[73]

To advance the Thorez candidacy, a furious propaganda effort was undertaken to enlist public opinion as a means of pressure on the SFIO leadership. In fact, an agreement was reached between the two parties, in which the SFIO leaders would ask support for Thorez as President of the Government in exchange for Communist support of the socialist Vincent Auriol as first President of the Fourth Republic.[74] Despite these precautions, 23 SFIO deputies defected from the

---

[73] "Interview de Maurice Thorez au *Times*," *ibid.*, pp. 1014–1016. And despite the fact that the idea of a reunified party was out of the question at this point, Thorez saw fit to add that "The French Workers' Party which we propose to constitute with the fusion of Communists and socialists will guide our new popular democracy" (*ibid.*, p. 1016).

[74] The Presidency of the Provisional Government would be temporary, perhaps only a month or two, until the new regime came into being; whereas the President of the Republic would be in office for seven years. This no doubt explains the SFIO's acceptance of Thorez. The communists, on the other hand, would have preferred a less pow-

agreement, abstaining in the vote which gave Thorez only 259 of the 310 required ballots.[75] But this was not decisive, however, for Thorez in any case would have lacked the necessary votes. Thus, even the large Communist success in the initial general election of the Fourth Republic—the last important PCF victory prior to *le grand schisme* of May 1947—was not sufficient to reverse the momentum that would soon flow completely away from all the Western European communist parties.

After Thorez failed to gain election, the MRP leader Georges Bidault was refused investiture as well. The reason for this was that the socialists, although weakened and lacking a positive tactic, nonetheless still refused to give up the tripartite idea—that is, to govern without the Communists—which would no doubt have resulted this time from an MRP investiture. After Bidault's defeat, negotiations toward another possible cabinet became quickly stalemated. This impasse was acceptable to the MRP, for whom time was an ally. But the Communists wanted above all to avoid a prolonged cabinet crisis, for the MRP leaders were now maneuvering to bring in the PRL and the Conservative Right, which would have meant the PCF's certain exclusion. At this point, Communist strategy had been effectively neutralized in almost all directions.

The PCF solution, though a stopgap at best, was to make the startling proposal of a homogeneous SFIO government. This, at least, would have the advantage of removing the MRP from government as well, if the Communists themselves had to go. The leader of the government was to be the aged Léon Blum.[76]

The former Premier, no longer a deputy and thus considered above the immediate parliamentary intrigues, himself had never successfully resolved the perennial socialist dilemma of choosing for bourgeois de-

---

erful personality than Auriol as President of the Republic, but they desired even more the extraordinary precedent that would have been created.

[75] Among them were André Philip and Gaston Defferre. See Thorez, *Fils du peuple* (*Oeuvres choisies*), p. 495.

[76] "This was the role of the patriarch in French political life: in 1924, one turned to Poincaré; in 1934, Doumergue; in 1940, Pétain; this time, it was M. Léon Blum." Jacques Chapsal, *La vie politique en France depuis 1940*, p. 127. This may have been the view of those from the SFIO rightward, but it was certainly not the Communist viewpoint.

mocracy or revolution in alliance options. Thus, both Thorez and Bidault could believe he was not likely to lean too far to either side. Blum was therefore chosen, on December 16, to form a government whose sole aim would be to run the affairs of state until the other institutions of the new regime were in place. This certainly did not solve the Communist's strategic problem, but it did buy some time, and although a continued ambiguous situation worked against Party goals, the proposal of a homogeneous socialist cabinet demonstrated that a certain degree of unused resourcefulness remained to be drawn upon.

As foreordained, after the election of the Council of the Republic and the President, Blum quietly resigned his government in January 1947, after one month in office. His SFIO colleague, Paul Ramadier, thereupon formed a new and enlarged tripartite cabinet on January 22, and it is this government which was legally the first of the Fourth Republic. Of the 26 ministers under Ramadier, 9 were SFIO, 5 were MRP, 5 were PCF, in addition to 3 Radicals, 2 UDSR, and 2 Independents.[77] The fact of socialist, and in particular Ramadier's, leadership of the cabinet had been important in securing Communist participation, but the successful constitution of a cabinet holding not only the three largest parties but a host of smaller ones as well was a decisive turning point: it revealed definitively that in terms of parliamentary arithmetic Communist collaboration in French government was no longer either inevitable or indispensable.[78]

From January through April 1947, the French Communist hopes of remaining in government—and thus their policy positions as well—completely disintegrated in the wake of domestic crisis and international conflicts. During these months the Communist ministers clashed increasingly with their colleagues over the beginning of a colonial war in Vietnam, which had first erupted during the 1946 Bidault

---

[77] The five Communist ministers were Thorez (Minister of State and Vice-President of the Cabinet), Billoux (Minister of National Defense), Tillon (Minister of Reconstruction), Croizat (Minister of Labor and Social Security), and Georges Marrane (Minister of Public Health and Population). Finally, after three years, a Communist had been named to one of the key ministries: Defense. Despite this sign of confidence in his allies, however, Ramadier "flanked Billoux with three 'bodyguards': Coste-Floret, Jacquinot, and Maroselli." Quilliot, *La SFIO*, p. 217.

[78] Rieber, *Stalin*, p. 308.

government, and over a difference on the attitude the French government ought to take in the face of a second colonial rebellion in Madagascar. Both problems had been answered with force by the metropolitan regime. The Communists refused to sanction the repression, and in March, all the PCF deputies with the exception of ministers abstained in a vote of confidence on the government's policy in Indochina.[79] At the same time, the East-West split had both deepened and widened. Since the end of the war, the royalist Right-wing government of postwar Greece had been besieged by guerrilla forces, largely communist and supported materially by the now communist-controlled governments of Albania, Bulgaria, and Yugoslavia, and behind them the Soviet Union. Turkey, though not faced with civil war, had encountered tremendous internal economic and political difficulties, and in both countries the Western Allied position was endangered, a situation threatening the Yalta status quo which came to a head in the spring of 1947. In consequence, on March 12, 1947, President Truman outlined what became known as the Truman Doctrine to a joint session of Congress, and the division of Europe into hostile blocs had become probably irreversible.

Despite these new pressures on communist participation in the French, Italian, and Belgian governments, the West European communists themselves did not talk of moving into opposition; their policy was precisely the opposite. Moreover, in France, PCF participation in the government was thought to be of particular importance in view of the March 1947 conference of foreign ministers, in Moscow, at which the American, Soviet, British, and French representatives were to discuss important questions such as the matter of German reparations and the Western proposal concerning French rights in the Saar.

The Moscow Conference ended in a bitter stalemate, however. The Soviet Union charged that the three Western Powers had failed to

---

[79] This was part of a more generally ambivalent attitude of the Communists on the colonial question: they supported retention of certain colonies on the pretext that in the case of separation from the mother country they would "not be certain of guaranteeing their own independence." In reality, to have called for total independence for the colonies at that point would have been to admit that this was a possibility under "monopoly capitalism" whose highest stage (wrote Lenin) is imperialism. In this sense it was a predicament similar to that of "structural reforms," and later that posed by the development of the Common Market.

honor the Potsdam agreements, citing as evidence the Anglo-American bizonal agreement. The Western allies, for their part, considered the Soviet position on German reparations unacceptably harsh, while the Soviets further refused to accept the French–Anglo-American proposal on the Saar and its crucial resources of coal. Within the French cabinet, the Communist ministers had fought Foreign Minister Bidault's policy of annexation of the Saar as well as the Marshall-Bevin-Bidault agreement on the transfer of Saar coal to France.[80] They had little influence however. The French government had chosen the West over a Soviet alliance, and every realistic observer knew this had never been in question.

Given the result of the Moscow conference, it was somewhat unexpected that the termination of Communist-non-Communist collaboration in France came not over a foreign policy issue, but over the question of wage demands.

In February 1947 a wildcat strike had suddenly erupted at the Renault auto works, one of the key industries.[81] Begun either spontaneously or as a result of Trotskyite and anarchist agitation, the strike was at first restrained by the CGT, which wanted to do nothing to endanger the Communist position in government.[82] This was highly frustrating to the rank and file, whose wage claims were justified. The rather lax financial policy of the government—dating from the 1944 debate over the Pleven and Mendès-France proposals at Algiers—had not adequately constrained prices as it had wages.[83] Things calmed for a month at Renault under CGT influence, but in late April the strike broke out once again and overflowed the bounds of Communist disapproval. The PCF Minister of Labor, Ambroise Croizat, and the CGT leader Frachon worked to try to achieve a quick compromise on

[80] Rieber, *Stalin*, pp. 342–43.

[81] In the postwar period, the common wisdom is that "when Renault sneezes, France has a cold." This was to be born out in May 1947 and May 1968.

[82] The constant battle of the Communists to limit Trotskyite and anarchist influence, that is to avoid being "turned on the left flank," is an often latent but always significant factor in strategic and tactical considerations. It is particularly apparent when the dominant tactic is collaboration rather than sectarian militancy, and is perhaps more apparent among syndicalist forces than among the parties, where the *gauchistes* are less potentially threatening, as shown in 1934–38, 1944–47, and 1968–72.

[83] The successful wage policy was of course to a great extent due to CGT moderation.

the basis of an immediate three-franc increase, but this was thrown back in their faces by the strikers. Sensing that the rank-and-file mood had become uncontrollable, on April 30 the PCF came out in favor of an across-the-board wage increase throughout the economy, arguing that price ceilings had been inadequately administered and that increases in production should now be transformed into a generalized salary increase for the workers.[84]

Ramadier and the rest of the cabinet rejected the Communist position, and when the PCF deputies voted against the government's economic policy in a question of confidence posed by the Premier, the issue was fatally joined. The Communist ministers refused to resign, hoping to throw the onus of rupture onto the Premier, and through him onto the SFIO as a whole. Thorez argued once again that the Communist Party wanted to remain a government party. This might even have been possible, had Ramadier seen a way to retain the Communist ministers without losing face. Instead, the SFIO leader, after consideration of several alternatives, chose to stand on the issue of cabinet solidarity and dismissed the PCF ministers abruptly by decree on May 4. The decree was published in the *Journal Officiel* on May 5, 1947.

After the exclusion of the Communists, the SFIO party executive as a whole was obliged to decide formally whether or not to remain in government without the Communists—in effect, whether or not to abandon the commitment to Tripartism which had been consistently endorsed by socialist congresses and meetings since the Liberation. The majority in favor of this option had steadily been diminishing since 1946, and now, by a majority of only 400 out of almost 4,700 ballots, the SFIO National Council accepted the policy of Ramadier.[85] And although some SFIO leaders such as Léon Blum (who had proven himself shortsighted before) at the time felt able to suggest that the event of May 5 was of temporary significance,[86] the logic of events was such that the French socialists had definitely opted against Communist participation, a policy that would soon be transformed by the pressure of international events into a policy of domestic "containment."

[84] *L'Humanité*, April 30, 1947, p. 1.   [85] Rieber, *Stalin*, p. 355.
[86] See Graham, *French Socialists and Tripartisme*, pp. 263–64.

Had the French Communists pursued the goal of a "people's democracy" during the Tripartite period? Surely, but only in the sense that they have always pursued the millenium at the same time as they have believed themselves acting within the limits of the possible. This is the very sense of the dual perspective, the dual program, which is the core of Marxist-Leninist strategy. Can one point to a way in which the strategy for a people's democracy might have been implemented tactically? There is probably very little speculation involved in citing the local Liberation committees, the Departmental Liberation committees, the CNR, and the militias as possible structures of "dual power" in the "maximum" Communist plans during this period. In fact, this much is almost admitted outright in the Thorez speech of January 21, 1945, in which he ratified the dissolution of the militias (see above), and indicated further that, in the same way as the militias were not to replace the police, "the local and departmental Liberation committees should not substitute themselves for the municipal and departmental administrations, any more than the CNR should substitute itself for the government." [87] Had events permitted, would the French Communists have attempted a *"coup de Prague"?* Again, the answer is no doubt affirmative, with the proviso that the possibilities for this kind of takeover were never such that a tactical plan for a coup could be part of an immediate program. Before the end of active hostilities in 1945, Lenin's successor had remarked: "This war is not as in the past; whoever occupies a territory also imposes his own social system. Everyone imposes his own system as far as his armies can reach. It cannot be otherwise." [88] In 1947, the French Communists once again affirmed the fusion of proletarian internationalism and Realpolitik according to Stalin.

---

[87] It is significant that Jacques Duclos recently chose to cite this passage with great emphasis in his *Mémoires*, vol. 3, book 2, p. 287.

[88] From Milovan Djilas, *Conversations with Stalin.*

Chapter Six

LE GRAND SCHISME: THE FRENCH COMMUNIST MOVEMENT IN EXCLUSION AND ISOLATION (1947–1962)

Before the Gaullist *treize mai* 1958, the date of May 5, 1947, was generally regarded as the most important in postwar French domestic politics, for the exclusion of the Communists from the government of Paul Ramadier on that day more than any other event shaped the contours of political life for the next decade. At the time, however, the extent of the separation was not immediately visible, and no one understood clearly that it was to be definitive. Yet within a year it was commonly recognized that the undeclared war between East and West would be reflected in Western European domestic politics. Of necessity France and Italy were the nations most affected, for in those countries communist movements occupied a much larger piece of the political terrain than in Britain, the North countries, or western-occupied Germany. Exclusion of the Communists from arenas of "normal" politics thus inflicted a broader gash in the flesh of French and Italian public life than in the politics of, say, Belgium.

Le grand schisme went finally so deep that during this fifteen-year period the PCF was to present the unlikely and even somewhat embarrassing spectacle of the largest political party (in terms of both votes and membership) being reduced to more or less completely symbolic actions, the most important of which, moreover, had to be carried out through ancillary organizations rather than the formal party organization itself. Furthermore, the Communist-controlled syndicate, also the largest in France, was similarly reduced to a level of

influence completely disproportionate to its size and representativeness, a fact still more anomalous when one considers the
weakness of the other syndicalist structures.

In short, the years 1947–62 were a period of exclusion of Communism by the non-Communist forces in French politics and society, a
position that one may liken roughly to the experience of both 1924–34
and 1939–41. However, there was now the new dimension of "containment" and the Cold War cleavage as a whole, which gave anti-
Communism in France a distinctly modern tone. For their part, the
French Communists responded in kind, encrusting the movement in a
Stalinist and sectarianist immobility, accentuated still further by re-
flex actions against attack from without and within.

Recent scholarship has suggested that, contrary to a once-dominant
view in the West, the origins of the Cold War were not entirely the
work of a single hand.[1] As will be shown in the present chapter, certain of the conventional interpretations of events in postwar France
likewise may bear reconsideration, at least insofar as the French Communists are concerned. This is not to say that the analysis here is a
priori an attempt to overturn entirely the *consensus sapientium*, but
merely to advise the reader that an effort has been made to place into
relief, simultaneously with the received word, certain elements that
have heretofore been left dark in the history of postwar communism
in France. Also, it may be useful to point out that, to a greater extent
than in earlier chapters, the present one is not a chronological recita-
tion but rather a thematic presentation; and because the major trends
of the period were consolidated during 1947–53, it is these years
which receive the closest attention. Finally because insofar as the
Communists are concerned the most suitable point at which to end
the presentation in this chapter is 1962 rather than 1958, the reader
may at first find himself somewhat disoriented. At its end, the 1958
change of regime notwithstanding, the reasons for this dislocation between the history of French Communism and the history of the rest of
France should be evident.[2]

In the most general terms, one may remark that the exclusion of the
PCF from a share in French government meant that the 1944–47

---

[1] I refer, of course, to the "revisionist" interpretation of the Cold War.
[2] The Communist reaction to the change of regime in 1958 is discussed in chapter 8.

Tripartite coalition, with its axis on the Left, gave way to the "Third Force," a coalition founded on the Center, "in between" fundamental oppositions of the PCF and RPF. The Third Force, which some analysts terminate with the general elections of 1951 while others consider it as extending at least up to the 1954–55 government of Mendès-France, was essentially a constantly shifting pattern of parliamentary majorities (and hence governments) forming and disintegrating on the basis of specific issues, rather than upon the terms of a general program. It was this peculiarity of the Fourth Republic which rendered popular the famous formula "one government per issue."

In terms of parliamentary geography, the Third Force coalition strategy, in contrast to Tripartism, meant on the surface merely the substitution of a Center-Right party, the Radical Party, for a party of the extreme Left, the PCF. Shortly after the Communists left the government, the *Rassemblement des gauches républicaines* (R.G.R.) as well as "moderate" and "independent" (conservative) deputies were also added to the coalition mixtures, and by abstracting the historical pattern of coalition formation in French republican politics since 1900, one might content himself with the remark that this "shift to the right" in the course of the first legislature of the Fourth Republic merely repeated a common practice of the Third Republic.

While accurate structurally as far as it goes, the comparison is nevertheless totally insufficient to convey the meaning of this particular shift to the right, because *le grand schisme* excluded not only the French Communist deputies from participation in coalition politics on the national governmental level, but it also—through what I have called a "vertical mirror effect"—excluded and isolated the entire range of Communist-organized or -dominated organizations within the context of the national community, permitting them coexistence but not participation. The result, to be analyzed at length in Part Two, was to sharpen the development of the French Communist movement as a "countercommunity" within the established society, as well as to emphasize the role of the PCF and the CGT as a sort of people's tribune or public advocate for the "little man" threatened by the inability or lack of will on the part of the governmental elites to smooth over the effects of reconstruction and modernization upon the more disadvantaged sectors of the population. Moreover a close examination of the development of French Communism during the period 1947–62 will both illuminate subsequent doctrinal changes in the ideology of the vanguard party role, and help to explain such apparently paradoxical judgments of French Communism as the following juxtaposition. The first opinion, written in 1952, concerns the danger of communism to the established French order:

France is, at the present moment, the weakest link in the European security system, because Communism is not merely a potential but an actual danger to the regime . . . the circumstances are such that, if the parties now governing France do not find some way of ensuring greater governmental stability, Communism cannot be prevented from creating a climate which could easily lead to civil disorder, or dictatorship, or both.[3]

The second, written in 1958 but before the arrival of General de Gaulle, concerns, once again, the potential of Communist activity in France:

[The PCF] has reached a dead center of compromise and synthesis beyond which there can be no movement in one direction or another without serious electoral and perhaps organizational and ideological dislocations. The Party is becoming progressively embedded in the social and ideological structure of France, and as a result is beginning to reflect within itself the very contradictions of the French society.[4]

Can it be that in 1952 the PCF actually threatened the existence of the regime, that in 1958 it had reached a state of inertia, and that by 1963, according to another well-known observer, its presence was both "cause and symptom" of the weaknesses in French democracy?[5] Possibly, for while at first glance such opinions seem contradictory, they may not be entirely so. Or still further, perhaps one's conception of the Communist movement in France must be broad enough to encompass many real and seeming paradoxes.

[3] Dorothy Pickles, "The Communist Problem in France," *International Affairs*, April 1952, p. 162.
[4] Roy Macridis, "The Immobility of the French Communist Party," *Journal of Politics* 20, no. 4 (November 1958): 627.
[5] Micaud, *Communism and the French Left*, p. ix.

The Events of May–September, 1947:
From Government Party to Pariah

In the midst of a growing tension that was soon to result in Cold War, the French Communist ministers were excluded from the government of the socialist Paul Ramadier on May 5, 1947. Nonetheless, for a number of months thereafter, the PCF leadership continued to emphasize its desire to remain in coalition politics, in the process seeking to appease its critics in what must be termed a surprisingly conciliatory manner. It was not until the formation of the Cominform and the proclamation of the Zdhanov line in late September that the Communists in France adopted the new Soviet posture toward the "bourgeois" West. Thus, while the non-Communists were in France the first to begin open hostilities, by September 1947 the domestic Cold War had been joined on both sides.

The tone of French politics from May to September 1947 was tenuous and even somewhat eerie, in the sense that Communists and non-Communists seemed to shadowbox politically, and few pretended to comprehend how deep and durable the new rupture in the political and social fabric was to be. Still, from the beginning it was clear that the future French domestic politics would be conditioned to a considerable extent by the evolution of international relations, in particular the attitude of the West toward the Soviet Union. Paul Ramadier was later to write that "The rupture with the communists occurred as a simple event of French domestic politics, and had no international ramifications." [6] While it is possible that a few totally naive individuals might have remained oblivious to the connection, it would seem that Ramadier's comment was a masterpiece of understatement or diplomatic dissimulation. [7] It would be impossible to believe as well that the Communist leaders had no inkling of the potential importance of the exclusion of May 5, which they had fought with considerable ef-

---

[6] In a letter of January 17, 1958, cited in Bruce D. Graham, *The French Socialists and Tripartisme*, p. 264n.

[7] Particularly in view of the exclusion of the Communists from governments in France, Italy, and Belgium within a few months of each other, the PCB on March 19, the PCF on May 5, and the PCI during the cabinet crisis May 18–30.

fort. Their minimization of the split may be explained both by the fact that the collaborationist-oriented line promulgated in the movement since 1941 had not yet been publicly jettisoned, and the knowledge that their only realistic hope for power over at least the short- and medium-run lay in strategies other than a frontal assault.

At the 11th Party Congress (June 25–28, 1947) for example, which was the first important convocation of the Party after May 5, the report of Maurice Thorez indicated the French Communists had no desire to abandon collaboration in "bourgeois" democracy for a policy of militant opposition:

> We are and we remain a government party, a party conscious of its responsibilities before the country. . . . We continue to think, to say, that "the most happy perspective for France is the prolonged maintenance in office of a democratic government of large national unity." . . . We continue to maintain the same willingness towards a union of all the working class and democratic forces. We have not changed and we will not change.[8]

Going somewhat overboard in his attempt to link the Communists with the past and present progressive traditions of the French people, Thorez asserted that, "We, who are the authentic representatives of the national interest; we, the legitimate heritors of the generations of manual and intellectual laborers who have made the grandeur and force of France; we, communists . . . we continue the rationalist and materialist tradition of the grand Encyclopedists of the eighteenth century."[9] At the end of his speech, the delegates rose to their feet chanting *"Thorez au pouvoir!"* and Marcel Cachin rhetorically asked the congress "through what aberration has [the government] deprived itself of such a statesman?"[10] As for the possibility that the Communists might retaliate violently against the regime, before the Cominform meeting in September the PCF leadership took pains to terminate all suspicion of the Party's intentions. On May 8, for example, Jacques Duclos remarked bluntly: "The people who are talking of a general strike in France are imbeciles."[11]

---

[8] Maurice Thorez, *Textes choisis*, p. 67. The passage in quotation marks is from his interview of November 1946 in the *London Times*.

[9] PCF–11, Thorez report, p. 43.

[10] Cited in Jacques Fauvet, *Histoire du Parti communiste français*, 2:199.

[11] *L'année politique*, 1947, p. 95. See also the remark of Florimond Bonte, a member of the Politburo, on May 5: "The French Communist Party, whether or not it partici-

Nonetheless, the summer months were marked by a mood of constant apprehension in France and the Western allied governments were also anxious over the situation, as France was geographically the key to Western defense in the event of conventional war.

In June, a rather large and menacing wave of strikes occurred in which the CGT was very active. The strikes were strongest at the SNCF (the government-owned railroads), several important bank networks, large department stores, the coal mines, and the Citroën automobile company. In August and September, a further series of strikes took place, hitting particularly the crucial automobile industry (Peugeot, Berliet, Michelin, and others). This apparent political offensive by the Communists through the CGT, however, was rendered ambiguous by the fact that on August 1 the CGT and the CNPF (the new organization of the *Patronat*) had issued a common declaration announcing a salary raise of 11 percent in the private sector. Altogether, the situation remained equivocal, and few observers were able to foresee the sudden change of late September.

On June 5, 1947, the Marshall Plan was made public. Secretary George Marshall remarked that "Our policy is directed neither against a country nor against a doctrine, but against hunger, misery, despair, and chaos." On June 22, the Soviet government accepted the invitation of Georges Bidault and Ernest Bevin to discuss the economic reconstruction of Europe. With the French Party muting its criticism of the Marshall proposal,[12] the tripartite conference went on until the Soviets finally rejected the American initiative on the argument that the projected aid program would infringe upon its sovereignty. This was to be the turning point for the French Communists, for with the Soviet-American negotiations having turned into "peaceful hostili-

---

pates in the government, will continue to consider itself as a government party, yet even more responsible before the country as it is the largest party in France" (*ibid.*).

[12] At first the PCF press service mistakenly sent out a declaration by Thorez to the effect that the Marshall Plan was a "trap." Immediately retracting the statement—and clearly embarrassed by the premature leakage of a condemnation obviously prepared for later release—Thorez insisted: "I repeat that we appreciate our responsibilities to too great an extent to create difficulties between the Allies or to do anything whatsoever to disturb the necessary agreement between [them] . . . ." (*Fauvet*, 2:200.). This snafu suggests the guarded PCF and CPSU reaction at this time was a ploy to enhance later rejection.

ties," Stalin was immediately to turn the screws on the national communist parties in terms of their relations to "bourgeois" power structures.

From September 22 to 27, two delegates each from the nine most important communist parties of East and West Europe met in the small Polish city of Szlarska Poreba; at this convocation, the Cominform was created.

Although they arrived at the meeting with some trepidation, PCF delegates Jacques Duclos and Etienne Fajon had no idea of the extent to which the French Party, along with the Italian Party, would become the scapegoats in the switch of international tactics. In essence, this first meeting of the Cominform was a "trial" of the collaborationist line of the preceding six years, a line the French and Italian Communists had fully implemented but which was now to become the object of "necessary fraternal criticism" because it no longer suited the foreign-policy interest of the Soviet Union. Duclos and Fajon played the role of the accused; and Zhdanov, acting for Stalin, occupied the position of prosecutor.

In creating the Cominform, Stalin essentially wanted the French and Italian parties to revert to hard-line postures in order to rouse the West European populations against development of an Atlantic alliance. As Isaac Deutscher has written:

So little did Stalin think of turning the Cominform into any genuine instrument of international revolution that he did not ask the Chinese and other Asian parties to adhere. . . . His chief concern, outside the Soviet "sphere of influence," was to adjust the policies of the French and Italian Communists to the new needs of his diplomacy.[13]

The report of Zhdanov introduced the new attitude which was to bear his name for a short time.[14] Basically, the Zhdanov line was an uncomplicated formula: the world had, as a direct result of World War II and in a more general way as a result of the unfolding of the

[13] Isaac Deutscher, *Stalin*, p. 570. For an account of this "trial" of the French and Italian Communists, see the book by one of the latter delegates, Eugenio Reale, entitled *Avec Jacques Duclos au banc des accusés à la réunion constitutive du Kominform à Szklarska Poreba, 22–27 septembre 1947* (Paris: Plon, 1958) ix + 203 pp. Maurice Thorez, through shrewd maneuvering, had avoided attending the conference himself, as had Togliatti.

[14] He died only one year later.

class struggle on an international level, become divided into two blocs: the imperialist, antidemocratic bloc and the anti-imperialist, democratic bloc. The former, directed by the United States, was pictured as the incarnation of capitalism, and therefore of war. The latter bloc, "fraternally protected" by the Red Army, was now a "decisive force" for peace and human progress. To achieve a "progessive" solution to this conflict, the role of the Eastern European parties was basically to link their countries closer to the Soviet internationalist patrimony, while the task of the French and Italian parties—operating within the "imperialist camp"—was to prevent American domination of Europe. In a word, this meant hindrance of the Marshall Plan's implementation, and later, to combat the Truman Doctrine. The great failure of the two large Western European parties was their failure to realize this, as a result of which they had committed "grave errors" during the preceding months.[15] The Yugoslav delegate Kardelj charged that the PCF had become impregnated by "Right-wing deviationism," while Djilas was even more demanding, asserting that the PCF leadership had, by not preparing a "true insurrection," "allowed de Gaulle to take over and then eliminate the French Resistance." Furthermore, they had supposedly "allowed themselves to be maneuvered by the Right-wing socialists Ramadier and Blum." In sum, the first Cominform meeting was a scathing critique of Western European Communist collaboration in "bourgeois parliamentarianism"—not that this was condemned as a contradiction of Marxist-Leninist *principles* however, but rather that circumstances had necessitated a change in tactics that the PCF and PCI leaderships had "failed to perceive" on their own. Duclos's reply, that "It is not just to say we did nothing. It was necessary to do more: that is all,"[16] failed to move Malenkov and Zhdanov, who considered this "self-criticism" extremely modest.

---

[15] As Reale, later a dissident, points out (*Avec Jacques Duclos*), the PCF and PCI were simply the victims of a situation in which scapegoats were necessary. Power transfers and policy changes in a Stalinist-type hierarchy have been generally neither smooth nor peaceful. If the leader (until his demise) is always correct, then to explain and justify a major change the cause must be placed in the realm of "objective" conditions. At the same time, it is useful for one or more heads to fall, both to provide cover and diversion for the top leadership and to insure that a change in policy or personnel is not perceived as a sign of weakness.

[16] Reale, *Avec Jacques Duclos*, p. 203.

Whether reasonable or not, the Soviet interest demanded a complete turnabout of attitude from the "principal task" (i.e., unity "at the top") of the second PCF reintegration into the national community.

At the same time, in addition to the immediate objective of hindering the Marshall Plan, one perceives another and more delicate objective insofar as the Soviets were concerned: Stalin must have seen the temptation toward a progressive embourgeoisement of the Western communist leaderships, a desire to remain in power that might be translated into a dilution of loyalty to the CPSU in exchange for a relegitimation of Communist governmental participation in the Western European regimes. From the Soviet point of view it was dangerous that Thorez, Duclos, Billoux, Grenier, and the other PCF leaders had become accustomed to the allure of power before they were able entirely to wield it.[17] And finally, a return to a hard-line public image would withdraw the Communists from association with the regime, necessary lest communist governmental action in "bourgeois" reforms compromise the credibility of the socialist utopia as a political symbol. It was partially for such a reason that the Communists had been much less interested in "structural reforms" in 1936 and 1945 than were the socialists, creating that bizarre alliance of circumstance with the Center (Radicals, then MRP) over the heads of the socialists whenever a program was discussed. The more the existing regime can be portrayed as reactionary, the less it competes with the historical perspective offered by the Communists. In 1947, accepting isolation and adopting a hard-line attitude in return presented the double advantage of heading off Trotskyite and anarchist attempts to outflank the Party doctrine on its left (thereby solidifying its mass and its militant supporters, if at the same time reducing their numbers) and reaffirming "international proletarian solidarity," the PCF-CPSU link, as the ultimate guide to French Communist action.

---

[17] Annie Kriegel cites the perhaps not irrelevant remarks of Albert Vassart, a Comintern representative in France, on Thorez's reaction to his election as deputy in 1932: "I accompanied him the day he made his first visit to the Chamber as a newly elected official, and his wide grin expressed much more than any speech. . . . In a few days' time he was thoroughly acquainted [with all the advantages of a member of parliament;] when, for example, we took a bus together . . . he experienced an infantile pleasure in getting on last in order to have the opportunity to show his card authorizing his right to ride even when there was a full load. (*Les communistes français*, p. 138).

All this notwithstanding, the creation of the Cominform was not announced until October 5, and the Zhdanov report itself was not made public until October 22. Probably this was out of deference to the PCF stake in the French municipal elections held on October 19–26, for an immediate revelation of the "Zhdanov line" would have undoubtedly ruined PCF attempts to achieve local alliances. Immediately after the first ballot, however, it became clear that the non-Communist left—and particularly the socialists—were in any case hostile to such initiatives. In this situation, the new line was made public on October 22 in an attempt to win votes through a show of force, since the opposite tactic was unworkable. Withholding the new line until the 22d indicates, nevertheless, that despite a decision to return to a more sectarian line, neither Stalin nor the French Communists wanted immediately to burn their bridges to "bourgeois" democracy as a matter of principle. Rather one must see their behavior in developing the Cold War as a reaction to circumstance.

Not surprisingly, the municipal elections of October 1947, indicated a definite anti-Communist trend, particularly when compared with the great success of 1945. Whereas in 1945 the PCF had won approximately 25 percent of the vote, in 1947 it won only about 20 percent; whereas in 1945 it had elected 36,517 municipal councilors in the 38,000 communes of France, in 1947 only 30,503 were elected; and in the most startling reversal, whereas they had won 60 of the 80 municipal councils in the "Red Belt" surrounding Paris in 1945, in 1947 they won only 27. Much of this decline, of course, can be attributed to the great successes of the new *Rassemblement du peuple français*, founded by General de Gaulle in April, and also to a new municipal electoral law designed to work against the PCF. Both the SFIO and the MRP also declined in the election of October 19–26, suggesting that, while apparently significant in absolute terms, the Communist losses were part of a general beating taken by the tripartite coalition. Later municipal elections would bear this out insofar as the Communists were concerned, although both the SFIO and the MRP had begun a permanent decline at this time.

At the meeting of the Central Committee on October 29–30, Maurice Thorez took stock of the situation—in other words, he made the necessary self-criticism on behalf of the Party and pronounced the PCF embrace of the Zhdanov line. Still, he attempted to blame the Central Committee as a whole for the "errors," in order to divert attention from his own role:

The root of these errors [is found] in the delay of the Central Committee itself in realizing and clearly defining the nature and the meaning of the changes occurring in the international situation. . . . From that time, we did not emphasize from the beginning and with the necessary vigor, that we had been excluded from the Government entirely upon the express order of the American reactionaries. [We] left the impression that it was a question of an ordinary ministerial crisis. . . . From that resulted the indecisions and waverings of our National Assembly group. . . . For a certain time, the Party seemed to hesitate in its opposition to a Government which misunderstood, with such gravity, the interests of the country . . . when we alone . . . have an attitude absolutely congruent with the interests of France.[18]

With his reemphasis on the Party's special legitimacy, Thorez was insolating the Communists on the level of doctrine as well as tactically. In other words, he was indicating that the French Communists were gearing up for a possibly long and hard period of sectarian activity, to which the idea of the unique legitimacy of the Party corresponded more than the doctrine of alliance between democratic and socialist leaderships: Consciously or unconsciously, in announcing the new doctrinal emphasis, the Communist Secretary-General put himself into costume for the role of pariah, which he and his Party would play for the next fifteen years. Because the non-Communist parties in France had elected to pursue the policy of "containment" on a domestic as well as an international scale, the French Communists were at that point condemned to suffer once again the consequences of their origins and allegiances. And although such would probably have been the case even without American pressure, it would be naive to deny the interplay of foreign and domestic factors in the exclusion of the Communists from French politics.

[18] Thorez report to Central Committee, October 30, 1947, pp. 26–28. "Défendre la République. Sauvegarder notre indépendance nationale."

The "Vertical Mirror Effect" in the Labor Movement: The Split of the CGT in December 1947

The question of wages and prices had been the immediate pretext for the exclusion of the PCF from participation in the national government in May 1947. Major strikes over these and other issues continued throughout spring and summer, in the process exacerbating tensions between Communist and socialist elements within the reunified CGT. The exclusion of the Communists from the government on May 5 set in motion a chain of events that led directly to a renewed split in the labor movement as well. As in 1920–22, 1936–39, and 1944–45, a "vertical mirror effect" was produced in French politics— that is to say, the nature of relations between Communist and socialist "families" in general implied either cooperation or cleavage all the way up and down a series of primary and secondary political organizations, including national political parties, syndicates, student organizations, and most other groups having some ancillary relation to the functioning of the political system.

Georges Lefranc has remarked that "From the month of May on, the strikes had never ceased, successively touching the most diverse sectors . . . and taking diverse forms. . . . The vacation period had seen a certain waning, but in October, the movement began again." [19] The massive series of strikes of November and December, which were to provide the immediate occasion for the schism, began on November 10 in Marseilles, where the newly elected RPF-dominated municipal council—having replaced a Communist-dominated council—decided to raise the fares on public transportation.[20] The local CGT federation and PCF organizations called protest demonstrations, and the demonstrators pillaged several chic cafés and nightclubs in the process. Several were arrested, one person was killed, and

---

[19] *Le mouvement syndical de la libération aux événements de mai–juin, 1968*, p. 52.

[20] In the new municipal council, the balance was 25 RPF, 24 PCF, 9 SFIO, and 5 MRP. The council elected as mayor, on the basis of a relative majority, the RPF candidate Carlini, a Gaullist victory made possible by the socialists, who refused to support the Communist candidate. See *ibid.*, p. 55.

later—when the arrested were brought to trial—several violent clashes occurred at the Palais de Justice and City Hall. On November 13, Premier Ramadier declared that "The demonstrators attacked the Palais . . . and City Hall at the instigation of a party. [This was] something more than a demonstration: It was a riot directed against the functioning of public authority." [21] Thus, at the highest level, the strikes of November were very early propagandized as "potentially insurrectionary" in character, as a direct manifestation of the Cold War. From Marseilles, the strike spread quickly, reaching the SNCF, the postal services, the coal mines in the northeast, and the Parisian metallurgy industries. Ramadier, his political credit drastically reduced, resigned on November 19, to permit the candidacy of Léon Blum. Having made clear his point of view on the "communist problem" since the very moment of his return from a Nazi prison, Blum's declaration to the National Assembly on November 21 sounded a familiar note, yet one that had taken on considerably more resonance during the preceding year:

The Republic is in danger. . . . Civil liberties, public peace, peace in general are threatened: the danger is double. First, international Communism has openly declared war on French democracy. Second, within France, a party has constituted itself whose objective, and perhaps only objective, is to dispossess the sovereign people of their fundamental rights. I am here to sound the appeal. I am here to try to rally all the Republicans, all those who refuse to submit themselves to the impersonal dictatorship, not of the proletariat, but of a political party; [and] all those who refuse to seek a recourse against this peril in the personal power of one man. [22]

Despite this invocation of both the PCF and RPF perils, the "personal equation" (as de Gaulle might have put it) of the old socialist leader had been somewhat tarnished by the time the Fourth Republic was born. Needing 309 votes for investiture, Blum was able to garner only 300. Six days later by a vote of 322–186, the Assembly invested Robert Schuman.

By the end of November, the number of strikers was estimated variously at between one and two million, and a "National Strike Committee" had been organized by twenty federations of the CGT.

[21] *Ibid.*, p. 55.
[22] *Ibid.*, p. 57. The last phrase is a reference to General de Gaulle.

At its head was the Communist syndicalist leader, Benoît Frachon. On November 24, the Schuman government attempted to employ a carrot-and-stick approach. The government simultaneously offered considerable economic and social benefits to the strikers and issued an order mobilizing certain sections of the military. The Communist-dominated strike committee refused the government concessions as insufficient, however, and the conflict was escalated on both sides. The strikes were extended, becoming in effect general strikes in seven departments (Alpes-Maritimes, Gard, Hérault, Haute-Garonne, Tarn-et-Garonne, Loire, and Allier), and instances of sabotage became serious (including, tragically a sabotage on the railroad, which resulted in twenty deaths and forty injuries). The government responded with seizures of newspapers and tracts, the approval by the Assembly of a series of "antisabotage" laws, and authorization of the police to clear out strikers from electric power plants in the Paris suburbs, which had been occupied for several days.

By December 1, the strike wave had begun to subside, particularly in sectors which had begun the movement, such as the postal services, the mines, and the railroads. No doubt many of the returning strikers were anguished over the acts of sabotage perpetrated under the auspices of the National Strike Committee, while others were merely tired of the general agitation in which they had been living for too long. On another level it seemed evident also that among the rank and file a broad sentiment was developing in opposition to Communist syndicalist tactics. On December 8, after a definite trend in favor of ending the strike had appeared, the Schuman government intervened to offer the following settlement: [23]

1. No sanctions were to be taken against strikers. Prosecutions would occur only in the case of infringements of existing penal law, in particular in cases of sabotage, extreme violence, and hindrance of the right to work.

2. Workers in the nationalized enterprises would not be paid for the days they were on strike but a sum of 1,500 francs was to be given to all workers, strikers or not, who had returned to work by December 10.

[23] *Ibid.*, p. 62.

3. Family allocations would be paid to all eligible workers.

4. The Government would proceed immediately to consultations with concerned organizations in order to arrive at a just relationship of prices to wages by June 1948.

5. Decisions in this regard were to be overseen by a delegation from the Economic and Social Council.

Although the Communist elements in the CGT were not prepared to end the strike on the basis of this offer, a mass movement back to work by the strikers themselves forced the Communists to concede. On December 9, Frachon announced a back-to-work order, and by December 12 industrial relations had returned to what had to be considered normal for the period.

Within the CGT leadership, however, the socialist elements had since the emergence of a reunified syndicate been both wary and apprehensive of their pact with the Communists. For many months, a non-Communist group organized by Léon Jouhaux, called *Force ouvrière*, had existed as a faction within the CGT and had come increasingly to consider a split with the Communists as the only hope of avoiding domination of socialist-oriented syndicalism by a "totalitarian enterprise." On December 19 the chain of events begun in May was completed when the *Force ouvrière* left the CGT. On April 13, 1948, the dissociated wing of the CGT announced its reconstitution as the *Confédération générale du travail–Force ouvrière* (CGT-FO).[24]

Unlike the splits of 1922 and 1939, however, this time the socialists were in the minority. In effect, the Communist element in the French labor movement, having completed in 1944–47 what it had begun in 1936–39, was now the dominant syndicalist force, a fact which was to prove of extreme importance in the pattern of postwar French politics, for, as Raymond Aron remarked as early as 1948: "The force of the Communist Party is not so much the number of its membership . . . as the authority it exercises, through the intermediary of the CGT, upon the working masses." [25] While this is only a partial truth, it

[24] For a more detailed account of the split of the CGT in December 1947, particularly as regards the formation of *Force ouvrière* within the CGT, see *ibid.* and Val Lorwin, *The French Labor Movement*.

[25] Raymond Aron, *Le grand schisme*, p. 191.

hints at a crucial aspect of the nature of the French Communist movement, to be explored more deeply in Part Two.

What had the Communists hoped to gain from the strikes of November–December? Why did the leadership take a hardline position such that it deliberately risked provoking a schism as an immediate result?

One common answer, already cited, was that the strikes were of an insurrectional character and ordered by the Cominform, a point of view reinforced by the fact that during the same period similar, though smaller, strikes had occurred in northern Italy.[26] Schuman and his Minister of the Interior, Jules Moch, considered that at the least the Communists had hoped for—if not actually planned—some sort of insurrection during those months. Its "successful prevention" by the French government was therefore hailed as a major achievement, and Schuman asserted that France had "rendered an incalculable service to the world . . . because this fearful maneuver was supposed to be the point of departure for a vast international agitation capable of placing in danger the security of the democracies or even world peace." John Foster Dulles, passing through Paris on December 5, was of the same opinion. He remarked to the press that "The events in France have greater importance for the future of Europe than the London Conference [on Germany]." [27] As to the question of the origin of the strike tactic and the creation of the National Strike Committee, there can be little doubt that it is correct to place the agitation of November–December 1947 in the context of the Cold War, and more particularly to understand it as one of the tools that Stalin hoped would turn French opinion against the government and the Western Allies in general. On the other hand, while this was the tactic of the Communist-committed elements in the CGT, it certainly does not explain the actions of the non-Communist majority among the striking rank and file, as well as the majority of socialist-committed elements. Here one must recognize the legitimacy of the economic and social demands presented,[28] and the fact that the Communists

[26] See, e.g., Thomas H. Greene, "The Communist Parties of Italy and France: A Study in Comparative Communism," *World Politics* 21, no. 1 (October 1968): 4.

[27] Both cited by Fauvet, *Histoire du Parti* 2:209.

[28] Cf. Lefranc, *Le mouvement syndical*, pp. 41–47, and Aron, *Grand schisme*, chap. 12, for relevant statistics on the disparities of wage and price rises, the effects of the black market, and the lax government financial policy.

were successful in using justified bread-and-butter demands to draw non-communist elements into a strike that the Party was able to render political. In effect, the problem posed by the events of November–December for the members of *Force ouvrière* was, given their conception of syndicalist activity as apolitical, how far they were willing to allow the CGT majority to lead them in violation of both their philosophy of syndicalism and their political sympathies.

The question of the "insurrectional character" of Communist intentions is of course a more complex problem, as it pertains to a matter about which no public evidence exists. This caveat made, if the historical analysis in chapter 5 is correct, it seems reasonable to assume that at no time after 1944 at the latest did the Communists consider an open insurrection capable of success, given the balance of forces in France and the unlikelihood of help from abroad. If one attempts to place oneself in the mood of the period, it is possible to believe that the Third Force governments and British and American foreign-policy makers, given a lack of information combined with the ideological distortions characterizing the first postwar years, might not have recognized the relative weakness of the USSR and the Western European Communist movements, and thus have been quite sincere in their visions of Thorez in the Elysée Palace. Nonetheless, the underlying constraints on the Communist movement in France, not only in terms of its taking power but also in terms of its merely standing pat, became manifest during the period 1948–49. The gradual Allied cognizance of this condition and its general reflection in the media is indicated by a series of articles written by André Géraud which appeared in the weathervane journal *Foreign Affairs* during this period, in particular his article of October 1949, entitled "Insurrection Fades in France." [29]

If not insurrectionary in any immediate sense of the term (although latently so in terms of the "maximum" strategy), what was the Communist goal in the strikes of November–December 1948? To answer this question implies a statement of the minimum program, the immediate and medium-term ends considered realizable by the leadership.

Aside from seeking to impart the strikes with a character of popular protest against the exclusion of the Communist Party from participa-

[29] *Foreign Affairs* 28, no. 1 (October 1949): 30–42. (See also vols. 26, 27.)

tion in the national power context, and aside from the legitimate character of the economic and social demands presented, the minimum
program was centered around the goal of hindering the application of
the Marshall Plan to France, and through that perhaps to prevent the
formation of an Atlantic alliance based on American military and political hegemony in Europe. A second goal was no doubt to produce a
mass movement of sufficient intensity to oblige the reintegration of
the Communists with governmental circles. A common PCF slogan at
this time was the demand for a "government of democratic unity and
national independence" in which "the Communist Party, the largest
party in France, would play its part." [30]

Why did the Communist leadership play the hard line in its relations with the government to the extent that one is tempted to conclude they consciously provoked a schism in the CGT at that point?
Here one is once again in the realm of psychologizing from hindsight,
but nonetheless one possible explanation seems more convincing than
others. For one thing, an eventual split in the CGT was, after May 5,
almost inevitable. Although not expressed in terms of a "vertical mirror effect" most observers had little doubt that, as had already happened twice previously, a split in either the party system or the labor

---

[30] Cf. the similar, though differently phrased, conclusions of the Minister of the Interior, Jules Moch: "We knew that, from afar, a recently created organization [i.e., the
Cominform] had decided to make a total effort on the international level, not with the
goal of bringing substantial advantages to the workers, but with the view of discourag-
ing America from furnishing the economic aid so generously and so usefully proposed
to Western Europe by General Marshall.

"Was this movement fused to a movement of general insurrection? I do not think so.
The documents in our possession show that the tactic was more subtle: to execute the
order from afar by creating disorder in the regions benefiting from American aid did
not necessitate a truly revolutionary action. However, these local translators of the general order must have interpreted it as authorizing them to work with a blank check, a
general rehearsal, even, if the attempt succeeded, to the point of exploiting to the end,
with that suppleness of tactic which is one of the characteristics of their manner. Let us
imagine the resignation of the existing government at the time, following by several
days that of its predecessor. In the discouragement of the crisis which might have
followed, would not occasions have arisen either to demonstrate the impossibility of
governing without the party which had earlier excluded itself from power, [and] therefore to impose its return to the affairs of state . . . or to channel the movement, to that
point peaceful in appearance, toward the goal of conquest of the State?" (From a speech
to the Anglo-American Press Club, February 18, 1948, cited in Lefranc, *Le mouvement
syndical*, p. 64.)

movement on the Left would necessarily result in a sympathetic cleavage all the way up and down the points of attachment between Communists and socialists throughout society. Furthermore, because the Communists had captured the CGT and were now in the majority, a split could be better absorbed by them than by the socialists. With regard to the strikes of May, Raymond Aron has written:

> From the Liberation on, the Communist Party followed a tactic that was at once subtle and dangerous, consisting of posing as a government party, while still maintaining a monopoly of revolutionary hope and action. . . . It had by no means renounced this unstable compromise between its tradition and the necessity of the moment in the spring of 1947; but the strike [of May], whether spontaneous or instigated by anticommunist syndicates, revealed to it the urgency of a peril which it will never be tempted to underestimate: the risk of being overtaken on the left.[31]

Considering the possible long-term effects of the Party's recent activity on its credibility among the rank and file, Frachon and the other Communist CGT leaders in control of the National Strike Committee appeared to be seeking more to protect the Communist left flank than to hold firm for the total demands of the strike. The government offer of December 8 was one of significant concessions and the rank and file was ready to go back to work. Thus, by playing upon the hard line all throughout the November–December strikes and by agreeing to issue a back-to-work order only after the rank and file had abandoned a more aggressive tactic, the Communists—gambling that they could successfully tie together the two themes of national independence (i.e., refusal of the "Marshallization" and "American domination" of France) and of fundamental opposition (i.e., refusal to compromise with "bourgeois" power except under duress)—sought to head off being turned on the left in the labor movement by the effervescent and ever-changing series of Trotskyite, anarchist, and "left socialist" groups that sprouted and withered. In this way, they hoped to ramify the basic Cominform tactic, which on the whole was geared to benefit immediately only the Soviet bloc. By refocusing attention toward their characteristics alien to the established order, they were, as usual, searching tactically to make the best of an unfavorable situation.

[31] Aron, *Le grand schisme,* p. 190.

A Paradigm of the Communist Movement in France 1948–62

Before going on to examine closely several specific aspects of the exclusion and isolation of the Communists in France during the period 1947–62, it will be useful first to sketch briefly and with very broad strokes a large canvas. The succeeding cameos will then highlight the most important details.

In addition to attack from the "outside," one of the most debilitating problems of the early 1950s was the emergence of an open conflict within the highest leadership ranks, which provoked a crisis that shook the internal stability of the entire party apparatus from top to bottom.

On October 10, 1950, Maurice Thorez was stricken by a cerebral hemorrhage, and a few days later a Soviet aircraft arrived in Paris to remove him to the USSR for a period of recovery that would last two and one-half years. Thorez did not return to France until April 10, 1953, slightly more than a month after the death of Stalin. Unlike the circumstances during his wartime absence, when Jacques Duclos and Benoît Frachon were able to provide unambiguous leadership insofar as such was possible during the Resistance, during Thorez's second absence his heir apparent, Auguste Lecoeur, had rather quickly involved himself in a series of controversial internal Party maneuvers, which resulted in his denunciation in January 1952 and his ultimate exclusion from the leadership in March 1954.[32]

In December 1952, a second internal crisis, involving André Marty and Charles Tillon, again shook the cohesion of the Communist lead-

---

[32] Essentially, Lecoeur's "crime" had consisted of seeking to set up a system of "cell political instructors" within the Party organization, in order to "raise the ideological competence" of the militants and the rank and file. Possibly, this was an attempt by Lecoeur to install himself inextricably in place of Thorez by the creation of a corps of key officials, the proposed "cell instructors," loyal to himself. See, on "l'affaire Lecoeur," his own book, *L'autocritique attendue* and the article by Jean Touchard, "De l'affaire Lecoeur à l'affaire Hervé," *Revue française de science politique* 6, no. 2 (April–June 1956): 389–98. Fauvet, *Histoire du Parti* (2:264) reports that Thorez remarked "Lecoeur wanted to bury me even before I was dead!"

ership. In appearance much more banal than the "affaire Lecoeur," [33]
it nonetheless furthered a certain sense of confusion and lack of cohesion throughout the Party structure, all the more as the two men were heroes of past glories—Marty for his supposed role in fomenting a mutiny on a French ship sent to intervene in the Russian civil war, and Tillon for his leadership in the FTP during the Resistance.

Only with the return of Maurice Thorez, who alone had the necessary Soviet support and personal authority to be able to arbitrate between factions and personalities, did the leadership begin to close ranks once again. Even so, the somewhat equivocal signals arising from the Soviet Party during the collective-leadership between the death of Stalin and the emergence of Khrushchev meant that at least until 1956 the initiatives of the French Communists toward finding a solution to their isolation and exclusion were weak and unconvincing.[34] For example, the Communists voted for the investiture of the Mendès-France government in June 1954, and voted with his majority on many occasions, the most important of which were the Indochina settlement (July 23, 1954), the grant of internal autonomy to Tunisia and Morocco (August 10, 1954), and the defeat of the European Defense Community (August 30, 1954). They also voted for the Guy Mollet investiture (January 31, 1956) and for many of the important bills during his ministry, such as a third week of paid vacation (February 28, 1956), special powers in Algeria (March 12, 1956), and the establishment of an Old Age Pension Fund (May 5, 1956). Finally, toward the final crisis of the Republic, the Communists abstained to permit the investiture of Pierre Pflimlin in May 1958. Moreover, all

[33] Essentially it was an affair of "personalities" rather than a battle for power per se. Significantly in the case of both Marty and Tillon a prime cause of their disgrace was open disagreement with Jeanette Vermeersch-Thorez, wife of the Secretary-General. For Marty's version of the affair, see *L'affaire Marty* (Paris, 1955). For Tillon's version see *Un procès de Moscou à Paris* (Paris, 1971). For a quick summary of the major events, see Fauvet, *Histoire du Parti*, 2:246–57. An old hypothesis, possibly true (and taken up again by Tillon and Annie Kriegel, *Les grands procès dans les systèmes communistes* [Paris: Gallimard, 1972], pp. 24–26) is that the Marty-Tillon affairs were a spinoff of the show trials of Slansky, London, and others in Czechoslovakia.

[34] In fact, retention of the posture of "defensive attack" established in the fall and winter of 1947 continued much beyond 1956. This is what Roy Macridis termed the "immobility" of the PCF.

during the Fourth Republic years the Communist leaders had repeated a desire to support or even to participate in a "progressive"
government.[35] Nonetheless, the Communist failure to make credible
these gestures of moderation is indicated by the fact that in his empirical study of parliament during these years, Duncan MacRae Jr. classes
the PCF deputies as "Permanent Opposition Vote" rather than "Potential Pro-Cabinet Vote" even when they actually voted for or abstained in three investitures and voted several important bills.[36] The
justification for MacRae's categorization of the Communists is in a
purely empirical sense obviously somewhat problematic. As a statement of assumptions, however, such a categorization is revealing for
its indication that although the Communists were in fact sometimes
"Potential Pro-Cabinet" supporters, the non-Communists considered
the Communists to be "Permanent Opposition"—or rather made them
so simply by refusing to form a government in which the Communists
would participate.[37] This was, for example, the case of Mendès-
France, who refused to count Communist votes in ascertaining
whether he had achieved an investiture in June 1954.[38]

In any case, the Communist abstention on the Pflimlin investiture,
among a host of other conciliatory actions in 1957–58 (e.g., a less than

---

[35] E.g., a declaration of January, 1956: "The balance of forces in the newly elected
Assembly indicates that conditions of change exist, but that today, as before, no majority or program of the Left is possible without the Communists. . . . The French Communist Party reaffirms that it is ready to come to an agreement with the Socialist Party
in order to promote a new program. . . . It is equally ready to come to an agreement
with other Left groups oriented in the same direction." (In *Histoire du . . . [Manuel]*, p.
593.) Even during the most difficult periods of the Cold War such proposals by the
Communists were constant.

[36] *Parliament, Parties and Society in France, 1946–58*, table p. 60. The March 1956 vote
in favor of special powers in Algeria was particularly controversial. The PCF leaders
hoped to push Mollet to honor his promise of peace and at the same time to further
their own proposal for a Left alliance.

[37] It might have been useful had MacRae made a distinction such as that between
fundamental and global opposition suggested in chapter 1 of this book. The term "permanent" opposition seems too equivocal. For example, on the Mollet bill to establish a
series of taxes to support a program of old-age pensions, the "Communist votes were
essential for the cabinet's victory on this roll call" (*ibid.*, p. 160).

[38] Counting the Communist votes, Mendès-France had a majority of 109 votes; without the Communists his margin over the necessary absolute majority of 314 was less
than 10. In addition to his own aversion to a coalition including the PCF, Mendès-
France was attempting to refute charges of fellow-traveling and neutralism.

virulent criticism of the French policy in Algeria), demonstrated that by then the PCF leadership had become willing to embrace even the defects of the Fourth Republic in order to avoid a "reactionary" solution—that is, a de Gaulle solution—to the crisis in which were opposed French liberal democratic principles and the reality of colonialism. From 1956 onward, the PCF tended to abandon its militant, hard-line Cold War rhetoric in favor of conciliatory propaganda, as in 1936–39, in order to save the coalition. Finally, in May 1958, the Communists, along with Mendès-France, Mitterrand, and a few others, wanted to appear the most resolute defenders of the Republic. Of course this defense of "bourgeois" democracy was partial, expedient, and ambiguous; yet in 1958 it was possible to consider the Communists among the most loyal of citizens when almost everyone else was defecting from the Republic.

In effect, de Gaulle, like the Communists, offered Frenchmen a dual conception of legitimacy, the halves of which might at some times coexist but which at others—as in 1958—might not. The first doctrine of legitimacy was what de Gaulle called "republican legitimacy," meaning essentially what Max Weber called the rational-legal legitimacy of a constitutional republic. To this, de Gaulle added a conception of "French" or "historic" legitimacy. This higher legitimacy was invoked when strict adherence to the constitution placed the "destiny" of France in danger. Considering himself the incarnation of this historic legitimacy, General de Gaulle believed himself justified in combating the regime if necessary to preserve the nation. It is part of the tragedy of the *Libération manquée* in postwar France that the Communist embrace of republican legitimacy could occur only when the Gaullists had abandoned the latter to pursue their own myths of the destiny of France.

However this may be, in May 1958, as in August 1939, the Communists "lost" the moment. The continued failure of the PCF to escape its exclusion and isolation in 1958 may be seen as a function primarily of the hostile context, which left almost no room for either radical or collaborative tactics. Even the SFIO leaders, in effect obliged to choose between, on the one hand, *Algérie française* and metropolitan civil war, and on the other hand, de Gaulle and the Communists, hesitated not a moment in rejecting the PCF offer to form a "government of republican defense." And, as always, the relation of the PCF and SFIO leaderships was crucial, for successful alliance tactics depended on the SFIO as the connecting link between French Communism and the rest of French society.

Having displaced Daniel Mayer as Secretary-General in 1945–46 to become leader of the Left-wing group in the SFIO (the faction favorable to alliance with the PCF), Guy Mollet after 1947 accepted the Cold War schism and developed into an adamant anti-Communist: It was Mollet who took up Blum's critique of the *parti nationaliste étranger* by stating that French Communist policy "looked neither Right nor Left, but to the East." The socialists under Mollet remained committed to the Center-oriented coalition formula after 1947, even during their largely self-imposed exile from government in the second legislature (1951–56). The return of a theoretical Popular Front governmental majority in the general elections of January 2, 1956, combined with three years of post-Stalinist rule in the USSR, gave the PCF leaders some hope that the SFIO might be tempted to move Left once again.[39] Therefore, during the period 1956–58 the Communists mounted several initiatives in the direction of the Socialists, particularly as the Republican Front of Mollet and the Radicals under Mendès-France broke open after Mendès was almost immediately isolated within his cabinet. Nonetheless, the immobility of the PCF leadership—in this case definable as the failure to present concessions or to invent effective camouflage tactics—foredoomed the alliance strategy of the last two years of the Fourth Republic.[40]

---

[39] In the elections of January 2, the PCF won 25 percent of the Assembly seats and obtained more votes than ever before [147 seats and 5,514,000 of 21,300,000 valid ballots].

[40] One may briefly cite the most significant of these attempts to convince the socialists of "the necessity of a government in the image of January 2." At the 14th PCF Congress (July 1956), a public message to the SFIO was issued, proclaiming that "It is an appeal for the unity of the Communist Party and the Socialist Party which [is necessary to] guide France towards socialism." (PCF-14, p. 13. See pp. 323–29 for the full text.) On October 6, 23, and 29, 1957, Thorez and Duclos wrote to Guy Mollet proposing a PCF-SFIO solution to the ministerial caused by the fall of the Bourgès-Maunoury cabinet on September 30. The PCF proposed that the Radicals, Progressives, UDSR-RDA, and RGR groups might also be part of such an alliance. The offer was renewed and made public in a speech by Thorez at the Cirque d'Hiver on October 24. In February 1958, as the final crisis of the Fourth Republic loomed

In its relations with the rest of the political system, then, the French Communist Party in the Fourth Republic remained locked into old tactical approaches, tied to the old hierarchy of symbols, and was singularly unimaginative in either reinvigorating the old ways or developing some turnabout to escape its isolation. In a word, the Party remained Stalinist. Whereas the Italian Communist Party chose to act almost immediately upon the implications of Khrushchev's denunciation of Stalin at the 20th CPSU Congress (February 1956), the French Party significantly at first even refused to accept the authenticity of the Khrushchev speech. The background to the French and Italian divergence in accepting the theory and practice of de-Stalinization have been examined numerous times, and need be no more than cited here.[41] First, the more or less continuous existence of the PCF had permitted the Comintern leadership to make its bolshevization— and the character of alliance with the CPSU implied therein—more thoroughgoing than that of the Italian Party, which was dispersed and underground from 1926 through 1942. Thus, the sheer weight of old ways and old models on the organization acted as a powerful gag on whatever innovative forces might have existed in 1956. Secondly, the PCF leaders, precisely because of their success in bolshevization and their consequent long and deep contact with the Soviet model, had become utterly impregnated with Stalinist doctrine and practice, a degree of mental conditioning so profound that for it to have been quickly and easily abandoned was simply impossible. Most important of all in this regard was Maurice Thorez himself, the *Fils du peuple.* Surrounded by a cult of personality perhaps unequaled among all the leaders of nonruling communist parties, the very life of Thorez was inextricably bound to the Stalinist past. (See chapter 9 for a more complete discussion.) To reject Stalinism openly would have meant

---

closer, Thorez wrote to Mollet, Daladier, Queuille, Houphouet-Boigny, Senghor, Mitterrand, Faure and others, asserting that it was necessary "to check the seditious enterprises together." On April 12, 1958, Thorez wrote Mollet again, proposing "unity in the face of the fascist menace." On May 28, 1958, Jacques Duclos wrote to all the left and left-center parties proposing the formation of a "government of republican defense" against the Gaullist coup. When the moment of decision arrived in May 1958, Mollet had not replied to any of the PCF initiatives. In June, he held a portfolio in the new provisional government of General de Gaulle.

[41] Both parties supported the Soviet invasion of Hungary, however.

for Thorez a public rejection of his own past. It is significant in this regard that the French Communists were the most vitriolic critics of the Titoist defection in 1948, for this was a symbolic measure of proof that the "errors" of May–September 1947 had not been a manifestation of lack of ardor toward the CPSU and Stalin.[42]

The failure of the Thorez leadership group to find a way out of the predicament of the 1950s was accompanied by an unusually equivocal pattern of change in Communist membership and electors. While the memberships of both the PCF and CGT were deeply cut down, their ability to command mass electoral support—after a drop from the circumstantially inflated levels of 1945–47—tended to stabilize and even to rise in the late 1950s and early 1960s (see chapters 9 and 10). In terms of Party membership itself, the decline was quite steep. Although membership figures are still camouflaged by the leadership, and despite the ubiquitous difficulties involved in calculating the membership of any political party, a reasonably accurate estimate is possible.[43] From a high of approximately 800,000 actual members in 1946, the figure by 1955 was somewhere around 250,000 or perhaps even slightly lower. This decline may be imputed to several factors: the decline of the Communist mystique from the Resistance years, France's economic development, the Party's lack of prospects for gaining power, the influence of the Cold War, and perhaps even rank and file disillusionment with Communist eschatology. However, when one notes that membership figures for the Italian Communist Party show a striking degree of stability,[44] while figures for the SFIO—the other would-be mass party in France during this period—show a decline similar to, or perhaps even greater than, that of the PCF, such

[42] It is no doubt also true that the PCF was motivated by a simple desire for revenge against the Yugoslavs, who had been the most extreme critics of the French Party line at the first Cominform meeting.

[43] On the problems involved in calculating the PCF membership, see Kriegel, *Les communistes français*, chapter 1, and esp. note 8, p. 262, for a comment on the figures given in Lecoeur, *L'autocritique attendue*, and the general relation between the figures published by the Party (membership cards sent out to the federations) and real membership (cards placed). The figures quoted here are those of Kriegel, p. 13.

[44] Thomas Greene's figures ("*The Communist Parties*" p. 36) are the following for the PCI: 1946, 2,150,000; 1949, 2,300,000; 1951, 2,112,000; 1957, 2,035,000.

hypotheses seem less likely.[45] Thus, while in some sense probably the result of a combination of factors such as the above, the decimation of PCF membership ranks appears correlated to a general decline in party membership in France, no doubt a reflection of the transition from the hope and optimism of the Liberation period to the widespread frustration and disgust with politics in general as the Fourth Republic increasingly came to resemble the Third Republic. Moreover, the PCF membership after 1956 stabilized at a point between 250,000 and 300,000, which was the approximate size of the Party during the Popular Front. One might well suspect, therefore, that there may be some sort of saturation point fixed by a combination of socioeconomic, historical, and psychosocial factors, past which the "hard core" of the Communist movement cannot expand without the intervention of some large-scale structural changes in society or some extraordinary event. Annie Kriegel has pointed out that in recent years the PCF has had to recruit approximately 30,000 new members per year merely to balance the normal turnover in Party ranks.[46] Thus, the relative stability of Party effectives since 1956 indicates that even events such as the crises of 1958 and 1968 have not worked to change the level of new Communist memberships to any great extent. Perhaps then, in Roy Macridis's term, the size of the PCF has become "encrusted" within a matrix of conditions that, all other things being equal, will constrain it from exceptional growth or decline. It would be unjustified to extrapolate previous and present stability very far, however, for important variables are not likely to remain constant very long. On the one hand, were the PCF to come to power in a coalition of the Left, its membership might inflate suddenly once again; on the other hand, if the PCF is unable to return to government within the near- or medium-term future, it is possible that frustration may diminish the saturation point of Party strength (see chapters 7, 8, 12).

The permanence of the French Communist electorate, despite the

---

[45] Christine Hurtig, *De la SFIO au Nouveau parti socialiste* (Paris: A. Colin, 1971), gives the following figures: 1946, 355,000; 1948, 223,000; 1949, 158,000; 1951, 127,000; 1960, 100,000; 1968, 81,000.

[46] Kriegel, *Communistes français*, pp. 16–17.

Cold War situation and the other factors that seem to explain the decline in Party effectiveness, has been one of the most constantly perplexing and marked phenomena of postwar French history. Throughout the Fourth Republic the PCF, which consistently won the most votes, could claim to be France's largest party. After having won 28.6 percent of the total vote in the election of 1946, it won 25.6 percent in 1951, and 25.7 percent in 1956. After dropping to 18.9 percent of the vote in the wake of General de Gaulle's return to power in 1958, in 1962 the Party rebounded partially to win 21.7 percent of the vote, and although no longer the largest party, its electoral strength continued to perplex observers for whom important indicators seemed to point to a more drastic communist decline. (In 1967 the PCF won 22.5 percent of the vote, in 1968 it won 20 percent and in 1973 it won 21.3 percent. See also chapter 10.)

The consistency of the Communist vote in general elections was not matched by a similar trend in the number of PCF deputies, yet the disparities from one legislature to another, despite their size, are accounted for rather easily. It was pointed out above that one of the reasons for the enactment of a new electoral law for the municipal elections of 1947 had been to limit Communist success. Likewise, the famous electoral law of 1951, permitting a complicated system of alliances called *apparentements*, owed its origin to the struggle for survival of the Third Force against the Communist and Gaullist extremes.[47]

In 1946, with 28.6 percent of the vote, the Communists had won 27 percent of the seats (169 of 621) in the first legislature of the Fourth Republic. In 1951, with 25.6 percent of the vote, the PCF won only 16 percent of the Assembly seats (99 of 627). In 1956, with a tremendous organizational effort, the Communists concentrated their votes and obtained more than ever before. The PCF also benefited from a strong leftward swing toward the "Republican Front," which consisted of the SFIO and the Radical Socialists under Mollet and Mendès-France, as well as a disaggregation of the Right caused by the

---

[47] Used in 1951 and 1956, it was a success only in 1951. For a brief explanation see Philip M. Williams, *Crisis and Compromise*, pp. 534–35. For a more detailed analysis see Peter Campbell, *French Electoral Systems and Elections 1789–1957* and Cotteret, J.-M., C. Emeri, and P. Lalumière, *Lois électorales et inégalités de représentation en France 1936–1960.*

Poujadist surge. Thus, in the 1956 elections the Communists were able to obtain 24 percent of the seats (144 of 596) with 25.7 percent of the vote.[48] In 1958, the incoming Gaullists revised the electoral law again. The new system was much like the one used during the Third Republic—single-member constituencies and two ballots. This, as was intended, damaged the PCF particularly.[49] Having won 18.9 percent of the vote, the Communists got only 2 percent of the seats in the first legislature of the Fifth Republic (10 of 465).

Thus, the determination of the non-Communist forces to exclude and isolate the Communists during this period was made operational in part through manipulation of the rules of the game. It has often been argued that these changes in the electoral law may have been necessary both to save the Fourth Republic from disaster before its collapse in 1958 (i.e., without the electoral law of 1951 an "antisystem" majority of Communists on the Left and Gaullists on the Right would have existed in the Assembly; what the results of this would have been, however, is difficult to say) and to launch the Fifth Republic with a solid parliamentary majority. (On the first ballot in 1958, the PCF received 3,870,000 votes, the UNR and allies 3,589,000 votes. Nonetheless, because second-ballot alliances were made by the latter—and denied the former—the Gaullists had 189 seats in the first legislature, the PCF had ten.) At the same time, one would be less than fair if one did not point out the degree to which the manipulation of electoral laws falsified the principle of representation of the electorate.[50]

[48] The 1951 law gave the government majority 97 more seats than would have been won under the 1946 law. (Williams, *Crisis and Compromise*, p. 534). The Gaullists, because of their greater capacity to make alliances (the parties and groups of the Right were not so anti-RPF as the SFIO was anti-PCF) were less hurt in 1951: with 22 percent of the vote they won 18% of the seats (117 of 627). By 1956, the RPF was no longer in existence. On the 1956 elections see François Goguel, "Les élections françaises du 2 janvier 1956," *Revue française de science politique* 6, no. 1 (Jan.–Mar. 1956): 5–17 and MacCrae, *Parliament, Parties*, ch. 8, 9.

[49] It was perhaps for this reason that Guy Mollet encouraged or at least tolerated passively the return to the *scrutin d'arrondissement* system, which damaged the SFIO as well as the PCF (See André Philip, *Les socialistes*, pp. 167–68). The SFIO won about 3 million votes in both 1956 and 1958, but had 99 seats in the former year and only 47 in the latter.

[50] Cf. the bizarre judgment of the 1951 law made by the vigorously antiCommunist English historian, Dorothy Pickles: "This [electoral] system may have had the merit of

With regard to representation in the upper chamber, during the Fourth Republic called the Council of the Republic, the effort to exclude and isolate the communists was overwhelmingly successful, as against the merely partial success in the Assembly.

Before the war, the PCF had been able to elect only two senators to the upper house. In the first postwar elections, December 8, 1946, the convergence of a congenial electoral law and the Liberation élan allowed the Communists to win 84 of 315 available seats (27 percent), whereas the SFIO had 62, the MRP 72, the Radicals 44, and various conservatives 44 altogether. For the election of November 7, 1948, the 1946 law—used only that year—was rewritten.[51] Primarily to weaken the Communists, the 1948 revision voted by the Third Force coalition drastically diluted the proportional representation aspect of elections to the Council.[52]

The result was that from 84 seats in 1946, the PCF fell to 19 seats in 1948. In the nine renewals since that time—all run on the basis of the 1948 law—the Communists have never held more than 18 seats (6

giving some satisfacion to the supporters of both the majority and the proportional principles. Its chief demerit was its extreme complexity. It was also on some points obscure and self-defeating." *French Politics*, pp. 137–38.

[51] It had been agreed among the Tripartite partners in 1946 that after two years the entire Council of the Republic would be reelected, and that the electoral law would also be reconsidered.

[52] Under the 1946 law, the upper chamber had turned out to be almost a replica of the Assembly. The 1948 law reverted to a system much like that used to elect the Senate during the Third Republic, in which conservative Radicals held the dominant force. Essentially, since 1948 delegates to the upper chamber have been chosen on a departmental basis by an electoral college made up predominantly of local councillors. "The distribution of seats among departments strengthens the countryside against the towns; and within each electoral college, the large towns are seriously under-represented. . . . Moreover, since most [delegates] need a clear majority of votes cast for election on the first ballot, and an ordinary majority on the second, the minority of urban electors can rarely win a seat. But proportional representation is used in the seven most populous departments. . . . This helps the rural minorities in urban areas—but also ensures that the Communists . . . win seats in their strongholds and so obtain some, although inadequate, representation in the upper house." (Philip Williams, *The French Parliament*, p. 30. See also the useful, though overly long, study by Jean-Pierre Marichy, *La deuxième chambre dans la vie politique française depuis 1875* (Paris: Librairie générale de droit et de jurisprudence, 1969), iv + 787 pp. For an account of the controversy surrounding the second chamber in the Fifth Republic, renamed Senate, see Jacques Georgel, *Le sénat dans l'adversité, 1962–66* (Paris: Editions Cujas, 1968) 221 pp.

percent of the total) at any one time.[53] The impotence of the upper chamber—above all during the Fourth Republic, slightly less during the Fifth—has relegated the underrepresentation of the Communists in that body to a manipulation of minor political importance. This exclusion nevertheless merits attention as part of the containment of Communist attempts to rebuild a united front.

A pattern similar to that in the upper chamber was found in the general councils, which represent the *canton* (the second-lowest unit of local government, directly above the *commune*) and which are constructed on a departmental basis. Because of the historical centralization of local power in the hands of the prefect, and through him in the hands of the national government itself, the general councils have traditionally held little power, being confined to a largely symbolic "advisory" role despite the fact that the departmental budgets are debated in those bodies.

Normally one-half the membership is elected every three years, but in the elections of September 1945, as part of the attempt to establish a clean slate during the Liberation, the entire membership stood for reelection. The favorable Communist image at this time, as in other elections, resulted in a relatively large Communist success; whereas in 1937 the PCF had elected only 74 general councillors out of a to-

[53] Following is the Communist strength in the Upper Chamber 1946–71.

	PCF Seats	Total Seats	Percent of Total Seats
1946	84	315	27
1948	19	320	6
1952	16	320	5
1955	14	319	4
1958	16	319	5
1959	14	307	5
1962	14	273	5
1965	14	274	5
1968	18	283	6
1971	18	283	6

Sources:
1946–59, Philip Williams, *Crisis and Compromise*, p. 532.
1962, *L'année politique*, 1962, p. 103.
1965, Philip Williams, *The French Parliament*, p. 29.
1968, Encyclopédies périodiques, *Le Sénat*, p. 283.
1971, *Le Monde*, September 29, 1971, p. 1.

tal close to 3,000 (approximately 2.5 percent), in 1945 the Party elected 320 (approximately 7 percent of the total of 4,500.[54] In 1949, denied the possibility of alliances, and despite winning an even larger percentage of the total vote (24 percent) than in 1945 (22 percent), the Communists dropped to about 2 percent of the total seats. By 1958 the PCF was down from 320 seats in 1945 to 90 seats, again between 2 and 3 percent of the total.[55] Only in the elections of 1964, in which they benefited from the change in the political climate over the preceding two years and were thus able to form "silent" coalitions with socialists and Radicals on the basis of anti-Gaullism, did the Communists make headway in the cantonal elections. From their total of 90 seats in 1958, they increased their membership to 139 in 1964.[56] However, even this total represented less than 5 percent of the available seats.

In order to limit Communist representation, it was unnecessary to change the electoral law for the cantonal consultations, as the majority system with two ballots had been used even in 1945. The author of the only detailed study has commented: "Disadvantaged by the mode of election . . . the Communist candidates, present in every canton, rarely succeeded in gaining entrance to the prefecture." [57] A further complication for them was that "The limited number of urban cantons, and the frequent dismemberment of urban communes into many

[54] The Communists had the most success, as was expected, in "the industrial and urban regions (the Paris region, the Nord and Pas-de-Calais confines, the urban cantons of Le Havre, Rouen and Marseilles, the poor and underdeveloped regions such as the interior parts of Brittany and some departments in the center, such as the Nièvre, Allier and Cher)," but also "bit into certain Radical strongholds in the Southwest compromised by the Occupation (the Charente, Dordogne, Lot-et-Garonne) and had a further large success in the Rhône-Alpes region and the cities of the Midi (seven Communist councillors out of twelve cantons in Marseilles; two out of four in Nice; three out of three cantons in Nîmes)." (Marie-Hélène Marchand, *Les conseillers généraux depuis 1945*, p. 79.)

[55] The Communists had been totally voided in 47 departments, and almost entirely eliminated in the Southwest, Franche-Comté, Bourgogne, the Rhône-Alpes and had also given back the Radical and Moderate positions it had won in 1945. Still, the PCF "bastions" held rather firmly, e.g., in the Paris region and the Northeast, in the Massif Central, interior Brittany, and in the "red countryside" areas of Haute-Vienne, Creuse, and Allier as well as in the urban cantons of Le Havre, Rouen, and Marseilles. (*Ibid.*, p. 82.)

[56] *Ibid.*, p. 85.   [57] *Ibid.*, p. 82.

cantons, each adjoining a small number of suburban or rural communes judged more moderate, limited . . . the chances of the Communist Party to have a large number of representatives." [58] The result of this was that the disparity between the percentage of Communist votes and seats was startling, particularly when compared with the reverse disparity as one moved rightward along the political spectrum. Table 3 gives such statistics for the cantonal elections of 1945, 1949, and 1958, illustrating that only for the SFIO was the proportion rather balanced, while the extreme Left was extraordinarily underrepresented more or less to the extent the Center and Right was overrepresented:

Table 3: Votes and Seats by Percentage in Cantonal Elections 1945, 1949 and 1958

	1945		1949		1958	
	Votes	*Seats*	*Votes*	*Seats*	*Votes*	*Seats*
PCF	23%	7%	24%	2%	22%	3%
SFIO	24%	25%	17%	15%	18%	16%
Radicals	15%	33%	14%	20%	16%	27%
MRP	14%	8%	9%	6%	11%	9%
Moderates-Conservatives	4%	13%	12%	30%	23%	35%

Source: Marie-Hélène Marchand, *Les conseillers généraux en France depuis 1945*, pp. 113–14, adapted. RPF not included for 1949.

The extraordinary underrepresentation of the Communists is mitigated somewhat by the fact that the size of the Communist vote is partially due to the ubiquitous presence of PCF candidates. No other party was prepared to run or was capable of running so many. "The candidate is often presented only to count the Party's votes in a canton where he has no chance of being elected." [59] This explanation also serves to account for the similarity of the cantonal percentage to the Communist percentage in national legislative elections. Nonetheless, in the general councils, as elsewhere, the period 1947–62 was one of maximum exclusion and isolation of the Communists by non-Com-

[58] *Ibid.*, p. 115.   [59] *Ibid.*

munist political forces, based on the electoral law mechanism and the refusal of any group to ally with them.[60]

The results for municipal elections—much more complicated than those for legislative, senatorial, or cantonal elections and therefore extremely difficult to interpret (a problem deepened by the lack of standardized and unimpeachable figures over time)—would appear to indicate a similar trend. Having won 36,517 seats (of approximately 435,000) in the 38,000 municipalities in 1945, the results for the next three municipal elections were: 30,503 (1947), 24,206 (1953), 19,872 (1959).[61] While part of these losses may be traced to the exclusion and isolation of the Communists, no doubt the *continual* decline—as opposed to the sudden drop of 1945–47 and then a plateau, as with Senate and cantonal statistics—is due also to two other reasons: a) to the large decline in party membership, making it more difficult to present candidates numbering in the tens of thousands; and b) to changes in the electoral laws governing municipalities.[62] In contrast to the general decline, however, once again the Communist bastions have held out against the trend, as evidenced by the results in the Paris area. After a serious drop from the 1945 results, the Communist Party in the three municipal elections between 1947 and 1959 succeeded in improving its position slightly on the Paris municipal council despite the Cold War: from 25 of 90 seats in 1947, the total rose to 28 in 1953 and 29 in 1959. In the General Council of the Seine (the 90 Paris municipal

[60] Although the electoral law was not (and did not have to be) changed to limit Communist general councilors, the cantonal election of 1949 had been put off from its scheduled date of October 1948 by the Third Force coalition out of political motives—essentially a desire to wait for a more propitious moment to confront the RPF and the PCF.

[61] Source: 1945 and 1947, *L'année politique* for 1947, p. 364; the figure for 1953 is from *L'année politique* for 1959, p. 33; for 1959 the citation is from *L'année politique* for 1965, p. 25. Normally, that volume uses the figures announced by the Ministry of the Interior.

[62] For example, proportional representation has been used in large municipalities, defined as such by setting an arbitrary population limit. By raising the limit, more municipalities can be elected on the basis of other electoral laws, as PR is favorable to the Communists, especially in large urban areas. Thus, the bottom limit for PR was 4,000 population in 1945 and 1947; it was raised to 9,000 in 1953 and in 1959 separate laws were constructed for populations beginning at both 9,000 and 30,000. The Gaullist majority has completely abolished PR for municipal elections in the Fifth Republic, and in addition has prohibited second-ballot alliances in cities over 30,000. The requirement of a first-ballot common list often works to the disadvantage of the Communists.

councilors plus 60 councilors elected from the Paris suburbs) the PCF total increased from 51 seats (of 150) in 1947, to 55 in 1953, and 59 in 1959.[63]

This brief review of the position of the French Communists in the parliament and in the two elected levels of local government indicates that during the period 1947–62 the division of the polity along Communist–non-Communist lines was fundamental at all levels of electoral politics. At the same time, one may say that this exclusion and isolation of the Communists, which tended to define the boundaries of the Communist–non-Communist cleavage in French society as clearly as during the class-against-class period (1928–34), in the process also "solidified" the Communist movement in its outlines, which had become blurred first during the Popular Front and then again during the war and reconstruction periods. (Some important implications in this regard are drawn and analyzed in chapter 9.) The Popular Front, Resistance, Liberation, and Tripartite epochs had to an extent seen a reintegration of the Communist movement with French society, a partial and illusory reconciliation of the conflict between Communists and non-Communists. The years 1947–62, on the other hand, saw the renewal and reinforcement of the Communist–non-Communist split extending vertically all the way up and down the primary and secondary organizations of political and social life.

The position of the CGT and its relations with the other syndicates (primarily the socialist-oriented CGT-FO and the Christian Democratic CFTC) paralleled the experience of the Communist Party itself during the period 1947–62. The membership suffered deep losses, whereas the "electoral" appeal of the CGT—as measured by elections to administrative organisms of certain social welfare institutions—remained remarkably stable. In this, the CGT was once again a reliable guidepost as a "mirror" of the PCF and of the entire relationship between Communists and non-Communists in France.

Although precise global figures are impossible to obtain, expert investigation has established beyond much doubt that the CGT in only the five years between 1947 and 1952 lost a *majority* of its mem-

[63] Sources: Results compiled and cross-checked from the following: *L'Humanité* of April 29, 1953, p. 4; *Ibid.*, May 19, 1953, p. 1; *Ibid.*, March 17, 1959, p. 1; *L'année politique*, 1947, p. 363; *Le Monde*, March 23, 1965, p. 2.

bership.[64] A further but more gradual decline continued throughout the late 1950s, and by the early 1960s most observers agreed that the membership of the CGT was between 1.5 and 2 million members. In terms of political influence, the position of the CGT—and French syndicalism in general—was considerably weakened during the Fourth Republic, particularly after 1951. On the one hand the 1947 split in the CGT had weakened the claims of both resulting syndicates, while on the other hand a general fatigue and frustration with almost warlike work relationships had produced a certain "apathy among workers, which made even Communists reluctant to strike." [65] Outside of an exceptional period during 1953, the extent of this calm is revealed in Table 4.

Table 4: Strike Days in France 1946–62 (in millions)

Year	Number	Year	Number	Year	Number
1946	374	1952	1,751	1958	1,137
1947	23,371	1953	9,722	1959	1,938
1948	11,918	1954	1,140	1960	1,063
1949	7,292	1955	3,078	1961	2,601
1950	11,710	1956	1,422	1962	1,901
1951	3,294	1957	4,121		

Source: Quid? 1970 edition, p. 1233. Figures are of course only approximately accurate.

The exception of 1953 began as a vast movement of spontaneous strikes in the public sector affecting several hundred thousand workers and launched for professional reasons. The original cause was to protest a series of decrees by the Laniel government jeopardizing certain workers' guarantees in state and nationalized enterprises (one rumor had it that Laniel planned to set back the retirement age by seven years) but the movement ended by making much larger demands, such as a general salary increase, an end to the Indochina war, and so on. The Communist leaders in the CGT, caught by surprise, could do no more than play an *attentiste* role, as the strikes were led by FO and the CFTC. The CGT rallied to the Government-FO-CFTC negotiated agreement. The leadership crises in both the French and Soviet parties were no doubt in large measure the cause of CGT wavering. "Thus the French Communist Party resigned itself to the inglorious miscarriage of the most powerful strike wave France had known since 1947–48." Fejtö, *The French Communist Party and the Crisis of International Communism*, p. 35.

[64] Georges Lefranc, one of the most reliable authorities on French syndicalism, gives the figures for these two years as 5,480,257 and 2,505,357 (*Le mouvement syndical*, p. 79).

[65] Val Lorwin, *The French Labor Movement*, p. 142.

While both the membership and influence of the CGT were thus considerably reduced during the 1950s, like the PCF, the Communist-dominated syndicalist confederation appeared to lose little of its electoral support, as revealed in the results of two of the most important types of elections for which the candidates are union-sponsored: those for the administrative organs of Social Security and Family Assistance organizations. For the four elections carried out during the period 1947–62 the results were the following:

Table 5: Distribution of Union Votes by Percent in Elections for Administrators of Social Security and Family Assistance Organizations

	1947		1950		1955		1962	
	SS	*AF*	*SS*	*AF*	*SS*	*AF*	*SS*	*AF*
CGT								
% of total votes	59.3	61.8	43.5	47.9	43.0	47.0	44.3	48.5
% of union votes	69.2	71.2	54.4	56.3	53.6	56.4	56.1	57.7
CFTC								
% of total votes	26.4	25.0	21.3	23.6	20.9	21.9	20.9	22.5
% of union votes	30.8	28.8	26.7	27.7	26.1	26.3	25.3	26.7
FO								
% of total votes			15.1	13.8	16.1	14.3	14.7	13.0
% of union votes			18.9	15.9	20.3	17.2	18.6	15.5

Source: Gérard Adam, *Atlas des élections sociales en France* (Paris, Armand Colin, 1964), p. 30.

The CGT totals for the period 1950–62 are strikingly constant, and at direct variance with the graph of membership statistics. Moreover, the decline apparent in the figures for 1947 and 1950 is explainable almost entirely by the creation of the CGT–FO and not by an autonomous defection of the CGT electorate. Thus, like the PCF the CGT lost a great part of its membership while retaining its electoral importance, a phenomenon related to the "tribune" role of the Communist movement in France analyzed in chapter 10.

In terms of relations between the syndicates, outside of a brief period in 1953 the Cold War influence was such that at both the national and federation level there was no "unity of action" to speak of. Although the largest and strongest union in France, during a period from 1947 through 1964–66 (the moment of the creation of a new socialist-oriented syndicate, the *Confédération française démocratique du travail* [CFDT], as a result of a split in the CFTC) the Communist-dominated CGT found itself somewhat isolated, while the CGT-FO and CFTC had rather cooperative, if ineffective relations. And despite the fact that of those workers unionized (about one-fifth to one-fourth of the working population) the CGT group was by far the largest single part, the small percentage of unionized workers in general tended to accentuate the ineffectiveness of the CGT because the *Patronat* and the government could always claim that syndicalism—and particularly Communist syndicalism—was not representative of the working class as a whole or of its "real" interests.[66]

The key to a successful policy of "unity of action" on the part of the CGT would have been cooperation from the CGT–FO. While the *Force ouvrière* rank and file was often interested in cooperating (for this reason common actions sometimes occurred on a purely local basis) the FO leadership—like that of the SFIO—remained adamantly hostile to overtures from the CGT. Thus, during the Cold War, the correspondence between Maurice Thorez and Guy Mollet on the one hand, and Benoît Frachon and Léon Jouhaux on the other, was strikingly similar: a series of proposals from the Communists rejected out of hand by the socialists.

In sum, after being successfully co-opted by the PCF during the Liberation period, the CGT was obliged to suffer its association with that party "not like the others," as one says in France. Given this, it could hardly avoid the same pattern of exclusion and isolation that was forced upon the PCF.

The Postwar Isolation of the French Communists in the French Parliament

Having outlined very broadly how the French Communists were excluded and isolated on the most important levels of political activity

[66] For histories of this period of French syndicalist disunity, the best source is the work of Lefranc, *Le mouvement syndical de la libération . . .* and also *Les expériences syndicales en France de 1939 à 1950* (Paris: Aubier, 1950). For studies of the other syndicates in particular see Gérard Adam, *La CFTC, 1940–1958* (Paris: A. Colin, 1964), and *La CGT-FO* (Paris: A. Colin, 1965). A less useful, though more general summary is found in Jean-Daniel Reynaud, *Les syndicats en France* (Paris: A. Colin, 1966). An excellent study which goes up only to the early 1950s is Lorwin, *French Labor Movement*.

in France during the period dating approximately from 1947 to 1962, it is worthwhile to examine closely how this quarantine was accomplished in a particular realm, that of parliament. Furthermore, it will be of interest to examine the Communist reaction to containment, for here one is able to see quite clearly the degree to which the PCF had been reduced to purely symbolic politics.

Unlike relations between Communists and non-Communists on both the party and syndicalist level, the non-Communist groups in parliament were obliged to sit with the former, to allow them to speak, to honor their constitutional right to propose laws, and to assign them to parliamentary committees. In a word, the Communists were impossible to quarantine. Yet while the persistently monolithic, and most often antigovernment, Communist vote was one of the ingredients of cabinet instability in the Fourth Republic, the non-Communists were nonetheless able to succeed significantly in reducing the extent to which the Communists were able to influence the actual conduct of business in the lower and upper chambers.

In the simpler case of the upper chamber, it should first be noted that the tremendous dilution of Communist representation in the Council of the Republic as a result of the elections of November 1948 made the task of their exclusion and isolation rather easier than in the lower chamber. One of the ways in which the non-Communists used their numerical advantage to completely neutralize their opponents was in assigning posts in the working bodies of the Council: the *Bureau,* or executive of the upper chamber; and the *Commissions,* structurally similar to the Committees in the American Congress.

Table 6 illustrates the number and title of Communist-held positions in the Commissions of the upper chamber during representative years since 1946. For the sake of demonstrating a continuing trend, the pattern is traced through 1970. The pattern in the Commissions is more significant than that in the Bureau for a simple reason. The Bureau is normally made up of a President,[67] four Vice-Presidents, and one Secretary from each group. Given that the Presidency was unavailable to the Communists for a combination of rather obvious

---

[67] From 1946 through 1968 the office of President was held by Gaston Monnerville (Radical), representing Guyane and then the Lot. In 1968 it was assumed by Alain Poher (MRP), who became President of the Republic during the interim period in 1969 after the defeat of the Gaullist referendum and the resignation of de Gaulle.

reasons, and given that the law assured the PCF of one Secretaryship in the Bureau, the only possible relevant measure of Communist participation might be found in the distribution of Vice-Presidencies. Not surprisingly, one finds that the Communists had one Vice-President in 1946 (Henri Martel) and none for twenty-three years after their exclusion from the government in 1947. Taken alone, this would be a partially misleading bit of evidence, however. In both the upper and lower houses a tradition, derived from Third Republic practice, required that the Bureau be constructed according to the numerical strength of each group within the chamber. Thus, with 27 percent of the seats in 1946 the Communists were entitled to a Vice-Presidency, while with 6 percent or less in each election since that time, they have lost their claim on such a position.[68] It was therefore only indirectly, through manipulation of the electoral law, that the Communists were denied a Vice-Presidency in the Bureau.

The trend revealed in the composition of the Commissions, as presented in Table 6, is much more relevant in demonstrating the exclusion and isolation of the Communists.

In the Fourth Republic Council of the Republic (1946–58) twenty Commissions existed, while in the Fifth Republic Senate their number has been reduced to six.[69] The large number of zeros—including a complete exclusion of the Communists from Presidencies and Vice-Presidencies of Commissions after 1948—is self-explanatory. Particularly in the Fourth Republic, the Communists should have acquired some, even if not many, positions other than simple membership on the Commissions. That the Communists held none—and hence held practically no power in the upper chamber—can be explained only as a conscious attempt on the part of the non-Communists to exclude them.

The pattern of anticommunism in the upper chamber was thus severe and quite successful, and the intentions of Communist opponents were facilitated by the nature of the electoral basis of the upper

[68] It should be pointed out here, however, that while such customary practices were honored when they worked against the Communists, such was not always the case when they would have worked in favor of them.

[69] This was a Gaullist innovation designed to "rationalize" the functioning of the Senate, but also to permit the Executive to reduce the scope of its action and to deal more effectively with oppostion in the upper chamber.

Table 6: Communist Participation in the Commissions of the French Second Chamber, Selected Years 1946–70

	Presidents of Commissions	Vice-Presidents of Commissions	Secretaries of Commissions
1946	6	10	about 20
1948	0	0	0
1953	0	0	0
1957	0	0	0
1959	0	0	0
1962	0	0	0
1965	0	0	0
1968	0	0	2
1970	0	0	1

Sources: 1946, "Deux années d'activité . . . ," pp. 157–58. 1948–70, Official Council of the Republic and Senate Register. The six PCF Commission Presidents were: M. Willard (Justice); N. Calonne (Industrial Production); S. Lefranc (Reapprovisionment); L. Dupic (Reconstruction); Henri Martel (Labor); P. Tubert (a PCF ally) (National Defense). The ten Vice-Presidents were C. le Contel (Economic Affairs); M. Dumont (National Education); G. Cardonne (Finances); A. Dujardin (Interior); A. De France (Merchant Marine and Fishing); F. Vittori (Pensions); A. Legeau (Press); A. Vilhet (Reapprovisionment); P. Franceschi (PCF ally) (Universal Suffrage and Rules); D. Maiga (PCF ally) (Overseas Territories).

It may be added that of the governmental positions in other bodies to which the Senate elected members, the same trend is revealed: of 18 judges elected to the Haute Cour de Justice each year, in 1970 for the first time one Communist senator was elected. Of the three Senators named to the Constitutional Council by the President of the Senate, none has ever been from the PCF. Of the twelve senators elected to the Consultative Assembly of the Council of Europe, none has ever been PCF. Of the twelve senators named to the European parliament, none has ever been from the Communist Party. (Sources: same as above.)

house. The problem of excluding and isolating the Communists in the Fourth Republic National Assembly was much more difficult, however, because of the size of the Communist Party's representation, considerable even after the famous *apparentements* election of 1951 and reduced significantly only with the Gaullist electoral law change of 1958.[70] Furthermore, the problem of the Communists in the lower chamber was more critical in the Fourth Republic than in the Fifth for reasons other than the mere fact of their number: the Assembly in the

---

[70] The percentage of Communist-held seats in the Assembly since the first postwar election has been the following:

Fourth Republic, as in the Third, tended to dominate the Executive: however, while in the 1875–1940 regime the conservative upper chamber was a significant constraint on the Left and extreme-Left, in the Fourth Republic this was not the case. In recognition of the role played by the Third Republic's Senate in frustrating the Popular Front, its powers had been much reduced in the Fourth Republic's Constitution. The partial veto power exercised by the large Communist group in the Assembly of the Fourth Republic was thus a significant factor in preventing the emergence of a strong, coherent, and continuing governmental majority, although it was certainly not the only important element.

The Assembly dominated the conduct of government business in many ways. For one thing, the standing orders of the Assembly were adamant that the chamber controlled its own agenda. The government was thus obliged to work not at its own speed and according to its own priorities, but rather mainly at the behest of the shifting and heterogeneous majorities that formed and dissolved with such rapidity during the Fourth Republic. Furthermore, ministers were not responsible for seeing their bills through the Assembly. It was the *rapporteur* of the relevant Commission who launched the floor debate. Moreover, the latter had the option of presenting an alternative to the government bill or, as sometimes happened, so amended a version of the bill that it no longer reflected the government's intentions. Often, the government could force the Assembly to debate and vote on the original bill only by making the issue a matter of confidence, which, because of the divisions in that body, the head of government was reluctant to do.

Thus, in administrative procedures crucial to the actual output of

1945 (First Constituent Assembly)	26%
1946 (Second Constituent Assembly)	25%
1946 (Fourth Republic)	27%
1951	16%
1956	24%
1958 (Fifth Republic)	2%
1962	9%
1967	15%
1968	7%
1973	15%

political decisions, parliamentary officials and Commissions played an extremely important role in the Fourth Republic.[71] Presidents and *rapporteurs* of the Commissions sometimes came to play the role of a quasi-minister (as in the American Congress), who had the power to place the government on the defensive and later to corner it in impossible positions resolvable often only through the resignation or disinvestiture of a cabinet.[72]

For all of these reasons, as the Cold War grew more intense after the French, Italian, and Belgian communists were excluded from their respective governments in 1947, and as the division of Europe into two blocs became more apparent with each new provocation by East or West, the Third Force coalitions came to consider as increasingly important the matter of isolating and neutralizing the Communist delegation in the National Assembly. Likewise, it became crucial for the Communists to avoid such an occurrence, if they hoped to influence the French government in the direction of Soviet foreign policy interests, and therein, the "future of socialism" as they perceived it.

We have seen above that the Communists were able to retain their popular vote throughout the Fourth Republic and regain in the 1956 general elections almost all of those seats lost to the *apparentements* electoral law of 1951. Footnote 70 carries this information up through the present in terms of percentages of total seats held by communists. Once again, it is helpful to begin a discussion of the neutralization of the Communists in parliament by discussing the composition of the Bureau and the Commissions of the National Assembly.

In the Bureau, because of the size of the Communist delegation and the traditional practice of composing the Assembly executive on the basis of proportional group strengths, it was much more difficult to attempt complete exclusion of the Communists than it was in the sen-

---

[71] Thus, while the PCF *régime d'assemblée* proposal was defeated in June 1946, the MRP-SFIO constitution did not provide for a solution to the problem of executive power either. It may be noted that one of the key reforms of the Fifth Republic parliamentary procedure has been to place the Assembly under the control of the government, for example on the question of constructing the agenda and with respect to the matter of whose bill shall be debated and voted upon (mainly through the introduction of the *vote bloqué*, by which the government may demand that a bill be voted upon in the form originally introduced).

[72] See Pickles, *French Politics*, pp. 276–77.

ate. Therefore, in all the Bureaus during the Fourth Republic the Communists had at least one Vice-President (of five or six) and one Secretary (of from six to fourteen). This representation was sometimes even exceeded; in 1947 and 1949, when the PCF had two Vice-Presidents of the Assembly (Jacques Duclos, the head of the Communist parliamentary group, and Mme. Madeleine Braun), and three Secretaries; and in 1956, when the Party again had two Vice-Presidents (Roger Garaudy and Mme. Paul Vaillant-Couturier).[73]

Nonetheless, the Communist claims in the Assembly Bureau came under attack from time to time when a crucial matter was at hand. For example, in constituting the Bureau in January 1948, the non-Communist deputies broke with a custom of the Third Republic and the Standing Orders of the Fourth Republic chamber to deny the Communists the Senior Vice-Presidency of the Assembly, which should normally have gone to the largest group. Marcel Cachin, the oldest deputy and therefore "Dean of the Assembly," retaliated for the Communists at the first session, by giving a speech that "abandoned the tradition of impartiality in his capacity as acting President." [74] His speech, which denounced the Marshall Plan and "American imperialism" in rather violent terms, was a deliberate perversion of his office and was designed to show that the Communists would not hesitate to retaliate. While hardly immaculate themselves, the non-Communist deputies nevertheless held the majority and quickly used this power to revise the Standing Orders so that the functions of Dean of the House as acting President were terminated immediately after he finished his opening speech.[75]

---

[73] As indicated by the choice of Communist Vice-Presidents, the PCF, of all French political parties, has traditionally had the most open policy regarding the participation of women. This is probably true of communist parties in general, although feminine participation is often merely formal at the highest levels. The influence of the wife of Maurice Thorez, Jeanette Vermeersch-Thorez, was a controversial exception however. For example, she is supposed to have had a decisive role in the exclusions of Auguste Lecoeur and Charles Tillon in the 1950s, and was also one of the few leading figures in the Party to insist on unyielding loyalty to the Soviet Union after the 1968 invasion of Czechoslovakia. She also vigorously opposed the beginnings of the birth control movement in France on the "scientific socialist" grounds that birth control was really a "neo-Malthusian" capitalist plot to restrain the number of births in the working class.

[74] Pickles, *French Politics*, p. 269. The Dean is named Acting President until the permanent President is elected.

[75] *Ibid.*

A repeat of the Cachin incident was expected in January 1949, because the Senior Vice-Presidency was again denied the Communists. This time, however, Cachin made a very conciliatory opening speech, stressing the possibilities of peaceful coexistence, avoiding direct criticism of the United States and the Marshall Plan, and calling for a meeting between Stalin and Truman to "settle peacefully the problems causing tensions between East and West." Moreover, the Communist group "accepted with good grace" two secondary Vice-Presidencies in place of the Senior Vice-Presidency.[76] One may surmise that this was less an admission of defeat by the Communists than a calculated move: they could not in any case have obtained the senior post and were at the time in the middle of a "peace campaign," whose main themes were a relaxation of East-West tension, a "ban-the-bomb" campaign, and so on. (See below, p. 219 f., on the relation of the Peace Movement and Communist tactics during the Cold War.)

From 1959 through 1962, when the PCF had only ten deputies, therefore not enough to form a parliamentary group (thirty members are necessary to form a group in the Fifth Republic Assembly) there was consequently no problem. All of the Communist deputies were *non-inscrit* during this period. After the 1962 general elections, when the PCF won 9 percent of the Assembly seats (41), the issue arose once again. This time, however, there was a strong Gaullist majority and, above all, a powerful President of the Republic long known for his strong anticommunist feelings. Dorothy Pickles had noted in 1953, concerning proposals for a new rule on staffing the Assembly Bureau, that "One of the [Standing Orders] which it is proposed to revise . . . requires the constitution of the Bureau of the Assembly to reflect party strengths in that House. The debate on . . . revision made it clear that the majority wanted this matter to be left for the Assembly itself to decide, thus enabling the number of Communist representatives to be restricted." [77]

[76] Marshall Shulman, *Stalin's Foreign Policy Reappraised*, p. 55.

[77] Pickles, *French Politics*, p. 269. It is significant that in the first constitutional proposal for the Fourth Republic, Article 56 stated that "Each of the two Chambers elects its Bureau each year, at the beginning of the session, according to the principle of proportional representation of the groups." Article 11 of the second constitutional proposal was revised to read: "Each of the two Chambers elects its Bureau each year at the beginning of the ordinary session, and according to the conditions foreseen by its governing rules." (Maurice Duverger, *Constitutions et documents politiques*, 5th edition, p.

The Constitution of the Fifth Republic said nothing new about the election of the Assembly Bureau. When the Communist "problem" arose once again in December 1962, the Gaullist majority repeated the response of the Fourth Republic coalition by excluding the Communists completely. After four years of Gaullist rule, however, a majority of the different socialist and Center-left groups had defected from the original coalition of 1958. Moreover, international events since the 20th CPSU Congress had somewhat diluted the extent to which the "Red peril" occupied men's minds. Thus, in a common protest against *le pouvoir personnel*, directed at once against de Gaulle's autocratic methods in presenting the 1962 constitutional referendum and the increasingly obvious submission of parliament to the executive branch of government, the socialists and Communists both adopted (though not officially in common) a policy of nonparticipation in some of the protocol connected with parliamentary life. For example they chose not to attend the annual dinner given by the President of the Republic in honor of parliament. This was, to be sure, a rather pathetic reprisal, but it was in fact one of the few legal avenues of protest left to the opposition. Ironically, however, the very strength of the Gaullists had united the Left on this issue, as it would continue to do in succeeding years.[78]

The exclusion of the Communists from the Assembly Bureau lasted until after the general elections of 1967, when they again were accorded one secondary Vice-Presidency and two Secretaries, in recognition of their increased numbers (73 PCF deputies, or 15 percent of the total), and the fact that an electoral coalition of the opposition (the PCF and FGDS—see chapter 7) nearly overcame the Gaullist major-

140.) Thus, even as early as the two constitutional referendums of 1946 the question of staffing the Bureau had been posed as part of the general debate over proportional representation, meaning, in context, strong PCF (and then RPF as well) representation. Generally, the period 1946–58 in France was a complete retreat from proportional representation elections to single-member constituencies and traditional forms of gerrymander.

[78] While it may have been unintentional, it is also quite possible that Gaullist leaders, including the General himself, undertook thereafter consciously to foster a united democratic socialist opposition. This would be done slowly enough not to endanger the continuity of Gaullist rule until the Fifth Republic's legitimacy and efficacy had been firmly established, but quickly enough—so the Gaullists hoped—to avoid stagnation among the opposition and its consequent domination by the Communists.

ity.[79] After the events of May–June, 1968 and the tremendous Gaullist landslide of June 1968, the PCF was again excluded from the Bureau, however. As in 1959–62, their weak representation (33 deputies or 7 percent of the total) rendered their potential claims almost nil, unless one chooses to consider the inequities of the electoral law, which was obviously not one of the burning Gaullist interests of the moment.[80]

In terms of the Assembly Commissions, one finds a pattern similar to the general trend so far uncovered. Table 7 represents Communist participation on the Commissions of the French lower chamber during selected years from 1936 to 1970.[81]

First and quite obviously, one notes that during the Popular Front the PCF had obtained a significant though not disproportionate share of formal power positions in the Chamber of Deputies from 1936 to 1939 (the PCF was declared illegal in September 1939). With three Presidencies, all of relatively nonpolitical and nonvital Commissions, and nineteen Vice-Presidencies, the Communist electorate (15 percent of the total) and Chamber group (12 percent of the total seats) were fairly represented. And even in 1939, after the breaking up of the Popular Front and the Munich Pact, the Communists still were accorded two Presidencies and twenty-one Vice-Presidencies.[82]

The figures for the First Constituent Assembly and the first legislature of the Fourth Republic reveal that the Communists again received a more or less proportional share of Assembly offices. Moreover, the fact that Communists were at one point or another at the

[79] It is possible the Gaullists became momentarily apprehensive that their own precedents might one day be invoked against them. However, in the wake of the landslide victory in 1968, the opposition was again denied all vice-presidencies. (During the 1973 electoral campaign, the Independent Republicans proposed that the commission vice-presidencies be reserved to the opposition.)

[80] In the 1968 election it took about 89,000 votes to "elect" one Communist deputy; in the same election about 24,000 votes elected a Gaullist deputy (dividing total second-ballot votes by deputies elected). Such a statistic is only approximately accurate, but the degree of the imbalance is evident.

[81] In the 1930s there were 24 Commissions, in the First Constituent Assembly 19, in the Fourth Republic 20, and in the Fifth Republic 6. Once again the Fifth Republic practice implies the Gaullist desire to deemphasize the legislative branch.

[82] The SFIO leadership played a large role in obtaining fair representation for the Communists. Blum considered it a better strategy to attempt to co-opt the Communists than to drive them underground, recalling his position on the 1939 dissolution.

*Table 7: Communist Participation on the Commissions of the
French Lower Chamber, Selected Years, 1936–70*

	Presidents of Commissions	Vice-Presidents of Commissions	Secretaries of Commissions
1936–37	3 [a]	19	27
1939	2 [b]	21	*c.* 25
1945	3 [c]	12	*c.* 15
1947	6 [d]	12	12
1950	0	4	4
1953	0	0	2
1956	0	8	9
1960	0	0	0
1963	0	0	0
1967	0	1 [e]	0
1970	0	0	0

SOURCES: For 1936–37, "L'action du groupe communiste au parlement: Rapport du groupe communiste parlementaire pour le 9ème Congrès" (Paris: PCF, 1937), pp. 21–22. For 1939, *Annuaire* of the Chamber of deputies; for 1945, *Annuaire* of the First Constituent Assembly; for 1947, "Deux années d'activité … ," p. 151; for 1950, 1953, 1956, 1960, 1963, 1967, 1970, *Annuaire* of the National Assembly for those years.

[a] Communist presidents of the Commissions on General, Departmental, and Communal Administration; Agriculture; Insurance and Planning.

[b] Communist presidents of the Commissions on General, Departmental, and Communal Administration; Agriculture.

[c] Communist presidents of the Commissions on Agriculture and Reapprovisionment; National Defense; National Education.

[d] Communist presidents of the Commissions on Foreign Affairs; Agriculture; National Education; Interior; Means of Communications; Rules.

[e] A Communist Vice-President in the Commission on Production and Exchange.

GENERAL NOTE: As was the case in the upper chamber, in the election of members to sit in other bodies, the Communists were generally excluded in the Fourth Republic after 1947 and completely excluded in the Fifth Republic. For example, in 1953 of 75 deputies elected to the High Court of Justice, 4 were Communist; of 11 deputies elected to the Superior Council of the Magistrature, none were Communist; of 7 deputies elected to the Constitutional Committee, none were Communist; of 24 deputies elected to the Consultative Assembly of the Council of Europe, none were Communist; of 10 deputies elected to the Common Assembly of the ECSC, none were Communist. Throughout the Fifth Republic, of the 24 deputies elected each year (22 in 1962) to the Consultative Assembly of the Council of Europe, to the European Parliamentary Assembly and of the 3 deputies named to the Constitutional Council by the President of the National Assembly, none have been from the Communist delegation. (Sources same as above.)

The "democratization" of European institutions, which would permit Communists to sit in the European bodies, has been a part of the PCF program throughout the 1960s. In an interesting doctrinal development, the French Communists, who until head of the Commissions on National Defense (although de Gaulle had diluted the potential impact of this commission by dispersing responsibility for defense through different ministries—see above), Interior, and Education indicates that during the first years of the postwar period the Communists played an active and effective role in the Assembly, which conclusion accords with PCF participation in immediate postwar governments themselves.[83]

---

the early 1960s were uncompromising in a demand that the Common Market structure be dismantled to await the unification of "all of Europe," have since that time "taken cognizance" of the EEC. In general, the Marxist-Leninists have had difficulty explaining the European phenomenon in doctrinal terms, since, according to the traditional interpretation, the capitalist nations are doomed to a mortal struggle among themselves. The modifications in the doctrine on the inevitability of war since the death of Stalin have not really solved the problem, for a "proof" of Marxism-Leninism still depends on a supposed inability of "capitalism" to evolve successfully. Were the Communists to give up the idea that capitalism is necessarily doomed, they would also be forced to admit that socialism is not necessarily the next step in the evolution of society.

[83] The meaning of an "active and effective" role can be made empirical to some extent by citing the following statistics given by the Communists themselves:

A) Activity of the Communist parliamentary group in the First Constituent National Assembly:

1. Foreign Affairs	7 speeches	no bills proposed.
2. Agriculture	15 speeches	19 bills proposed.
3. Veterans and Prisoners	8 speeches	14 bills proposed.
4. Constitution	16 speeches	
5. National Defense	16 speeches	
6. Nationalizations	11 speeches	3 bills proposed.
7. French Union	8 speeches	11 bills proposed.
8. Labor and Social Security	11 speeches	

B) Activity of the Communist parliamentary group from December 1946 to March 1947:

1. Foreign Affairs	1 speech	no bills proposed.
2. Agriculture	17 speeches	37 bills proposed.
3. Veterans and Prisoners	No speeches	17 bills proposed.
4. National Defense	7 speeches	no bills proposed.
5. Nationalizations	No speeches	3 bills proposed.
6. Work and Social Security	5 speeches	4 bills proposed.
7. French Union	5 speeches	7 bills proposed.

(Compiled from *Deux années d'activité* . . . , pp. 49–114. Statistics for the Second Constituent are similar to the First and are not included for reasons of economy of space.)

The figures for the period since 1948 are quite another matter how-ever. The preponderance of zeros after 1947—less significant in the first years of the Fifth Republic than in the Fourth because of the reduced Communist delegation, but significant once again after 1962—indicates the degree to which the Communists have been ex-cluded and isolated from even formal power in the French National Assembly since 1947.

The Problems of Parliamentary Immunity and Parliamentary Obstructionism: Some Examples, 1947–53.

Although certainly not the only and perhaps not even the most im-portant division in the French parliaments of 1947–62, the cleavage between Communists and non-Communists was the sharpest and least complex of all. Given the stakes involved, it is not surprising that as a result of the isolation and exclusion of the Communists the actions of the two opposing blocs moved very far toward the extremes of parlia-mentary behavior where the other was concerned. For the non-Com-munist group, which had other things to do as well, this was but part of the time. For the Communists, who were constantly and every-where faced with "containment," the use in parliament of extremism by way of reprisal became almost a norm, particularly during the period 1947–53, because use of the most unusual weapons in the arse-nal of parliamentary tactics remained practically the only recourse for the Communists. In light of this, an examination of the questions of parliamentary immunity and parliamentary obstructionism proves in-teresting to underline further the bizarre situation of the Communist movement and the frustration of its strategy and tactics. Once again, as a detailed history is impossible in the context of this study, one must be content with the analysis of a few representative cases.

The Problem of Parliamentary Immunity. The speeches of Maurice Thorez were naturally scrutinized with utmost care throughout his thirty-year leadership of the French Communist Party. This was par-ticularly true during the early years of the Cold War, when men were prepared to believe apocalyptic predictions that in calmer and less emotional times would have been immediately dismissed as nonsense, and when Thorez, as one of the leaders of the "international Communist conspiracy," was thought by many to be concealing plans for the last fearful conflagration.

In early 1949, in response to a question that had been, as one newspaper put it, "in the wind" for many months, a question that concerned fears of a Soviet attack on Western Europe and the attitude that the PCF would adopt in such a situation, Thorez replied at the February 22–23 meeting of the Central Committee in the following terms:

The enemies of the people, thinking to embarrass us, pose the following question: "What would you do if the Red Army occupied Paris?" Here is our reply: . . . The Soviet Union is never found and never could be found in the position of being an aggressor toward any other country. The country of socialism could not, by definition, practice a policy of aggression and of war as do the imperialist powers. . . . However, since the question is put to us, let us say clearly this: if the common efforts of all Frenchmen devoted to liberty and peace do not succeed in bringing our country back into the camp of democracy and peace, if later our people should be dragged against their will into an anti-Soviet war, and if under these conditions the Soviet Army, defending the cause of the people, the cause of socialism, should be brought to pursue the aggressors onto our soil, could the workers and the people of France act toward the Soviet army otherwise than did the workers and the people of Poland, of Rumania, of Yugoslavia . . . ?" [84]

It would be difficult to imagine more inappropriate timing than in this tactical blunder by Thorez, for this statement came at a time when the communist movement internationally had recently launched a "peace" campaign (see below) designed to rally "the Western peoples" to the aims of Soviet foreign policy, and when the PCF was attempting to play down events of the previous year in Czechoslovakia. As André Philip has noted, "after the coup de Prague (February 24, 1948), the fear of a Russian invasion began to agitate [popular] opinion." [85] Apparently "a grand gesture of loyalty to" the USSR in the context of the Soviet campaign against Tito and "bourgeois nationalism," the Thorez statement was also an ill-timed provocation, given the Communist interest in preventing the signature of the North

[84] *L'Humanité*, February 23, 1949, p. 1. See also *Histoire (Manuel)* . . . pp. 523–24.
[85] André Philip, *Les socialistes*, p. 146.

Atlantic Treaty.[86] The dominant Party slogan of this period, "The people of France will not, will never, go to war against the Soviet Union," had been moderately acceptable to public opinion because its implication that the danger of war lay in the West neatly sidestepped the question of Soviet intentions and actions. The Thorez scenario of February 22, on the other hand, by taking up an unlikely set of hypothetical conditions and raising the possibility of the French people suffering a fate similar to the Polish, Rumanian, and Czech populations, was nothing short of a tremendous blunder: it was one thing to charge the Allied powers with warmongering; it was quite another to speak in glowing terms of the possibility of Soviet tanks rumbling down the Champs Elysées!

As a deputy, Thorez was normally protected from prosecution, but a group of noncommunist deputies demanded that his parliamentary immunity be lifted, that a full investigation be launched, that Thorez be prosecuted for treason, and that the PCF be declared illegal. However, despite his bold talk, the PCF Secretary-General had been careful to put his prognosis in the conditional tense, thus rendering prosecution extremely difficult.[87] Furthermore, as the mandatory sentence for treason was death, it was likely that any trial of the Communist leader on such grounds would end in acquittal. Therefore, after an agitated debate the Assembly passed a resolution, 386–182, condemning the Thorez declaration and "calling upon the Government to defend national independence and apply the law." [88] Rather than pursuing the lifting of parliamentary immunity, therefore, the Third Force governments chose to use the climate created by the Thorez incident as a basis for a campaign of repressive actions against Communist organizations in general. There soon followed, for example, police raids on Communist publishing centers; a raid on the Paris headquarters of the CGT, where several militants were interrogated, and some were later prosecuted for "passing military information to hostile nations" or for "possession of documents of military interest"; and

[86] Shulman, *Stalin's Foreign Policy*, pp. 60–61.

[87] One speaker, condemning Thorez in the Assembly, noted: "Each word is so marvelously weighed and placed in hypothetical form. . . . Yes or no, has M. Maurice Thorez posed his candidacy to the succession of M. Pierre Laval?" (Cited in Fauvet, *Histoire du Parti*, 2:228.)

[88] Shulman, *Stalin's Foreign Policy*, p. 115.

searches of the coal mines in the Nord revealed a number of caches of Molotov cocktails in this bastion of CGT strength, which many concluded implied plans for sabotage.[89] Also, the government announced a ban on street demonstrations and made it illegal to distribute handbills calling for them. In the Assembly, a motion was passed in early March lifting the immunity of Roger Garaudy for a provocative article he had written in *L'Humanité*, but the non-Communist majority refused to lift Marcel Cachin's immunity as well, on the basis that he was only the nominal editor of the paper.

A second incident that shed light on the problem of parliamentary immunity, and thus on the question of the legitimacy of Communists in the French National Assembly during the Cold War, was the celebrated arrest of Jacques Duclos in 1952. The occasion of this arrest was a demonstration organized by the Communists against the visit of General Matthew Ridgway to Paris on May 28 of that year. Ridgway had arrived from Korea to replace General Eisenhower as Supreme Commander of the NATO forces. In the days before his appearance several provocative incidents had already occurred, and on May 25 an editor of *L'Humanité* (André Stil) was arrested, on the basis of a law dating from 1848, for having written articles praising the action of militants who defied the ban on demonstrations. The demonstration on the 28th turned quickly to a violent clash between many thousands of communist militants, armed with poster boards made of iron, and an almost equal number of police and army forces. More than seven hundred arrests were made and more than fifty people were injured; one demonstrator, an Algerian, was killed in the Place de Stalingrad.

That evening, when the streets had been cleared of all but police and army guards, Jacques Duclos was stopped on his way home from the offices of *L'Humanité*. On the front seat of his car were found a club and a revolver, and on the back seat two dead pigeons. On the basis of this find, he was arrested, his immunity eventually lifted, and prosecution begun. With the potential of the demonstration "up-

---

[89] The Communist efforts to hinder military deliveries during the formation of the Western military alliance were numerous but not very effective, despite the spectacular attention given them in the press. For example, the CGT was unsuccessful in preventing the unloading of the first shipments of arms under the Mutual Defense Assistance Program, a "test case" indicative of later developments.

graded" because of the arrest of a top PCF leader, the Minister of the
Interior denounced the event as "a real attack on the security of the
State . . . criminal action pursued by the leadership of one party
against the republican and democratic regime." [90] Though he spent
two months in prison, Duclos was eventually acquitted of the charges
against him. The implications of the arrest of Duclos and the action of
the government thereafter have been commented upon piquantly by
the well-known journalist Jacques Fauvet:

[It was] a perfectly illegal and completely stupid arrest. The demonstration
had ended, and the instance of *flagrante delicto* demanded by the law in the
apprehension of a deputy was not established, except for the carrying of a
weapon. The capture was delightful but encumbering, and the government,
which often dramatized, made itself somewhat ridiculous: in the course of
that night the two fowl became "two homing pigeons hidden under a blanket"
and the car radio was capable, they assured one, of intercepting police calls.
At dawn the two pigeons became once again what they had been, good when
accompanied by sweet peas, and the radio as well, good for listening to the
news. . . . [However] this did not undo the fact that the Party had placed itself in a compromising situation, and the Government profited from it. . . .
During the next year prosecutions, perquisitions, seizures, and arrests were
numerous throughout the country. [Nonetheless], none resulted in the conviction of a single leader. The Government could do nothing against the Party;
nor, for that matter, the Party against the Government." [91]

Of course, the problem of whether or not to lift parliamentary immunity involved more than simply a strictly legal matter insofar as the
non-Communist majority of French deputies were concerned. [92] In effect, the attempt to deny legitimacy to Communist deputies was an
integral part of the non-Communists' general strategy of exclusion and
isolation, during the early years of the Cold War. [93]

[90] Fauvet, *Histoire du Parti*, 2:243.

[91] *Ibid.*, p. 243. David Caute, *Communism and the French Intellectuals* (p. 360) concurs,
asserting that Duclos was arrested on a trumped-up charge.

[92] This is indicated by the numbers involved: in November 1950 there were 256 outstanding demands for suspension of immunity, 217 of which related to Communists
(Pickles, *French Politics*, p. 270). At the time, there were 169 PCF deputies.

[93] Writing in 1953, Dorothy Pickles observed that: "Perhaps the largest loophole
which the Constitution of the Fourth Republic offers to Communist activity is that
provided by Article 22 governing the conditions of parliamentary immunity" (*French
Politics*, p. 269). This would seem to be somewhat imprecise: in effect, the largest "loophole" was, for her, to have given the Communist movement legal status in the first

The Problem of Parliamentary Obstructionism. In the pursuit of their dominant goal of simultaneously serving both Soviet foreign policy interests and the "ultimate" Communist revolution by hindering the development of the Western alliance and the success of the Marshall Plan, the French Communists had been denied almost all parliamentary weapons by the noncommunist majority. Left with little from which to choose, the Communists frequently adopted extreme tactics in the Assembly—tactics of obstructionism and, on occasion, violence. It need hardly be said that the choice of such tactics was not one of principle, for obstructionism promised to achieve little of the Communist program. The disruption was rather a last-ditch defense of Communist prerogatives in the French parliament, and was at the same time designed with the hope of winning popular sympathy by drawing attention to the denial of participation to the Communists and seeking to portray the movement as a sort of persecuted tribune of the people whom the regime refused to legitimize. Furthermore, the use of obstructionism as a parliamentary weapon was by no means limited to the Communist Party. Not only did the Right-wing RPF and Poujadist extremists seek to gain their way through blockage of the machinery of government, but sometimes even governing parties themselves did likewise. Such were the "rules of the game" in the Fourth Republic. Nonetheless, given the transformation in Eastern Europe and the avowed Communist intentions in France, PCF obstructionism could not avoid presenting a "special" problem quite unlike that which characterized other movements of opposition.

The techniques of parliamentary obstruction (e.g., the proposal of interminable amendments requiring debate and vote; the demand for the more time-consuming methods of voting; the succession of deputies making long speeches designed to wear out opponents or stall until the end of a session; proposals to suspend debate; proposals to table; "occupation" of the rostrum and refusal to leave) do not need

---

place. Pickles's real criticism would seem to be her assertion that "the Courts were surprisingly, indeed sometimes disquietingly, lenient towards cases in which Communist Deputies were brought before them" (*ibid.*, p. 294). Once again, it is not out of place to note the ambivalence of communism as parliamentary opposition and the dilemma posed an established liberal order in regard to such questions as parliamentary immunity.

detailed explanation. Rather, once again the most effective method of presentation would seem to be the discussion of a selection of cases that raise the major questions involved.

As an example of the use of the various methods of voting to stall passage of a bill one may cite the instance of November 1947, at which time the Communists attempted to combat the enactment of measures to deal with sabotage of Western defense preparations in connection with the great strike wave of November–December 1947. It will be remembered that the French, Italian, and Belgian Communists had recently been excluded from their respective governments, that the Truman Doctrine had been announced on March 12, that the Marshall Plan had been proposed on June 5, and that the Cominform had been created in late September. The strikes of November 1947, in which CGT-controlled dock workers had refused to unload military shipments and other "traitorous" or "antimilitarist" (depending on one's point of view) acts had occurred, were termed of "an insurrectional character" by the head of government, Robert Schuman. Thus, the Assembly debate on sabotage had taken on a particularly vitriolic tone.

Since they were certain to lose a vote, the Communists' tactic was to stall. They repeatedly demanded open ballots at the rostrum (*scrutin public*), which required each deputy to vote in person and which consumed 1½ hours or more of parliamentary time. Given the large number of amendments proposed by the Communists, during the first day of debates 10 hours out of 23 in session were occupied merely in counting votes. Immediately, however, the noncommunist majority moved to close off this tactic by voting to amend the Standing Orders of the Assembly the very next day: the amendment provided that no single group might request more than one *scrutin public* during the course of a single debate.[94]

Another form of interruption of the work of the Assembly was a suspension of the session due to uncontrollable scenes, generally caused by the Communists. We may take as an example of this the events of November 16–25, 1948. During this period, tension was still extremely high, because of the outbreak of an unusually bitter strike

---

[94] *Ibid.*, pp. 268–69.

of the coal miners (generally controlled by the CGT) on October 4, the heated Big Four discussions over Berlin and the future of Germany, the tremendous advances being made by the Chinese Communists against Chiang Kai-Shek, and above all, in terms of French opinion, the still very fresh memory of the Prague coup of February 24. In late October, the mood of the anti-Communist majority was mirrored in a front-page *Le Monde* editorial signed by Rémy Roure, entitled "The Insurrection." Writing of the miners' strike and its larger implications, Roure voiced a general feeling:

We praise the government at once for its moderation and for its firmness. It has on its side law, force, and reason. It must avoid the trap set by the Communist Party, which consists of transforming the strike into open insurrection. . . . What is going on in France is an episode of the "Cold War," which is perhaps the prelude to an immense catastrophe.[95]

Le Monde of October 27 headlined that "In case of a Russian Attack, Washington Says the Frontier of the Rhine will be Held," and six days later the same paper somewhat anxiously quoted *The Observer* of London, whose editorialist had stated flatly that "France is an ally on whom we cannot count." [96] Thus, the newspapers of the period permit one to recapture somewhat the public's near panic fear of possible war, domestic insurrection, or at least widespread sabotage, which were imputed to the Communists, French and Soviet.

On November 16, the National Assembly opened a debate on "Communist activity," and the first speaker, Minister of the Interior Jules Moch, charged the Communists with sabotage, insurrectional plans, and "receiving funds from abroad" to finance the CGT-controlled strikes and sabotage in the defense and related production industries. Another speaker called upon the Minister to dissolve the PCF, "which is no longer a French Party, but a party of traitors." [97] Replying for the Communist group, Auguste Lecoeur began his own speech with a virulent denunciation of the government and particularly its use of the C.R.S. (special riot police) against demonstrators and strikers. The following incident occurred, reported by *Le Monde:*

LECOEUR: The barbarity, without name, of the CRS, comparable to that of the SS. . . .

[95] *Le Monde*, October 23, 1948, p. 1.   [96] *Ibid.*, November 2, 1948, p. 2.
[97] *Ibid.*, November 20, 1948, p. 3.

HERRIOT (President of the Assembly): Such allegations are injurious and unjust! . . .

(In the midst of the uproar, M. Lecoeur speaks of lynchings and of "assassinations by rifle-butts.")

MINISTER OF THE INTERIOR: It's not true.

LECOEUR: You defend the CRS. I defend the miners. (The Communists rise and applaud.)

MINISTER: You know well. . . .

LECOEUR: That you are a professional liar!

(The tumult is at its height. MM. Moch, Lacoste, and André Marie leave the chamber followed by many deputies. Several of the latter, in passing near the rostrum, express their sentiments to M. Lecoeur with raised voices; the latter then pretends to get ready to attack them; the ushers interpose themselves; the President suspends the session and leaves his chair.) [98]

Such provocations gained the Communists little, however, for whatever else may have divided the non-Communist deputies, they always united against Communist provocations. For example, after the incident described above, the session was resumed after forty minutes, and a series of antisabotage measures was passed the first week of December after being introduced on November 29—extremely rapid action for a national parliament.

Perhaps the most definitive incident of this type, however, incorporating the largest number of tactics of provocation and obstruction, occurred during debate on a second series of antisabotage measures in March 1950. Because of its relevance in describing in one incident a broad pattern of behavior, a reconstruction of a series of eyewitness reports of the incident follows:

The communists, in order to delay the debate, first asked for suspension of the session, and then for priority for a proposition of . . . M. Dutard (PCF). A vote was taken, and while the tallying was being done, despite protests by the [communists], the Assembly undertook the examination . . . of the bill concerning . . . the social security and family allocation institutions. . . . M. Duprat then began a long speech provoking incidents throughout, after which the President announced the rejection of the suspension request, 409–182, and the adoption of priority for the proposition of M. Dutard, 309–180.

The discussion concerning the social security [bill] continued and another vote . . . occurred after added speeches by MM. Duprat and Musmeaux (PCF) on an amendment. . . . The communists then demanded still another vote, which decided, by 415 votes against 182, that the session was suspended. The debate was resumed at 3 P.M. under the Presidency of M. Roclore, who announced that the Musmeaux amendment was defeated. . . . The communists then asked for a verification of the quorum. . . . After several minutes delay . . . M. Roclore then put the bill as a whole to a vote, despite communist protest.

M. Duprat indicated that he wanted to explain the vote of his party, despite the fact that the [new] vote had already begun, and he tried to mount the tribune. The ushers prevented him. Seeing this, M. Musmeaux leaped onto the staircase leading to the Presidential rostrum and from there, jumping over the secretaries, landed on the tribune. As for M. Duprat, he climbed . . . the ramp of the tribune staircase and hoisted himself up to the position of M. Musmeaux. The disorder was at its height. M. Roclore suspended the session. . . . Soon, incidents of extreme violence occurred on the floor. The communists moved toward the benches of the right and center. Insults were exchanged, soon followed by a series of fights. The ushers attempted to intervene, but were immediately overwhelmed; they were immersed in a general battle, in the course of which several deputies rolled on the benches and under the desks. . . . The incidents then went on behind closed doors, but to judge from the ushers passing between the floor and the corridors, they remained very violent. . . . It was only at 4:50 P.M. that the session resumed. One noted that in the MRP ranks two rows of desks were missing, and that M. Duprat still occupied the tribune. M. Edouard Herriot . . . asked M. Duprat to leave the rostrum: the deputy . . . refused . . . The President declared that . . . the Bureau of the Assembly . . . had decided to seek the censure, with temporary exclusion of M. Duprat. . . .

The deputies voted his censure and temporary exclusion by a standing vote. [Duprat] continued to "occupy" the tribune, while the other deputies left the chamber, except for the communists who brought him a chair and a sandwich and "occupied" the staircase of the tribune themselves. This lasted from 7 until 10:15 P.M., when the Republican Guard arrived and evacuated the floor in a 15-minute scuffle with the communist group. The session was finally resumed at 11:30 P.M., and immediately M. Musmeaux (PCF) began a speech lasting 2½ hours. At 2:30 A.M. a motion of censure and temporary exclusion was voted against him as well, and Musmeaux also refused to leave the tribune. Again the Republican Guard was called, and succeeded in removing him with somewhat less violence. The session resumed at 3 A.M., and the bill on social security . . . passed 567–0, with even the communists voting for it; the galleries registered astonishment. Finally, at 3:45 A.M., the Assembly took up the "sabotage" bill.

At 5 A.M., the PCF forced a vote of procedure on a prejudicial matter, which was rejected 322–180 at 5:40 A.M. Roger Garaudy (PCF) then spoke for 1½ hours. At 7:20 A.M., the Assembly refused another communist request to postpone further discussion of the bill, until Tuesday, by 302–218. At 8:20

A.M. a communist motion to suspend debate until Monday was voted down 308–278. Immediately thereupon, the communists moved that debate be suspended until 3:00 P.M. that afternoon, "to allow the Assembly staff personnel to get some rest." This was refused 309–278. After several hours of further debate on procedure the Assembly voted a motion of cloture, 315–180, and debate was begun on the articles of the bill itself. In a last-ditch move, Jacques Duclos (PCF) deposited a motion of censure against the government, but it was unacceptable on procedural grounds.[99]

The bill to repress acts of sabotage was discussed and finally passed on March 8, by a vote of 393–186. Thus, the Communist efforts to obstruct parliamentary business, although spectacular, ultimately failed. For one thing, the Standing Orders did not permit a filibuster tactic to go on for long, and for another, "when the Communists exceed the bounds of toleration, the result was to produce [temporarily] a degree of unity among the other parties which it was one of their chief purposes to destroy."[100]

Another parliamentary weapon used by the Communists at times was the device, well-known in American politics, of the news leak. From the fall of 1947 on, Communist participation on parliamentary commissions, in particular the Commission on National Defense, became a matter of extreme controversy, simply because the Communist members would undoubtedly pass on relevant information to the Soviet Union. The work of the National Defense Commission was thus paralyzed for much of the next year.[101] Finally, in the fall of 1948, the nonCommunist majority on the Commission adopted an informal policy of refusing to deliberate in the presence of Communists.[102]

[99] Reconstructed from reports in *Le Monde*, March 4, 1950, p. 12, and March 5–6, 1950, pp. 3, 8.

[100] Pickles, *French Politics*, p. 268.

[101] See Jaques Fauvet, "La situation politique," *Le Monde*, November 19, 1948, p. 1.

[102] *Le Monde*, November 17, 1948, p. 3. The implications of these events had been drawn in an article of October 29: "[This] poses the question, avoided until now, of the judiciousness of the presence of communists on certain parliamentary organisms" (p. 4).

At the opening of the winter Assembly session, two suggestions were advanced as to how to deal with the problem of the National Defense Commission: either a subcommission would be created, or else a supercommission, consisting of the Commission on Finance and the Commission on National Defense, would be established. In either case, the commission would be chosen by majority (i.e. non-Communist) rule. As Jacques Fauvet remarked, "In either case the Communists will surely remain outside the door" (*ibid.*, November 19, 1948, p. 1). Finally, the Assembly solved the problem of

Another use of the leak, in the sense of a public disclosure rather than passing secrets to a foreign power, occurred in connection with the "affair of the Generals," which took up much newsprint during the early months of 1950. In January of that year, the Assembly had set up a commission to investigate the responsibility of two Generals, Mast and Revers, in the transfer of a confidential report on the Indochina situation to the Viet Minh. The "affair" had potentially large political as well as military implications, for the two men responsible for presenting the commission's report were both MRP, as was the Minister for the Colonies during the time the scandal broke in the newspapers. The situation was especially delicate because the testimony received by the commission implicated several socialists, and even went so far as to question the responsibility of the SFIO Ministers of Interior and Defense in 1949. The "affair of the Generals" thus implied the possibility of a political crisis in the Third Force coalition. And with general elections being scheduled for the next year, complicated by the threat of an RPF-PCF antisystem majority, it seemed in the interest of all those favorable to the Third Force that the greatest secrecy be maintained.

The Communists however, had other ideas. They saw in the affair a chance to damage the government's policy in Indochina and perhaps to drive a wedge between the MRP and SFIO, which they hoped, forlornly, to force into a turn to the Left. Therefore, the Communist member of the special commission regularly leaked information to *L'Humanité*, in effect forcing all the other newspapers to pick up the story to counter the communist viewpoint. This damaging publicity was one of the factors that was gradually driving a wedge between the MRP and SFIO toward the end of 1950. The problem of state aid to religious schools, taken up during the last half of 1951, would eventually split the coalition partners: The so-called *loi Barangé*, supported ferociously by the RPF in order to pressure the MRP to break from the SFIO and turn to the Right, finished the original Third Force alliance. The SFIO remained out of all governments during the second legislature of the Fourth Republic (1951–56), although it would some-

---

the National Defense Commission in effect by simply reducing its role until its functions were more or less nonexistent.

times support a government without participating in it. Nonetheless, the SFIO did not veer to the Left, and the MRP did not fall into an open embrace of the RPF.

In sum, the obstructionist tactics of the French Communists in the postwar French parliament, which reached their height during the period 1947–53, the years of greatest tension, had at times some marginal effect on the conduct of government. On the whole, however, they were merely a rearguard action designed to cover so far as possible an inglorious retreat amid a decline in the organization and its leadership. The Communists' attempt to disguise the Party's weakness and ineffectiveness was more successful than it might have been, because the anxious political context made men much more inclined to imagine the Communists as stronger than they actually were, as more potentially dangerous than they actually were, as nearer the implementation of their revolutionary goals than they actually were.

Toward the end of the Fourth Republic, however, after the death of Stalin and after the 20th CPSU Congress, a more realistic picture of the Communist movement domestically and internationally began to be drawn in both scholarly and public opinion. It was at this time that fears of the Communist hard line, so prevalent during the early years of the Fourth Republic, began to resurface as criticisms of Communist "immobility." During the last years of the Fourth Republic the dilemma of a large and influential Communist opposition in France was thus reaffirmed with striking clarity: dangerous to govern "with," yet debilitating to govern "without," the French Communist movement posed a challenge to governmental legitimacy and effectiveness ambivalent to such an extent that the only possible method of dealing with it seemed an uneasy truce. That the truce was established on the basis of a near total exclusion and isolation of the Communists from legitimate and effective participation in the polity fundamentally weakened the institutions of the Republic. Yet to the leaders of the Third force, a policy of containment of the Communists seemed a justified method of preventing the subversion of liberal institutions, a possible dislocation of the Western alliance, and ultimately the possible reduction of France to the position of a Soviet fiefdom.

Symbolic Politics: The Peace Movement

For the French Communists the Cold War period was one of near-total tactical frustration, as well as considerable erosion of organizational strength and vitality in the Communist Party and its ancillaries. One result was that a political party representing one-fourth of the French electorate found its only productive outlets in activity of an almost entirely symbolic nature.

One of the most interesting uses of symbolic politics at this time was the *Mouvement de la Paix*. With Communist access blocked to most of the habitual forms of political participation in a liberal parliamentary regime, the tactical implementation of strategy depended more than usual on the ancillary or "front" organizations.[103] And previous research has demonstrated a definite tendency among the Western European Communist parties at this time to de-emphasize the Party itself in favor of the more acceptable ancillaries—in particular the Peace Movement.[104]

The Peace Movement was at first not a Communist ancillary in any sense of the term, but it gradually became so owing to infiltration. The Movement had its beginnings in February–March 1948, in the creation of an organization called *Combattants de la liberté*. Yves Farge, its creator, had been an important figure in the Resistance, and, as Minister of Food in 1946, he had to limit the black market.[105] In early April 1948, the Cominform endorsed the *Combattants* in the *Cominform Bulletin*, asserting that it sought "to defend national independence, to thwart the machinations of the neofascists, and to strengthen the Republic, to prevent the reentry into public life of traitors and collabo-

---

[103] For one of the classic discussions of ancillary organizations in Leninist strategy see Selznick, *The Organizational Weapon*, pp. 113–125.

[104] See Shulman, *Stalin's Foreign Policy*, chaps. 4 and 9. The following analysis is based largely on his account.

[105] Apparently Farge founded the *Combattants* in an attempt to prevent General de Gaulle from identifying the Resistance completely with the Gaullist movement. This had been a widespread sentiment particularly among Left-wing Resistants, and many of them had earlier joined the *Union démocratique et socialiste de la Résistance* (*USDR*), a small party founded in 1945. In any case, the program of the "Combattants," based on a policy of "anti-fascism," was rather clearly directed against de Gaulle and the RPF.

rators, to create a genuine people's army, and to end the war in the French colonies." [106]

The first sign that the Cominform was interested in developing an "international peace movement" came in August 1948, when the Polish communists organized a "World Council of Intellectuals for Peace" at Breslau. During the last week of November, a "National Congress for the Defense of Peace and Freedom" was held in Paris, the purpose of which was to establish the Peace Movement and to organize local peace councils throughout France. By this time, it had become clear that the issue of "peace" was a rallying point at which the Communists could integrate with non-Communists. [107] In a complicated series of events the *Combattants* and the new Peace Movement became merged, and Communist leaders such as Laurent Casanova and Charles Tillon worked in uneasy coalition with Farge and the non-Communist leaders. The "cover" of non-Communists in the organization was essential to Communist intentions and thus, for example, when a dispute between Farge and Casanova threatened to bring open crisis into the Movement, Maurice Thorez decided against Casanova. [108] By the beginning of 1949, however, because of vigorous activity and the packing of the local and higher level councils with communist militants, the latter had come to dominate the activity of the Peace Movement.

The idea that the Peace Movement was now the potentially most efficacious outlet for support of Soviet foreign policy became rather quickly accepted among the Communist leadership. On December 15, Georges Cogniot wrote in the *Cominform Bulletin* that, given the lack of response to professional and social issues and the broad decline of the CGT on all fronts, it was the possibility of mass action based on the peace issue which "opens up a perspective for the unification of the democratic forces on a far wider scale than that achieved in the

[106] Shulman, *Stalin's Foreign Policy*, p. 85, from the *Cominform Bulletin*, April 1, 1948, p. 3.

[107] For example, although the Breslau congress had been Communist-organized, many non-Communists interested in peace and "banning the bomb" attended nonetheless—among them Julian Huxley from England, O. John Rogge from America, and the Abbot Jean Boulier from France. This sort of relationship was the basis of many "fellow traveler" accusations in later years.

[108] Shulman, *Stalin's Foreign Policy*, p. 89.

past." Although embarrassed by the Thorez statement of February 1949 about the possibility of welcoming the Red Army into Paris, the Peace Movement tried to mount a large-scale campaign on an international level, "confidently led by the French Communist Party," as one Soviet commentator wrote.[109]

The center of the Peace Movement was indeed France. As Shulman has indicated,

There its political objectives could be declared more openly and its prospects were more promising. The French still felt a lingering fascination for the concept of the Third Force, not only in domestic politics but also as a French mission to mediate among the Great Powers. The profound fear of a revived Germany and of an aroused Soviet Union struck a powerful chord in French hearts. Moreover, the tradition of French intellectuals' identifying their progressive aspirations with the Soviet cause went back to the *Clarté* group in the early twenties, which included among others Anatole France, Romain Rolland and Henri Barbusse. These factors rapidly made the Peace Movement a political force of considerable portent in France. There at least the Soviet Union could hope that the commitment of the government to the Western alliance could be reversed by popular resistance.[110]

Ultimately, however, although Communist opposition made somewhat more difficult the already complicated and bitter cleavages surrounding the issues of German rearmament and the nature of the Western alliance, the position of France in the American-dominated Atlantic community was solidified.

Yet the Peace Movement nonetheless achieved some moderate success in terms of mass action. It served as one of the few points of connection between Communists and non-Communists in France during the Cold War. Its main tactical weapon was the signature campaign, which, before the extensive development of public opinion polls, was a dramatic method of making a public show of mass strength. Its great advantage as far as the Communists were concerned was that the proposition to be signed could be phrased broadly enough so that it could not be identified as a Party slogan. For example, the first of these signature campaigns, which produced a letter to President Truman denying that the French government represented the will of the

---

[109] *Ibid.*, pp. 91 and 93, the latter citing E. Rubinin in *Trud*, March 16, 1949, p. 4.
[110] *Ibid.*, p. 93.

French people in adhering to the North Atlantic treaty, was said to have produced "hundreds of thousands" of signatures. Undoubtedly, many people thought they were signing a simple pledge of desire for a neutralist position.

In April 1949, the "First World Congress of Partisans for Peace" took place in Paris, with delegates from some fifty countries attending and the meeting room decorated with doves done by Picasso. The chairman of the Congress was Professor Frédéric Joliot-Curie, French High Commissioner for Atomic Energy and a member of the PCF.[111] Among the speakers were Pietro Nenni, Yves Farge, and Alexander Fadeyev. To continue the work of the Congress, a Permanent World Peace Committee was named, with its headquarters in Paris, and a magazine, *In Defense of Peace*, was created to publicize the "peace" point of view. During the following months the Peace Movement kept active, with a demonstration against General Bradley on August 5 and a signature campaign for a "Peace Ballot" in October, which supposedly gathered some seven million signatures for "international peace" by the end of 1949.[112] In November 1949, the Cominform adopted a resolution presented by Mikhail Suslov, declaring the Peace Movement should now become the "pivot of [the] entire activity" of the communist parties; [113] and by 1950, the World Peace Movement undoubtedly constituted a tool of greater immediate tactical value to

[111] One year later, on April 28, 1950, Joliot-Curie was dismissed from his position for having stated that "no communist scientist could ever use his knowledge in a war against the Soviet Union."

[112] At the same time, the PCF leadership was having some trouble prevailing upon its militants to emphasize the vague issue of "peace" at the expense of economic and social demands, particularly since such a tactic obliged them to make what they considered to be humiliating overtures to socialists, Catholics, and others who had recently excluded the Communists from other organizations. Moreover, during the last half of 1949, food prices began to rise considerably, industrial production was off, and the franc had been devalued—all of which made the rank and file once again extremely nervous about the security of their daily lives. One partially successful remedy was to merge the two issues, as in the first months of 1950 when the CGT called a series of strikes in defense and defense-related industries which, because based publicly upon demands for higher wages, fell outside legal restrictions on strikes in vital industries. This was the immediate stimulus for the second series of antisabotage measures posed in the Assembly in March 1950.

[113] Cited in Shulman, *Stalin's Foreign Policy*, p. 132.

the Soviets than the Western European Communist parties themselves.

The importance of the peace issue in France was illustrated at the 12th PCF Congress (April 2–6, 1950). One gets an idea of the tenor of this Congress, held in a tense Cold War atmosphere, from the "Manifesto to the People of France," in which the congress delegates proclaimed that "The government is betraying the interests of the homeland. . . . The imperialists want to attack the country of socialism, the Soviet Union. . . . The American imperialists. . . . want to make of France a reservoir of cannon fodder. . . . Peace hangs by a thread!" [114] Only if one is sensitive to the moment—in particular to the profound fears of renewed war in both West and East blocs—can one empathize with the chord of public feeling upon which the Party sought to improvise. The priority of Party tasks was outlined by Maurice Thorez: "The report of the Central Committee . . . makes it a duty of the organizations and militants of the Party . . . to place all effort into (1) participating actively in the signature campaign for the interdiction of the atomic bomb; (2) developing a mass action against the handling, transport, and fabrication of war materiel; (3) making known . . . the eleven-point program." [115] Among the eleven points were denunciation of the Marshall Plan and the Atlantic alliance; reaffirmation of the 1944 Franco-Soviet agreement (theoretically still in effect, though in reality a dead letter); the conclusion of a peace treaty between France, the United States, the Soviet Union, Britain, and the People's Republic of China; recognition of the East German State; recognition of the insurgent government in Vietnam and repatriation of the French Expeditionary Force. [116]

The role of the Peace Movement in the hoped-for achievement of these objectives was to be large. Ultimately, however, the Peace Movement could not but fail to demonstrate its fundamental weakness as a Communist tactical weapon, and one can say that no significant policy decision was more than marginally influenced by "peace" agitation. Although moderately successful in its efforts to rally mass sup-

[114] "Documents du 12ème Congrès" *Cahiers du communisme* (May 1950): 51–52.
[115] "Résolution sur le rapport du Comité central, *ibid.*, p. 18.
[116] "Programme de rénovation nationale du PCF," *ibid.*, pp. 49–50.

port, the Communists' intentions would have required an organization of a size impossible to create. Thus, it was noted in the *Cahiers du communisme* of May 1950 that despite certain progress, "The number of Committees for Defense of the Peace and of local councils, and their activity in liaison with the masses, are not sufficient in terms of the demands of the hour and the existing possibilities." [117]

In sum, what did the Peace Movement achieve for the French Communist movement? For one thing, it provided psychological sustenance for the rank and file, occupying their energies when other outlets were denied them. In this sense it did much to preserve the morale of the beleaguered movement and reaffirmed the sense of a definite Communist "community," which had come under attack from the "outside" (See chapter 9). For another thing, it provided a means of action for the Communists, which, although more or less purely symbolic in terms of results, nonetheless could be used to measure success, for example, in terms of thousands of signatures. Finally, the Peace Movement, as all aspects of Communist organization, could be worked into the millenarian predictions of Marxism-Leninism in the manner of Thorez: effective use of the Peace Movement would reverse the Third Force coalition in parliament, thus resulting in the return of the Communists to power,

In a government of democratic unity which will satisfy the demands of the working people, restore and extend the freedom of the people, and bring France back to the camp of democracy and peace. In this way we shall lead our country along the road toward socialism. . . . The Cominform Resolution holds that the mass peace movement can lead to power, [that it is] a formula broader, if possible, than our slogan of a Government of Democratic Union. . . . Read that again! . . . It is not a question of beginning all over again with 1934 or 1936.[118]

By hinting at the potential of a "step toward socialism" through the Peace Movement, Thorez was playing on the eternal desire of the Communist mind to believe that "the revolution" is only a matter of time, that its inevitability is only a matter of when, not whether. For the true believers, the exclusion and isolation of the French Commu-

[117] *Ibid.*, p. 40.   [118] *L'Humanité*, December 13, 1949, pp. 3–4.

nists during the Cold War was therefore perceived either as merely a temporary setback, as a proof that the final cataclysm was being prepared, or both.[119]

[119] This chapter, which has been concerned mainly with the exclusion and isolation of the Communists in France during the Cold War, in consequence has not dealt with the problem of de-Stalinization to any great extent. This is intentional, for the dominant pattern 1947–62 is best understood apart from the question of de-Stalinization. The French Communists have been the slowest of the Western European parties to de-Stalinize, and thus it has seemed more useful to discuss the question of de-Stalinization 1956–62 as a preface to the post-1962 evolution. Aspects of the problem are therefore discussed in the next chapter and in chapter 9.

Chapter Seven

TOWARD WHAT "UNITY OF THEORY AND PRACTICE"? (1962–1972)

If he compares the Fourth and Fifth Republic's constitutions in the abstract, an uninformed reader might be inclined to wonder exactly what the "change of regime" was all about. Notwithstanding, political institutions and practices in France have been fundamentally transformed in at least two ways since the Gaullist *treize mai:* First, as opposed to the Fourth Republic's unstable and incoherent pattern of governmental majorities, the Fifth Republic has been dominated by a consistent and relatively unified political coalition. Moreover, the Gaullist coalition of 1958 soon thereafter transformed itself into what the late Otto Kirchheimer was the first to call a catchall party. The UNR–UDR is relatively unencumbered by doctrine, is interested fundamentally in winning elections, and has based its essential unity upon a powerful President of the Republic, whose electoral legitimacy was rendered direct and universal by the constitutional reform of 1962.

Secondly, and related to the first in ways to be explained shortly, the nature of political opposition in French politics has been at least partially transformed from the Fourth Republic pattern. For one thing, during the period 1958–62 the socialists and part of the Center seceded from the initial Gaullist majority. At first they returned to a form of quasi-fundamental opposition, then—after the bitter quarrel over the constitutional referendum of 1962 had somewhat attenuated—both groups accepted the fact of a popularly elected President and once more began to seek their goals within the new institutional context.

At the same time, from 1956 onward the French Communist Party progressively revised essential aspects of its doctrine and strategy. Known by the code terms "de-Stalinization," "peaceful coexistence," and "peaceful transition to socialism," this transformation of Communist doctrine has helped the PCF to partially escape from the sterile position to which it was confined during the period 1947–62. The French socialists—pushed by the Gaullists, pulled by the Communists, and threatened with permanent decline—have in effect decided to reopen the "dialogue" with the communists that failed three times previously: in 1921–22, 1934–38, and 1944–47. The most significant result of this new dialogue, the Commom Program of June 27, 1972, is at once a symbol of renewed Left-wing unity—one of the oldest myths in the French political culture—and a sign of a strong tendency toward a bipolarization of the French party system around two coalitions.

The uncertain future of the new Communist-socialist coalition will be discussed in more detail at the conclusion of this study. The important point here is rather that the second great modification in French politics since the advent of the Fifth Republic—the continuing transformation of the French Left—has worked to such an extent that while still excluded from effective participation in national political institutions, the French Communists are no longer isolated. It may not be an exaggeration to say that resolution of the double exclusion from power of the Communists and the non-Communist Left is at present the most important remaining obstacle to an eventual consensus on political institutions in France—if not with regard to French economy and society as a whole.

1958–62: The PCF and the Change in Regime

Isaac Deutscher argues persuasively that Stalin's conception of "the building of socialism" (i.e., the Soviet interest) was extended, owing to the increased Soviet influence resulting from World War II, from a doctrine of "socialism in one country" to what Deutscher labels "socialism in one zone." From the beginning there was implicit in this conception, which Churchill chose to call "the Iron Curtain," a cynical utilitarian attitude toward the Western European communist parties, which was expressed as a tacit diplomatic policy that allowed the "Socialist state to adhere to such international pragmatic sanctions as the division of zones of influence, by which the Socialist state strengthens the position of capitalism in one part of the world, provided that, as *quid pro quo*, it is allowed to strengthen its own position and expand in another." [1] We have seen how the Communist movement in France received (however voluntarily) precious little from the "two bloc" situation. Thus, when the crisis of May 1958 occurred, the French Communists were hardly in a position to consider that a revolutionary situation, *their* revolutionary situation, had arrived.

In one sense, this entire study is an analysis of the nature and action of a communist party that is waiting for the revolutionary moment in a liberal capitalist society. The way in which the PCF attempted to explain the change of regime and justify its own results in 1958 is of particular interest in this regard. The PCF's analysis of de Gaulle's return to power was conditioned by doctrine. It asserted that the key change was the modification of the relation of class forces, a retrograde event that was detrimental to the working class and adventitious to the capitalists. [2] Communist doctrine had considered the Fourth Republic to be a fully developed capitalist bourgeois regime, and while not the best of all possible regimes, it was said to be more advantageous to the "unfolding of the long-term proletarian struggle" than would a Gaullist-style republic, characterized by "authoritarian personal" rule, which might even "open the way toward fascism." Thus, after May 1958, because a socialist revolution remained a pipedream, the PCF took up "the battle for democracy" (albeit "bourgeois" democracy!) as its "primary task" in France. Maurice Thorez, during the referendum campaign that was to give popular sanction to establish a Fifth Republic, made the following declaration of this change in direction:

The working class is far from indifferent as to the form in which the bourgeois state presents itself. It knows the advantages of bourgeois democ-

[1] Isaac Deutscher, *Stalin*, p. 537.
[2] For a similar point, see Bon in Bon et al., *Le communisme en France*, p. 125.

racy, the rights which this democracy assures it. We know well that the bourgeois Republic, Parliament, and universal suffrage represent enormous progress, progress which permits the proletariat to become conscious of itself and to organize itself. Our Party . . . declares openly that the choice which is now presented is between personal dictatorship and democracy. . . . In the advent of [this] dictatorial regime . . . it is clear that the only question posed was the defense of democratic liberties and institutions against personal power, against reactionary dictatorship.[3]

In typically ambiguous fashion, when the distinction between "bourgeois" and "proletarian" democracy did not suit the present purpose, the Communist line defended merely "democracy" against the threat of "reaction" in the class struggle. While the PCF urged defeat of the referendum, however, it did not advocate a simple return to the Fourth Republic after the temporary emergency rule of General de Gaulle:

The cause of the evils from which France is suffering is neither democracy nor the parliamentary regime; but on the contrary the permanent violation of the will of the universal suffrage and of the principles of the representative regime through anticommunism. . . . To refuse to take into account the votes of six million Frenchmen and to exclude their representatives from participation in the institutions is to falsify the normal working of democracy. . . . The remedy to the disorder and governmental impotence does not consist in throwing democracy overboard, but rather in assuring its normal functioning . . . in giving the working class and its Party the place which they are due in Parliament and in the government at the side of the others.[4]

This line was the basis, during May–November 1958, of a Communist proposal for a "government of republican defense" against Gaullist intentions, a platform which received but little attention among the population in general.[5] Only such a government, asserted the

[3] From a speech by Thorez to the PCF National Congress of July 17–18, 1958, "Union et action pour le 'non' au referendum-plébiscite," p. 10.

[4] From a resolution of the Central Committee, June 10, 1958, published in "Contre la dictature, la guerre et la misère," brochure, 24 pp. (pp. 23–24).

[5] The perpetual ambiguity of Communists' analyses and their convoluted proposals have often worked to make them either unintelligible or contradictory in the eyes of popular opinion. François Fejtö noted how in 1958 many were "bewildered to see the PCF limit itself to the defense of the Fourth Republic, which it had attacked so violently for many years. . . . The negative vote [on the referendum of September 28] requested by the Communists not only seemed destined to entail . . . the reestablishment of the old constitution but also seemed to be a show of solidarity with the to-

Communists, could preserve the (bourgeois) republic, the best possible regime given the balance of class forces in France. Thus, for them:

Despite the veil of legality in which he covered himself and the apparent respect of the formalities of investiture, de Gaulle has been carried into power not by the free will of the National Assembly, but by the *coup de force* of Algiers and Ajaccio. His is a fundamentally illegitimate government, resulting from violence and a reactionary menace.[6]

The Gaullist landslide in the referendum of September 28, 1958 (79 percent "yes") created a serious doctrinal problem for the Communists: "the people" had pronounced themselves resoundingly in favor of the Gaullist coup and the idea of a new regime; how could the Party deny that the referendum of 1958 was not so legitimate as those of 1946? Thus, as the Fifth Republic became stabilized and showed signs of endurance in the course of its first half-decade of existence, the PCF was forced to change its line to a point at which its attitude toward the Fifth Republic resembled closely its attitude toward its predecessor. The Fifth Republic was no longer pictured as a "retrograde" regime, a regression from a more advanced stage, but rather as a classic bourgeois regime, which could directly precede a transition to socialism.

The original slogan used by the Communist Party to characterize the new regime was "a presidential regime oriented toward personal dictatorship and opening the way to fascism." [7] In reporting on the formulation of this slogan to the 15th Congress, Georges Cogniot noted that the connection with fascism had been added on to a less extreme charge in order to emphasize the "new dangers" of Gaullism.[8] As it became apparent that the epithet was of little political value and as the extreme right moved into opposition to de Gaulle on the

---

tality of the regime that had just failed." *(The French Communist Party and the Crisis of International Communism*, pp. 98–99.)

[6] From a widely circulated pamphlet "De Gaulle: Ce qu'il est, ce qu'il veut," dated June 11, 1958 and signed by the Central Committee, pp. 2 and 8. In July, Thorez again took up the question in terms of a denial of legitimacy to de Gaulle: "Since June 1, France has known a regime of personal and military dictatorship, which was imposed on it by threat and force. . . . The establishment of such a government represents . . . a rupture with the legitimacy, with the very bases of the Republic. . . ." See "Union et Action . . . ," pp. 3 and 14–15.

[7] PCF–15, (June, 1959), *Thèses*, p. 518.   [8] PCF–15, p. 501.

Algerian question between the years 1959 and 1961, the charge of fascism was quickly dropped. Also in 1959, the Party line began to call for "the restoration and renovation of democracy" [9] the means to which was to be the summoning of a new Constituent Assembly in order to "restore" democracy (i.e., restore a parliamentary republic free of "personal power") and to "renovate" it (e.g., through the introduction of proportional representation and a unicameral parliament). [10] That even all this would merely imply an "advanced" form of a regime that already had existed is indicated by this excerpt from the "Political Resolution" of the 16th Congress:

> The restoration and the renovation of democracy is a stage in the struggle for socialism. . . . But an essential step. Not because such is our will but because such is the logic of history. . . . Only the revisionists . . . can confuse the restoration and the renovation of democracy with the arrival of a socialist republic. . . .. The program proposed . . . is not a socialist program, it is a democratic program. [11]

Thus, because the Fifth Republic consisted of a "retrograde" set of institutions, a return to "authentic" or "true" bourgeois democracy was posited as a "necessary" step on the road to socialism, whereas during the Third and Fourth Republics a further intermediate regime was not cited.

As the Fifth Republic established itself during the period 1959–62, the Party's demand for a "restoration and renovation" of democracy caused fears among the leadership that it was projecting a reactionary image, since, on the surface at least, it did seem to imply a soft spot for the Fourth Republic. De Gaulle's successful conclusion of the Algerian war and the people's approval in 1962 of the proposal that the President be elected by universal suffrage were both evidence of the permanence of the new institutions, and in the light of these constraints, the Party dropped this slogan and began to use a less explicit phrase, "a true democracy," to indicate the general goal of the minimum program. The presidential election of 1965, in which the PCF participated and supported the "united Left" candidacy of François

---

[9] E.g., PCF–15, Duclos report, p. 277.

[10] See also the 1945 PCF constitutional project, chapter 5.

[11] PCF–16, pp. 573–74. See also the PCF line in 1944–46 and in 1936–38, and the present Communist analysis of the "advanced democracy" stage (see chapter 8).

Mitterrand (see below) was a further turning point in the Communist attitude toward the Fifth Republic, for the electorate had ratified the new institution by its large participation (only 15 percent of the voters abstained) and high general interest.[12] Furthermore, in the 1965 election General de Gaulle was forced into a runoff which was widely perceived as a victory for the Left. It was however at the same time a blow to the original Communist position because it tended to further legitimize the regime in the eyes of the public—a legitimation for which Communist participation in the election was in no small way responsible.[13] Finally, from the early 1960s onward the Communists had been finding it increasingly difficult to oppose de Gaulle on foreign policy questions: his disengagement of France from rather complete subordination to American foreign policy and his spectacular gestures (acceptance of independence for Algeria and other French colonies; withdrawal from the unified command structure of NATO; recognition of the People's Republic of China; the blocking of European political integration) were of such a character that the Soviet leadership publicly endorsed French policy.[14]

Altogether, by 1965 the French Communists had been constrained to admit that the origins of the Fifth Republic had become a moot point, and that the regime had been accepted by popular opinion to an extent that more or less obliged its recognition as an authentic form of "bourgeois democracy." While "the falsification of the normal functioning of democracy" in the Fourth Republic had been complicated in the Fifth by the new element of "personal power," it was no longer

[12] See esp. the comprehensive volume edited by the Centre d'étude de la vie politique française, *L'élection présidentielle de décembre 1965*, in particular pp. 99–284 on the campaign itself.

[13] The runoff itself was not forced by the united Left candidacy alone however; without the candidacy of the Centrist Jean Lecanuet, de Gaulle would have probably been elected on the first ballot.

[14] Whereas in 1964, Thorez was still attempting to rationalize these positive aspects of Gaullist policy as the result of force of circumstance ("If we pronounce ourselves resolutely against personal power, we are not a priori against one or another measure which may be dictated to it by an uncontrollable conjuncture," PCF–18, p. 31), by 1967 the new Secretary-General, Waldeck Rochet, had admitted that some aspects of Gaullist policy were "positive" in and of themselves. ("The French Communist Party is opposed to the negative and grave aspects of . . . Gaullist policy." *Ibid.*, p. 33.) The "Servin-Casanova group" had been condemned as revisionist in 1961 in part for having adopted such an attitude too soon.

either convenient or realistic for the Communists to assert that the Fifth Republic was an example of "bourgeois dictatorship." And whereas for most Frenchmen this subtle and involved doctrinal evolution had neither much sense nor much significance, for the communists it meant that they were no longer struggling to regain lost ground, so to speak. Rather, they were working once again with "opening the socialist transformation" in mind as "the next step." [15]

In sum, the changes in Communist doctrine regarding the Fifth Republic, and PCF participation in its institutions (so far as this participation has gone) have resulted in a partial and ambiguous legitimation of the regime in the manner of the Communist attitude toward the parliamentary republics of 1875–1940 and 1946–58.[16] Whereas during 1958–65 the French Communists considered the Fifth Republic to be completely illegitimate because "retrograde," since that time their doctrinal line has come to accord it the ambiguous justification characteristic of the Marxist-Leninist perspective on authentic bourgeois democracy. And while Communist behavior within the institutions themselves has, because of the constraints upon it, not evolved a great deal, the transformation of doctrine that occurred during the first years of the Fifth Republic deserves close scrutiny from the observer interested in comprehending the psychology of Communist movements of opposition. In general terms, one may consider this doctrinal evolution as evidence that the Marxist-Leninist view of the dynamic of social change—a progressive and inevitable unfolding of the class struggle on ever-higher levels of dialectical synthesis—still anchors the French Communist mentality and implies an ambivalent relation between the Communist movement and the status quo.

[15] The evolution of the PCF doctrine regarding the "socialist transformation" itself is analyzed in chapter 8.

[16] For a similar point see Lavau in Bon et al, *Le communisme en France*, pp. 38–55. Lavau, however, argues this "partial legitimation" on the fact of Communist participation itself. While participation is not in itself legitimacy insofar as the Communist perspective is considered, it is reasonable to argue that Communist participation may influence others' attitudes, and even, as Lavau suggests, that participation may be eroding the PCF position itself. This question would bear a study of the Communist rank and file attitude.

A Permanent Transformation
of the French Left?

One may pass rather quickly over the statistics on Communist "penetration" of the institutions of the Fifth Republic, for with one important exception the Fourth Republic patterns have not undergone changes implying significant modification of structure or function. For example, after having stabilized around 1955, the PCF membership varied until a few years ago between 250,000 and 300,000.[17] Since the events of May–June 1968 a slow upswing has occurred, so that the limiting figures are now 300,000 to 350,000. Statistics from the various elections since 1958 show a retention of somewhat over one-fifth of the total votes cast, and a somewhat lower percentage of total registered voters.[18] The percentage of Communists elected in the Senate has remained below 6 percent of the total, while the figures for the General Councils show that the Communists continue to hold between 5 and 7 percent of the total available seats.[19] The figures for municipal elections continue to demonstrate the concentrated and localized character of Communist power in the country as a whole. Nonetheless the last three municipal elections (1959, 1965, 1971) seem to show a steady progression of Communist strength among the opposition parties, adding weight to the PCF claim to be the preeminent opposition to Gaullism.[20] Only in terms of represen-

[17] Kriegel, *Les communistes français*, p. 13.

[18] Of votes cast since 1958, the PCF has had between 20–22 percent of the total; of the total registered voters, the PCF electorate has represented from 14.3 percent (1962) to 17.8 percent (1967). The difference in figures is accounted for by the fact that much less of the potential PCF electorate abstains than does that of other parties.

[19] Both figures have gone up slightly since 1962. In the cantonal elections to the General Councils in 1967, the Communists—for the first time—won an absolute majority in a department, that of Seine-Saint Denis. Also in 1967, they "governed" another General Council in coalition with the SFIO, that of Val-de-Marne. Both are in the "red belt" surrounding Paris. In 1970 the PCF-SFIO coalition in the Val-de-Marne was replaced by a Gaullist coalition.

[20] For example, in the 1971 municipal elections the Gaullist coalitions won eight new municipal majorities while the Communists won five. Of the 192 municipalities of over 30,000 inhabitants, the opposition had 114 in 1965 and 119 in 1971. *Le Monde* commented therefore "it appears in a striking fashion that this evolution is imputable essen-

tatives in the National Assembly has a significant change occurred in the Fifth Republic pattern, and because this change is tied in closely with the recent evolution of the French Left as a whole, it will be better to discuss it further on in context.

The partial reintegration of the French Communists into the political system of the Fifth Republic, after the exclusion and isolation of the Cold War years, is essentially the story of the attempts at unity of the Left undertaken since 1962. This still tenuous and incomplete reconstruction of a link between Communists and non-Communists has followed what one might accurately term a dialectical pattern.

The first events in this process were catalyzed more by the pressure of Gaullist domination of the fragmented Left opposition than by a sudden desire on the part of the French socialists to seek once again to move beyond the split at Tours. In respect of alliance, whether electoral or otherwise, the PCF naturally looked first toward the SFIO (it was not merely a banal statement to remark that the PCF could not expect to vault into parliamentary politics again on the backs of the MRP and Radicals). Thus, Guy Mollet, the SFIO Secretary-General until 1969, was probably the single most important figure in Communist plans to break out of isolation and exclusion (at least up to the presidential election of 1965, when François Mitterrand became an equally dominant figure). Mollet's control of the SFIO organization was to prove the key that fit the lock in Communist chains.

Having in 1958 been one of those who were instrumental in de Gaulle's return and therefore having assured Communist impotence at that moment, during the next few years Mollet first left the cabinet and then moved into fundamental opposition, partly over the Gaullist policy in Algeria (Mollet himself was an advocate of *Algérie française*) and more basically over *pouvoir personnel*.[21] Although Mollet did

---

tially to the gain of the PCF" (March 23, 1971, p. 1). Having declined from 19,872 total municipal councilors in 1959 to 16,254 in 1965 (*L'année politique*, 1965, p. 25), the PCF made a gain of several thousand in 1971 (*Le Monde*, March 23, 1971, p. 10, citing PCF figures).

[21] In 1958, Mollet's support of de Gaulle, in defiance of both the SFIO militants and the Party congress (its "antidemocratic" action also isolated the SFIO leadership in the Socialist International), had led to a splinter faction of the SFIO forming the *Parti socialiste autonome* (PSA), which would soon be transformed into the *Parti socialiste unifié* (PSU). At the same time, numerous members of the Radicals and the UDSR formed a

not admit that his opposition to de Gaulle had become intransigent until September 1962,[22] during 1960 and 1961 his increasing disenchantment was fairly apparent. The PCF leadership, whose slogan "Unity of the Working Class at All Costs!" had fallen on deaf ears in May–June 1958, now sought to take advantage of the situation by attempting to present the Gaullist regime as a common enemy. At the 16th Congress (May 1961) Maurice Thorez stated the theme almost brazenly:

Our Congress calls all republicans to rally to the working class in order to combat the [Gaullist] regime of arbitrary power. . . . This is a point on which socialists and communists are in agreement.

Given that, why not come to an agreement, to move to action on this question? A united front is nothing more than that: common action regarding a problem on which there is unanimity. If we were of the same opinion on all questions, we would not speak of a united front. Unification would be a fact. [But there is] a point of agreement. On this point we propose therefore that action be undertaken from a common accord between the Communist Party, the SFIO, the PSU, and the other groups seeking democracy.[23]

Despite the SFIO decline and despite the offer from Thorez, Mollet still refused to deal formally with the Communists. Nonetheless, during 1962 several important signs of a trend toward unity developed out of opposition to de Gaulle. The PCF, SFIO, Radicals, PSU, UDSR, and MRP parliamentary groups all went on record opposing the constitutional referendum of October 28, 1962: some because they opposed a universally elected President and some because of the manner in which de Gaulle had presented the referendum.[24] The Communists were opposed on both grounds.

Although the SFIO refused to undertake a common campaign against the referendum, the PCF, through its slogan "Let us march side by side and strike together!" was able to draw attention successfully to the mutual goal, and thereby to score a minor psychological

---

Union des forces démocratiques (UFD). In 1958, like the SFIO, neither the PSA nor the UFD would consider an alliance with the PCF, despite entreaties of the latter.

[22] Jean Ranger, "L'évolution du PCF et ses relations avec la SFIO," RFSP, 16, no. 1 (February 1964): 78.

[23] PCF–16, Thorez speech, p. 614–615.

[24] In bypassing parliament, de Gaulle violated the spirit, if not the letter, of the Fifth Republic's Constitution.

coup for its unity policy. Then in the legislative elections of November, the PCF announced an unforeseen and rather bold tactic: despite the lack of a formal PCF-SFIO electoral alliance, Communist candidates were to stand down unilaterally on the second ballot in favor of better-placed socialist candidates. In between the first and second ballots, Mollet unexpectedly took up the initiative, announcing that "The Communists [say] we must beat the UNR on the runoff ballot. I find that, in this domain, the Communists and we are speaking the same language." [25] Thus, for the first time since local elections at the end of World War II, the Communists had achieved a reciprocal electoral tactic. Because of this tactic, the PCF's representation rose from 10 to 41 seats, the SFIO's from 40 to 65 seats, and the Radicals' from 35 to 43. Therefore at the Central Committee meeting at Malakoff on December 13–14, 1962, Waldeck Rochet, quoting the Gaullist Minister of the Interior, Roger Frey, noted that Communist support was the determining factor for 35 seats obtained by the socialists, while the Radicals owed 10 of their 43 seats to the Communists. [26] At the same meeting, Maurice Thorez drew the conclusion that the Cold War atmosphere on the French Left had begun to mellow and that the great lesson of the referendum and election campaigns was an end to sectarian behavior. This implied, he concluded, "the most diverse forms of the united front." [27] The corollary of this new situation was that "revisionism," the "principal danger" to the Party line in 1961, when the Servin-Casanova group had been condemned for its "positive appreciation of certain aspects of Gaullist policy," had now become a secondary focus of "vigilance," while "dogmatism" and "sectarianism" were the new "principal menaces to the hopes of the working class." In other words, the French Communist Party— moved both by the general evolution in international affairs since 1956 and the specific impetus of electoral imperatives—was espousing ever more openly some of the changes characteristic of the process of de-Stalinization.

The tendency toward return of the Communists to the national po-

[25] Ranger, "L'évolution du PCF," p. 79.

[26] Rochet report at Malakoff, p. 4. In a shocking victory, the Radical Berthoin bested the former Gaullist Prime Minister, Michel Debré, with the aid of Communist votes.

[27] Thorez speech at Malakoff, p. 39.

litical mainstream was not welcomed by all, or perhaps even most, of the non-Communist Left. In particular, a reformist and center-oriented wing of the SFIO, headed by Gaston Defferre, the Mayor of Marseilles, remained opposed to even purely electoral bargains with the PCF. It was Defferre's attempt to create an opposition *rassemblement* of the Center-Left that stalled Communist hopes for further progress during the next three years.

While probably immediately motivated by a desire to halt the incipient rapprochement of socialists and Communists, the action of Gaston Defferre during the period 1963–65 quickly became focused upon the presidential election of 1965, the first to be held under the provisions of the October 1962 referendum. His presidential candidacy eventually developed into a two-year effort to transform the French party system on the Left by uniting the disparate non-Communist parties and groups into a new political force, the Democratic Socialist Federation.

Originally sponsored by an independent group of political clubs and journals rather than by his own party, Defferre at first had to be more or less "persuaded" to run for President. After months of discussions he announced his candidacy in December 1963.[28] Despite considerable hostility from the old-guard Mollet leadership, who had been handed a *fait accompli*, a special SFIO congress convened in February 1964 endorsed the Defferre candidacy out of consideration for the probable effect an intraparty struggle would have upon both militant and public opinion. In fact, the idea of a renovation of the non-Communist Left and the Center, which after five years were showing the strain of attempting to survive between Gaullism and communism, had by now seized the interest of the rank and file. Because of this, a small group of clubmen and journalists were able to impose a Defferre candidacy on the SFIO and eventually on other parties as well. At the same time, a bitter feud simmering just below the surface of events was opened between Defferre and Mollet, who correctly perceived the former's presidential campaign as an open challenge to

---

[28] It appears that the Club Jean Moulin was the first to urge a Defferre candidacy. Later, other clubs joined in, as well as the magazine *L'Express*, run by Jean-Jacques Servan-Schreiber. See Frank L. Wilson, *The French Democratic Left*, pp. 110–11, which contains the most useful account of the Defferre coalition attempt.

his preeminence in the SFIO and his power among the leaders of the non-Communist opposition.[29]

The Defferre proposal to unite the groups and organizations backing his candidacy into a new Democratic Socialist Federation was not made formally until April 1965. In the meantime, apart from his program [30] and the contacts and negotiations he began with groups who had not previously worked together before,[31] the great innovation of Defferre's activity was a new attitude toward the Communists.

Since the Congress of Tours, Communists and socialists had demonstrated to each other either hostility and mutual exclusion, or temporary alliances at the top among the existing parties (as had been the case during the Popular Front and Tripartism). Defferre's idea, based on an innovative strategy developed largely in the Club Jean Moulin,[32] was to create a new and dynamic political formation between the Communists and Gaullists, which, while not allying formally with the PCF, would attract a large part of its electorate and win over a significant part of the younger militants and cadres. The strategy was that such losses would oblige the PCF leadership to accept a decisive liberalization, and that ultimately the "Communist problem" might even be eliminated by co-optation of its social bases. Concurrent with Defferre's efforts, however, Guy Mollet continued the socialist-Communist contacts begun in 1962.[33] This meant the SFIO again presented an ambivalent alliance posture. It was simultaneously negotiating two possible approaches toward the Communists, and in the end was pitting Defferre and his "new men" against Mollet and the SFIO *ancien régime*.

By the time he actually made public his proposal for a Democratic Socialist Federation in April 1965, Defferre's presidential candidacy had become "irrevocably tied" to the success of his plan for a new

---

[29] *Ibid.*, pp. 111–12.   [30] Outlined in *Un nouvel horizon* (Paris, 1965).

[31] See Frank L. Wilson, *The French Democratic Left*, pp. 117–19; Jean André Faucher, *La gauche française sous de Gaulle*, pp. 133–59. Raymond Barrillon, *La gauche française en mouvement*, and Jean Poperen, *La gauche française: Le nouvel âge, 1958–1965* are also useful.

[32] See their collective work, *Un parti pour la gauche* (Paris, 1965).

[33] For example, in January–February 1964, *Le Populaire* ran a series of articles entitled "Les communistes et nous," answering a series of articles in *L'Humanité* of December 1963. See Wilson, *French Democratic Left*, pp. 122, 231.

party.[34] Outside of the continuing struggle for dominance between himself and Mollet, Defferre's major strategic problem was to negotiate a coalition of socialists and Christian democrats (MRP) in support of his candidacy. However, the dominant sentiment in the SFIO was against allying firmly with a "clerical" party, and the MRP itself was split among a rather minor Gaullist faction, a strictly centrist group, and a group favorable to the Defferre plan. In May 1965, both the SFIO and MRP congresses endorsed Defferre for President, but this apparent victory was merely the lull before the storm. When negotiations about the creation of the new party organization began on June 15, it soon became clear that the MRP (led by Joseph Fontanet) and the Mollet faction in the SFIO had merely been playing a waiting game. Within three days, the negotiations had reached a deadlock and were broken off. In consequence of the failure of the Democratic Socialist Federation, one week thereafter Defferre withdrew his candidacy for the presidency.

The Communists, to be sure, had opposed the Defferre plan all along, and had announced they would enter their own candidate in the presidential election if the socialists chose to move toward the Center parties rather than toward themselves.[35] Yet the PCF leadership was hesitant to present a Communist candidate, for this would no doubt be viewed as a *de facto* legitimation (through wrongly) of the new presidential institution, which Party doctrine continued to characterize as unconstitutional, or at least unconstitutionally established. Moreover, since the Communists had little to gain in the election, it was tactically preferable to build another bridge to the non-Communist opposition, as this was more fundamental to the long-term strategy.

Nonetheless, it had become clear by the spring of 1965 that a Communist would be presented, if only to prevent the Center-Left Defferre candidacy from making a strong enough showing to weaken the case for an alliance of the Left and Extreme Left. During the first

[34] *Ibid.*, p. 124.

[35] In a rather bizarre tacit coalition, the Gaullists and Communists had allied in the municipal elections of March 1965 to attempt to defeat Defferre in Marseilles, and thus to permanently damage his candidacy for the presidency. The attempt was unsuccessful. No doubt the Gaullists at this time did not believe a PCF-SFIO presidential alliance was conceivable.

years of the Fifth Republic, the Communists had sought to gain acceptance for the contention that any new political majority had necessarily to include themselves. The failure of Gaston Defferre in May–June 1965 had now lent credence to this claim and the sudden and spectacular emergence of François Mitterrand as a Left unity candidate in the summer and fall of 1965 was the clearest sign that after a two and one-half year hiatus the momentum in favor of unity had swung once again toward the Communists.

As part of the de-Stalinization of Communist doctrine that had developed slowly in the PCF after the 20th CPSU Congress, the PCF had by 1965 affirmed several key revisions, which closed at least some of the theoretical distance between themselves and the socialists. Moving from the most fundamental revision, the doctrine of "peaceful coexistence," the French Communists went on to embrace the doctrine of "peaceful revolution," or "peaceful transition to socialism," along with the corollary that this peaceful transition could be accomplished in a "multiple party" situation both during and after the revolution.[36] Although the sincerity of these doctrinal changes was at first highly in doubt almost everywhere, this evolution in words was evinced in such deeds as Khruschev's successful, though politically inconclusive, visit to France from March 23 to April 3, 1960, and the Soviets' behavior in ending the Cuban Missile Crisis and in signing the Partial Test Ban Treaty.

These solid pieces of evidence of Communist intentions rendered discussion, and perhaps even negotiation, with the domestic and the foreign Parties somewhat more plausible than it had been at any time since 1947. For the next three years François Mitterrand was to be the center of a series of events that would consolidate the informal initiatives of 1962, and would in effect reintegrate the French Communist Party into national politics, at least to the limited extent permitted by the Gaullist majority.

Only one month after the stillbirth of Defferre's Democratic Socialist Federation, a group of leaders of the non-Communist Left demonstrated both that the idea of a realliance was not dead and that the so-

[36] See chapter 8 for a detailed analysis of the transformation of Communist revolutionary doctrine. Here we are concerned primarily with the doctrine's effects on PCF capacities for coalition.

cialist disagreement with the Christian democrats was serious. The form of this proof was that the SFIO, the Radical Party, the USDR, and the Convention of Republican Institutions (CIR) agreed to form a *Fédération de la Gauche démocrate et socialiste* (FGDS) without the MRP. Founded primarily on what remained of the organizational strength of the SFIO and the Radicals (both were much weaker than in former times), the public leadership of the FGDS was assumed by the CIR, partially because of its "new look" but mainly because of its own leadership, in particular Mitterrand.[37] The CIR had already indicated its preferred strategy during the municipal elections of March 1965, when it attempted to foment alliances that would include the PCF. The prominent place it occupied in the new FGDS was a signal that the strategy of electoral alliance with the Communists, favored especially by Mollet and Mitterrand, would determine the orientation of the new organization.

During the summer of 1965, both the formal incorporation of the FGDS and the Mitterrand presidential campaign were prepared. The former went rather smoothly, as the Defferrists did not seek to sabotage the Federation. However, the arrangement for Communist support of a Mitterrand candidacy was more difficult because the Communists insisted that a "common program" be agreed upon beforehand, in order that Left-wing support for Mitterrand be more than simply an electoral strategy. On the other hand, the SFIO leadership intended to make the alliance precisely one of electoral support and nothing more, arguing that conditions had not yet matured sufficiently to talk of a governing coalition. Mitterrand has described the result:

The Executive Committee of the SFIO, which had supported me formally, allowed me to work at the end of a tether which it expected to hold firmly from the opposite end. All contact with the communists was forbidden me under a penalty of disavowal. . . . I did not see emissaries from the commu-

[37] The CIR had been created in 1964. Because it was essentially a federation of the then-flourishing movement of political clubs, it presented a quite dynamic image when compared with the traditional organizations. It is almost certain, however, that Mitterrand's assumption of the presidency resulted from a compromise between the leading Radical and SFIO figures, René Billères and Guy Mollet. It is thus also probable that there was no immediate causal link between the creation of the FGDS and the Mitterrand national presidential candidacy, although they became immediately reinforcing.

nists . . . [until] my last press conference, at which Waldeck Rochet was present. It would have been too much strain on the connection with the socialists.[38]

The primary goal of the Communists was to become part of the Left alliance, however, and by September they had agreed to drop their demand for a common program and had accepted the indignities of a purely electoral alliance conducted mainly in the form of public exchanges in the respective party newspapers.[39] As for their participation in the presidential campaign, Mitterrand himself has said that the Communists were "a loyal and active ally." [40] This was indeed true, despite the fact that during the campaign *Pravda* published an editorial endorsing de Gaulle because of his foreign policy. Immediately thereafter, the new PCF Secretary-General, Waldeck Rochet, had restated publicly his support of Mitterrand, and *Pravda* censured the report of his speech.[41]

Mitterrand's candidacy was successful. It was not a Centrist but the Leftist Mitterrand who had gained a place in the runoff against de Gaulle; furthermore, the electoral alliance held firm, which gave impetus to further negotiations. Moreover, the Communists' support of Mitterrand—despite the wishes of the Soviet leadership—was an in-

[38] *Ma part de vérité: de la rupture à l'unité*, pp. 49–50. Nonetheless, several Mitterrand advisors, notably Roland Dumas, Charles Hernu and Claude Estier, had unofficial contacts with Communist leaders, among them Waldeck Rochet's personal emissary, Jules Borker. Borker is a well-known lawyer, and acts as an "advisor" to the PCF Central Committee.

Waldeck Rochet was by 1964 the effective leader of the PCF. Thorez was ill in 1962–63, and Rochet gradually took over his functions, becoming Secretary-General in 1964. Thorez's death on July 11, 1964, caused neither a power struggle nor a change in policy. For this reason I will not focus on the event.

[39] One may follow the daily events in *L'Humanité*, *Le Populaire* and the CIR paper, *Le Combat républicain* for June–September 1965.

[40] *Ma part*, p. 50.

[41] Mitterrand, *Ma part*, pp. 55–56. Apparently, the role of Waldeck Rochet on the Communist side was as decisive as the role of Mitterrand on the non-Communist side in promoting the rapprochement, and it involved a certain risk, particularly in obtaining agreement from the Politburo hard-liners to drop the demand for a common program. As André Barjonet (an important Communist figure who resigned after May 1968) has revealed: "Waldeck Rochet made his first significant political gamble at the end of 1965, when he prevailed in the Politburo and Central Committee in achieving active support for François Mitterrand as 'unity candidate of the Left.' " (*Le Parti communiste français*, p. 200).

dication that the French Communist Party had moved a step away from unconditional "proletarian nationalism," or more precisely, had perhaps begun to redefine the Stalinist connotations of the term.

The relative closeness of the second ballot (Mitterrand gained 45.5 percent of the vote to de Gaulle's 54.5 percent) had demonstrated, furthermore, that while a Center-Left coalition probably could never become a majority, an alliance between the Left and the extreme Left probably could. Therefore, after 1965, the "Communist problem" was once again of immediate consequence in the highest stakes in French politics.[42]

After the presidential election of December 1965, the Communists immediately showed their desire to continue and deepen the alliance. On January 11, 1966, Waldeck Rochet wrote Guy Mollet asking once again that negotiations begin on a joint governmental program. Mollet, however, while interested in further electoral cooperation, insisted that discussion on a common program would have to come after a previous debate, "a resumption of the public dialogue engaged in 1944 on fundamental questions, notably concerning the objectives and the character of working class action in a capitalist regime and the conditions and guarantees of political democracy."[43] The Communists, while insisting that such a discussion was no longer necessary "since [our] differences are largely resolved,"[44] realized that further gestures would have to be made if the alliance with the socialists, necessary to the new strategy of a peaceful transition to socialism, was to be expanded.

[42] *Results of the presidential election of December 5 and 19, 1965: (percent of valid ballots)*

	1st ballot	2nd ballot
de Gaulle	43.7%	54.5%
Mitterrand	32.2	45.5
Lecanuet	15.8	—
Tixier-Vignancourt	5.3	—
Marcilhacy	1.7	—
Barbu	1.2	—

[43] *Le Monde*, January 28, 1966, p. 1, quoted in Alain Duhamel, "Le Parti communiste et l'élection présidentielle," *Revue française de science politique*, 16, no. 3:545.

[44] *L'Humanité*, January 27, 1966, p. 1. The Communists had in mind their doctrinal acceptance of a multiparty system in a future socialist society in France. While a considerable doctrinal concession, this certainly did not resolve the Communist-socialist differences. See chapter 8.

Thus, during the early months of 1966 a new dialogue on doctrine was undertaken in *L'Humanité* and *Le Populaire,* and while the Communists had not achieved their goal of getting Mollet to discuss a common program, they achieved a minor victory by shifting the discussion from a debate on the "historical necessity" of the Soviet experience (the subject of the 1963–64 dialogue, see note 33) to a discussion of present remaining doctrinal disagreements.[45] In March, a "Week of Marxist Thought" was organized by the Communists. The list of invited speakers—quite diverse—was meant to demonstrate an increasing openmindedness.[46]

The next step in the rapprochement of Communists and non-Communists was an electoral agreement signed between the PCF and the FGDS on December 20, 1966.[47] This agreement formalized the policy of second-ballot withdrawals—practiced informally in 1962 and later in the cantonal elections of 1964 and the municipal elections of 1965—in the coming legislative elections of March 1967. And although the Communists had not yet succeeded in obtaining discussions on a common program, their actions in 1965 indicated their awareness of the significance of even purely electoral alliances: as late as the summer of 1965, a coalition with the Communists had been possible only on a tacit basis. For the first time since the collapse of Tripartism, they now had a formal coalition agreement. Moreover, the document of December 1966 symbolized that the noncommunist Left had agreed to ally with the Communists at the top, in the manner of the Popular Front, rather than to attempt to absorb them, as Defferre's strategy implied.[48]

---

[45] PCF–18, Rochet report, p. 62, and a letter from Mollet to Rochet, February 1, 1966.

[46] The PCF published the week's debates in an interesting volume, *Démocratie et liberté* (Paris, 1966), edited by Roger Garaudy, the symbol, so to speak, of the French Communists' "extended hand" and willingness to dialogue. Garaudy has since been expelled from the Party.

[47] See *Le Monde,* December 22, 1966, p. 1. Waldeck Rochet noted (PCF–18, p. 55) that the meetings of October–December preceding the agreement were the first in which Communists participated openly with other parties in twenty years.

[48] A participant in the negotiations has written of the cooperative atmosphere in which the accord was reached: "Everything went without difficulties. In the Radical Party . . . [the] friends of Félix Gaillard ratified the agreement made with the communists. . . . The most Right-leaning Radical incumbents, Robert Hersant, André

The success of the FGDS-PCF alliance in the 1967 general elections was another proof of the electoral strength of an alliance between the Left and the extreme Left, despite fears that the presence of Communists would frighten away the non-Communist electorate from the coalition. In fact, the substantially fewer abstentions in 1967 than in 1962, indicated the electorate had not been dismayed by the Left coalition, but on the contrary was eager to endorse it. Additional proof of the alliance's success could be found in the electoral gains of both members of the coalition. The PCF increased its share of the vote to 22.5 percent (up from 21.7 percent in 1962), while the FGDS increased its share to 19 percent (up from the approximately 16 percent gathered by the FGDS parties individually in 1962). And most importantly, in terms of seats won, thanks to the mutual withdrawals and the second-ballot rally of a large fraction of Centrist votes (25 to 45 percent, depending on specific cases), the Left alliance could claim extraordinary gains: the PCF rose from 41 to 72 seats, the FGDS from 87 to 118 seats; while the Centrists and *non-inscrits* fell from 49 to 46 and the Gaullist coalition from 276 to 232. Votes from the overseas territories and the rally of several *non-inscrit* deputies were the only means by which the Gaullist coalition was able to preserve a slim majority: 245 seats in a chamber of 487.[49]

Gauthier and Guy Ebrard, [even] imitated this example. . . . Mitterrand, Mollet, and [René] Billères [the Radical leader] had been very firm in their positions" (Faucher, *La gauche française sous de Gaulle*, p. 216). Despite this optimistic evaluation, Frank Wilson is probably more correct that "Of the Federation's political families, the Radicals were the most hostile to the privileged alliance with the PCF . . ." and that "In most cases, the alliance with the PCF was accepted for lack of a better alternative," *The French Democratic Left, 1963–69*, pp. 167–68. Still, Wilson himself notes that "only one or two Radical deputies could claim after 1967 that they had been elected without the help of the PCF voters" (*ibid.*, p. 167). Perhaps this also explains their cooperation.

[49] Chapsal, *La vie politique en France depuis 1940*, p. 586. Still, the Centrist deputies would have prevented a Left cabinet. Within the FGDS, all the members had gained: the SFIO won 10 new seats, the CIR 15 seats, and the Radicals 6 seats. As for the discipline of the electoral alliance, Philip Williams has noted: "Discipline within the Left was more effective than ever before." The PCF was less generous than in 1962, but still withdrew in 15 cases where they had more votes than the FGDS candidate on the first ballot but where the nature of the electorate indicated a Communist could not win. The FGDS, in return, made little use of an "escape clause" by which it could support a Center candidate where a Left candidate had no chance. "The alliance therefore applied almost everywhere, and it was honored. . . . Only four Federation candidates broke discipline and stayed in against a Communist with more votes; they were disavowed by

After the election, on the initiative of the FGDS, a coordinating parliamentary group was formed in the National Assembly. It was called the *Délégation permanente des gauches* (after the coordinating group set up by the *Bloc Républicain* in 1902). The group leadership met before each important vote in the Assembly, and owing to its efforts "the FGDS and PCF voted together on all the major political votes taken in the legislature elected in 1967. And all censure motions (except one on foreign policy introduced by the FGDS) were jointly sponsored by the Federation and the PCF." [50] The success of this parliamentary cooperation on the heels of the 1967 electoral success demonstrated with even greater urgency the necessity of placing the relationship between the PCF and FGDS on a fuller basis, for the noncommunist Left was not yet prepared to take power with the Communists as allies. [51]

At the instigation and continued insistence of the communists, discussions were thus finally initiated, after the elections of March 1967, on the idea of a common program. Begun thanks to articles in the respective party newspapers, the dialogue soon developed into formal negotiations, and after several months of closed-door bargaining, on

---

the Federation, expelled from the Socialist party, and abandoned by between a fifth and a half of their first-ballot voters" *(French Politicians and Elections, 1951–1969*, pp. 218–19.)

[50] Wilson, *French Democratic Left*, p. 162. The three most important censure motions during this period won 236, 237, and 233 votes; 244 would have been sufficient to defeat the government. The Communists could take all the more pleasure in their new-found parliamentary strength given their previous isolation. A close statistical study of Communist participation in the second legislature of the Fifth Republic (1962–1967) revealed that "Despite an unfavorable relationship of force, the initiatives of the Communist group from 1962 to 1967 were . . . numerous; the chances for adoption of most of these projects were almost nil." (Herbert Maisl, in Pierre Ferrari and Herbert Maisl, *Les groupes communistes aux assemblées parlementaires Italiennes [1958–63] et Françaises [1962–67]*, p. 177.) In five years, the Communists saw three of eighty measures they introduced accepted by the Assembly; all of them were of extremely minor significance.

[51] This is stated explicitly in *Ma Part*, p. 60, where Mitterrand explains why the communists refused to step aside for approximately 10 less-well-placed candidates. Had the Communists withdrawn, the Gaullist majority might well have been overturned *(ibid.*, p. 144). Mitterrand asserts that the Communists were afraid the FGDS would have opted for a Third Force coalition in the event of a Left majority; nonetheless, Mitterrand does not explain what he would have done in the event of a Left victory in 1967. He may have considered a 1936-style solution: Communist support without participation. The Communists would no doubt have opposed this, however, although they might eventually have accepted it.

February 24, 1968, the two groups made public a document, "Déclaration commune de la FGDS et du PCF," a joint statement that took the first step toward a common program.

Despite the Federation's new commitment to the Communists, its individual groups and factions still retained Centrist orientations, as is indicated in Mitterrand's description of the difficulties in merely deciding what to call the new document:

> We made considerable use of the dictionary in baptizing the text. . . . . This quarrel over terminology of course presupposed a political choice. The optimists of unity of the Left at any price called it a common program; those nostalgic for the Center, a report; those of the negotiations who desired a long pause after this trying effort were content with the static definition of "enlarged agreement," in reference to the agreement of December 20, 1966; those who saw in the enlarged agreement the proof that a continued evolution was possible said it was a platform.[52]

Nonetheless, the relative depth of the negotiations and of the "Joint Declaration" were extraordinary events, unquestionably bearing out Mitterrand's assertion that, "In truth . . . the Left had never gone so far in the discussion of a program."[53]

Divided into three sections—Institutions and the Defense of Liberties, Economic and Social Problems, Foreign Policy—the document was essentially a catalogue of similarities and differences in points of view. Where differences existed both positions were given in the text.

The two organizations were able to show agreement mainly in the area of Institutions. That section began: "Irreducibly hostile to the regime of personal power in whatever form it may take, and determined to combat it until its elimination, the FGDS and the PCF will act in common to establish an authentic and modern democracy, capable of responding to the ideal of our people, to the interest of our country, and to the demands of our time." There followed a long list of constitutional revisions, the most important of which were to be the abolition of Article 16, concerning emergency powers; a change in Ar-

---

[52] *Ibid.*, p. 66. Rochet and Mitterrand alternated in presiding over the working sessions during the negotiations. Their personal rapport apparently facilitated the discussion considerably. The "Déclaration Commune . . ." is a brochure dated February 28, 1968 (n.p.).

[53] *Ibid.*, p. 77

ticle 11 to prevent referendums from becoming "plebiscites"; an in-crease in the area of legislative competence (article 34) and greater con-trol of the prime minister by the Assembly (Article 49); the creation of a supreme court (Articles 56–63) and other measures to reform the ju-diciary.[54] Finally the declaration proposed reduction of the presiden-tial mandate to five years, thereby tying it to the election of the As-sembly and permitting the establishment of a "legislative contract" between the executive and legislative branches.[55] Regarding economic and social reform, a similar catalogue of changes was enumerated, including several important new nationalizations (here some disagree-ment was expressed; the PCF wanted more than the FGDS), a lower-ing of the retirement age, and a full employment policy. The greatest open disagreements were in the area of foreign policy, where the FGDS expressed a desire for the economic and political unification of Europe while the PCF argued against a "supranational authority dom-inated by huge capitalist forces." The document ended on the rather optimistic hope that the two parties would consider it desirable to at-tempt to resolve their differing points of view, "notably in questions of foreign policy, with the aim of exploring the possibilities of further rapprochement." [56]

Of course, in mentioning an "authentic and modern democracy" as the goal, the document studiously avoided discussion of both social-ism and revolution, a tactic necessary in light of the fact that the Radi-cals were involved.[57] Despite the limited nature of the topics dis-

[54] For example, Article 65 would be revised to create a Superior Council of the Magistracy independent of the Executive, habeas corpus would be introduced, and the *Cour de Sûreté de l'Etat* would be abolished as would the practice of "preventive deten-tion." The detailed concern with judicial reform can be attributed largely to Mitter-rand. See his long analysis in the "livre de combat" written for the 1965 presidential election, *Le coup d'état permanent* (Paris, 1965), Part III, pp. 151–232.

[55] The "legislative contract" is an idea which in France was first associated with the name of Pierre Mendès-France. See his *La république moderne.*

[56] *Déclaration commune.* See also the commentary of Waldeck Rochet in *L'Humanité* of February 26, 1968. The FGDS had had earlier drafted its own "Programme de la Fédé-ration de la gauche démocrate et socialiste," July 14, 1966, 61 pp.

[57] The Radicals had accepted "the Joint Declaration of February 24, 1968 without much opposition; they were not much concerned about programs at any time, and the Joint Declaration was very close to the FGDS Program they had already endorsed." Wilson, *French Democratic Left*, p. 168. See also Barrillon, *La gauche française en mouve-ment*, pp. 59–60 ff.

cussed in this regard, however, the Communist leadership chose to emphasize the positive aspect, in effect to treat the "Joint Declaration" as only a beginning. On February 24, in a report to the Central Committee, Waldeck Rochet had this to say:

This text does nòt contain all the dispositions which figure in our [own] program . . . but it contains no measure which is in opposition to our program. In other words, in adopting this document our Party has not renounced any of its fundamental positions. . . . The new document undeniably constitutes a step forward on the road toward union of the Left forces. It constitutes a particular progress because the points of agreement have become more numerous and also because the existing disagreements are clearly described. . . . The document . . . constitutes *a minimum platform of action.* [58]

Thus, at the end of February 1968, the prospects for continued movement toward a union of the French Left seemed rather good, with two factors in particular motivating the trend: first on both sides the desire to return to power was strong. For the Communists, whose doctrine of peaceful revolution stated explicitly that alliance with the non-Communist Left was now the first step in "the socialist transition," the alliance orientation was clear and unambiguous, even if, as always, its ends were dangerously not so. Within the non-Communist Left, however, it was still not definite that the goal of returning to power implied an alliance with the PCF, although a trend had developed toward this understanding. The second factor was thus also necessary: this was the failure of the Defferrist Center-oriented leadership to create a plausible challenge to Guallism, and the emergence of François Mitterrand supported, at least provisionally, by Guy Mollet. Furthermore, the replacement of Maurice Thorez by Waldeck Rochet on the Communist side appeared to open the way still more, for with Thorez died the most important symbol of the French Communist link with Stalinism and the "cult of personality." Although Thorez personally had always leaned more toward tactics of participation and unity than those of sectarianism, the mere presence of his person, the residue of the charismatic role of the *fils du peuple*, had been an impediment to de-Stalinization and credibility of the peaceful revolution and multi-party doctrines. His death was in this sense a

---

[58] "Un pas en avant." *L'Humanité*, February 26, 1968, pp. 3–4. Emphasis textual.

last service rendered the organization to which he had devoted his life.[59]

The February 1968 situation was optimistic insofar as the enthusiasts of an alliance between the Communists and non-Communists were concerned.[60] The moment, however, proved to be short lived. The events of May–June 1968 in effect interrupted the march toward unity. These events disrupted both the Federation and the rapprochement of Left and extreme Left.

No observer contests that the student strikes and demonstrations, which led into a general strike of some 9 to 10 million workers, caught everyone by surprise, including all the supposedly revolutionary parties.[61] On May 3, for example, *L'Humanité* attacked the "German anarchist" Daniel Cohn-Bendit, and by May 11 the PCF had done little more publicly than to call for a special session of the Assembly to discuss the riots after the "night of the barricades" on May 10.[62] Four days later the PCF and FGDS jointly submitted a motion of censure against the government, but the motion was defeated by 11 votes on May 23. At the same time, the CGT sought vainly to gain control of a vast and eventually unprecedented wildcat strike movement, of which the syndicates had lost control. The rejection by the rank and file of the Grenelle Accords negotiated by syndicalist and government leaders on May 27 was merely the most visible piece of evidence in this regard.

The first significant initiative from the Left parties came on May 28, and it was to prove a crucial miscalculation. On that day François Mitterrand called a special press conference and announced dramatically that the unspecified referendum proposed by de Gaulle on May 24 would surely be defeated and that as a result of this de Gaulle

[59] Curiously and coincidentally, the two mandarins of West European communism, Thorez and Togliatti, died within six weeks of each other, July 11 and August 21, 1964.

[60] The Gaullist Prime Minister Georges Pompidou expressed the considerable anxieties of those opposed to any alliance involving the Communists by denouncing the Common Declaration as "a program of anarchy leading to dictatorship."

[61] In the immediately following discussion, I shall once again be concerned mainly with the pattern of attempted unification of the French Left. The events of May–June are commented upon with respect to Communist revolutionary doctrine and practice in chapter 12.

[62] See *Le Monde*, May 12–13, 1968, p. 5.

would be forced to resign, an event that would imply the "disappearance" of the Pompidou government as well. The Left, he said, was prepared to "assume its responsibilities," and Mitterrand thereupon proposed the formation of a caretaker government, which would include Communists and centrists in addition to the FGDS. This government, he went on, might be headed by himself or by Pierre Mendès-France. Furthermore, he announced solemnly that he would be a candidate for the Presidency, which he "expected" would soon be vacant.

This bold move was a tremendous gamble that was lost only two days later when, after a puzzling trip to Baden-Baden, Germany, General de Gaulle announced on television that he had decided to dissolve the National Assembly and hold new elections, rather than to continue with the referendum project he had proposed one week earlier. Immediately following the broadcast, a crowd moved to the Champs Elysées to demonstrate either in favor of de Gaulle or simply for a return to order, which seemed to the people to amount to the same thing. At that point, the government had regained the normal consent of the people to accept established authority, and within a few days the strike movement had lost its *élan*. The solemn Mitterrand initiative had by a stroke of the Gaullist magic wand been rendered farcical.

Furthermore, the press conference of May 28 had aggravated relations between the PCF and FGDS. Mitterrand had made known his intentions to the executive of the FGDS, but had not explicitly informed the Communists of his plans despite having met with two PCF leaders the night before his press conference.[63] Moreover, the Communists had sent Mitterrand a letter on May 27 asking the Federation to rally to a vague PCF proposal for a "popular government," made the day before.[64] The FGDS leadership, in the persons of Mitterrand, Mollet, and the Radical René Billères, considered this an "unwonted procedure," and informed the Communists that they

[63] The meeting was attended by himself, Claude Fuzier, Roland Dumas, and Waldeck Rochet and Georges Marchais from the PCF. It was held at Mitterrand's home. Mitterrand, *Ma part*, p. 106.

[64] See *L'Humanité* of May 26 and May 27, 1968.

could not accept any sort of "ultimatum." [65] Still another point of disagreement was Mitterrand's suggestion of Mendès-France as head of the interim government. The Communists opposed this because of the latter's recent *gauchisant* evolution and his presence at the huge rally at Charlety Stadium on the evening of May 27, where the PCF and CGT had been held up to ridicule as "revisionists" and "objective allies of the regime." [66]

Nonetheless, the Left alliance held tenuously through the moment at which de Gaulle's return from Baden-Baden rendered the Mitterrand and Rochet initiatives equally moot. From that point on, the PCF and FGDS became preoccupied with the general elections and attempted to guarantee their 1967 positions. This proved to be impossible; the "great fear" that characterized popular opinion at the time of the elections visited electoral disaster upon the Left, much as the rank and file had disavowed the syndicalist leadership one month earlier.

In the first ballot of June 23, the Gaullists, having chosen to rename their organization the Union for the Defense of the Republic, won over 9.5 million of the 22,140,000 ballots cast, and the Gaullist-led coalition won 142 of the 154 seats decided in the first round. [67] Moreover, the Gaullists won tremendous victories in some of the strongest bastions of the Left. The PCF, with 4,435,000 votes, declined by about 600,000 from its 1967 total, while the FGDS, having obtained 3,650,000 votes, had itself lost almost as much. Most of the defectors from the Left apparently either voted for the Gaullists or abstained. [68] On the second ballot the rout of the Left was completed: in the final

---

[65] Mitterrand, *Ma part*, p. 106.

[66] It has often been asserted that Communist leaders "negotiated" secretly with the government. It appears highly probable that secret meetings occurred between leaders of the CGT and government minister Jacques Chirac to achieve a return to order, the price being the Grenelle Accords. Did the government thus "buy off" the CGT, a secondary effect of an "objective alliance" between the Communist movement and the regime? No easy categorical answer is warranted. (See Chapters 8 and 12.)

[67] Of the 142, the Independent Republicans won 28.

[68] See François Goguel, "Les élections législatives des 23 et 30 juin 1968," *RFSP*, 18 (1968): 837–58; Alain Lancelot, "Les élections des 23 et 30 juin 1968," *Projet*, No. 15 (May 1967): 549–62: and Frank Wilson, "The French Left and the Elections of 1968," *World Politics* 21 (1969): 539–74.

totals the Gaullist coalition won 358 of 485 seats, of which 294—or an absolute majority—belonged to the UDR alone.[69] The other 64 seats belonged to the Gaullist allies, the Independent Republicans led by Valéry Giscard d'Estaing. The FGDS-PCF alliance, operating as in 1967, failed both to obtain the same discipline among their electorates and to capture the Center vote, which on the second ballot this time went to the Gaullists. The communists won only 34 seats, and the FGDS 57, a loss of 39 and 61 respectively: Whereas the Left had begun to approach a majority in 1967, in 1968 it was thrust into a very weak minority position.[70] This was self-evidently due to the very exceptional circumstances in which the elections were held, for popular opinion would not normally have changed to such a degree in a single year. In any event, the electoral defeat provided an opportunity for those who had opposed the FGDS-PCF alliance to make their move.

The first target of the Radicals and the Right wing of the SFIO was Mitterrand himself, ostensibly because of his gambler's behavior during the May–June crisis but at least equally because of his crucial position in the alliance with the Communists. At first, the FGDS parliamentary group voted to demand his resignation as President of the Federation, but Mollet and some other SFIO leaders blocked the move, partially out of a sense of commitment to the Mitterrand policy but probably more out of a desire to avoid a public split at a delicate time.[71] In any case, this was but a temporary success, for the electoral defeat had robbed Mitterrand of his power and prestige within the FGDS. On November 8, 1968, he resigned the Presidency.[72] The

[69] The first time one party had ever held an absolute majority in the history of the French republic.

[70] The alliance tactic in 1968 included the PSU as well, and for the second ballot there were 3 PSU, 134 FGDS, and 160 PCF candidates. Whereas the Communists had stood down in 13 circumscriptions in 1967 where their candidates led a Federation candidate, in 1968 they "made only three such gifts—to MM. Estier, Dayan (both close to Mitterrand), and Malvy. . . . All the candidates of the Left had observed their alliance; unlike 1967 . . . no one broke discipline in 1968." (Philip Williams, *French Politicians*, pp. 277–78.)

[71] See Wilson, *French Democratic Left*, pp. 183–84 and Mitterrand, *Ma part*, pp. 119–20.

[72] "I quit the Presidency of the Federation when I realized that the Federation had ceased to exist" (Mitterrand, *Ma part*, pp. 120–21).

Federation itself suffered a lingering, and quite unofficial, death over the fall and winter of 1968–69.

The second target of those interested in reversing the trend of 1965–68 was the Communist Party itself, and the Soviet invasion of Czechoslovakia on August 20, 1968, helped to discredit the French Communists as coalition partners. The unequivocal condemnation of the Soviet action by Rochet in the name of the Central Committee on the day following the Soviet entrance into Czech territory appeared to signal a clear break with the USSR. Shortly thereafter, however, the Party backtracked somewhat by endorsing Soviet coercion of the Czech leaders as a "negotiation," and when the "agreement" between the two governments was announced on August 26, 1968, the French Communists stated that they accepted the "normalization" of relations between the two countries.[73] Yet the French leadership has continued to affirm its condemnation of the invasion, on the grounds that it was a violation of the integrity of a fraternal state and party, an interpretation of the doctrine of "proletarian internationalism" opposite to that espoused by Brezhnev and the other Soviet leaders. Nonetheless, the French Communists have refused to raise the issue clearly in international communist councils, for this would throw into question the "fraternal" attachment between the PCF and CPSU.[74]

However this may be, relations between the Communists and their former electoral partners cooled significantly after August 1968, as did, for that matter, contacts between the CIR and the SFIO after the Federation had disappeared. The two organizations negotiated during the winter and spring of 1968–69 toward the formation of a renovated "pure" socialist party (i.e., without the Radicals), but, unable to agree

[73] This ambiguous attitude was the result of a compromise after furious disputes within the Communist leadership between a faction supporting unconditional loyalty to the USSR (a faction led, among others, by Jeannette Vermeersch-Thorez) and a faction seeking complete disavowal (led by Roger Garaudy). Waldeck Rochet himself was apparently severely shocked by the Soviet action, and he had apparently tried to warn Dubcek of the danger of invasion during a visit to Czechoslovakia a short time earlier.

[74] Mitterrand and those others still favorable to a Communist alliance argued consistently that the PCF condemnation of the invasion was of great significance.

The Radicals and the Defferre-oriented socialists took the position that the measure of ambivalence in the PCF position implied the link with Moscow remained unacceptable. This PCF position regarding the Czechoslovakian crisis and the PCF-CPSU relation in general is treated more deeply in chapters 8 and 12.

on the terms of a merger, the negotiations were broken off at the beginning of the summer of 1969.

In the meantime, while the CIR-SFIO negotiations were at an impasse, the fateful referendum of April 27, 1969, provoked the resignation of General de Gaulle. A presidential election was scheduled for June. Complicating matters still more was the previously announced SFIO congress on May 4 at Alfortville in the suburbs of Paris, the purpose of which was (yet again!) to lay the foundations for a renovated party. In addition to its own problems, the departure of de Gaulle had now left the socialists with the further problem of having to select a presidential candidate. The dilemma was unexpectedly "resolved" when Gaston Defferre, hoping to accomplish in 1969 what he had failed to do in 1965, announced his candidacy; after a bitter battle at the Alfortville congress he emerged with the endorsement of the SFIO, against the opposition of both Guy Mollet and those in the SFIO still loyal to Mitterrand. The Gaullist candidate, Georges Pompidou, was a strong favorite from the very inception of the campaign, while Guy Mollet hoped for either a weak socialist candidate or none at all, so that the socialist votes could go to the interim President, Alain Poher, a Centrist, on the second ballot. Mollet's attitude showed that he was prepared to sacrifice the possibility of a strong socialist showing for the goal of holding the Party together. Secondly, he also simply opposed Defferre's challenge for the leadership. The Communists, waiting to see if a united Left candidate would emerge, quickly nominated Jacques Duclos, who at the age of 70 plus projected the grandfatherly image of what one might call benevolent militancy, as the PCF standard-bearer. Also running were Michel Rocard, Secretary General of the PSU; Alain Krivine, a Trotskyite leader among the *gauchistes;* and Louis Ducatel, a conservative businessman with almost no support. At one point, both Rocard and Defferre offered to withdraw in favor of Pierre Mendès-France. Georges Marchais, already emerging as the successor to Waldeck Rochet, who had fallen ill in late 1968, violently denounced this new attempt to forge a unity candidacy without the Communists, but in any case Mendès-France had previously announced his unwillingness to stand in the presidential election, and therefore Defferre remained a candidate. (For some reason, Mendès-France later agreed to be Defferre's Prime

Minister if the latter were elected, and thereafter the two campaigned together).

The election was a clear victory for Pompidou. More important insofar as the pattern of opposition on the Left was concerned, the Defferre candidacy proved to be a total fiasco. He obtained barely 5 percent of the vote. Rocard, Ducatel, and Krivine obtained even less. On the other hand, with 21.5 percent of the vote, Jacques Duclos demonstrated that the PCF could conserve its electorate even in a presidential election. The Center candidate, Alain Poher, garnered 23.4 percent of the vote on the first ballot, which earned him the right to oppose Pompidou in the runoff. The PCF was thus denied the chance to force the non-Communist Left to choose between a Gaullist and a Communist. On the second ballot, therefore, the PCF leadership advised abstention: there was no choice, said Duclos, between *bonnet-blanc* and *blanc-bonnet*. With the normal abstention rate increased by the Communist initiative, 35 percent of the electorate abstained or handed in void ballots, and in one of the lowest turnouts of the Fifth Republic Pompidou was elected with 57.6 percent to 42.4 percent for Poher.

For the communists the 1969 presidential election could legitimately be considered a step forward, for it revealed that a Defferre-type strategy was no more viable in 1969 than it had been in 1965. In effect, this was the stimulus for a return to dialogue by the SFIO with the Communists, and it soon led to negotiations concerning a program.

The SFIO Alfortville Congress of May 1969 had been the scene of an ambiguous victory for Defferre but a second SFIO congress had already been scheduled for July at Issy-les-Moulineaux, in order to take stock of the post-presidential campaign situation. At this congress a number of significant events occurred: for one thing, the Defferre faction was a clear minority, and Mollet, who had come to stand for dialogue (if not yet outright alliance) with the Communists, was replaced after 21 years as Secretary-General by Alain Savary, a former "clubman" who was an even warmer advocate of an alliance with the PCF, "if certain guarantees were forthcoming." Furthermore, at the Issy Congress the SFIO's name was changed after 64 years to the simpler title of Socialist Party (P.S.) in order to symbolize the "renewal" of the organization. Finally, the congress mandated the new Executive Committee to draw up a "Socialist Plan of Action" based on the positions developed in the FGDS-PCF declaration of February 1968[75] A draft program was published in February 1970,[76] and adopted at the special Epinay congress of June 20–21, 1970.[77] Despite their continuing divisions,[78] a determined though narrow majority seemed to be leading the socialists toward a more purely Marxist doctrinal position and toward a definitive option of governmental alliance with the Communists.[79]

During 1970, the new Socialist Party agreed to resume the negotiations begun in 1968 between the FGDS and the PCF for the purpose of defining a possible joint program. After months of negotiations, led by Savary and the Assistant Secretary General and now preeminent PCF spokesman, Georges Marchais, a "First Summary" (*Premier bilan*) was made public on December 22, 1970.[80]

This document was of considerable importance for it broached the problem of a socialist–Communist alliance in a "socialist transition"— a problem that was of necessity avoided in the FGDS-PCF statement three years earlier. In effect it represented the first consideration of the terms under which the two parties might eventually ally to pro-

[75] See *La documentation socialiste*, No. 8, February 1970, p. 1.

[76] See *Ibid.*, for the complete text.

[77] See *Le Monde*, June 21–22, 1970, p. 1 and June 23, 1970, p. 1.

[78] The Savary motion proposing closer ties with the Communists won only 52 percent of the delegates' votes, where a similar motion had won 66 percent at the July 1969 congress. Furthermore, the conflict between Mollet and Defferre had been replaced by a conflict of a similar character between Savary and Pierre Mauroy, leader of the Nord federation. *Le Monde*, June 21–22, 1970, p. 1.

[79] The final version of the "Socialist Plan of Action," a program covering approximately ten years and supposedly situated "in between a declaration of principles and a statement of electoral tactics," was published in the *Bulletin Socialiste*, N. 92, September 8, 1970.

[80] The change in the French Communist leadership had been accomplished as smoothly as the 1963–64 change, when it had been apparent that Waldeck Rochet would succeed Thorez and when the manner of succession had been made gradual by Rochet's appointment during Thorez's progressive physical decline. Rochet's own illness, which incapacitated him completely by the end of 1969, resulted in Marchais being named Assistant Secretary General, while Rochet remained officially in his post. At the 20th Congress (December 1972), Rochet was elected President of the PCF (as Maurice Thorez had been) and Marchais was elected Secretary General.

mote a peaceful socialist revolution in France.[81] Nonetheless, while the Communists expressed rather extreme enthusiasm about the areas of agreement, the socialists were less forward. The Communists declared:

The Central Committee . . . approves the First Summary . . . of conversations engaged with the Socialist Party concerning the fundamental conditions of a political alliance. It ratifies the disposition . . . under the terms of which (the two parties) "decide to pursue their conversations. . . ." It reaffirms the determination of the Party to do all . . . in order to arrive at a durable political alliance with the Socialist Party.[82]

The Socialist Party leadership, however, did not "ratify" the document:

The Executive Committee of the Socialist Party takes cognizance of the summary presented concerning the state of the dialogue engaged between the Communist Party and the Socialist Party. It recalls that the Congress of Issy-les-Moulineaux decided that the dialogue could not "result in a political alliance" unless "satisfactory responses are brought forward regarding certain fundamental questions." In these conditions, it is the party congress which must consider the total balance sheet and decide either to end the dialogue or to engage itself toward the eventuality of an alliance.[83]

The summary of the 1970 socialist-Communist dialogue was indeed lacking insofar as the former were concerned. The aftermath of the Czechoslovakian tragedy had raised new demands for further Communist guarantees of acceptance of the rules of political democracy as they are understood in liberal regimes. The earlier disagreement over foreign policy was once again also prominent; the socialists advocated the economic and political unification of the EEC and passed quietly over the future of the Atlantic alliance, whereas the Communists rejected both in quite strong terms.

Nonetheless, the extent to which the new Socialist Party had committed itself to pursue contact with the Communists during 1970 was

---

[81] This document is analyzed in detail in chapter 8. It is found in *Le Monde*, December 24, 1970, pp. 10–11. Communist leaders have alluded to a broader and more detailed document than that made public, hinting that it demonstrates deeper agreement as well. If such exists, it remains secret.

[82] *Ibid.*   [83] *Ibid.*, p. 10.

made clear at the next congress, held again at Epinay, in June 1971. At this meeting the project to fuse the CIR, still led by François Mitterrand, and the Socialist Party—a project which had failed only two years earlier—was this time completed. What is more, the leadership of the Party was conferred upon Mitterrand himself. The delegates, in line with the decision taken in regard to the December 1970 "First Summary," voted on what attitude to take toward the Communists. A motion excluding "all Third Force strategies" (i.e., a Defferre-style orientation) was passed, as was a motion proposing the formulation of a "program of government," which would be rendered public at the beginning of 1972 and which would thereafter be discussed with the PCF.[84] Although the leadership of the Socialist Party remained seriously divided, the battle seemed to revolve more around personalities than around the orientation toward the Communists.[85] For example, the most prominent figures in the Party, Mitterrand and Savary, had vied for preeminence in the leadership, but both favored the pursuit of a dialogue with the Communists.[86] The Communist leadership chose to play coy, arguing that the Mitterrand resolution still contained some ambiguity as to how far the socialists were prepared to move in the direction of the Communists, and expressing regret that a resumption of the negotiations on fundamental principles had been put off until 1972.[87] Despite these reservations, however, it was clear that the PCF unity strategy had regained considerable ground since the disaster of 1968–69, and that its chances of achieving the long-sought "program of government" were once again on the rise.

[84] *Ibid.*, June 15, 1971, p. 1.

[85] The final motion proposed by Mitterrand won only a narrow victory over that submitted by Alain Savary and Guy Mollet; a further motion, also obtaining a strong minority vote, was that of the Center-oriented faction headed by Pierre Mauroy and Defferre; finally, four lesser motions were submitted.

[86] A further indication of the orientation of the new party was the presence at the June 1971 congress of a delegation from the CGT. The latter had not been represented at a socialist congress in 25 years. *Le Monde*, June 12, 1971, p. 40.

[87] See, for example, a speech by Georges Marchais reported in *L'Humanité*, June 28, 1971, p. 4.

The End of Cold War Among the French Labor Unions

French labor unions, which five times previously had reflected the cleavage and fusion in relations among the political parties on the Left, after 1959 once again displayed the "vertical mirror effect," which has worked along the Communist–non-Communist boundary in politics and society since 1920. After the CGT had split in December 1947, the next few years saw the CGT-FO and the CFTC establish themselves durably and independently in postwar France, when only a few years before some had thought possible a completely reunified syndicalist movement. From the beginning of the Fourth Republic, political pluralism was therefore established and with the isolation of the CGT—still the largest union of all—organized labor in France added its own bitter internal divisions to the structural weaknesses characteristic of the movement as a whole.

From 1948 on the CGT-FO avoided all contact with the CGT, and apart from a brief period of cooperation between the CGT and the CFTC in 1953, the Communist-dominated syndicate was unable to interest the latter in continued "unity of action." It was not until 1959 that the CGT-CFTC contact was renewed. The beginning of de-Stalinization, the partial East-West detente already apparent (if continually interrupted), and the weakness of the Communist position in France, revealed most recently by the 1958 crisis, were undoubtedly influential in a March 1959 agreement to engage in a week of mutual CGT-CFTC protests in favor of a series of purely economic demands. Common action thereafter continued to remain limited to isolated cases, however, and at its 31st Congress (October 1960), the CFTC leadership refused to accept an across-the-board offer of cooperation from the CGT. The leadership issued a statement that concluded: "We have certain objectives in common with the CGT, but not a common destiny." [88]

During the important miners' strike of January–March 1963, the

---

[88] Lefranc, *Le mouvement syndical de la libération*, pp. 165 ff. The CGT-FO continued to refuse all contact with the CGT. One of its leaders (Bothereau) asserted that "Unity [with the CGT] creates the road to Prague and to Budapest" (*ibid.*, p. 160).

pattern of limited CGT-CFTC cooperation and total FO refusal to deal with the Communists was continued. A turning point came in November 1964 when, after almost 25 years of internal struggles, the clerical majority in the CFTC was reversed and the union split: a laicized *Confédération Française Démocratique du Travail* (CFDT) and a minority organization that continued to use the old name resulted.

The new CFDT, led by Eugène Descamps, from the beginning sought to reverse the quietist posture of the 1950s and to emphasize its new nonclerical coloration. From the end of 1964, a certain number of interunion committees were formed with the CGT according to professions. These committees permitted the CGT to demonstrate its desire to cooperate, and they worked rather well during 1965. Then, on January 10, 1966, long negotiations resulted in the first broad "unity of action" agreement in the postwar period.[89] The FO strongly opposed this development, and Descamps himself was careful to insist that unity of action did not imply present or future reunification. Nonetheless, during 1966–67 the Descamps faction had to contend with increasing internal dissension regarding his policy toward the CGT, and when the strikes of May 1968 erupted, the problem of syndicalist unity suffered the same modifications as that of unity among the parties.

In effect, with the CGT and PCF seeking to prevent the strike movement from becoming a political "adventure," the increasingly activist and aggressive CFDT leadership moved to outflank the Communist syndicate on the left, notably with demands of "broad structural reforms," a greater recognition of the syndicalist role in the enterprise, and the continuation of contact with the *gauchiste* student strike leadership. The CGT, on the other hand, openly criticized the student leaders as provocateurs and limited its economic and social demands so that they fell far short of "structural reforms." The CGT in effect adopted the standard Communist position that these would become possible only in a new regime. With the CGT appearing more and more as a force for order, its relations with the *gauchisant* leadership of Descamps had disintegrated by the time de Gaulle recaptured the initiative.

[89] *Ibid.*, pp. 193 ff.

The break after May–June 1968, as with the parties, proved to be only temporary, however, because the long-term forces pushing a rapprochement were of such considerable strength. During 1969–70 the practice of limited common actions was renewed, and at the May 1970 CFDT Congress the delegates voted a platform manifesting a serious doctrinal radicalization. Among other things the platform adopted class struggle terminology and came out openly for a regime of ·"democratic socialism." In December 1970 and September 1971 broad CGT-CFDT agreements for unity of action were once again signed, and Descamps's successor as Secretary General, Edmond Maire, declared that "the policy of unity of action with the CGT is irreversible, but at bottom this unity cannot exist without a [continued] evolution in existing conceptions." [90]

Thus, syndicalist cooperation, like that between the political parties of the Left, has apparently become the dominant tendency of the 1970s, rather than the exception—at least insofar as the CGT and the CFDT are concerned—despite such difficulties as the present concern over the proper attitude toward *gauchistes*, as well as certain kinds of workers' demands. The smaller *Force ouvrière*, however, continues to join the Left-wing unions only for limited purposes and only when constrained by circumstances.

In Guise of a Conclusion

At this point we have reached the opportune moment to close—provisionally—this broad history of strategy and tactics in the French Communist movement, pausing only long enough to note the major events leading to the Communist-socialist "Common Program" of June 1972.

At its meeting of December 5–6, 1968, the PCF Central Committee adopted a statement of principles to be implemented in a future governmental program. Entitled "For an Advanced Democracy, for a Socialist France," this document contained ideas developed since the publication of the first program sketch, "The Goals of the Party," in

[90] *Paris-Match*, August 28, 1971, p. 7.

1959 (see chapter 8). In May 1969, a mass-circulation edition was published under the audacious title "Manifesto of the French Communist Party," which indicates the significance attached by the PCF leadership to the common-program tactic and the peaceful revolutionary strategy it is meant to implement.[91] On October 9, 1971, the Central Committee adopted an enlarged and more detailed version of the Manifesto, which was published as *Program for a Democratic Government of Popular Unity.*[92]

Then, in January 1972, the leadership of the new Socialist Party also published a government program, which was adopted in March at the National Convention (after heated debates and revision of certain sections—in particular those concerning workers' control and the French nuclear force). This program appeared under the title *Government Program of the Socialist Party,* with an introductory chapter by François Mitterrand.[93]

In April 1972, the Communist and socialist parties found themselves in disagreement over the referendum on the future of Europe, proposed on the initiative of President Pompidou. Evidently the Pompidou referendum was conceived with the dual goal of reinforcing the authority of the French government in European councils (in the immediate future at the first summit conference of the nine-nation EEC in October 1972), and of slowing the momentum of the Left parties toward an agreement on a program, particularly in view of the general elections scheduled for March 1973. The socialists called for abstention. They favored the goal of a united Europe but refused what they called a plebiscite. The Communists called for an outright negative vote. On April 23, only 55 percent of the French electorate cast ballots, and in spite of a relatively large majority of favorable votes, the Pompidou initiative was at best a half-success.

The most striking proof that Pompidou's success was less than total was the meeting, on April 27, of Communist and socialist delegations to open what turned out to be a decisive series of negotiations. During

[91] "Manifeste du Parti communiste français: Pour une démocratie avancée, pour une France socialiste." (Paris: Editions sociales, 1969) 79 pp.

[92] *Changer de cap: Programme pour un gouvernement démocratique d'union populaire* (Paris: Editions sociales, 1971) 251 pp.

[93] *Changer la vie: Programme de gouvernement du Parti socialiste* (Paris: Flammarion, 1972) 249 pp.

the night of June 26–27, 1972, Georges Marchais and François Mitterrand announced that agreement had been reached on a Common Program of Government.[94] On July 12, the program was also signed by a dissident group, consisting of about one-third of the Radical Party leadership, which organized itself soon thereafter as the "Movement of the Radical-Socialist Left."

The PCF-PS-Left Radical alliance provided the dominant point of focus in the March 1973 legislative elections, which the united Left did not win, but in which the hypothesis of a Communist return to government was apparently consecrated as one of the givens of French political life in the 1970s. An analysis in detail of the Common Program is beyond the scope of the present work, although in chapter 8 some of its implications are considered in terms of French Communist revolutionary pretensions. At this point let us merely remark that the Communists' achievement of the alliance has bound them more tightly than ever to the post-Stalinist revolutionary strategy, which is the subject of the following chapter.

Obviously Communist doctrine and practice should not be equated mechanically: what any political party says it is doing and what it is in reality accomplishing are often two different things. The French Communists, after fifty years, have neither made a revolution nor universally imposed the conviction that they are capable of doing so. More than this, since 1968 the challenges to Communist hegemony in the matter of revolutionary claims have become more telling than ever before: the French Communist Party is accused of being not only not revolutionary, but frankly conservative. Yet, even as popular opinion appears to take the French Communist revolutionary pretensions increasingly less seriously, it is the first task of the serious observer to refuse popular stereotypes and easy conclusions. After a half-century of strategic and tactical maneuver, the contradictions at the most fundamental levels of French Communist doctrine and practice remain at the heart of the movement. It is these contradictions which are to be considered in the following chapters.

[94] *Programme commun de gouvernement du Parti communiste et du Parti Socialiste* (Paris: Editions sociales, 1972) 192 pp. This Communist edition was followed by Socialist and Radical Party publications.

Part Two

THE "FACES" OF COMMUNISM IN FRANCE

Chapter Eight

VANGUARD OF THE REVOLUTION

The logic of Part Two of this study underlies and emerges from the historical interpretation of the French Communist movement presented in Part One. We begin with an examination of the PCF attempt to fulfill the role of *revolutionary vanguard*, which is its raison d'être. Whether or not one believes that the French Communists have successfully preserved a radical or revolutionary potential in the absence of congenial conditions, the several "faces" or role patterns of the communist movement as a whole are fully significant only when understood in the context of a fundamental referent—the desire to be the motivating force in the fulfillment of man's destiny to revolutionize his condition according to the prediction of Karl Marx. Both historically and functionally, one must understand the roles of *counter-community*, *tribune*, and *government party* as developing from a common origin, the will to ignite the socialist movement in France with the Bolshevik revolutionary spark.

The focus of this chapter will be the transformation of French Communist revolutionary doctrine in recent years, the stimulant to which was the all-important 20th Congress of the CPSU, which began on February 14, 1956. First opening the door to de-Staliniza- tion, through the attack on "cult of personality" in the Khrushchev secret speech, the 20th Congress also consecrated both the doctrine of "peaceful coexistence among countries with different social systems" and its corollary doctrine of a "peaceful transition to socialism" as the new strategic model for the still nonruling communist parties.

As we have seen above, the ideas of peaceful coexistence and peace- ful revolution had appeared sporadically and ambiguously in commu- nist doctrine before. The difference after 1956, however, was that the strategies of peaceful coexistence and peaceful revolution were said to have become the *dominant* modes of communist revolutionary struggle.

We have seen in chapter 1 that Leninist revolutionary strategy contained a fundamental ambivalence in its simultaneous counseling of partial collaboration and radical sectarianism. A communist party in action emphasizes one of these strategic postures, while not eliminating but merely rendering latent its complement. For example, it has been possible to demonstrate that the French Communist Popular Front tactic of 1934–39 did not "negate" the militant and sectarian posture of 1924–34, nor did radical sectarian support of the Nazi-Soviet Pact during the period 1939–41 negate the Popular Front. In the same way, the 1941–47 reintegration was not a refutation of the earlier "treason" any more than the 1947–62 period of exclusion and isolation negated either the second (1941–47) or third (1962–) periods of alliance at the top. All the tactical *grands tournants* in French Communist history have been "Leninist" insofar as the conception of Leninist-style strategy presented in this study is valid, and can be usefully compared to the practice of Communist movements in Western Europe over a half-century. (The often fruitless debates as to the "Leninist" or "revolutionary" qualities of parties such as the PCF and the PCI assume the validity of such a comparison. The extent to which it can be legitimately developed deserves more prior consideration.)

Likewise, although Marxist-Leninist revolutionary doctrine unquestionably stresses the necessity of a violent conclusion to the class struggle of bourgeoisie and proletariat, the often-cited statements of Marx, Engels, and Lenin on the existing, "though rare," possibilities of peaceful revolution have made it possible for contemporary Communists to advocate a peaceful transition to socialism on the basis of new world conditions without being obliged publicly to cede the heritage of the "prophets," the Maoist criticism notwithstanding. The French Communist doctrinal transformation in this regard was summarized in the "Theses" of the 14th PCF Congress (1956):

As early as 1950, the report of the Central Committee to the 12th Congress . . . while underlining the very grave danger of war . . . took note of the possibilities . . . of peace. The [1956] Central Committee report of the CPSU, presented by comrade Khrushchev, . . . constituted a decisive contribution to the study of this question. . . . . Within the new historical conditions, there exist . . . political and social forces strong enough to prevent the imperialists from beginning war. Thanks to their presence, the time has come when the Leninist principle of peaceful coexistence . . . must and can acquire a decisive importance in international relations.[1]

And while some equivocation persisted for a short time as to whether or not the PCF leadership would accept the definitive replacement of peaceful coexistence and peaceful transition for the concepts of inevitable war and violent revolution,[2] after the Soviet leadership demonstrated the change was a matter of international solidarity, the new dominance of "peaceful modes of struggle" was made the foundation of French Communist doctrine and strategy. Along with the other aspects of doctrinal evolution to be discussed below, this fundamental revision thus changed the Communist presentation of the contemporary epoch and the "course of history;" and one could not but realize the extent to which the classic Bolshevik model was implicated. In 1966, in a short and otherwise unremarkable book entitled *Le marxisme et les chemins de l'avenir*, the PCF Secretary General Waldeck Rochet declared:

With regard to France, no one can tell with precision at this moment in what way socialism will be realized tomorrow. But the position and the desire of the French Communist Party are clear: all its activity is oriented to the goal of creating conditions favorable to a peaceful passage to socialism.[3]

Since this statement was written, a rather large literature has sprung to life devoted to the question of whether or not the French Communists have "really changed" in their revolutionary pretensions. At this point such a question is out of place, for it involves essentially a judgment of the psychology of the leadership; it is more useful now to evaluate the several transformations of the pre-1956 model, for this

---

[1] PCF–14, "Theses," pp. 371–72. See also *Ibid.*, Thorez report, pp. 37 ff. For the pre-1956 Soviet tendency toward a foreign policy of nonconfrontation see especially Shulman, *Stalin's Foreign Policy Reappraised.*

[2] For example, Etienne Fajon said that the possibilities of peaceful transition were "continually growing" as opposed to being "decisive." Other hard-liners argued similarly. See his speech "Nécessité et conditions de la revolution socialiste" of June 4, 1956.

[3] Paris, 1966, p. 65.

will limit the problem to which the ultimately unanswerable interrogation of Communist intentions must remain the final key.

Until the consecration of the peaceful coexistence doctrine at the 20th CPSU Congress, the general model of revolution proposed by the communists had not been officially reformulated since the time of Lenin. In *State and Revolution* and *Imperialism* particularly, Lenin had pictured the necessary "revolutionary situation" as arising in connection with war or economic crisis, both of which would serve to weaken the incumbent regime to the point at which it could not prevent a mass rising led by the communists and would be vulnerable to such "vanguard" action. The experience of the Bolshevik revolution was presented as a proof of the theory, and despite the interwar failure of all communist revolutionary hopes the creation of the communist regimes of Eastern Europe as a result of World War II was understood as a still further verification of the Leninist prediction. Despite the lack either of revolutionary conditions or of a leadership attempting to formulate the Leninist model in terms suitable to the particular case of France (as Antonio Gramsci attempted for the Italian Communists), the French Communists, until the Khrushchev revision, continued to live with the classic 1917 model as their own. One may, for example, take as a simple statement of the PCF revolutionary doctrine the statement made by Thorez to the 8th Congress (1935) in connection with the negotiations to fuse the PCF and the SFIO: "We consider that the unified Party must . . . recognize the necessity of a violent overthrow of the power of the bourgeoisie and of the installation of the dictatorship of the proletariat *through the means of soviets.*" [4]

The period 1934–39 saw the Party goal structure dominated by the "battle against fascism" and its tactical godchild, the Popular Front. We have seen in chapter 3 that the Communists presented the Popular Front as a possible stage in a socialist revolution, but that neither the nature of the final revolutionary movement (violent) nor its consequences (dictatorship of the proletariat through the means of soviets) was redefined. Furthermore, in order to forestall a sort of "hundred flowers" campaign in terms of revision of the revolutionary model, the Communists—as only a party of absolute discipline can do—decreed a

[4] PCF–8, Thorez report, pp. 128. Emphasis textual.

freeze on "ideological generalizations" during the Popular Front. Still, the Popular Front concept was new in 1934–35, and the Communists were fearful that it would compromise their revolutionary credentials among the masses (even if they themselves regarded it as only a temporary tactic). Once the Popular Front was finished, however, the French Communists "had discovered an unsuspected political truth: the possibility of situating themselves concurrently *within* and *without* the established power structure while avoiding the accusation of petit-bourgeois Machiavellianism. The masses understood and approved." [5] In other words, Communist participation in the Popular Front compromised neither their own sense of the minimum-maximum strategic perspective or that of their clientele. In fact, it would not be too much to say, given events after 1938, that few people at the time believed the experience of the Popular Front had "changed" the PCF. Once again, it is not out of place to point out that, had the maximum Communist hopes been realized in 1936–37, one might now be writing of their participation in the Blum majority as the equivalent of the Bolshevik dual power tactic of February–October 1917.

During the war the Communists were at first primarily occupied with the military goals of the Resistance, although during the Liberation a medium-range goal, to be implemented if conditions permitted, was the establishment of a "people's democracy," and even, in the long-range perspective, a soviet-style society.

Of course, conditions did not permit, and the French Communists developed no new revolutionary perspectives, either doctrinally or practically, out of the war. At the Liberation, if anything, these perspectives had been narrowed, in that France was securely a part of the Western military alliance and the French Communists were assigned the task of doing nothing that might cause the Americans and British to reconsider the Yalta understandings before they had become *faits accomplis.*

Thus, for the first time since before 1934, the French Party leadership after May–September 1947 found itself once again "free," so to speak, to reconsider how the conditions of France might permit a revolution. The absence of any real innovations in the documents of the

---

[5] Michelle Perrot and Annie Kriegel, *Le socialisme français et le pouvoir*, p. 145.

period 1947–56 demonstrates that its theoretical consideration of revolution remained tightly limited by the character of the international movement. Aside from a few rather vague tactical novelties such as the notion that the Peace Movement would help lead the way to socialism, the French Communist revolutionary program retained the character of the Soviet Bolshevik experience and its supposed verification in Eastern Europe at the end of World War II.[6] For example, the themes of impending war and economic crisis were dominant in Party propaganda, the first quite naturally because of the condition of international relations during the height of the Cold War, and the second more probably because it was necessary to the Marxist-Leninist prediction of the general decline of capitalism. With regard to the latter doctrinal imperative, one notes furthermore that it was during the middle 1950s—in the face of considerable contrary evidence—that the French Communists tried for a while to prove the Marxist tenet that the working class would become pauperized under capitalism as one of their major propaganda themes.[7]

The impetus to the long-awaited transformation of revolutionary doctrine and strategy as it applied to individual national contexts was given by the Soviet Party leadership at the 20th CPSU Congress, as a corollary to the doctrine of peaceful coexistence. The thesis on peaceful coexistence was essentially that, although wars between the "capitalist-imperialist" countries themselves might still be inevitable, the establishment and stabilization of a powerful bloc of socialist countries after World War II had provided a new and "decisive" means of preventing world wars—i.e., wars between the capitalist and socialist blocs. The same reasoning was transferred into the model of future national revolutions. The political resolution of the 20th Congress asserted that "given the changed conditions, revolutions are quite feasible without civil war." Given the proper degree of class consciousness, the necessary will, and the guidance of a Communist party, the working class would be able to:

[6] From the time of the bolshevization on, the French Communist leaders doubtlessly discussed among themselves what a revolution in France would be like as compared with 1917. One can only speculate on such matters, which, in any case, had little autonomous effect on either doctrine or practice.

[7] See e.g., Maurice Thorez, "La situation économique de la France,—mystifications et réalités," *Cahiers du communisme* 31, no. 3 (March 1955, 259–279).

Win a solid majority in parliament, transform it from a tool serving the class ingerests of the bourgeoisie into an instrument serving the working people, launch a broad mass struggle outside parliament, smash the resistance of the reactionary forces, and provide the necessary conditions for a peaceful socialist revolution.[8]

In terms of practical application of the doctrine of peaceful revolution, the most promising arenas were said to be those underdeveloped countries which possessed reasonably effective parliamentary institutions.[9] In effect, this seemed to prejudice the French and Italian movements, and possibly, as the Chinese later came to say, the entire movement as a whole, by playing down the role of violence in revolutionary change.[10]

At any rate, the French leadership chose to follow the Soviet lead. The proposals made by the Communists during the 1956–57 government of the socialist Guy Mollet for a "government in the image of January 2" (meaning a government including the Communists and built around the Left majority that existed, at least mathematically, after the general elections of January 2, 1956) have been discussed in chapter 6. The crucial lack in these proposals was that they contained no innovations that might have demonstrated that the PCF leadership had decided to apply the idea of de-Stalinization further than an acceptance of the notion of peaceful revolution. In particular the notion of the dictatorship of the proletariat still implied the eventual absorption, interdiction, or castration of all political forces but the Communist Party itself. To accept the thesis of peaceful revolution did not mean, as in the Italian Communist movement, a simultaneous reconstruction of both the one-party model and the Stalinist conception of proletarian internationalism.

However, the effect of the change in regime and the reshuffle of political alliances in 1958, which still left the Communists out in the cold, combined with the originally condemned Italian example to mo-

---

[8] From the proceedings of the 20th CPSU Congress in *Essential Works of Marxism*, Ed. Arthur Mendel (New York, 1961, p. 401), also in Robert Tucker, *The Marxian Revolutionary Idea*, p. 141.

[9] The recent events in Chile are interesting in this regard.

[10] See, on the Chinese viewpoint, *The Origin and Development of the Differences Between the Leadership of the CPSU and Ourselves* (Peking, 1963) and especially, *The Proletarian Revolution and Khrushchev's Revisionism* (Peking, 1964).

tivate some doctrinal reconsideration.[11] And at the 15th PCF Congress (1959), the French Communists showed their first serious reformulation of the revolutionary model insofar as it concerned alliance with other political forces.

For one thing, the 15th Congress produced the outline of an elaborate program, entitled "The Goals of the Party." This was the first time the Communists had shown a concrete plan for the beginning of socialism, to occur after the "restoration and renovation of democracy." While parts of the proposal were unquestionably unacceptable to all possible allies, it was nonetheless a basis for negotiation, which was apparently the reason why the Communists presented it. More important politically than the various policy aspects of the program, however, was the first concession in terms of the one-party doctrine:

The requirement of working class unity stems from the development of the class struggle. . . . The national and democratic renaissance in France, just as the march toward socialism, cannot be the work of a single party; they demand a loyal and durable alliance between the working class, the laboring peasantry, the intellectuals, [and] the urban middle classes. They presuppose an alliance between the Communist Party and the other democratic parties.[12]

This brief reformulation was the first French Communist break with the mystique of monist or one-party rule, the model of revolutionary society as developed in the Soviet Union and adopted by all the Communist parties. Nonetheless, the new formula was still weak and ambiguous. It suggested a multiparty structure for the "national and democratic renaissance" and for the "march toward socialism," but it did not state how far down the socialist road the parties would need to travel together. As a result, few among those who had either refused an alliance with de Gaulle from the beginning (the PSA-PSU, UDSR) or who were returning to opposition during the period 1959–61 (the SFIO, notably, as well as some Radicals) felt that negotiation of the 1959 Communist program would have been worth the effort.

At the 16th PCF Congress, held only two years later, in May 1961,

---

[11] The PCF leaders had condemned Togliatti's enunciation of the "polycentrism" thesis in 1956. On the less than cordial PCF-PCI relations of this period, see François Fejtö, *The French Communist Party and the Crisis of International Communism.*

[12] PCF-15, "Theses," p. 535. The program outline "Les buts du Parti" is found on pp. 535–40.

the Communists took yet another step toward abandonment of the one-party doctrine. After repeating that a multiparty situation could exist in the march *toward* socialism, Waldeck Rochet went on to add:

Better, taking account of the conditions of our epoch and of the democratic traditions of France, we believe that cooperation between our Communist Party and the other democratic parties is possible and necessary, not only to put an end to the regime of *pouvoir personnel* and to reestablish a renewed democracy, *but also afterward in the realization of socialism.* [13]

The apparently minor difference in phraseology was in fact an ideological proposition of absolutely fundamental importance. However the SFIO, under Mollet, had at this point not yet turned to complete opposition to de Gaulle (see chapter 7); moreover, the Communists' offer to cooperate did not satisfy the socialists, because one might help to realize socialism and then find oneself unable to enjoy the fruits of one's labor. The Czech coup of 1948 was still vivid in the minds of the French social democrats.

Finally, at the 17th PCF Congress (May 1964), with the presidential election already in view and the Defferre initiative temporarily occupying center stage on the French Left, the Communists completed the long and grudging concession on the question of a single party versus multiple party regime as applicable to a socialist society:

The 17th Party Congress considers that agreement between the democratic parties on a program to realize in common is, at the present stage, the major condition of progress in the struggle for democracy. . . . It is therefore of the greatest importance that common action be developed and that this unity go further than what it was in 1934 and 1945. . . . It is necessary to surmount all the obstacles blocking the road to unity of action without restriction. . . . The Communist Party . . . has proposed and proposes the agreement of [communists and socialists] *not only for today, but for tomorrow.* . . . It has affirmed that it is ready to maintain unity tomorrow in order to implement together a program elaborated together. It has rejected the idea that the existence of a single party is an obligatory condition of the passage to socialism. This idea, supported by Stalin, constituted an abusive generalization of the specific conditions in which the Revolution of October took place. [14]

---

[13] PCF–16, Rochet report, pp. 67–68. Emphasis mine.

[14] PCF–17, "Résolution politique," pp. 522–24, emphasis added. I should add that in choosing to quote from the Party congresses I have done some minor violence to chronology; in fact, trial balloons on each revision were sent up before the Congresses, which then consecrated the doctrinal changes.

Once again an apparently minor reformulation of a key phrase expressed a fundamental revision of doctrine, for in admitting the idea of multiple parties "tomorrow," the French Communists had come to admit the idea of many parties in a full-fledged socialist regime. Yet, although among other things the length of time and the controversy involved in the Communist doctrinal transformation attested to its sincerity, an SFIO response was still not immediately forthcoming. There were two reasons: Defferre continued to offer a solution to the "Communist problem" without alliance, and, more important for many, it was by no means certain that the Communists would execute in practice what they had come to admit in doctrine.

For one thing, to document the idea that a coalition with a Communist Party was possible in a socialist regime, the Resolution of the 17th Congress had referred to an "experience abroad," which supposedly had proved such an alliance was possible and durable. "Thus this theoretical innovation was limited to such an extent that it seemed to refer to the examples of the people's democracies such as Czechoslovakia or the German Democratic Republic, which formally admit the existence of several parties." [15] Given this, the social democrats could hardly accept this apparently final concession on the single-party problem as valid without a complex of complementary guarantees, which the Communists were not yet prepared to give, and one of which (practical experience) they could not give at all a priori.

Rochet had tried to meet such objections in advance: he argued at the 17th Congress that the Communist position had in the past been "generally poorly interpreted and often caricatured." [16] Yet even the successor to Maurice Thorez, who was perhaps the Communist leader prepared to go the farthest in negotiations with the socialists, may have unwittingly fueled such suspicions when he remarked that "The merit of the thesis [on multiple parties] submitted to our Congress is that it raises one of the essential barriers on the road to unity." [17] In citing as the benefit of the ideological revision a greater chance to achieve alliance, rather than recognition of the desirability of political liberties in and of themselves, Rochet (no doubt unintentionally) once again focused attention on the barrier separating democratic central-

[15] Fetjö, *French Communist Party*, p. 169.
[16] PCF–17, Rochet report, p. 63.   [17] *Ibid.*, p. 65.

ism and liberal democracy, and therein the classic question of ends and means.

One further development at the 17th Congress tended to nullify the apparently serious concession on the question of multiple parties. This was a revision of the Party statutes relative to the organization of democratic centralism within the Party itself. Essentially, the reforms introduced in a report by Georges Marchais,[18] involving minor alterations in the organization of party discussion and the introduction of secret ballots, were what a Marxist would call changes of a purely "formal" nature, no doubt designed to convince the socialists of the Communists' democratic intentions. Since the changes in methods of discussion did not alter the monopoly of the Secretariats and the Politburo over control of proposals and candidacies, and since the introduction of a secret ballot did not alter the fact that only one slate of candidates was presented in an election, Marchais' somewhat gratuitous assertion that the reforms meant the Party would "be able to put more of an emphasis on democracy than on centralism" did not add to the credibility of the multiparty thesis, nor did a remark to the Congress by René Piquet to the effect that "To develop democracy in our Party is not to admit, as certain individuals indicate, a sort of bourgeois liberalism." [19] Still, Rochet attempted to limit the scope of the problem posed by the internal role of democratic centralism in terms of Communist-socialist cooperation: "It is true that the two parties are run on the basis of different organizational principles. But if such a question can present difficulties in case of reunification of the two parties, it is not of a nature to prevent the two parties from collaboration, from realizing a unity of action." [20]

Eventually, this was the understanding under which the Communists were accepted into the presidential campaign of François Mitterrand and into the electoral alliance of December 1966 for the general elections of March 1967, although the socialists did not consider the matter of whether or not the Communists expected to extend the principle of democratic centralism into a future society resolved by Ro-

---

[18] See PCF–17, pp. 286–330 and esp. pp. 307–324.
[19] Quoted in Jacques Fauvet, *Histoire du Parti communiste français* 2:323. Piquet was a candidate member of the Politburo.
[20] PCF–17, Rochet report, p. 67.

chet's statement. One aspect of this problem was raised by Guy Mollet just a few days before the second ballot of the presidential elections of December 1965:

As far as we [democratic socialists] are concerned. . . . our conviction is that a progressive republic demands simultaneous expansion of political democracy and the realization of economic democracy. . . . The communists will have to say . . . whether they choose to guarantee the continuity of this democracy, given their analysis of industrialized countries and of political democracy.[21]

The French socialist conception of democracy in the twentieth century has remained closely bound to political liberalism, and it was for Miollet and his colleagues self-evident that nonsocialist parties should be allowed all political liberties in a socialist regime, including the liberty to return to power. The Communist reply to Mollet's question, reasonable on the surface, was in fact ambiguous and disquieting in the implications it presented: "While fully guaranteeing the development of the largest possible democracy for the immense mass of the people, it will be necessary that the new [socialist regime] adopt laws tending to protect and defend the new social organization and take measures in order to insure respect of the laws." [22]

The Communist Party was by far the largest and best-organized of the socialist-oriented parties. Implicit in this statement, therefore, was the possibility that the PCF, which would most likely dominate a Communist-socialist parliamentary majority, could with perfect legality propose and vote for laws that would restrict political liberties as the socialists understood them.

After this new confrontation over the nature of democracy, the dialogue between Communists and socialists was interrupted for a year, during which time doctrinal positions were reexamined on both sides.[23] The successful conclusion of an electoral alliance between the

[21] *Le Populaire*, December 16–17, 1965, p. 1.

[22] Waldeck Rochet, "Après les élections présidentielles," brochure, Jan. 1966, p. 22.

[23] Frank L. Wilson has remarked that, "During the three years of the Federation's existence, its members conducted virtually continuous negotiations on a common doctrine" *(The French Democratic Left*, 1963–69, p. 142). During the early part of 1966, the Federation members negotiated the program presented on July 14 of that year. In 1967, further discussion led to the Charter of Bondy, outlining the doctrinal basis for a fusion within the FGDS. The Communists, while reflecting on further possible ideological

FGDS and the PCF in December 1966 revived the impetus of 1965. After the considerable gains by the Left coalition in the legislative elections of March 1967 demonstrated its potential to win a majority, a new doctrinal confrontation seemed almost imperative.[24] The FGDS and PCF leaderships therefore began to meet in order to discuss a common program; the result of these meetings was the Joint Declaration of February 24, 1968.

The broad outlines of this document and the reasons why it did not deal with the question of a "socialist transformation" have been discussed above. Its importance in the transformation of Communist revolutionary doctrine stems mainly from the first section of the statement, concerning institutions. In effect, by accepting that a series of constitutional revisions would act to "restore and renew" French democracy, as well as to permit the Left parties to move to the stage of "advanced democracy," which would supposedly be the prelude to the transition to socialism, the French Communists accepted that a transformed social system need not imply a priori a new political regime. This superseded the demand for a new constitution, which had first been made explicit in the original peaceful revolutionary program of 1959 and which had reappeared in the succeeding programs as well.[25]

Although treated in Marxist doctrine as part of the formal and ideological "superstructure" of a "bourgeois" capitalist system, the differences between various types of "bourgeois" regimes had not been

---

concessions of their own, could do little more than wait until the FGDS was prepared to reopen discussions.

[24] A complication in the conclusion of this alliance, as in 1965, had been the Communist insistence on prior discussion of a common program. The FGDS leadership avoided this, however, and the December 1966 agreement concerned only mutual withdrawals on the second ballot. The Communists used their own program on the first ballot. Much of it dated back to the first draft program presented at the 1959 Congress. See *Cahiers du communisme*, February–March 1967, pp. 580–86, for the text of the 1967 program. The FGDS did not publish its own program until July 14, 1966, after the elections. Rochet remarked later that "At its June session—when it had received still no positive response from the Federation of the Left—our Central Committee put together its program for the legislative elections." (PCF–18, Rochet report, p. 49).

[25] In the pre-1956 revolutionary model, this sort of question was not necessary to pose.

totally glossed over by the Communists. For example, of the Fourth Republic constitution Jacques Duclos had once asserted: "Certainly, we know well that the present Constitution is the Constitution of a country still subjugated to capitalist domination. . . . But the Constitution of October 27, 1946, . . . nonetheless demonstrates considerable progress in comparison to the constitutional laws of 1875." [26] Other statements have been cited elsewhere to document the Communist thesis that ideally "the democratic republic is the shortest route" to socialism,[27] but the impact of the PCF concession in the Joint Declaration was that, as the multiparty thesis would imply, the French Communists were now claiming that their version of socialism could be built on the basis of a basically "bourgeois" or liberal constitution.[28] Of course, given the possibility of amendment and the relation of, for example, the Soviet constitution and Soviet reality, this might have been of little significance.[29] However, in the context of contemporary international events, particularly of the developing relations between communists and socialists, it would have been as shortsighted to dismiss the meaning of this concession out of hand as to believe the French Communists had suddenly and completely abandoned the Stalinist heritage.

After the Joint Declaration of February 24, 1968, unforeseen events once again interrupted the dialogue between the PCF and the FGDS. The invasion of Czechoslovakia by Warsaw Pact troops in August was even more significant than the domestic crisis of May–June in this regard, for it brought once again to the surface the PCF-CPSU relation, throwing into question all the steps toward the alliance that had been achieved over the previous decade.

---

[26] Duclos speech to the National Assembly, January 6, 1953. See also this statement by Thorez: "The communists refused to proclaim falsely (during the life of the Fourth Republic) that all the evil came from the 1946 Constitution, of which assuredly [we] wanted to correct the defects, but which gave a reflection of the social and political forces of the country much more exact than the present caricature of national representation" (PCF-15, p. 64).

[27] See also, e.g. PCF-15, Thorez report, p. 62.

[28] Whether or not the Communists would eventually seek a unicameral legislature, as in 1944–46, is not part of the contemporary discussions although it apparently remains part of the Communist constitutional perspective.

[29] Cf. the analysis of Raymond Aron, *Démocratie et totalitarisme* [Paris: Editions Gallimard, 1965], chapter 13.

The Problem of the "International" Character
of the PCF; Communist and
Social Democratic Internationalism

The new French Socialist Party of the Socialist International has never ceased to claim an international character for itself.[30] In the famous "Declaration of Principles" written by Léon Blum just after the end of the Second World War, to which French socialists still pay homage, the aged leader of the Popular Front described the character of the SFIO in the following manner:

It is a party which is *at once national and international.* National essentially because there is no freedom for labor in a slave or subject nation, because the workers, who tended to be rejected out of the patrimony due to the abuses of capitalism, have reintegrated themselves by a century and one-half of efforts and sacrifices, because the patrimony is today their property. . . . Essentially international because the laws of economy have taken on a universal character, because the interests of all workers are at one with the rights and duties of all men, because the first of these interests, peace, cannot be assured outside of their organization and action on an international dimension.[31]

The vague character of Blum's conception of internationalism and the loose character of the Socialist International itself show the degree to which in both theory and practice the idea of internationalism has meant a different thing for socialists and Communists. Nevertheless, the nature of the link between the PCF and the rest of the Communist movement, as we have often seen above, has been somewhat more complicated than the idea of a simple master-servant relationship. The most relevant perspective on the question is the following rather de-

[30] The present postwar Socialist International was created at the Frankfurt Congress of 1951. Its heritage dates back to the Vienna (or "2½") International of 1919, which was organized by German, Austrian, and Swiss independent socialists, and which was joined by other groups (including the French socialists) at Hamburg in 1923. The organization and functions of the Socialist International were designed to contrast with the Third International (and later the Cominform).

[31] "Déclaration de principes et programme fondamental," adopted February 24, 1946 (cited from a brochure of the same name, supplement to the "Bulletin intérieur," n. 125, 1962, n.p.).

finitive statement from a French sociologist and historian with intimate knowledge of a subject difficult for "outsiders" to penetrate:

> From 1920 to 1943, the Party was the French Section of the Communist International. Not to understand the precise significance of this and to treat the history of the PCF as the history of an independent totality is probably less sensible even than to analyze the history of French catholicism by putting into parentheses the fact that it is a partial element of a church with a universal mission. . . . [Yet it] *is not a question . . . of knowing whether the policy of French communism was decided in Paris or Moscow,* but to begin with the major given, the only serious point of departure respecting the originality of the communist phenomenon: the worldwide dimension of the enterprise in which French communism placed itself.[32]

It is only in the framework of this insight that one may appreciate the full significance of a statement such as that by Thorez at the November 1960 Conference of Eighty-one Parties in Moscow condemning the Togliatti thesis of "polycentrism" as a new basis for proletarian internationalism:

> We reject any position which might tend to weaken the unity of the socialist system and the international communist movement by considering that they might have several centers. Our party has fought this erroneous point of view before . . . [based on] recognition of the vanguard role played by the Communist Party of the Soviet Union. . . . [All] the unity that we need is the voluntary but *real unity,* of all the detachments of our movement *around the Communist Party of the Soviet Union.*[33]

Thorez's emphasis on the voluntary element in relations between the PCF and the CPSU is important, because the acquiescence of the PCF leadership to Soviet policies—given an absence of physical sanctions available to the Soviets—has been based always on a voluntary

---

[32] Annie Kriegel, *Les communistes français,* p. 177, emphasis mine. For accounts of relations between the PCF leadership and the various Comintern representatives in Paris (demonstrating, by the way, how the Comintern's directives were treated sometimes as "pieces of advice," sometimes as "orders") see Drachkovitch and Lazitch (eds.) *The Comintern: Historical Highlights,* in particular the article by Lazitch himself. On the methods by which Stalin acted through the Comintern, see Isaac Deutscher, *Stalin,* pp. 392–93, 399 ff. After the dissolution of the Comintern in 1943, relations with the "fraternal" parties were transferred to a department of the Central Committee of the CPSU. Kriegel, *Les communistes français,* pp. 185–86.

[33] From Thorez's speech to the meeting of Eighty-one Parties, cited in Fetjö, *French Communist Party,* pp. 123–24. Emphasis textual.

recognition of the legitimacy of the Russian Communist leadership and party as the most authoritative incarnation of proletarian legitimacy internationally. Faithful to that revolutionary model, which sees the worldwide revolution as *necessarily* the work of a group of closely cooperating Bolshevik-style parties, the French Communists have believed that allegiance to the Soviet Party, and therefore to the Leninist-Stalinist idea of proletarian internationalism, is necessary for the practical success of the entire Communist project begun in 1917. In one sense, the bolshevization of the PCF in the 1920s meant the French Communists had come to accept that their obligation to proletarian internationalism might require support of policies unfavorable to the revolutionary movement in France but beneficial (supposedly) to the eventual worldwide success of communism. One might argue plausibly, on the other hand, that in accepting Stalin's version of proletarian internationalism the French Communists simply condemned themselves to impotence.

In any case, with the above in mind one can best understand the development of relations between the French and Soviet parties in the 1960s. Fighting both the Chinese and Italian deviations in the movement, the French Communists have acted vigorously to limit fragmentation of the international movement built around the CPSU. Their goal has been to preserve that version of proletarian internationalism structured upon a belief in the special legitimacy of the Soviet leadership as the "most battle-hardened and experienced detachment" of the international movement. To the PCF, retention of the international community of communist parties—i.e., solidarity with the CPSU—still appears to be fundamental if the movement is to carry out the historical principles of Lenin throughout the world.

The simplistic charge that the French Communists are "under the orders of a foreign power" has in any case been rendered less credible in recent years by several events, which have demonstrated a certain willingness by the PCF leadership to allow a measure of disagreement with the Soviets to be made public. Combined with the development of a theory of a specifically "French road to socialism," this subtle detachment of the French movement from its Soviet *maître d'école* may legitimately be termed a nationalization or patriotization of French Communism.

The nationalization of French Communism, part of what has come to be called de-Stalinization, is in a conceptual sense a breakdown of the principle of democratic centralism as it was implemented in the international movement under Stalin. Its discussion must be dated from 1956, when the 20th CPSU Congress consecrated the de-Stalinization campaign. At the end of chapter 6, it was noted that the French movement was the slowest of the Western organizations to accept the implications of the 20th Congress. We shall now examine de-Stalinization's effect upon the international character of the PCF.

To set the argument, it is useful first to cite the response of the PCI, enunciated by Togliatti, for the Italian line was nearly the complete antithesis of the PCF's. The most famous of Togliatti's early commentaries on the critique of Stalin was his interview published in the June 16, 1956, issue of *Nuovi Argomenti*.[34] In this interview, as François Fejtö has remarked, the Italian Communist leader "completely authenticated from the international Communist point of view, as it were, the text of Khrushchev's secret speech."[35] For one thing, Togliatti expressed strong and unambiguous feelings on the issue of the "cult of personality:"

The least arbitrary of the [Khrushchev] generalizations is the one which sees in Stalin's errors a progressive encroachment by personal power on the collective entities of a democratic origin and nature, and, as a result of this, the pileup of phenomena of bureaucracy, of violation of legality, of stagnation, and also, partially, of degeneration at different points of the social organism. . . . It seems to us that undoubtedly Stalin's errors were tied in with an excessive increase in the bureaucratic apparatus in Soviet economic and political life, and perhaps, above all, in Party life.[36]

Not only did the Italian leader attack negatively, however; in this same interview he also asserted the famous thesis of "polycentrism," since known as the "Italian line:" "the Soviet model cannot and must not any longer be obligatory. . . . The whole system becomes polycentric, and even in the Communist movement itself we cannot speak of a single guide."[37]

---

[34] "9 Domande sullo Stalinismo," *Nuovi Argomenti*, No. 20, June 16, 1956, in *The Anti-Stalin Campaign and International Communism*, pp. 97–139.

[35] Fejtö, *French Communist Party*, pp. 64–65.

[36] From "9 Domande . . . ," cited in *ibid.*, p. 65.   [37] *Ibid.*, pp. 65–66.

The Italians had, in effect, openly broken the chain of Communist Party legitimacies leading to the CPSU both as a matter of doctrine and of fact. Although the PCI leadership would continue to express its "fraternal" agreement with the CPSU on most major issues after this moment,[38] the Italians had taken a step that made it clear that the dominant role of the CPSU, while once believed historically "necessary," had come to an end insofar as they were concerned.

Available evidence suggests that in the PCF leadership ranks a very animated and conscious debate on the question of whether and how far to go in the direction of the Khrushchev secret speech took place immediately upon its publication, and that the French Communists did not simply follow blindly without seeking to weigh the consequences of their acts.[39] Nonetheless, they decided to adopt the most cautious approach of all the Western parties. For example, while accepting the criticism based on the Stalinist "cult of personality," a position of some ambivalence was maintained: "It was wrong, while Stalin was still living, to shower him with dithyrambic praise and to give him the exclusive credit for all the successes in the Soviet Union. . . . Today it is wrong to blame Stalin alone for every negative act of the CPSU." [40] Furthermore, and again in contrast to the Italian response, the thesis of "polycentrism" was rejected, all the more explicitly because the PCF counterargument rested precisely on the same criteria that the PCI considered outdated: "In fact, our profound attachment to the Soviet Union is precisely conditioned by the fact that we are dealing here with the first socialist country, with the base of the international workers' movement. . . . The cause of the Soviet Union is the cause of the international workers' movement." [41] In brief, whereas the Italian Communists had rejected the legitimacy of the CPSU as the "authentic guide" of the Communist movement on the international level, the French Communists had chosen to reaffirm the continuity of this role.

Their choice of grudging and limited acceptance of the criticism of

[38] E.g., the Hungarian invasion of August 1956.

[39] This conclusion is based on personal interviews.

[40] Statement of the Politburo of June 19, 1956, cited in Fejtö, *French Communist Party*, p. 66.

[41] From a speech by Thorez to the Central Committee, in *Cahiers du communisme*, June, 1956, and quoted from *ibid.*, p. 58.

the "cult of personality" and the "abuses of democratic centralism" under Stalin was well displayed at the 14th PCF Congress. Commenting on the proceedings of the Congress in his closing speech, Waldeck Rochet could say with some justification: "Comrades, our Congress has been in the end the Congress of fidelity to principle. Certain elements, under the pressure of bourgeois ideology, would have liked to draw our Party into the opportunist rut. Our Congress, unanimously, has expressed its fidelity to the grand ideas of Marxism-Leninism." [42] Thorez, feeling himself personally implicated in the "cult of personality" critique, asserted that it was against the principles of Party organization to discuss "continually" fundamental questions, "as if we were a club, a school of controversy." [43] After a "yes, but . . ." critique of Stalin, which went on for three pages in the printed text of his report, Thorez then came to the key point insofar as his own previous role and influence were concerned: "In the discussions [preceding the Congress], the comrades considered that the criticism of the cult of personality established around Stalin and the consequences of this cult cannot be in any case mechanically transferred to us, applied just as it is, to our Party, which did not suffer similar defects." [44] Thorez's case was aided by the fact that the CPSU leadership, seeking to maintain the allegiance of the foreign parties and to help them through the crisis "from on high" insofar as possible, had sent Mikhail Suslov to the PCF Congress. This was the first time a high CPSU representative had spoken at a French Communist congress,[45] and Suslov made a point of underlining the closeness of the PCF-CPSU tie and the particular place of Thorez in this relationship. Thus, although uneasily, the PCF leadership had successfully turned the 14th Congress into what the well-known *Le Monde* reporter, Raymond Barrillon, called a "litany of approval."

During the next years, despite their acceptance of the doctrinal implications of de-Stalinization, the French Communists continued to drag their feet in the matter of the organizational implications. The PCF attempted to attribute Stalin's errors to circumstances, in order to sidestep, if possible, the accusation that Stalinism was implicit in the Communist organizational psychology itself. A representative ex-

[42] PCF–14, Rochet speech, p. 420.   [43] PCF–14, p. 62.   [44] *Ibid.*, p. 60.
[45] *Ibid.* Stalin had no doubt never thought it necessary to make such a gesture.

ample of this line of argument was given in Rochet's report to the 17th Congress (1964):

Certainly, we do not ignore that the birth of the new regime in Russia was accompanied by enormous difficulties and even by great suffering. It was because the former Russia was a very backward country. It was necessary to undertake the construction of socialism in the conditions of capitalist encirclement, in the midst of unprecedented difficulties.[46]

Rochet went on to argue that the great merit of the Russian Revolution was to prove it was possible for the working class to construct socialism, and that the social-democrat criticisms of the process were somewhat in vain because they had nothing to offer in the way of opposition to the Soviet model. Thus, despite the cult of personality and certain "violations of legality" which gave a "deformed character to the dictatorship of the proletariat," Rochet asserted that the difficult success of the Soviets obliges one to admit there was no other way to do it at the time, and, in any case, the "necessary self-criticism" of the excesses of the Stalinist period had been made. Thanks to the trail-blazing experience of the USSR, he concluded, "it is possible now for other roads to socialism to be followed." [47]

The French Communist criticism of Stalinism, ambivalent as it was, by 1964 had not yet convinced many people that the PCF had given up its tie to the CPSU to an extent that might permit one to assert with some finality that the French movement had really changed. Thus, when Rochet said that "of course the PCF has the closest fraternal ties with the CPSU, but we do not separate nationalism and proletarian internationalism, and we make our decisions in complete independence in the interests of our people and our country," [48] there was as yet little evidence that would incline observers to accept this remark ·at face value. At bottom, perceptive analysts in all camps realized that for the PCF leadership something much larger than the criticism of one man was involved in the question of de-Stalinization, for in fact both the principles of democratic centralism and the nature of the international movement, which I have explained in terms of a

[46] PCF–17, Rochet report, p. 59.
[47] Paraphrased from *ibid.*, pp. 59–61. For a contemporary and contrary analysis of the "necessity" of Stalinism, see Zbigniew Brzezinski, *Between Two Ages*, pp. 126–34.
[48] *Ibid.*, paraphrased from p. 61.

mentality of hierarchical legitimacies, would suffer irreparable damage
if de-Stalinization were to go too deep, for the phenomenon of Stalinism, however one chooses to regard it, indicted the Communist movement as a whole.

Since 1964, however, two events of rather major importance and
several of lesser importance have indicated that the French Communist leadership is indeed seeking to promote evolution in the nature of
proletarian internationalism without actually giving up the global
focus of the Leninist-Stalinist model and the place of the CPSU
within it. First, the PCF support of Mitterrand in 1965 indicated that
in certain cases the leadership was prepared to place national interests
above those of the international movement as defined by the Soviet
leadership. However, since victory was already more or less conceded
to de Gaulle, this cannot be taken as a limiting case. In February
1966, the PCF allowed its "poet in residence," Louis Aragon, to criticize the trial of the Soviet writers Siniavsky and Daniel, and in December 1970, the PCF publicly criticized the "Leningrad trials" of a
group of Jews who had planned to hijack a plane to flee the country.

These were rather peripheral events, however, and while they are
of some significance, it is unquestionable that the most characteristic
and telling aspects of the evolving PCF-CPSU relationship were to be
found in the French Communist reaction to the invasion of Czechoslovakia on August 20, 1968. On August 21, the Politburo of the PCF
issued a communiqué expressing its "surprise and reprobation" at
the event, and there is, moreover, little doubt that Waldeck Rochet,
who had expressed the French Party's endorsement of Dubcek's "socialism with a human face" in meetings with the Czech leader in July,
had attempted to convince Dubcek that the Soviets might act against
him. Despite this, on the day following the first, unequivocal condemnation of the invasion, the French Party leadership began to tone
down the terms of its criticism, though not its sense. This moderation
suggests that the hard-line group, led by Etienne Fajon and Jeanette
Vermeersch-Thorez, had gained a hearing in opposition to those
who sought to maintain an undiluted position, in particular Roger
Garaudy. Furthermore, the French Party was the first non-Warsaw-
Pact party to send a delegation to Moscow (in November 1968) to
renew ties with the Soviets once the "normalization" had begun, and

on July 5, 1971, it became the first party which had disapproved the invasion to sign a bilateral communiqué with the Soviet Party. Yet, in spite of the later exclusion of Roger Garaudy from the leadership and then from the Party (though not entirely because of his position on the invasion) [49] and the French Communist acceptance of the subsequent "normalization" of Soviet-Czech relations, the PCF leadership has held fast to its denunciation of the original action, and has even strengthened it by force of repetition.[50]

While an estimate of the significance of these events in terms of the PCF-CPSU relationship must remain a matter of judgment, even if two observers agree on the facts, it is of particular interest to note the evaluation of François Mitterrand, at the present time the crucial figure in future Communist-socialist relations:

In reality, [in August, 1968] for the first time in its history the French Communist Party disavowed the Russian Communist Party. No doubt it had already marked a certain retreat . . . when Pravda supported, in 1965, the candidacy of General de Gaulle. But never had a difference of this amplitude been publicly avowed. This evolution is in my opinion very significant, and to slight it . . . seems to me neither positive nor just. The Communists began a long way away! I continue to think that on the occasion of the Czechoslovakian drama the Communists in our country moved away from Russia.

[49] Garaudy, excluded from the leadership at the 19th Congress (February 1970) was "guilty" of other heresies as well, such as revision of the working class concept, of a flirtation with the idea of workers' self-administration and of overly open relations with non-Communists—all of which implied the essential "deviation" of publicly diverging from the Party line.

[50] The trials of opposition figures in Czechoslovakia during the first eight months of 1972 reinvigorated the controversy over the PCF position. In February 1972, a PCF delegation headed by Roland Leroy—regarded as the second most influential PCF leader—went to Czechoslovakia to report on the situation. During its sojourn, *L'Humanité* reprinted the PCF's "well-known positions" on the crisis of 1968 (see the issue of February 12) and after the delegation returned to France, the PCF Politburo simply "took note" of Czech Party leader Gustav Husak's denial that political trials were occurring. After the trials and the sentencing of Jaromir Litera and Milan Huebl (leading figures in the Dubcek period), the PCF declared: "our information indicates that the trials going on in Czechoslovakia are not aimed at . . . truly subversive activities. And when it is a question of political or ideological oppposition, we consider that it is through the means of an intense political and ideological struggle . . . that one should act" (*L'Humanité*, July 29, 1972, p. 2). Gustav Husak denounced Western condemnation of the trials as "old Goebbel's propaganda," and the PCF's position in particular caused great "displeasure" in Czechoslovakia. (*International Herald Tribune*, August 8, 1972, p. 5.)

That they have not moved far enough away, I am convinced as much as my censors. But the important thing is to know on which slope of the mountain runs the source.[51]

In sum, in condemning the invasion and political trials while ratifying the "normalization" of the situation in Czechoslovakia, the French Communist leadership has demonstrated a refusal to make any irretrievable commitment on the issue of the relation between the "fraternal" parties and the CPSU. Behind the attempt to safeguard what is left of the unity of the movement, however, one is inclined to believe the French Communists have finally drawn the conclusion of over three decades of "cooperation" in pursuing the Soviet interest, even while they remain adamant in attempting to preserve the sense of solidarity and legitimacy within the organization of the international movement. This strongly ambivalent position no doubt issues from a recognition of the depth of the dilemma and of its implications for the nature of the communist phenomenon as a whole. At the same time, merely by facing the question, the French Communists have begun to move toward a position that was achieved earlier and more forcefully by the Yugoslavs: charismatic authority, once seriously questioned, is irretrievably compromised.

The Question of Alternation in Power After the Construction of Socialism

As is evident from the above discussion, many of the issues dividing the French Communists and socialists are more symbolic than actual. The Communists are now asked to give verbal guarantees of beliefs no one can be certain they will honor should they find themselves in a position to do otherwise. Most of these kinds of assurances concern the "dictatorship of the proletariat," the nature of which has histori-

---

[51] Mitterrand, *Ma part de vérité*, pp. 137–38. On another occasion, when questioned about his capacity to "control" the Communists, Mitterrand replied, "Don't worry. I have no desire to play the role of Masaryk." In a television interview in October 1971, Mitterrand asserted a theme he has since often repeated, that "There will not be, there cannot be a Prague coup in Paris." He and the Socialist Party leadership declared themselves satisfied with the PCF attitude toward the 1972 political trials in Czechoslovakia and Mitterrand himself sent a telegram of disapproval to Czech President Svoboda.

cally given rise to the most bitter disagreements between Bolsheviks and social democrats.

The phrase itself occurs only rarely in the works of Marx. The best known of these is his assertion in the "Critique of the Gotha Programme" that during the transition from capitalism to socialism the state "can be nothing but the revolutionary dictatorship of the proletariat." We have seen above that between 1959 and 1964 the French Communists adopted the multiparty theses of plural parties "during" and "after" the construction of socialism, but the dialogue between themselves and the socialists on the constitution of such a regime had by 1966 reached an impasse over the extent to which such a regime would permit an opposition and its eventual consequences.

Taking stock of the fact that the phrase itself had shown itself in 1936, 1945, and 1970 to be an impediment to discussion, the Communists as before have sought to make the symbolic concession of making the phrase appear to be somewhat less extreme. At the pivotal 17th Congress (1964), the question was publicly raised for the first time in the discussions, and the Party leadership even permitted consideration of a motion from a local cell suggesting that the term "dictatorship of the proletariat" be dropped entirely from the Preamble to the Party Statutes.[52] The reasons given were that the term could be wrongly interpreted by the public to mean a single-party dictatorship, and that Marx's and Lenin's use of the term had been distorted by the later advent of the Hitler and Franco dictatorships, in the sense that while the former meant dictatorship of the majority, the latter meant dictatorship of a minority. One may assume that the leadership had decided in advance to permit a public discussion. Georges Marchais was instructed to explain that to remove the phrase from Party doctrine would be a "grave political error," because

to place in question the concept of dictatorship of the proletariat in order to replace it by "political power," as the Rabelais cell proposes, would be to slide onto the terrain of bourgeois democracy, because the class content of the State charged with the building of socialism would disappear.[53]

[52] The motion originated in the "Rabelais Cell," which is part of the "Section d'Orsay" in the Seine-et-Oise.
[53] PCF-17, Marchais report, p. 295. Although a minor point, one is amused by the following statement by Marchais in an interview with *Der Spiegel* in August 1972: Asked

The problem, he asserted, was not to give up the idea itself, but rather to "explain" its positive aspects, so that the working class and its allies could attain the level of class consciousness necessary to understand that such a dictatorship would be in their own interest.[54]

This task fell to Waldeck Rochet, whose report to the 17th Congress contains most of the themes that dominated the unity negotiations during the 1960s. The essence of his remarks was that, because of the democratic and revolutionary traditions of the French people, the French form of the dictatorship of the proletariat could be "new, less violent, and of shorter duration" than that experienced in other countries. Furthermore, Rochet attempted to underline the seriousness of this doctrinal device by using a euphemism for the term—such as "This proletarian regime, by which the working class exercises its political direction in alliance with the laboring peasantry and the urban middle classes"—more often than the term itself.[55] Over the next years euphemisms continued to be used. One example is the Theses of the 1970 Congress, which attempt to present the dictatorship period as something of an idyll:

The socialist regime of the working class and its allies, which the founders of Marxism-Leninism called a dictatorship of the proletariat, will place the productive forces into the service of the French people. . . . It will respect and encourage . . . the specific contribution of the small farmers, small merchants and artisans, and small and medium size private enterprises, in the development of the national economy. . . . It will guarantee and extend the democratic rights and liberties gained by the French people in the course of its history. It will assure scrupulously the separation of Church and State, just as it will guarantee the freedom of belief and religion.[56]

------

why the 1971 PCF program did not make reference to the "dictatorship of the proletariat," Marchais replied that "We no longer employ that expression, because, as a result of fascism, the word dictatorship evokes a regime which excludes democracy and liberty." (See *Le Monde*, August 8, 1972, p. 5.)

[54] One of the periodic internal opposition movements in the Party gained attention with the publication in 1962 of *Le pari démocratique*, published under the collective pseudonym "Jean Dru." One of the main targets in the volume was the concept of "dictatorship of the proletariat," which the authors charged was "inadequate to Western reality" (see esp. pp. 143–60). They proposed a "peaceful, pluralist transition to socialism," urging the PCF to give up entirely the idea of a one-party regime. (See esp. pp. 165–70.)

[55] PCF–17, Rochet report, pp. 66–67.   [56] PCF–19, *Theses*, pp. 431–32.

While the French socialists have not shown themselves insensitive to these Communist attempts to emphasize the democratic aspect of the future socialist regime,[57] it is with respect to the remaining classic Communist conceptions and practice of "proletarian dictatorship" that the dialogue and negotiations have been carried on since 1966.

In 1956, while introducing the first hesitant consequences of the peaceful coexistence and peaceful transition doctrines into French Communist doctrine, Maurice Thorez had chosen to place emphasis on the future society promised by the PCF: "The variety of forms . . . has nothing to do with the content of the dictatorship of the proletariat. This content must always be the same. It is not different from one nation to another. Its model was and remains furnished by the country of the October Revolution. . . . [and is] based on the soviet system." [58] The crucial question was, of course, what exactly was the essence of the October Revolution and the "soviet system"? In one sense the matter was highly arbitrary, since its content could be defined in various ways and a phrase or two from Marx and Lenin could still be found to justify the formula: This was part of the beauty of the prophetic legacy. As defined since 1956, we have seen that for the French Communists, apparently neither the creation of "soviets" nor the single monopolistic party nor the appellation "dictatorship of the proletariat" itself was of the essence of this content.

Rather, the essence lay elsewhere, and one had the suspicion in 1969–70 that this time, finally, the Communist-socialist dialogue had reached the vital center of the debate, for in addition to verifying the erosion of the "chain of legitimacies" on the international level the discussion came to settle on the last remnant of the special legitimacy of the Communist party in the national revolutionary struggle; that is to say, the French Communists agreed to debate the fundamental Leninist addition to Marx: the necessity of the Party and the extent of its distinct role in the transition from capitalism to socialism.

[57] They themselves have not used the dictatorship concept to any great extent since 1920. Blum developed a revised notion of *vacances de la légalité* (suspension of the law) during the early 1930s, but this too fell into disuse.

[58] Thorez report to the Central Committee, in *L'Humanité*, November 22, 1956, p. 4. This remark is all the more enlightening when one considers that it is found in a passage in which Thorez attempts to "explain" the Hungarian revolt!

The classic theory of the vanguard role of the Communist party, developed embryonically by Lenin and completed and codified under Stalin, was examined in chapter 2. Essentially, this doctrine stated that the socialist revolution will *necessarily* be made by the working class as proletariat and that the "guide" of the working class in its revolutionary task is *necessarily* the Communist Party. The important Declaration of the Congress of Eighty-one Parties in 1960 reaffirmed the Party's vanguard role even as the congress confirmed the idea of peaceful transition and condemned the hard-line Chinese heresy:

More and more the possibilities of . . . peaceful transition will come to light. A particular case of peaceful transition is represented by the use of an authentic democratic parliament, given of course that there exists outside of parliament a forceful revolutionary élan in the masses, *oriented and directed by the communist vanguard*, given the condition that there exists a crushing superiority of forces on the side of the working class and its allies, and that the isolated bourgeoisie finds itself obliged to cede.[59]

Even in developing the theses of multiple parties and limited opposition in a socialist regime in his key report to the 17th Congress (1964), Waldeck Rochet remarked significantly that in rejecting the thesis of the single-party regime it was nonetheless not a question.

of reducing the essential role of the Marxist-Leninist party in the struggle . . . but [rather] of uniting and making cooperation possible between the democratic parties. . . . At the side of the party of the working class might exist other democratic parties representing certain social groups and collaborating in the construction of socialism.[60]

Finally, even as late as the February 1970 19th Party Congress, the *Theses* insisted that "The possibility of constructing and defending socialism is linked to the capacity of the Communist Party to play the role of vanguard in the socialist society." [61] And further on in the same document appears as concise a statement of the "chain of legitimacies" on a national level as one could hope to find. Linked in a chain of logical implication are the interests of the "nation," the "working class," and the Party:

[59] Quoted from PCF–16, Rochet report, p. 76. See also the 1957 Declaration of Communist Parties at Moscow. Emphasis added.
[60] PCF–17, Rochet report, p. 65.   [61] PCF–17, *Theses* (brochure), p. 26.

The French Communist Party is the representative of the national interest. In struggling against the power of the monopolies, for profound democratic transformations in society, for socialism, the proletariat does not defend only its class interests: it expresses the needs of national development, the future of the nation, and the desire to assure the liberty, grandeur, and prosperity of France.[62]

In the classic model of a Soviet-type socialist society, the chain of legitimacies identifying Party, proletariat, and nation meant that in the transition from capitalism to communism the Party is necessarily and alone the most legitimate representative of the polity; that is, once this stage is reached, once "the working class and its Communist Party" are in power, the problem of public authority has been definitively settled, at least until that still theoretical point at which the state will supposedly begin to "wither away" and political power "as such" will come to an end. The classic Soviet model does not take into consideration a situation in which a Communist Party, once in power, should give it up voluntarily; according to the doctrine there cannot be any more legitimate representative of the proletarian and public interest than the Party. Therefore, the classic model defines an "authentic" socialist regime as one in which the Communist Party is the guide, vanguard, and orienting force: in short, the dominant ruling power.[63]

Philosophically and historically socialists and social democrats have opposed this conception of a revolutionary transition to socialism. The French socialist idea of the nature of the revolution was summed up concisely in the "Declaration of Principles" drawn up by Léon Blum in 1946:

The Socialist Party is an *essentially revolutionary* party: it has the goal of realizing the substitution of the capitalist regime by a regime in which natural resources as well as the means of production and exchange will become the

[62] PCF–19, *Theses*, p. 455. Thorez had expressed the same idea in somewhat more poetic terms in 1958. "A Party which occupies such a place in the heart of the people, a Party which is the flesh of the flesh of the working class, which is the recognized interpreter of the nation, will know how to fulfill its duty" ("Union et action," p. 30).

[63] The fact of allowing other parties with no effective independence to coexist with the Communist Party, as is the case in some East European regimes, does not alter the essential structure of the classic model.

property of the collectivity and in which, in consequence, classes will be abolished. This transformation . . . can be the work only of workers themselves. *By whatever means it is accomplished, it constitutes in itself the social revolution.* . . . The Socialist Party has the particular function of grouping the mass of workers of all types . . . on the political—economic terrain, with the goal of the conquest of public power—*a necessary but not sufficient* condition of the social transformation.[64]

In the discussions between French Communists and socialists, this most fundamental level of doctrinal difference, focusing on a radically different view of the role of the revolutionary party, was finally reached in the negotiations that resumed in December 1969, after the largely unilateral Communist doctrinal concessions of 1959–64, the discussions of 1964–68, and the interruption of the dialogue after May–June 1968. The question of the necessity of a particular party in the building of a socialist society took the form of a related question as to the possibility of an alternation in power in a socialist regime; the following problem was posed: if, in the context of free elections, a Left coalition government were voted out of office, would that alliance return to the opposition?

This question had been posed early in the Soviet regime, when, after the trials of the civil war and the failure of "war communism" to resolve the economic difficulties of the people, a resurgence of the still officially sanctioned non-Bolshevik groups occurred in 1920–21. The Mensheviks and Social Revolutionaries, who had been in almost total eclipse for three years, showed a considerable renewal of popular support, while anarchists and anarcho-syndicalists also found sympathy for their denunciations of the Bolshevik government. The anti-Bolshevik trend had become so strong by the end of 1921 that "If the Bolsheviks had now permitted free elections to the Soviets, they would almost certainly have been swept from power." [65] This turn of events challenged their naive and tacit assumption that once the revolution had begun, the working class would inevitably and willingly support the Communist Party throughout the "construction of socialism." The bond between class and party had been taken for granted, and in all the literature of Russian Bolshevism and European socialism

---

[64] Second and third emphasis added.
[65] Isaac Deutscher, *The Prophet Armed*, p. 504.

in general, "the question of what socialists in office should do if they lost the confidence of the workers had hardly ever been pondered." [66] The Bolshevik response to the weakening of their mass base, as discussed in chapter 1, was simply to ban all organized opposition, creating the single-party dictatorship model which the French Communists then inherited. In the French Communist-socialist "First Summary" declaration of December 22, 1970, the result showed that neither side had compromised its fundamental doctrine on this point. The Socialist Party inserted this statement of principle:

For the Socialist Party, the plurality of parties, freedom of opinion and of contestation, as well as that of candidacy, must remain guaranteed. The parties and organizations contesting the socialist society participate in the electoral consultations, organized on the basis of direct and secret universal suffrage, in the same conditions as the parties concurring in the construction of socialism. In the case that a majority of the population should express its disapproval of the action undertaken, the latter would give up office. If this eventuality should arise, it would prove either a clear insufficiency of the parties and organizations favorable to socialism, or excessive haste in the passage to socialism. . . . The Socialist Party reaffirms that, if the freely expressed confidence of the [people] were refused the majority parties, they would renounce office and take up the struggle once again in the opposition. [67]

The Communist Party, on the other hand, refused to envision even the possibility that their legitimacy might be contested once in power:

For the Communist Party, liberty of thought, of expression and of association, and the right to criticize and to contest will be recognized for all [in the socialist regime], minority groups included. . . . At the same time, the Communist Party considers that, faced with hostile actions of the dethroned exploiters, it will be the duty of the organizations proclaiming themselves socialist to call upon the masses to defend and to reinforce the socialist state, emanation of the working people, and to preserve and enlarge the conquests of the new regime. . . . The Communist Party considers that the democratic regime, whose existence implies the support of a popular majority, will have for its principal task the satisfaction of the laboring masses, and will thus be firm in the ever more active confidence that they will bring to it. [68]

---

[66] *Ibid.*, p. 505.
[67] The "First Summary" declaration of the Communist and Socialist parties, reprinted in *Le Monde*, December 24, 1970, p. 10–11.
[68] *Ibid.*

In other words, the Communists in December 1970 chose once again to define the socialist and democratic regime as that in which the Communist Party is in power. Furthermore, their adamant attitude in this regard had apparently given some cause for alarm to their socialist interlocutors, a degree of alarm not expressed in the February 21, 1968, Common Declaration in which both parties had stated their agreement "to examine in common the measures to take in order to check any attempts to prevent a government of the Left from implementing its program." [69] In the document of December 1970, only the Communists repeated this phrase concerning "the defense of socialism." [70]

Thus, although the foundation of the Marxist-Leninist conception of the vanguard role was debated more openly than ever before by the Communists and socialists during 1970, neither party showed a willingness to compromise on this absolutely fundamental issue. During the early months of 1971, the Communist leadership, obviously eager to continue discussions, tried to deflect the focus somewhat by offering that in a future socialist regime in France there might be an alternation of power among socialist parties, but not of socialist and capitalist parties. [71] This proved a weak diversionary tactic in the debate,

[69] This was the famous *petite phrase*, which the Gaullists used to such advantage in the legislative elections of June 1968. They claimed that an opposition victory would risk a "totalitarian regime" in France.

[70] Mitterrand was reproached in many circles for having accepted such a phrase in the February 1968 declaration. Perhaps this was a reason leading Alain Savary, who led the Socialist Party delegation in 1969–70, not to commit his party in this respect in the December 1970 statement. Another reason may be the change in the Communist leadership: there are many reasons for believing that Waldeck Rochet, whom Mitterrand has referred to as a "man of reflection and rectitude of thought" *(Ma part,* p. 71), was much more able to create an atmosphere of confidence than Georges Marchais. Also, relations between Rochet and Mitterrand personally were much more cordial and trustworthy than were relations between Marchais and the Savary leadership.

[71] See for example *Le Monde,* January 31–February 1, 1971, p. 6, which reports Georges Marchais's speech at the Central Committee meeting of January 28–29, 1971. In *Ma part* Mitterrand notes that Waldeck Rochet had argued the same idea in a television interview in 1968: "The effect of what he said was that he admitted a multiplicity (of parties), on the condition that the competing parties had adopted the socialist construction, which implied that the parties hostile to socialism would not have the right to express themselves, if they had even the right to exist" (p. 70). On June 10, 1971, Jacques Duclos still asserted that "one cannot envisage a coming-and-going in power of

but nonetheless, with this ambiguous "concession" to liberal conceptions the Communist leadership for the first time had admitted a theoretical situation—albeit farfetched— in which the PCF might voluntarily give up power once having acquired it and having begun the "transition to socialism."

The Socialist Party, under the brief tenure of Alain Savary, had "renewed" itself in the spring of 1969, and in June 1971 had "rere-newed" itself in fusing with the CIR, the organization led by François Mitterrand. The resolution passed at the June congress advocated a resumption of dialogue with the Communists at this point, but deferred the next meeting until the spring of 1972. This was to allow the new Socialist Party, with Mitterrand as Secretary General, to draft a program and to consolidate the changes in political strategy and tactics then in a process of tentative development.

Somewhat surprisingly, the Communist leader, Georges Marchais, announced directly after the socialist congress that the Communists wished to resume negotiations immediately; and furthermore, he added in an interview, if the socialists would agree to adopt an electoral law calling for proportional representation, the Communists would accept the principle of majority rule and thus alternation in power. Moreover, the next day Mitterrand, reversing the socialist practice in effect since Mollet made the decision to accept the Gaullist electoral law in 1958, announced that he himself was personally in favor of a return to PR. (This did not commit the Socialist Party as a whole, however.) In an interview on the radio station France-Inter on June 24, 1971, Marchais then went further. He proposed that the Communists and socialists begin a vast propaganda campaign in favor of a change to PR:

I am happy to see François Mitterrand take a position in favor of the proportional representation system; I consider that it is an important step forward by the Socialist Party. Until now we have been the only party in favor of proportional representation. And I will take this occasion to say, in the name of our Politburo which has mandated me to do it, that we propose to the Socialist

---

socialism and capitalism. . . . Thus it is necessary to render this question no longer pertinent by implementing policies which respond to the aspirations of the . . . people" (*Le Monde*, June 12, 1971, p. 9).

Party as of now . . . . to engage a large campaign across the country in order
to impose consideration of [the PR] system, the only just system, on the
present [governing] majority.

And at this point Marchais added apropos of the alternation in
power question: "The people will be called upon to pronounce themselves regularly on the government; the [socialist] parties will respect
the popular verdict." [72] Although still rather tentative, and although
he had not said it in so many words, Marchais appeared to be sig-
naling a decision of the Politiburo that the vanguard role of the Communist Party (or rather what remained of the Soviet Party example insofar as the PCF would attempt to apply it to the conditions of
France) was now considered no longer a matter of "historical necessity," but rather a function of electoral results; that the implied principle of proletarian legitimacy, which Trotsky once expressed as the
"historical birthright" of the Party, had been relegated to the dustbin
of history. [73] In the June 1972 Common Program, finally, the statements of the December 1970 "First Summary" were combined, but in
such a way as to render unequivocal the Communists' acceptance of
alternation in power:

The parties of the majority as those of the opposition will respect the verdict
expressed by universal suffrage.

If the confidence of the country were refused the majority parties, they
would renounce power to take up the struggle once again in the opposition.

But a democratic government whose existence implies the support of a popular majority, will have for its principal task the satisfaction of the laboring
masses, and will thus be firm in the ever more active confidence that they
bring to it. [74]

Although further changes are not to be excluded by any means, it
seems indisputably premature to conclude, from the Communist-
socialist Common Program of June 1972 (and up to the general elec-

[72] Both citations are from *Le Monde*, June 26, 1971, p. 8.

[73] This commitment was then made quite official in the PCF *Program* (October 1971):
"The regular organization of elections . . . is one of the essential means permitting the
people to express their judgment on the activity of the parties. The parties will respect
the popular verdict. There will be no identification of the parties with the State apparatus." (p. 128)

[74] *Common Program*, p. 149.

tions of March 1973), that the contradiction between the French Communist movement and liberal democratic procedures has been resolved, and that the French Communists have abandoned, as unapplicable and thus "historically unnecessary," the one-party concept.

In essence, the Communist acceptance of liberal party politics and their commitment to return to the opposition if defeated remains tied to the Common Program, and is interpreted by themselves and by their opponents as relating only to the period envisioned in the Program—that is, the so-called "advanced democracy." In speaking of what will happen once the "advanced democracy" becomes the "transformation to socialism," those Communists (such as Jacques Duclos and André Wurmser) who have spoken on this question since the signature of the Common Program have insisted that it will be "impossible" to retreat.[75] Thus, whereas the long negotiations to bring the French Communists to admit the principle of an alternation in power may indicate that they had originally conceived of the "advanced democracy" and the Common Program as part of a "maximalist" maneuver—that is to say, they had perhaps hoped to lead the socialists into an intransigent attempt to make of the next Left-wing government a revolutionary government—the events elapsed since the original commitment indicate a retreat to a "minimalist" conception, and even a certain preparation of the ground for a disengagement from a future Left-wing government by having already created a doctrinal justification for a failure once again to transform society. Would this

---

[75] In terms of the one-party doctrine, it is of significance that even Waldeck Rochet could write in his last book (1969): "The communists aspire logically [sic] to complete unity, that is to say, to organic unity. . . . But in a country such as France, it is possible that, alongside the Communist Party, a Socialist Party may continue to exist for a long time." *L'avenir du Parti communiste français*, pp. 114–15. (*Note:* At the time this book went to press, two new elements were added to this debate regarding the goals of the PCF. First, the coup d'état of September 1973 in Chile met with relatively little violent opposition from the Popular Unity coalition, and in particular from the Chilean Communist Party. The relevance of the Chilean experiment and failure for the case of France is not unequivocal, however. Second, in a new book by Georges Marchais, the PCF Secretary-General appears to go beyond previous statements on the alternation in power doctrine, asserting that the French Communists are prepared to leave power if voted out at any time, without qualification. See *Le défi démocratique* (Paris; Grasset, 1973).

be from motives of "revolutionary prudence," or the result of a chronic incapacity to resolve the contradiction of alliance politics and revolutionary pretensions?

In the early paragraphs of this study the following judgment, shared by nearly all observers, was expressed: that in the absence of some sudden and unpredictable change in the balance of political and military forces in Europe, the French Communists will not attempt revolution in the classic sense of insurrection or civil war. In this sense, and in the absence of such a change, the French Communists are no longer revolutionary, whatever their intentions or revolutionary élan, and assuming they prefer survival out of power to a foredoomed attempt to implement the classic strategy.

There is no conclusive way for political analysts to determine whether the often Byzantine transformation of revolutionary doctrine has been merely camouflage, and whether past priorities and present strategic constraints have rendered irrelevant the French Communists' revolutionary pretensions. Moreover, the approach taken here is not the only or necessarily the most fruitful way to study the matter. However, if the distinctions between fundamental opposition, radical capacities, and revolutionary action made throughout this study are valuable, the following conclusions may be interesting.

In the absence of a limiting case (for example, an open attempt at holding power once having returned to government; an open disavowal of the monist conception of socialist society combined with an actual practice of liberal alternation in power; or, a less definite limiting case, a refusal to accept the domestic consequences of an eventual renewal of the Cold War) one cannot be certain of the extent to which the French Communists retain the capacity for radical actions capable of implementing their fundamental opposition to the established order in a transformation of society—especially if one considers the strategic constraints on their potential for action. Nonetheless, the content of the present Communist program and the Communist-socialist Common Program both imply radical changes in the established order, politically, socially, and economically. Moreover, the Communists have defined the "advanced democracy" as a temporary stage toward a further transformation, which appears to retain as its essential characteristic the classic tautological definition of socialist society as one in which a Communist movement is hegemonic. It seems justified to assume that should the present Left coalition, or some future version of it, gain power in an election, the Common Program, or its inheritor, would at least be begun. At such a point, political scientists might be led to redefine the distinction of radical change from revolutionary action, at least in the context of an advanced industrial society. Such a discussion is quite beyond the context of the present work. Rather, let us draw the very limited conclusion that the French Communist Party at the present time appears quite capable of at least initiating unquestionably radical changes in French society by means of the Common Program tactic and the peaceful transition strategy.

The PCF and Public Opinion

If one keeps in mind that the present PCF strategy depends first of all on an electoral success, it is interesting to consider briefly the evolution of popular opinion regarding the PCF in certain key respects. The attitude of the public toward a Left government including the Communists will be a crucial factor in determining the nature, depth, and above all, the duration of such an alliance.

After the Left's remarkable gains in the legislative elections of 1967, it was generally assumed that the alliance had a good chance to continue and to solidify. There was at that time no reason to expect the events of May–June and August 1968. Thus, a SOFRES poll of February 1968 revealed that 65 percent of the sample believed that should Mitterrand win the presidential elections then scheduled for 1972, he would bring Communist ministers into the government, while only 6 percent thought definitely not.[76] And while only 25 percent of the sample as a whole believed that a leftist coalition including the Communists could form a durable government, more importantly some 58 percent of the Communist-voting sample and 45 percent of the non-Communist Left sample said this would be possible.[77] Moreover, according to a series of IFOP polls in recent years, the percentage of French people (44 percent) believing the Communist Party will gain

[76] See Lancelot and Weill in Bon et al., *Le communisme en France*, p. 294.
[77] *Ibid.*, p. 300.

ground in the next ten years is larger than the percentage for any other party.[78]

The defeat of the Left in the elections of June 1968, the ensuing breakup of the FGDS, and the "hibernation" of the Left alliance after the Soviet invasion of Czechoslovakia had a predictable effect on public opinion. A SOFRES poll in December 1969 revealed that in contrast to the apparent trend of 1967–68, only 28 percent of the sample as a whole would say the Left had a "rather probable" chance of winning the next legislative elections. Moreover, within this response, only 48 percent of the Communist voters and 31 percent of the non-Communist Left voters answered affirmatively.[79]

Even in the December 1969 study, however, one could still note signs of the growing acceptance of an increased Communist role in national politics, which has been developing among French people since the early 1960s. Besides the generalized sentiment that the Communists "ought" to have a larger role in political life,[80] the interview sample showed a startling jump in the percentage favorable to Communist ministerial participation: A July 1964 poll showed 31 percent were in favor of Communist ministers; a 1966 poll showed a result of 38 percent, a poll in February 1968 showed 48 percent, and the 1969 poll showed no less than 69 percent of the entire sample favorable to a return of the PCF to national government.[81] Furthermore, within the favorable responses, the all-important percentage of non-Communist Left voters who were in favor of PCF participation increased from 70 percent in 1968 to 89 percent in 1969, an increase that appears all the more significant in that it was recorded only one year after the Czechoslovakian invasion.

From these data one may conclude that French public opinion considers eventual Communist participation in government once again to be a highly probable event; moreover, it is increasingly in favor of such an occurrence.

[78] Monique Fichelet et al., in *Ibid.*, p. 263.

[79] SOFRES 1969, pp. 33–34. Three major SOFRES polls will be cited as SOFRES 1968, 1969, 1971. (See bibliography for full references.) SOFRES and IFOP are the initials of two major survey research organizations in France.

[80] Fichelet, in Bon et al. p. 262.

[81] *Sondages* 28, No. 1 (1966): 66, for 1964 and 1966; Lancelot and Weill, p. 295, for 1968; SOFRES 1969, p. 37, for 1969.

However, with this increased desire to see the Communists participate, the public has demonstrated a desire to delimit the nature and
extent of this participation. In the 1968 poll, 44 percent of the sample
opposed the idea of a Communist Prime Minister. In 1969 the percentage had risen to 54 percent. As for a Communist President of the
Republic, the 54 percent negative response of 1968 had jumped to 65
percent by 1969.[82] The trend was apparent even among the non-Communist Left voters, although the 1969 poll showed 40 percent in favor
of the idea of a PCF Prime Minister and 42 percent opposed.[83]

Finally, two sets of questions in the surveys concerning the scope of
Communist intentions revealed that the PCF leadership has made considerable progress in its attempt to gain public confidence, in particular as regards the non-Communist Left voters, but that the present
trend remains tenuous still.

Four different SOFRES polls, the last dating from July 1972, asked
the following question: "If the Left won the next elections, would the
PCF be a loyal partner, or would it seek to maneuver to its own
profit?" For the entire sample the results were as follows:[84]

	Loyal	Disloyal	No Response
1972	23%	50%	27%
1971	31%	50%	19%
1969	22%	57%	21%
1968	24%	35%	41%

From these figures it is clear that events since 1968 have had the effect
of crystallizing the public image of the PCF in a significant sector of
opinion previously undecided or refusing to express an opinion. Taking the total sample one notes that between 1968 and 1971 those formerly offering no response were now twice as likely to feel the Communists would be disloyal than they were to feel the Party would be
loyal to its allies. Then, in July 1972—a few weeks after the Common
Program alliance was ratified—responses to the same question showed
an 8 percent decrease in those believing the Communists would be

[82] Lancelot and Weill, in Bon et al., pp. 296–297; SOFRES 1969, p. 37.
[83] SOFRES 1969, p. 39.
[84] SOFRES 1971, p. 6; SOFRES 1969, p. 35; Lancelot and Weill, in Bon et al., p.
298. The 1972 poll is cited in *Le Figaro*, July 24, 1972, p. 4.

loyal. A similar trend is found among those voters who identify themselves as of the non-Communist Left.[85]

	Loyal	Disloyal	No Response
1972	30%	43%	27%
1971	43%	44%	13%
1969	27%	56%	17%
1968	39%	30%	31%

In these results it is noteworthy that the 1971–72 decline in the "Loyal" category among the non-Communist Left voters is 5 percent higher than for the sample as a whole. An explanatory hypothesis for such changes in opinion, and particularly applicable to the non-Communist Left voters, is that there exists a strong correlation between change in the popular image of the European Communist parties and their proximity to power: during electoral periods, particularly during those in which a Communist party has a chance of gaining entrance to government, the public expresses greater distrust of Communist intentions than during other periods, when responses to opinion polls have a tendency to be more abstract or theoretical.[86]

The second set of questions concerning the sincerity and depth of Communist doctrinal transformations revolved around the problem of the single-party regime and the principle of competitive party systems.

In the 1968 and 1969 polls, interviewers asked the following question: "If the PCF came to power, would it abolish all other parties?" In 1968 the sample as a whole contained 30 percent who said the Communists would indeed ban all opposition, 36 percent who said not, and 34 percent without an opinion. The response of non-Communist Left voters was 24 percent yes, 52 percent no and 24 percent no opinion.[87] In 1969 the total sample contained an inverse balance: 48 percent said the Communists would ban the opposition, 33 percent said they would not and only 19 percent offered no opinion. The non-Communist Left answered 39 percent yes, 51 percent no and 10 per-

---

[85] *Ibid.*, p. 7, p. 36, p. 298.
[86] This hypothesis, recently resuggested by Professor Juan Linz, demands close investigation on a comparative basis.
[87] Lancelot and Weill, in Bon et al., p. 288.

cent no opinion, indicating that although a majority of this group still believed in the sincerity of the multiparty thesis, a majority of those formerly offering no opinion had arrived at the belief that the Communists could not be trusted in this regard. Once again, the influence of the two great catalytic events of 1968 is no doubt the origin of this shift.

Finally, the 1971 poll demonstrated that the question of alternation in power, at the center of the Communist-socialist dialogue since 1969, still remained a large barrier between the PCF and public confidence. Only 19 percent of the sample said the PCF would leave power once in government again, while 61 percent believed that the Communists "would seek to remain there by any means." [88] Among the non-Communist Left voters only 27 percent said the Communists would give up power voluntarily in an election, and 42 percent of the PCF voters said they believed the Party would seek to remain in power by any means. [89]

In sum, the recent evolution of French public opinion indicates that the "peaceful transition" strategy linked to the Common Program tactic is not closed off entirely a priori, in the sense that the public is apparently prepared to encourage and to accept Communist participation in national government on a limited scale and in the context of a Left-wing government led by the socialists. *When* the French people would be led to elect a Left majority and *how far* they would be willing to support it are two of the major question marks in the future of French Communism and France itself.

A communist party in opposition justifies itself only by the future it promises. Yet it also seeks to adopt this promised future to the struggle to gain power. The tradeoff between ideological images of the future and political strategies of the present manifests in French communism the attempt to resolve the contradiction of a potentially revolutionary party in a nonrevolutionary situation.

[88] SOFRES 1971, p. 8.   [89] *Ibid.*, p. 9.

Chapter Nine

THE COUNTERCOMMUNITY AND THE ESTABLISHED SOCIETY

In his remarkable study of the revolutionary tradition in Europe, *To the Finland Station*, Edmund Wilson attempts to give an idea of what life was like for Marx and Engels as political exiles in London:

The life of political exiles becomes infected with special states of mind which are unimaginable for men who have a country. Those precisely whose principles and interests have raised them above the ordinary citizen, now lacking the citizen's base and his organic relation to society, find themselves contracted to something less. . . . For communists the situation is even harder. . . . Since the communist has set himself against the whole complex of society, he must try to live in it without being of it. . . . He is thrown in upon his few comrades and himself, and they develop bad nerves and bad tempers; they are soon wasting their mental energies and their emotions in sterile controversies and spiteful quarrels. Group enthusiasm turns to intrigue, and talent becomes diseased with vanity. The relationships of revolutionary brotherhood become degraded by jealousy and suspicion. Always braced against the pressure that bears down on them both as aliens and as enemies of society, the self-alienated man gives way to impulses to round upon his associates and accuse them of selling out the cause.[1]

It is not very farfetched to compare the existence of a political exile forced to leave his country to that of a political exile who remains within its borders, at least in the very important sense of attempting to "live in society without being of it." And, in effect, particularly with respect to the 1920–34, 1939–41 and 1947–62 periods in the history of French Communism, social scientists and general observers alike have often remarked or analyzed the movement as a separate community or society—what I will call here a *countercommunity*. Even

[1] (Garden City, N.Y.: Doubleday and Co., Inc., 1940), pp. 221–22.

more than the Italian movement, in the prewar period clandestine and in the postwar period characterized by considerably more open contact with the rest of Italian society, the French Communist movement has long been recognized to constitute a community within a society.

Still, while the French Communist community has been analyzed both with regard to its internal structures and its social bases,[2] its historical development and the political implications therein have been but little drawn, in particular insofar as the countercommunity dimension is compatible or incompatible with the PCF's other roles.

In the present chapter, after some preliminary remarks on the nature and general demarcations of the countercommunity (essentially an extension of Kriegel's analysis) these political implications will be examined. Chapter 12 will treat the relations of the countercommunity and the other "faces" of the Communist movement in France.

In the following two chapters we shall examine the Communist movement as it has played the roles of government party and peoples' tribune. It is precisely because the Party has played these two system-oriented roles that one finds the expression of partial and transitional acceptance of the status quo characteristic of communist parties in opposition. It is the two antithetical roles of countercommunity and revolutionary vanguard that manifest the fundamental opposition of the Communists to this same status quo.

The French Communist countercommunity can be envisioned as an alternative minisociety, founded on the organizational structure of the Party and "living" within the existing national society. As the choice of terms would indicate, however, the countercommunity is more than merely a society. The classic distinction between *Gemeinschaft* and *Gesellschaft*, first drawn in detail by Tönnies, informs us that

---

[2] On various aspects, see Bibliography for works by Kriegel, Duverger, Micaud; André Barjonet, *Le Parti communiste français*, parts 2 and 3; Alain Brayance (pseud.), *Anatomie du Parti communiste français;* Jean-Marie Domenach, "The French Communist Party," in Mario Einaudi, et al., *Communism in Western Europe.* For a contemporary analysis of the PCF internal structure as static bureaucratic centralism, reasserting this old theme particularly with regard to May–June, 1968, see Richard Johnson, *The French Communist Party Versus the Students* (New Haven: Yale University Press, 1972). See also the interesting set of memoirs of militants published by the PCF under the title "Souvenirs," in particular, Florimond Bonte, *De l'ombre à la lumière;* Virgile Barel, *50 années de lutte;* Léo Figuères, *Jeunesse militante;* and Laurent Naves, *Mon chemin.*

whereas a society may be said to be a human association bound together by a body of rules, a community is a society pervaded by certain shared values and objectives outside of the rules themselves. In terms of this distinction, there are serious reasons to consider that the French nation, even today, forms a society but not a community.[3]

Within the boundaries of French society, on the other hand, one would be justified in pointing to the existence of many subnational communities. They are most easily identified when one considers certain manifestations of region, race, and religion, and perhaps also the classic political "families" in France. However, there is probably no single community in France more closely knit and more active than the Communist community, for no other community has a more explicit and uniform code of membership, values, and goals; and no other community has such a high degree of participation in and enforcement of the general norms.

In effect, the establishment of a countercommunity was historically understood by the communists as the beginning of a "dual power" double circuit of French "bourgeois" society as a whole, just as the Party institutions themselves were an embryonic double circuit of the state institutions. After the revolution, they believed, the countercommunity would grow and be enfranchised with the new revolutionary legitimacy to become the new Establishment. Conversely, the expansion of the countercommunity to become the Establishment (under the guidance of the Party) would be merely another way of saying the revolution had occurred.

Within the PCF countercommunity were thus already contained certain model practices and norms of the future regime. As Kriegel has put it: "A communist party, imbedded in a country in which it does not hold power, functions as a party-society: the countersociety which it constitutes in the interior of the global society prefigures the

[3] For example, Stanley Hoffmann remarked in the early 1960s in his striking contribution to the collective volume *In Search of France*, entitled "Paradoxes of the French Political Community": "Indeed, the fundamental question I must try to answer is whether France *is* a political community" (pp. 1–2). On p. 116 he concludes "my answer would have to be no," and on p. 102 he says that "the worst aspect of the present vacuum is that France is left without any legitimate (i.e., generally accepted) set of institutions." Hoffmann wrote at the end of the Algerian war.

socialist society which it wishes to substitute for the established society after the conquest of power." [4]

On an individual level, entrance into the Communist countercommunity is surely sometimes the result of what Erik Erikson has termed an "identity crisis." By joining the Party the individual resolves his personal search for identity in some decisive and radical action, as did Martin Luther in taking the fateful decision: "Here I stand, I can do no other."

Probably no one who has had personal contacts with members of a communist party would deny that the "identity crisis" is an apt conceptualization for a number of entrances into the movement. Yet, this pattern would seem to hold true mainly for intellectuals, and the range of people to whom it applies has probably diminished even more since the beginning of de-Stalinization, because the Communist Party has thereafter declined as an intellectually acceptable vehicle for redemption.

The identity crisis notwithstanding, the most common route into the French Communist community is much less dramatic. In the working-class milieu of the Paris suburbs and the industrial Nord, and in underdeveloped agricultural areas like the Cher and the Haute-Vienne, joining the Communist Party or the CGT remains a normal event—certainly remarkable but in no sense remotely approaching the implications of joining the Communist Party in the United States or England, for example.[5] For the normal new Party member, however radical a decision to join may appear to the outsider, in particular the foreigner whose own country does not know a strong Communist movement, it is in a personal sense a radically conservative decision. For Martin Luther, resolution of his identity crisis led him to a new position of radical individualism, of total independence from the Church, whereas for the normal new member of the Communist community the decision to join manifests a choice in exactly the opposite

[4] Kriegel, "Les communistes français et leurs juifs," *"L'Arche* 167 (January 25–February 25, 1971) :47. This conception does not imply, however, that the future regime is to be an exact reproduction of the Party institutions or the future society an exact reproduction of the countercommunity.

[5] Cf. the still relevant data and conclusions in this regard in Gabriel Almond, *The Appeals of Communism.*

direction: the substitution of one imposing authority for another. The individually conservative choice to join the Communist movement is given a radical content only at the social or collective level—only insofar as the Party leadership is able to render the entire organization radical in opposition to the established order.

As in any structurally solid community, the strength and foundation of the Communist community is not to be found at the summit of the structures of power and authority. Rather, its resilience is created in the mundane existence lived by most of its members most of the time.

One of the fundamental characteristics of a true community is the extraordinary amount of time, energy, and commitment the individual member expends within it, so much so that the most solid, if not necessarily the happiest, communities are no doubt those in which people tend to live out their entire lives. And indeed, the French Communists have attempted to create an entire life as much as possible for the community, to the extent that when they are not within its boundaries they feel themselves on foreign terrain. Quite obviously this can be only a partial success, for two fundamental reasons.

First, the community is a physical as well as a psychological phenomenon. Physically, the French Communist community exists within the greater French society with which it is obliged to enter into necessary and crucial relationships, in particular those of work and extended family. This is perhaps the most obvious limiting factor on the degree of community to which the Communist movement can aspire. To the degree that the lack of physical isolation can be overcome or ignored, the Communist community can more easily create and sustain a mass psychology conscious of itself as without and in fundamental opposition to the established "bourgeois" order. Conversely, to the extent that the Communist movement becomes intermingled with the established patterns of daily life practiced by the rest of society, its own cohesion is weakened.

The second limiting factor is the reticence or resistance of potential members of the community to allow themselves to be completely immersed within it. One may conceive a gradation of emotional, intellectual, and material commitment to the community along the following lines: *electors, sympathizers, supporters, members, militants, "apparatchiks."* One would expect the latter three categories to be well integrated into the community, although it is probably valid to assume that somewhere between 20 and 50 percent of the Party members are much less than fully integrated: one must keep in mind that the annual turnover in the membership is 30,000, and must also allow for a number of marginal members who belong to the Party but do not participate in the community.[6] On the other hand, it is also no doubt justified to assume that the great majority if not the quasi-totality of the PCF electorate outside of its own membership does not belong to the Communist community, or if so, only in a marginal way. The boundaries of the countercommunity, given that they are essentially psychological and not physical in nature, are thus seen to be rather fluid, wending their way amorphously through the marginal group of actual party members into the groups of supporters and sympathizers, or "fellow travelers" as they used to be called. Yet, although the community boundaries are not extremely rigid, it would be an error to believe that the community does not exist. The problem is rather the extreme difficulty in identifying the limits in any strict empirical sense, a task which would be of no great interest in and of itself.

The party as a community attempts to blur as much as possible the distinction between the public and private life of the individual. Its aim is to organize his daily life into Party life.

First of all, his working life becomes absorbed into the Party framework. At his place of work he is expected daily to spread the ideas of Marxism-Leninism as well as the *mots d'ordre* of the Party. In this he works within his local cell, which transmits the Party line from higher up; he also takes his cues from the matters emphasized in the urban Party newspaper, *L'Humanité*, or the rural paper, *La Terre*. Furthermore, he is expected to join the CGT, although a significant number

[6] In explaining the unexpectedly significant number of Communist abstention votes in the April 23, 1972 referendum on Europe (i.e. adopting the Socialist Party tactic), PCF analyst Leo Lorenzi referred directly to this type of attachment: "And the Communist 'abstentions'? . . . Why should there not be some? . . . . They are those who are the furthest from Party activity, who show themselves susceptible to reformist ideas, who are less prepared to resist them. . . ." (*Le Monde*, May 5, 1972, p. 9).

of Party members are not members of the latter.[7] In the CGT, as in all the ancillary organizations in which Communists and non-Communists are found together, he is expected to attempt to attract new members into the Party fold, and the entire gamut of ancillary organizations is treated as one of the most useful transmission belts for recruitment purposes. It is not correct to say that the CGT is a "communist" organization, however, as a simple comparison of CGT membership (1.5–2 million) with PCF membership (350,000–400,000) tends to prove. The Communists claim to be active (*militant*) in the CGT, but this is as much an understatement as the above is an overstatement. A more accurate phrase is to say the CGT is Communist-dominated, as Party members hold almost all of the key positions.[8] The CGT weekly, *La vie ouvrière*, normally contains the Party's *mots d'ordre*, sometimes slightly reworded, as do the local factory papers. Thus, the feeling of community among the Communists can be effectively sustained at their place of work by Party activity carried out within the CGT.

Leisure time is also much taken up with Party activities. One may be attending Party or syndicate meetings, working with another ancillary organization (such as the Peace Movement), or participating in a Communist sports group or youth association. The Party also sponsors such events as fairs, picnics, and carnivals, which the member's entire family is expected to attend. The key Party social event is *La Fête de L'Humanité*, held each autumn in a Paris park. This carnival and propaganda platform draws between 500,000 and 1,000,000 peo-

[7] For example, at the 8th Congress (1954), Marcel Servin asserted that of 96,733 Party members eligible for the CGT, 23,177, or almost 24 percent had not joined. See Kriegel, *Communistes français*, p. 86.

[8] Since the 1947–48 split, the two Secretaries General of the CGT, Benoît Frachon and presently Georges Séguy, have both been members of the Politburo. As of 1971, 7 members of the 15-member Confederation Executive belonged to the PCF. In Italy, syndicalist autonomy from the parties, at least structurally, became total in 1969, when reunification was envisioned. The Communist-socialist CGIL accepted the CSIL and UIL condition of interdicting dual membership at the leadership levels. The CGIL Secretary General, Luciano Laura, gave up his seat in the PCI Politburo, and from 1969 forward CGIL leaders no longer were candidates in political elections. (See Peter Weitz, "The CGIL in PCI Strategy," a paper presented to the Conference on French and Italian Communism, October, 1972.)

ple, as well as the participation in recent years of such enterprises as IBM and Bull General Electric.

Finally, the Party as a community attempts to penetrate the nuclear family entirely. The wife of a militant may likely be a Party member herself, and may perhaps also be affiliated with the Union of French Women and various Party Housewives' Committees. The children are often enrolled in the Communist youth organizations, and are thus raised within the confines of the community from almost the very beginning.

Outside of the activities in which the members of the Communist community are expected to engage in perpetually, there are other temporary activities also of great importance. Perhaps the most significant of these is the network of "schools" or short courses run under Party auspices. Because many adult Communists left school at an early age, received a poor education, or did not do well themselves, the notion of a return to a sort of formal education is often appealing, and particularly so since they are sure to learn "the answers" and since attendance at a Party school is one of the informal requirements for promotion within the hierarchy.

Various forms of a Party educational system have been tried over the years, ranging from correspondence courses to monthly educational conferences, graduated reading guides to the encouragement of "personal study." However, the most successful formula, which has been most used, is the "short course," the purpose of which is to give "a systematic introduction to the doctrine" to selected militants.[9] There are three basic types of Party short courses, or schools: *elementary* schools, which take place on the level of Party sections in the form of a series of evening courses; the *federation* schools, which take place at the federation level, sometimes during the evening, sometimes during the day; and *central* schools, for which the location is the Central Party School, until recently located just outside of Paris in the former home of Maurice Thorez. The central schools, which last from one to four months, sometimes are directed to a specific audience of specialized cadres, such as syndicalist militants, peasant militants, or

[9] Kriegel, *Communistes français*, pp. 167–68. The following section is based on her analysis, pp. 166–76.

women, and at other times are directed to groups whose members are approximately equal in the responsibility they exercise "in civilian life" (for example factory foremen).[10]

During recent years, approximately one out of every six new Party members attended an elementary school: 18 percent in 1967 and 15.6 percent in 1968.[11] The increase in the number of students in federation schools is similar to that of the increase in Party members since World War II. In 1946, there were 235 such schools with 4,473 students enrolled;[12] in 1955–56, there were only 57 federation schools with 737 students enrolled, and by 1957–58 there were 90 schools and over 900 students.[13] In the Period 1967–69, there was a total of 408 such schools teaching 5,036 students.[14] During the same period, there were 30 central schools, which were attended by 997 militants. The cumulative effect of this system of schools was that, despite the fact that only one of approximately six new members attends an elementary school, indicating that the nonmilitant membership tends to avoid them, "it seems that a very large majority of the existing cadres have attended a school, federation or central. . . . Of the 960 delegates to the 19th Congress in January 1970, 750 had attended one or more schools."[15] As a training ground for the Party elite, the internal school system is thus of considerable importance; and with respect to the strengthening and preservation of the countercommunity values and norms, the evaluation of Annie Kriegel is quite profound:

In sum, it is not impossible that its system of schools is for the Party what the system of primary schools was for the Third Republic: a forceful agent of cohesion, a mold of exceptional quality. In assuring first of all the formation of cadres, it fulfills more broadly a triple function within the interior of the communist subsociety: it assures the "social purity" of its leadership class; it assures the general mobility of the social body in such a way that this leadership class is constantly irrigated with new blood; and finally, it assures the transmission and the circulation of collective archtypes and tradition. A triple role having a comon character: that of being conservative. . . . In this case, the conservation of Bolshevism . . . and in any case, of a revolutionary per-

---

[10] *Ibid.*, p. 168.   [11] *Ibid.*, p. 175.

[12] PCF–11, Thorez report, p. 82.   [13] PCF–15, Thorez report.

[14] Léon Feix, "Les cadres communistes," *Cahiers du communisme*, February, 1970, p. 185.

[15] Kriegel, *Communistes français*, p. 175.

spective, state of mind and language, contrasting with the reformist practice of daily militant life. If the Leninist themes . . . still induce so many echoes after fifty years, it is because they are *taught*, even if it be abstractly and in an unorganized manner, thus replenishing in depth a current of eschatologic and millenarian fervor.[16]

Of course, the ideal-type conception of the party as community sketched above does not exactly correspond to the reality of the French Communist movement as it has existed over the past half-century. Despite the inevitable gap between political theory and political reality, however, the degree to which the French Communist movement has evolved into a cohesive community strikes the observer so forcefully that it appears to be of the essence of the particular form the Marxist-Leninist-Stalinist conception has taken in France. The Bolshevik Party, for example, before taking power was very much unlike the French party in terms of size, continuity, and degree of participation in the established political institutions. In fact, with respect to these criteria, the PCF resembles more the CPSU in power than the Bolshevik Party in revolutionary opposition. To explain the rise of a countercommunity one is once again led back to the "accident" of 1934–36, in which the rise of Nazism led indirectly to the ballooning of the French Communist Party from a declining sect of about 30,000 to a mass movement of 300,000 members. This transformation, although it may not have been realized at the time, fundamentally altered the nature and perspective of the Communist movement in France. From that point onward, the French Communist (and Comintern) leaders were obliged to calculate strategy and tactics on the basis of a large and unwieldy permanent movement (the period 1939–43 excepted), which had the effect of rendering the 1917 model, still retained at least in theory, totally unrealistic in fact, although the illusion was not finally given up until long after.

It is possible to pinpoint the time of the emergence and solidification of the Communist countercommunity. Although one is naturally inclined to consider the 1934–36 period, there are nevertheless good reasons to place the genesis further on. For one thing, to fulfill the criteria of a community the common attachments and beliefs unit-

[16] *Ibid.*, pp. 175–76.

ing the members must be rather solid and must revolve around a set of values and goals effectively internalized by the membership. Furthermore, one is disinclined to apply the term community to any grouping that has not demonstrated its durability over a period of time. The Communist movement before 1939 cannot be said to have satisfied either of these requirements. The overwhelming majority of the 1936–38 membership was too recent and the proportion of militants to members too small for one to consider the movement effectively integrated around a well-internalized set of common beliefs and norms.[17]

The years of the Resistance, the Liberation, and Tripartism brought the rebirth of the French Communist movement and the reinflation of its membership ranks and influence after the dissolution and decimation of 1939–40. During these years, however, the movement was at the same time too enmeshed with the rest of society to constitute a separate community of reasonably definable proportions, a problem aggravated once again with the fact of a tremendous percentage of new and untrained members who had only weakly internalized the norms of what was still the protocommunity. One might even say that the Communist tractic of emphasizing collaboration over the hard line at this time was too successful to allow the countercommunity to emerge. There were basically too many points of attachment and too much lack of definition in the boundary between Communist and non-Communist organizations for the mass of the movement to have internalized a "without" psychology based effectively on the Marxist-Leninist-Stalinist perspective. Moreover, the Liberation *élan* was precisely one of intense participation and desire to recast the fundamentals of the ancien régime such that, once it was decided that the Communists would not attempt insurrection, the movement adopted a psychological "within" posture more strongly than ever before.

We thus are led to *le grand scheme* of 1947–53, during which time the French Communists were obliged to accept the implications of their

---

[17] The matter of the proportion of militants to members can only be discussed in the most general terms. However observers do seem to agree that in the postwar period approximately 35 to 50 percent of the PCF's membership can be termed militant, a very high ratio compared to other parties. The prewar percentage was somewhat lower.

ouster from government in May 1947, when the exorcism of communism in the West became rigid and widespread. It is because of the
special character of *le grand schisme* that one is inclined to date the consolidation of the French Communist countercommunity from this
period. For one thing, the tremendous contraction of Communist
memberships in the Party, in the CGT, and in the ancillary organizations, was a clear indication that the marginal members of the community were being driven out by the pressure from the rest of society.
Furthermore, pressure was being exerted at the same time for a purifi-
cation from within, for it is a common reaction of a community, when
being attacked, to close ranks and to demand unusual demonstrations
of loyalty and conformity to the rules and values. Those who had
joined the movement during 1941–47 but who could not accept what
David Caute has termed "intellectual Stalinism" were driven out or
left of their own accord. Evidence from Caute's volume on *Communism
and the French Intellectuals* supports this conclusion. Caute found that
aside from two periods in its history, and aside from specific cases
which contradict a general trend (such as the expulsion of Roger
Garaudy in 1970), the French Communist leadership "has made consistent and strenuous efforts to gain the support or cooperation of intellectuals, the periods 1924–32 and 1949–52 being . . . exceptions to
this rule." [18] For the years 1924–32—that is, during the bolshevization of the movement—such an attitude is easily explained: the demand for conformity and strict adherence to Comintern directives in
the interest of protection of the Soviet Union and hopefully revolutionary action was given increasing priority over the "creative" but
self-defeating Marxism characteristic of the PCF before 1924. The
years 1949–52 are described by Caute as follows:

Despite the immensely effective propaganda surrounding the Peace Movement . . . for the next few years a definite hardening of attitudes was apparent, the general sentiment being that intellectuals as a class had once again
proven their inherent unreliability, failing to adopt correct "class positions" on
such subjects as Titoism, the trials in the Popular Democracies, Zhdanovism,
and Soviet labor camps.[19]

The Peace Movement was at the time the PCF leadership's major
attempt to treat with the outside non-Communist world, and was in

---

[18] p. 34.   [19] *Ibid.*, p. 28.

fact its only productive tactic of this period. On the inside, however, within what Louis Aragon had idealized as *la Famille*, all "deviations" that tended to question or revise the doctrines of Marxism-Leninism-Stalinism were meeting with stern repression. While this strengthening of "intellectual Stalinism" was peripherally a reflection of the struggle against the Titoist deviation, its deeper motivation was the necessity to reaffirm the values of the Communist community, to protect the ideology, and eventually the organization itself, from the intentions of its enemies in a situation of domestic Cold War. Finally, this development in French communism, comprehensible even from the point of view of the internal situation in France alone, was confirmed and encouraged by a similar tendency in the Soviet Union: it was during Stalin's last years that, as he became increasingly paranoid, the use of psychological and physical terror against the Soviet population became once again much more widespread and arbitrary than during the years of the Grand Alliance, and at this time the Stalinist system took on a visage similar to that of the 1930s, the years of the Great Purge.

In the French movement, the Stalinist phenomenon known today as the "cult of personality" was also realized to a degree, built around the figure of Maurice Thorez—the *Fils du peuple*, as his autobiography would have it. During the late 1930s and after his return to France in 1944, a definite cult of personality or blind idealization had settled over the person of Thorez; but it was only after 1947, however, during the difficult period when the countercommunity was reduced and consolidated, that this form of leader worship became one of the significant facts of Party life. The French Communist congresses of this period closed with tributes to Stalin and Thorez hardly comprehensible today. Such sensitive men of letters as Paul Eluard and Aragon wrote paeanic verse in their honor permeated with a fanatic religious fervor. And on the occasion of Thorez's fiftieth birthday (1950), the Party circulated, in the style of letters, special membership forms: "Dear Maurice Thorez, I wish you long life and good health, and on the occasion of your fiftieth birthday I am joining the French Communist Party. . . . I hereby join the Party of Maurice Thorez." [20]

[20] Cited in Duverger, *Political Parties*, pp. 180–81. See the original membership form attached to the Thorez report to the 12th Congress (sold as a brochure), p. 97. On the

The strengthening of the "cult of personality" around Maurice Thorez was a fact of importance in the consolidation of the Communist community, for it gave the membership a focus and a point of unity desperately necessary during a period of extreme external pressures. His sudden illness in late 1950, which was to last for over two years, was thus not surprisingly a crucial factor in the confusion and indecision that characterized the movement in the early 1950s. Still, by 1950, the point of greatest danger had been passed and, though weakened, the countercommunity was able to survive.

In sum, during a period roughly encompassing the years 1948–53, the French Communist countercommunity was consolidated and demonstrated that it could survive in the national political life. The boundaries separating it from the rest of French society became more recognizable and rigid; the allegience of its members became more dogmatic and absolutist; those who were either unwilling to resist the pressures of the "outside world" or who refused to make the greater sacrifice of personal independence demanded in connection with the reaffirmation and tightening of the community belief structure were separated from the group. The reduction of Party membership to between 250,000 and 300,000 by 1954–55 and its stabilization at that point represents the bottoming out of the curve—in effect the stabilization of the countercommunity at a point that events since 1956 have not fundamentally altered.

Having characterized very generally the nature of the French Communist countercommunity and its historical development, we may now turn to the question of the significance of this role in terms of the relationship between the communist movement and the society at large.

In the Introduction we made a distinction between different forms of opposition and we contrasted *fundamental* opposition with *total* or *systematic* opposition. In the following two chapters, which analyze the Communist movement in the roles of government party and tribune, we shall make evident the analytical yield from the distinction of fundamental and total opposition. In effect, given the influence that the roles of government party and people's tribune have played in the his-

---

blind adoration of Stalin and Thorez by certain French intellectuals at this time, see especially Caute, *Communism and the French Intellectuals*, pp. 215–24.

torical development of the Communist movement in France, it would be a simple and gross inaccuracy to assert that the PCF has been totally and systematically opposed to the status quo. Yet at the same time one must account for its persistent resistance to becoming part of the Establishment. *Fundamental opposition* is a term that accurately reflects this resistance. The anchor of this resistance is the counter-community, which in effect provides the structural basis of the perpetual negation of the status quo by the Communist movement, a perpetuation of the "without" psychology, and a continuing support for the movement's ultimate role of vanguard of the revolutionary transition.

One of Lenin's major preoccupations as he developed his theory of a "new-type" party was to create a means by which to combat the first "revisionism," that of Bernstein, Kautsky, and their followers in the Second International. Aside from the all-important introduction of the ideas of conscious organization and strategic planning into proletarian revolutionary doctrine, as opposed to the *attentiste* attitude of the social democrats who held to the original Marxist notion that the economic revolution must necessarily precede the political revolution, Lenin's organizational propositions had still another aim: to develop a way to prevent the progressive integration of the working class into the status quo, or as Herbert Marcuse has put it, "to save Marxian orthodoxy from the reformist onslaught." [21] All the Marxists tended to agree that the working class was by nature conservative and reformist, and would continue to be so until the "contradictions of capitalism" had more deeply "ripened." [22] The overenthusiastic espousal of partial gains by the social democratic parties and syndicates, what Lenin called "economism," had to his mind diverted the working class from achieving greater consciousness of its supposedly inevitable revolutionary role. To transform the "economist," integration-oriented nature of the social democratic working-class parties once more into a political nature, into a revolutionary nature, was thus the goal of Lenin's theory of the "new-type party."

In short, by design the "new-type" Bolsehvik-style party, in addition to playing the positive role of revolutionary vanguard, had also

[21] *Soviet Marxism*, p. 32.

[22] A common argument in this regard was that "the great majority of the working class will gain revolutionary consciousness only in the revolution itself."

the negative task of restraining the normally nonrevolutionary working classes from accepting and legitimating the established order, which would have retarded the revolutionary process. The key factor to this end was to be the example set by the Bolsheviks themselves, a small, pure group of "new men."

Of course the pre-revolutionary Russian Bolshevik Party, being itself extremely small and composed mainly of dedicated radicals, had only minor problems restraining integrationist tendencies in its midst. For the French Communist movement, the problem has been of a totally different character, however. For one thing, by the time the Bolshevik Party became large in size (1924–25) the political revolution itself was completed. With regard to the PCF, during the period 1924–32—when the French Party was more concerned with creating an effectively Bolshevik movement than with retaining its loose and heterogeneous membership—the problem was hardly posed; for the Party had begun in 1920 with a membership so large and so divided that to approximate the Russian model meant undertaking both an organizational and ideological self-transformation, both aspects of which implied a narrowing and homogenizing of the membership.

By the late 1920s, when the earlier Bolshevik hopes of imminent revolution in the Western European industrialized countries had been set aside in the face of obviously nonrevolutionary conditions, the French movement was faced with the serious problem of what to do. In the Russian situation the question "what does a revolutionary party do while waiting for a revolutionary situation?" had been answered in reality without the Bolsehviks having to make difficult choices: the movement was small and more or less always illegal. Those leaders who remained within the country were conspirators hounded by the authorities; the rest were in exile. The French situation was decisively different: the party was legal and begun from a very large base; even by 1932 it had enough members left to continue its legal and parliamentary action.

The "accident" of 1934–35, by burdening the Party with a large mass membership—which it was obliged to nurture in the interest of the "struggle against fascism" and the Soviet foreign policy regarding prewar coalition maneuvers—in effect provided the French Communists with an answer to the question of what to do: *conserve and stabilize*. It is unlikely that this result of the Popular Front initiative had been foreseen in 1933–34, when it was being pondered in Comintern circles, and in any case after that point it became extremely difficult to envision a return to the revolutionary-sect type of organization the Party was tending toward by 1932. Instead, the leadership consciously or unconsciously sought to make a virtue of a defect: the "prerevolutionary" movement became a mass movement and size (membership, electoral, and syndical) came to be taken as a significant measure of tactical and strategic progress.

With the foreshadowing of the PCF countercommunity in 1934–38 and 1941–47 and its consolidation during the years 1948–53 the nature of the Party's role in directing the proletariat and preventing its assimilation within the established society underwent a profound change; from the example of a small tightly organized sect of dedicated professional revolutionaries (or so the Bolshevik model would have it) the Party had become an entire community within itself. Whereas Lenin and the other Bolsheviks attempted to live lives totally dedicated to the practice of revolution in an immediate sense, the members of the French Party as community had now to conceive the example of a lifestyle in which the greater part of the individual's time was spent in obviously non revolutionary activities (the very contradiction of a classic revolutionary life), in which even wives and children took part, and yet which could still be presented to the masses as a fundamental rejection of the status quo.[23] But even if the form of the Party and the nature of its role were decisively altered by the events of 1934–36, the function of the Party as educator remained the same: to set an avant-garde example of "radical proletarian consciousness" until the decisive moment arrived, and until then to restrain the militants, and, by organization and by example, to restrain the working class from the temptations of assimilation. Thus, the post-1947 mass countercommunity became the foundation of the continued resistance of the French Communist movement to the precedent of the social democrats. It became the cornerstone of the continued fundamental opposi-

---

[23] Compare with pre-1917 Bolshevik practice this statement by Thorez: "The Communist Party is not interested only in its militants. It takes care of their families, their wives and their children. It does not tear the combatant . . . away from his family. It integrates the family in the fraternal phalanx. . . . How much more joyous and easy the accomplishment of his task appears to the communist when he feels, when he knows that the Party does not forget those who are dear to him!" (*Fils du peuple*, 1949 edition, p. 252).

tion of the Communists to the established order in the absence of revolution.

The effect of the Communist countercommunity on French political and social life has been a matter of dispute. Robert Wohl represents the point of view of many:

This explains what must otherwise remain a mystifying paradox: why the effect of Communism on French national life has been so unfailingly reactionary. Instead of breaking through the walls of non-communication that separated Frenchmen, Communism deliberately set out to reinforce them. It is thus no mere *jeu d'esprit* to call the PCF the greatest bulwark of the bourgeois status quo.[24]

A critic of such a point of view might well ask how the Communist actions of 1936–37 and 1944–46—periods of great social reform and the only periods in which the PCF was associated with the national government—fit into such an argument. Yet at the same time it is significant that these periods of governmental participation have been precisely those times during which the Communist community has been the least rigid. While Wohl's judgment is overly categorical, it provokes a criticism leading to a deeper understanding of the PCF as a countercommunity.

Another type of evaluation of the French Communist movement suggests that because the Party is "already in power" within the countercommunity and because of the success of its electoral role as tribune, the desire to take power throughout society has been lost or given up.[25] This sort of judgment, which is criticized in chapters 8 and 12, rests upon a rather arbitrary denial of the sincerity of the doctrine of peaceful transition to socialism. However, a less arbitrary if more modest evaluation is perhaps possible, without merely taking a stand on the basis of unnecessarily vague formulations or unverifiable conclusions about the Communist psychology.

Essentially, the conclusions to be drawn from the above analysis are rather uncomplicated. From the time the French Communist Party

[24] Robert Wohl, *French Communism in the Making*, p. 446. See also, for example, Michel Crozier, "La France, terre de commandement," *Esprit*, December, 1957; Charles Micaud, *Communism and the French Left*; Roy Macridis, "The Immobility of the French Communist Party."

[25] See (e.g.) Georges Lavau in Bon et al., *Le communisme en France*, and André Barjonet, *La CGT*. More than a half-century earlier Robert Michels had made a similar argument concerning the SPD.

became a mass party, thereby transforming Lenin's conception of the Communists in opposition as a small group of enlightened professional revolutionaries into a miniature version of the future socialist society as a whole, the Party as community became the infrastructure re-straining the Communist movement (if not the working class as a whole) from resolving the ambivalent position it occupied within the status quo in imitation of the social democrat assimilation.[26] The factors most important in the success of this function were three: the totalist (some would prefer totalitarian) structure of the movement internally; the successful perpetuation of a millenarian psychology; the interna-tional character of the revolutionary enterprise, permitting the ratio-nalization of failure or containment in France by identification with supposed successes on a "higher" level.[27] Success in perpetuating this fundamental opposition has meant that the gap between theory and practice, between a revolutionary future and a nonrevolutionary present, has been kept open. In context, this is a positive accomplish-ment, for, given the absence of revolution, to be able to say the gap was closed would imply that it had been closed in the direction of present practice, of nonrevolution.[28]

In terms of the relation between the Communist movement and the society at large, for the Communists the problem is not one of com-municating with other Frenchmen, but rather of irreducible conflicts with a ruling class whose interests are understood as diametrically op-posed to their own. Thus, to argue that the Communists deliberately set out to reinforce these conflicts and have been successful in doing so certainly can be no condemnation of Communist action in terms of their own goals.

---

[26] The only social democratic party of the Second International to have constituted a community structure was the German Social Democratic Party. The SPD example was of great interest to the Comintern leaders in this regard. Lenin wrote in *Left-Wing Com-munism*, for example, "We are apprehensive of an excessive growth of the Party, be-cause careerists and charlatans . . . inevitably do all they can to insinuate themselves into the ranks of the ruling party" (*Selected Works*, p. 537).

[27] For a similar argument, cf. Kriegel, *Communistes français* and in Michelle Perrot and Kriegel, *Le socialisme français et le pouvoir*.

[28] A further alternative would be to adapt the theory so that the concept of revolution is so redefined that what would not have been called revolutionary in previous doctrine becomes so in the revised version. This is one common interpretation of the post-1956 transformation in French communism.

In non-Leninist categories, one may say that persistence of the Communist countercommunity has successfully continued the schism in the polity that broke open in 1789, and which has been renewed repeatedly over the next 130 years in different forms. Transformed by the growth of democratic politics from the original horizontal schism separating the powerful from the powerless to a vertical cleavage separating two forms of politics—Communist and non-Communist—this "pillarization" of the conflict between the Marxist-Leninist-Stalinist theory of history and all other doctrines of legitimacy, has remained one of the predominant characteristics of French political life. The effect of this cleavage is such that so long as the French Communist movement holds to the "chain of legitimacies," what I have called the "vertical mirror effect" will continue to be the pattern of the practical relationships between itself and the rest of society.

Tocqueville and countless others since have stressed the factor of overlapping memberships and loyalties in the achievement of consensus on the legitimate forms of politics in democratic society. By dividing one's loyalties between many organizations, no one of them claims all of one's allegience or represents all of one's interest. Citizens are thus led to compromise in political life, accepting that a given loss will sooner or later be made up by a compensating gain. The persistence of the Communist countercommunity in France, based on an exclusive and revolutionary principle of legitimacy, has made impossible the consummation of such a polity and social order. And while not the unique or even most successful challenge to the legitimacy of French regimes in the 20th century, the Communist movement remains now the most significant segment of the polity outside the generally accepted rules of the game.

There are several directions in which the countercommunity might evolve as a structure, all of which depend on the concomitant evolution in the other "faces" of Communism, nationally and internationally. First, should the Party, in its role of revolutionary vanguard, progress in its present aim of "guiding" a governmental coalition of socialist parties, the countercommunity would risk being weakened by enlarged and deepened contacts with other political forces and the disenchantment of finding itself a nonpermanent government party. Nonetheless, it is not likely that the community dimension of the

French Communist movement will disappear, for even in the absence of a strict single-party mentality, it would be naive to suppose the special historical role claimed by the Communists would easily or quickly evaporate. And in particular they would consider themselves invested with the task of "guaranteeing" the ideological and practical vigor of a Left coalition in a manner foreclosed to the more humble social democrats. Even in the "pluralist" climate of the Common Program after June 1972, Communist statements such as the following by L'Humanité editorialist René Andrieu have not been exceptional: "It is up to the Communists especially to raise enthusiasms and to galvanize energies. Their only ambition is to show themselves the best in the grand combat." [29]

A second way in which the countercommunity might evolve without a success of the Left coalition would be through economic development and structural transformations within the society as a whole. It is at least a matter of doubt whether such changes alone would act to break down the "without" psychology of the Communist community, in that rapid social change contains within itself sufficient strain and cleavage for the Communist outlook to be replenished.[30]

Of all the probable influences, however, the most significant might well be a continued evolution of international politics toward greater détente and perhaps one day entente. Should the Soviet Union progressively open its society to free contact with the Western world, it is difficult to see how the French Communists could resist the example. On the other hand, should there occur a renewed international political or economic crisis (with the resurgence of the political extremism of the first half of the twentieth century) one might expect the PCF countercommunity to return to a more self-enclosed and hostile posture vis-à-vis the rest of French society.

[29] July 8, 1972, p. 1.

[30] Communist propaganda, under the modernizing direction of René Piquet, is being imaginatively transformed to take up contemporary themes such as the environmental crisis and the role of computers, combining them with classic class struggle vocabulary (viz. an exhibition including IBM at the Fête de l'Humanité entitled "Computers in the March to Socialism!"). Moreover, as S. M. Lipset has remarked, the PCF and more particularly the CGT leadership are often able to claim successfully that improvements are a result of opposition agitation Revolution and Counter Revolution (New York: Basic Books, 1968), p. 237.

Chapter Ten

THE COMMUNIST MOVEMENT
AS TRIBUNE

Historically, one of the most extraordinary aspects of the Communist movement in France has been the persistence of its mass influence despite a lack of governmental power or a set of pressing revolutionary conditions. In the first part of this study one encountered again and again the cardinal fact that the electoral and social clientele of the PCF and CGT has been neither directly nor evenly related to the "hardness" or "softness" of the Communist line at any given moment. Whereas the hard core of the movement, the counter-community, has undergone tremendous variations in size according to the degree of tension along the cleavage between Communists and non-Communists, the electoral and mobilization capacities of Communist organizations have remained considerably more stable over time. While less true in the gestational period before 1934, during which time the nature of the movement was still in the process of definition, the pattern of Communist influence in the post-World War II period particularly has demonstrated that the PCF and CGT sustain a large number of supporters who neither expect the Party to exercise government power nor desire a Communist revolution.

The problem of attempting to define the limits of this category of supporter will not be of concern here. Because of the methodological problems of investigation involved, as S. M. Lipset has written, "How many of the French Communist voters actually adhere to a class-war perspective and a generally Communist view of politics is a question that is impossible to answer." [1] Various knowledgeable observers have given estimates as different as one-fourth to two-thirds.

[1] S. M. Lipset, *Revolution and Counterrevolution*, p. 228

Nor shall I attempt to determine precisely the motivation of such
supporters, who continue to back the Communist movement despite
blockage of the normal outlets of both reformist and revolutionary organizations. Here as well the problem cannot be resolved. Various
hypotheses have been advanced, many of which undoubtedly approach the heart of the matter. André Siegfried and François Goguel,
for example, see the Communists as the current heritors of the myth
of 1789, who have assumed the mantle from the Radicals and later the
SFIO. As the Communists have been perceived as the most "red" of
twentieth-century parties, they have inherited the support of those
who are revolutionary in sentiment but not in practice, a significant
clientele in French politics since the beginning of the nineteenth century. Others have proposed that one of the factors for the mass influence of the Communists is their acquisition of the support of an indigenous utopian socialist and anarchist clientele, which, while not
becoming Communist, nonetheless supports the Communist movement for its antiestablishmentarian qualities.[2] Still another attempt to
explain Communist mass support has delved for its answer into the
consequences of the industrial revolution in France. This argument
contends that an incomplete assimilation of the working class and
peasantry into the socioeconomic establishment as it developed in the
last half of the nineteenth century, as well as the human sufferings accompanying the industrial modernization of the twentieth century,
have created a broad group of disadvantaged individuals whom the
Communist movement has successfully brought within its sphere of
influence. In recent years the techniques of survey research have detailed to some extent this sort of historical-sociological explanation.
They have demonstrated, for example, that in addition to being seen
as "the party of the working class," and despite the negative aspects of
its popular image ("takes too much account of the Soviet interest"; "totalitarian tendencies" etc.), between 40 and 50 percent of French people express the opinion that the "Communist Party above all interests

---

[2] In the Introduction it was suggested that one of the continuing concerns of the
PCF has been to avoid being "turned on the left" by an organization (e.g. Trotskyite,
Maoist, anarchist) whose image is more extreme than its own. The danger of being
outflanked has made its relationship to the sentimental utopian socialist or anarchist-
inclined voter always problematic.

itself in the well-being of the people." [3] Still, only a much smaller group—between 20 and 25 percent—responds that "one can have confidence in the Communist Party for the economic prosperity of France."

The broad range of complementary data of this type suggests that Communist action in favor of the disadvantaged is perceived as essentially defensive in character (to be discussed further on) and, more importantly in this context, suggests the important hypothesis that the total number of supporters of this quite diverse Communist role is significantly larger than the Communist electorate alone—although a corollary hypothesis would be that the intensity of support for Communist organizations is less strong among the non-Communist voters than among the Communist electorate. Nonetheless, these figures may indicate a partially favorable—perhaps one ought to say not entirely unfavorable—Communist image already extending into certain sectors of non-Communist society whose support or neutrality the Party may be able one day to negotiate.

Finally, a variation of the socioeconomic development hypothesis focuses on political development specifically, arguing that the emergence of greatly expanded political participation before the achievement of stable and responsive institutions provoked a broad-based disillusionment with the established order upon which the Communist movement was able to capitalize. [4]

I have by no means exhausted the list of possibly and probably contributory variables. But such an analysis is not my interest here. I propose rather, to assume the existence of this support, based neither on the governmental nor revolutionary pretensions of the Communist movement, in order to argue that, *in toto*, one may speak of the relationship in terms of a role of political *tribune:* Essentially, the relationship of the PCF (and CGT) as tribune to these supporters is that the Communist movement has succeeded in establishing itself as the public advocate for those who are neither members of the Party

[3] See (e.g.) Lancelot and Weill in Bon et al., *Le communisme en France*, p. 290 (48 percent in 1968); SOFRES 1969, p. 28 (42 percent); and SOFRES 1971, p. 4 (52 percent).

[4] See Mark Kesselman, "Overinstitutionalization and Political Constraint: The Case of France," *Comparative Politics* 3, no. 1 (October 1970): 21–44, and the broad theory suggested in Samuel Huntington, *Political Order in Changing Societies* (New Haven, Conn.: Yale University Press, 1968) 488 pp.

itself nor supporters of the Communists' methods or their ultimate goals, but who nevertheless see themselves as disadvantaged, oppressed, repulsed by the Establishment, or who, for various other sentimental or practical reasons, refuse to accept the established order: a liberal capitalist society in the Western political and military community.[5]

This line of argument will not surprise those who have studied communist opposition movements however briefly, and in particular the French and Italian movements. First, in the early 1950s, Hadley Cantril explored the mass psychology of what he termed the "protest" vote in France and Italy. In his conclusion to *The Politics of Despair* Cantril painted the following composite portrait of the "protest" voter: The typical protest voter experiences more or less severe economic or social disadvantages (at least in his own mind); he considers that his personal situation is bad, but still not so disadvantaged as it might be; that he and his family deserve more out of life but that things are getting slightly better; that the "system" is contemptible, but that revolution, particularly on the basis of Communist methods, is neither desirable nor necessary; that the Communists are correct, however, in saying that no other party represents so much the point of view of the disadvantaged; and that therefore to vote for the Communist Party is the most effective and immediate way to express one's dissatisfaction with the status quo. However, such a voter feels that in the ultimate a communist system is evil; he will therefore support the Communists in their role of tribune by his protest vote without believing that it would be desirable for them to come to power.[6]

Whether or not the hypothesis of the protest vote is adequate, it

---

[5] See also the article by Lavau in Bon et al., esp. pp. 25–37.

[6] See Cantril, *The Politics of Despair*, pp. 115–16. In his *Affluence and the French Worker in the Fourth Republic*, Richard Hamilton (on the basis of a secondary analysis of a set of surveys done in 1952, 1955, and 1956) modified this explanation by correlating a radicalized vote partially with the "revolution of rising expectations," and demonstrating that a rise in the standard of living did not correlate with significant defections from the Communist electorate. The "protest" vote hypothesis has often been attacked. See in particular the recent article by Thomas H. Green, "The Electorates of Non-Ruling Communist Parties," *Studies in Comparative Communism* 4, nos. 3, 4 (July, October 1971): 68–103.

would appear that a key aspect of those who look to the Communist movement as their tribune is their fundamentally ambivalent orientation to the relationship. (In the conceptual framework developed in this study, this ambivalence is suggested by the ambivalence of Communist behavior itself.) The failure of other French parties for the most part to successfully attract and support those who desire a party that plays a tribune role has in the past left the PCF with little competition for their allegiance. Yet the tribune's supporters have demonstrated an equivocal tendency to adopt or accept the Marxist-Leninist mentality and show even less desire for a genuinely revolutionary program. Thus, since at least the time of the Popular Front, when the Communist movement in France was transformed into a mass movement, a significant part of its popular base has been simultaneously a support and a drag on its political strategy.

During the 1950s and early 1960s (before de-Stalinization was undertaken earnestly in the PCF) the thrust of Cantril's analysis was nowhere denied, although the significance of the tribune role was generally considered as secondary to what was taken to be the main concern of Communist strategy—revolution. As it became apparent after 1956 that the Communist movement was in some sense blocked and perhaps even immobilized politically, however, many observers came to the conclusion that the Party had become preoccupied with retaining popular support to the extent that its ultimate objective of revolution had become secondary. The PCF was supposedly so committed to electoralism and "economism" that it was no longer psychologically prepared to consider taking power. It had become, said many perceptive critics, a prisoner of its clienteles. Thus, it was during that time that social scientists of such eminence as Maurice Duverger and Stanley Hoffmann began to speak of the ubiquitous Communist defense of the disadvantaged in society as "Poujadism of the Left," drawing a parallel with a brief surge of protest, largely among small shopkeepers and peasants, which had produced considerable impact on public and electoral opinion during the period 1955–57. Carrying this argument to the extreme, one could argue that the Communists had become conservative, in fact reactionary, in their political outlook. They had chosen to become one of the bulwarks of the established order, while they retained a pseudorevolutionary rhetoric that poorly disguised the fact that they had become a force against change.

A judgment on this point of view was implicit in chapter 8 and will be formulated more explicitly in chapter 12, where the several "faces" of the Communist movement are considered together; for only at that point will we gain the necessary perspective for an accurate evaluation. For the moment let us limit ourselves solely to a consideration of the Communist tribune role; we shall first approach the subject historically and then discuss its importance in the global Communist strategy.

We should note first of all that the tribune aspect of communist activity was by no means an invention of the French Marxist-Leninists. Lenin himself had asserted that a Bolshevik party must in part operate like a Roman tribune, mirroring the demands of the masses and making certain that they are well-publicized and propagandized. Yet while this sort of action might actually result in certain reforms, for Lenin the essential significance of this strategy was that it would rally the masses behind the communists. Of course, once the communists had come to power the relationship between the Soviet Communist Party and the Russian masses was completely reversed.

For the communist parties not in power, however, the problem remained the same, and one finds in the history of French Communism from the very beginning an attempt to capture what later was to become known as the protest vote, to make of the Party the tribune of popular grievances against the government and society. One may even cite in this regard the 1928 electoral program, drafted under the slogan of "class against class" in the context of the most purposefully sectarian tactic ever practiced by the Communists in France. This program did not fail to condemn a "corrupted parliamentary regime, which, under the hypocritical and lying cover of democracy and popular sovereignty, permits the piratee of the banks, industry, and commerce to dupe and exploit the laboring masses," and asserted that "it is necessary to shatter . . . the bourgeois state through violence" in order to "replace it with a true workers' democracy . . . in the Soviet form." However, the same program contained a list of "immediate demands," including housing reform, paid vacations, an eight-hour working day, a forty-four hour work week, and unemployment insurance! [7] It is no doubt true that during the pre-1934 years the French Communists concerned themselves less with their electorate than at any time since, but nonetheless, not to remark upon the perennial attempt to create an electoral clientele of the nonrevolutionary mass majority (and thus, theoretically, to raise their revolutionary potential) would be to ignore one of the fundamental strategic premises of Marxism-Leninism in a structurally well-developed parliamentary setting.

In the terms of our analytical framework, the tribune role can be played toward either pole of strategy, and one can cite historical cases of each. For example, whereas during the Popular Front the "Ministry of the Masses" manifested the external aspect of the dual Communist strategy at a time when the dominant tactic was collaboration, during the postwar period of exclusion and isolation the PCF tribune worked in the opposite direction, implementing the goal of penetrating the domestic *cordon sanitaire* by demonstrating the broad representativeness of the movement. In effect, to win between 20 and 25 percent of the vote was to argue the illegitimacy of containment.

The political payoff for supporters of the tribune role is largely psychological, since the tribune possesses only limited power to extract outputs (essentially material benefits) from the authorities. This was clearly demonstrated in Cantril's work and in countless other interviews with Communist voters since that time. In a recent article emphasizing the importance of the tribune role in French Communist activity, Georges Lavau sums up the argument rather succinctly, writing that the tribune role "is principally to organize and to defend plebian social categories . . . and to give them a feeling of strength

[7] "Les buts révolutionnaires du Parti communiste: Programme électoral du Parti," (Paris, 1928, 22 pp.). One of the "opportunists" of 1927–28, Renaud Jean, noted the contradiction at the meeting of the "Latin secretariat" during the 6th Comintern Congress: "I permitted myself to criticize the program the Communist Party sent to 10 million voters. . . . In this program, in effect, there is not one word concerning the revolutionary goals of the Communist Party. . . . On the other hand, [there are] two complete pages on immediate demands. In a word, at the same moment as we took an extremely rigid position in terms of tactics, from the point of view of propaganda we took a reformist position which clashed strangely with this tactic." (Semard comments: "It's true.") *Classe contre classe.* p. 134.

and confidence. . . . [The] political program proposed and the political action undertaken acquire less importance from their [practical] value and their net results than from what they signify in the eyes of the plebian masses who are represented." [8] By voting for or being mobilized by the PCF or the CGT, supporters are psychologically able to strike back at the Establishment. They can at least force recognition of, if not necessarily improvement in, their position in society and they can achieve a feeling of power (essentially illusory), which they feel unable to accomplish through other means.

The fundamentally psychological payoff to the supporters implies that the Communist movement can achieve success in the role of tribune even without actually producing the goods, or, one is tempted to conclude, precisely because it does *not* produce the goods. On the other hand, the action of the CGT has been more often perceived as producing real material benefits. We have here an apparent difference in the nature of the two principal groups of supporters, which calls for an empirical study in depth.

The present leader of the PCF, Georges Marchais, has asserted that the Party's success as tribune is the primary explanation for the continued importance of the French Communist movement:

Honestly, no one can deny that the French Communist Party has become a central factor in the political life of our country. If this is so, it is because our Party, an essentially proletarian party, has affirmed itself in the course of struggle ever more . . . as *the veritable tribune of the entire people*. . . . Yes, our Party appears more and more in the eyes of the people as a truly popular party, which struggles with passion in favor of democracy, to defend the noble cause of peace, the vital interests of the people and of the nation. [9]

Marchais' evaluation is a convenient point from which to consider the interest of the Communists in maintaining the tribune role, for while it is possible to easily imagine various motivations for the supporters, the benefits derived from such a political commitment by a supposedly revolutionary party are less immediately intelligible.

A first distinction suggested by Marchais' statement is that the relationship of the Communist movement to the protest voter and to the merely sentimental revolutionary is assigned a dual significance in the

[8] Lavau in Bon et al., p. 18.
[9] PCF–17, Marchais report, p. 286; emphasis added.

eyes of the leadership, depending on whether one considers the short term or the long term, the minimum program or the maximum program.

In contemplating its prospects from the point of view of a minimum or prerevolutionary strategy, the French Communist leadership has always recognized the advantages of extending its mass influence as widely as possible.[10] Most importantly, in its struggle to dominate the other political forces of the Left, including the social democrats on the right flank and the Trotskyite-Maoist-anarchist splinter complex on the left flank, the success of the PCF and CGT in gaining votes and increasing membership have reinforced its claims to be the "principal force of the working class and its allies in the revolutionary struggle."[11]

Originally, communism in France developed in a context in which a significant minority of the working class placed itself within an anarchosyndicalist tradition, having rejected both bourgeois democracy and Jauressian parliamentary socialism. At first, such a syndicalist militant might have accepted the necessity of a temporary dictatorship in the Leninist fashion, because it was represented to him as simply an unavoidable step toward the utopian proletarian democracy of which he dreamed: factories without bosses and a society without a state. During the 1920s, in consideration of the authoritarian manner in which the Soviet regime developed, this anarcho-syndicalist wing deserted the Communists or was "re-educated." Moreover, the pre-World War I SFIO, which had never been able to create a strong organization in the centers of heavy industry, as a result had failed generally to represent the syndicalist movement in politics, and the gulf between the union movement and the party had been one of the most striking characteristics of French socialism before 1920.

In its progressive infiltration of the CGT, first during the reunification of 1936–39 and later during the Liberation and Tripartite experiences, the Communist Party was therefore able to achieve a double

[10] Even if in 1924–34 the goal of bolshevization was more important, as was the 1939–41 goal of supporting the Nazi-Soviet pact.

[11] Public opinion polls affirm unanimously that of all the PCF claims, that of being "the Party of the working class" is the one most widely accepted, even more so (by far) than that of being "the Party of revolution."

goal: on the one hand, the influence of anarcho-syndicalism had about disappeared more or less independently between 1920 and 1945, permitting the Communists to integrate much of their former social bases within the new CGT; on the other hand, by 1946 the social democratic wing of the labor movement was also brought under Communist influence, albeit only temporarily. When it emerged from its transitory union with the Marxist-Leninists, it too had been dealt a considerable blow: the consequence of the syndicalist split in 1947–48 was to reveal that the Communist movement had become the largest single force in organized labor, and that to this extent, as George Lichtheim has put it, "for the first time in French labor history, the mass movement and the political party were brought together, with the party in the controlling position, instead of being a rarely tolerated adjunct of the 'real' workers movement." [12]

In terms of the electoral and membership strength of the parties themselves, the events of 1934–39 and 1944–47 had the result of introducing the Communist Party into the role of the most influential of all the organizations of theLeft as well. And not only have the French socialists in the postwar period been denied much of the social bases of the SFIO they had under Jaurès and Blum, they are no longer able even to use the working-class mystique as a propaganda platform, a point of considerable importance for a party that still attempts to appear Marxist and that addresses an electorate that thinks largely in Marxist categories, whether consciously or not. The new leader of the Socialist Party, François Mitterrand, has quite frankly admitted "I know of only one working class party in France, and that is the Communist Party." [13]

[12] *Marxism in Modern France*, p. 72.

[13] Although such a classification can be only approximate, following is the breakdown of the PCF electorate by occupation according to IFOP surveys in 1967–68: manual and skilled workers, 49 percent; functionaries and office workers, 15 percent; cadres and professions, 2 percent; small business owners, 5–6 percent; peasants, 8–9 percent; inactive, 18–19 percent (*Le nouvel observateur*, February 2, 1970, p. 43). This may be compared with a similar classification for the year 1948 (also based on IFOP surveys, cited by Ranger in Bon et al., p. 243): workers, 37 percent; functionaries and office personnel, 13 percent; cadres, liberal professions, and small business owners, 50 percent; peasants, 22 percent; inactive, 22 percent. The working-class character of the movement is not surprisingly most pronounced in the Party itself. In 1966, for example, Georges Marchais gave the following classification of the membership: manual and skilled workers, 60.1 percent; lower-and middle-level office personnel, 18.57 percent; peasants, 6.56 percent; intellectuals, 9 percent; small business owners and artisans, 5.77

Because of the Communists' success as tribune, the socialist parties and groups have had to seek other clienteles, generally competing for the same potential supporters or focusing on small and specialized sectors of the electorate. The Convention of Republican Institutions had aimed its pitch at the growing number of middle- and upper-middle-level office workers and technicians, while the more militant PSU has become, in spite of its wishes, a sectarian party of intellectuals in which internecine feuds are perhaps the dominant characteristic.[14] The former SFIO, renamed if not yet renewed in 1969, had until that time demonstrated neither the desire nor the ability to restructure its social bases under the leadership of Guy Mollet. The leader during 1969–71, Alain Savary, attempted to reorient the Socialist Party during his short reign toward "those massive groups of intellectuals and technicians which are spawned by modern societies." [15] The merger of the Socialist Party and the CIR in June 1971 under the leadership of François Mitterrand promises at least the elimination of some of the confusion and dissension among the socialists at the leadership level, but it remains to be seen whether the renewed Socialist Party will be able to develop a mass following sufficient for it to counterbalance the PCF. In any case, Mitterrand's "fundamental objective" is avowed: At the June 1972 meeting of the Socialist International in Vienna he outlined the goal of "remaking the grand Socialist Party on the terrain occupied by the Communist Party itself, in order to demonstrate that of the five million Communist voters, three million could vote socialist." [16]

Thus primarily through its success in the role of tribune, within

percent. (See PCF–18, Marchais report, p. 273, also cited in Annie Kriegel, *Les communistes français*, p. 35.) Kriegel comments that because retired workers were counted according to their previous profession, and housewives according to the profession of their husbands, Marchais's statistics are somewhat distorted. Nonetheless, no one seriously disputes that members of working class origin predominate among the Party's membership.

[14] It is a common sarcasm that the PSU is a party "with six members and seven tendencies."

[15] *Pour le nouveau parti socialiste*, pp. 33–42.

[16] See *Le Monde*, July 1, 1972, p. 9. At the PCF National Conference of November 20–21, 1971, Georges Marchais warned strongly of the PS and CFDT challenge to Communist organization of the working class, and in reponse to the Mitterrand Vienna statement an editorial in *L'Humanité* replied that "one can be legitimately astonished (after signature of the Common Program three days earlier) that Mitterrand situates his main interest at this level" (June 30, 1972, p. 1).

342 *The "Faces" of Communism in France*

the context of the Third, Fourth, and Fifth Republics, the PCF has indeed become, as Marchais indicates, "a central factor" in French political life, reinforcing its progressive domination of the French Left and in the Fifth Republic permitting it legitimately to claim the title of "the principal force of the opposition." This very success, however, has implied always the potential problem of being *too* successful, that is, of becoming so enmeshed in defending the disadvantaged within the present regime that the revolutionary impetus, the *raison d'être* of the movement, would find itself in danger of extinction.

While the role of tribune as acted out within the established order can be said to be a partial legitimation of that order, reflecting the temporary justification accorded a bourgeois regime in Marxist doctrine, and therefore the minimum program of the dual strategy, the attempt to extend Communist influence among the masses by means of the tribune role has still another function—one connected with the maximum program and the ultimate strategy of revolution. In effect, it is only at the level of revolutionary theory and the vision of the future society that one can appreciate why a supposedly revolutionary party would involve itself so deeply with nonrevolutionary practices— unless, of course, one believes the French Communist pretensions to radical change are no longer relevant.

In pre-Leninist socialist doctrine, the dominant conceptions of the socialist revolution held that the working classes themselves would prove to be the immediate revolutionary force. The social democratic parties were to be somehow propelled into control of political power after the masses had accomplished an economic and social revolution, which, it was assumed, had necessarily to precede the former. This was the view of the Second International in which the German Social Democratic Party of Kautsky held sway. Lenin, in opposition to this *attentiste* conception, introduced the great strategic innovation of stalking the revolution "consciously" through the political weapon of the Party, the result of which was a reversal of the revolutionary sequence: Bolshevik strategy was based on the theory that the political revolution could precede the economic and social transformation. Even better, the political revolution, directed by a new-type vanguard party, would be the necessary key to the economic and social revolution. This changed the revolutionary equation in line with Lenin's dictum that "Majorities are not counted but won over." [17] Yet while he had made of the "vanguard party" a necessity according to Bolshevik revolutionary theory, even for him the masses still remained the ultimate and decisive factor in determining whether or not a revolution would be successful. This seemed to be born out by the events of 1917–20 in Russia, and in *Left-Wing Communism—An Infantile Disorder*, most of which was written in April 1920, Lenin asserted with regard to the dangers of the civil war between Reds and Whites:

> The proletarian vanguard has been won over ideologically. That is the main thing. Without this, not even the first step towards victory can be made. But . . . victory cannot be won with a vanguard alone. To throw only the vanguard into the decisive battle, before the entire class, the broad masses, have taken up a position either of direct support for the vanguard, or at least of sympathetic neutrality towards it and of precluded support for the enemy, would be, not merely foolish but criminal. [18]

Lenin (as Marx) considered that because of the natural tendency to conservatism among the majority of the lower classes, the masses would be won over only in the revolutionary struggle itself. And this was indeed the pattern in the Russian Revolution; before the Bolshevik takeover, the degree of mass support for the Party was more or less negligible.

Before 1934, and particularly as the "bolshevization" of the movement progressed after 1924–25, the French Communists found it not very difficult to think in terms of the Bolshevik model in many crucial respects. The size, organizational structure, leadership, and relationship of the French movement to the establishment order during this period came increasingly to resemble the characteristics of the Bolshevik Party before the revolution, although the political, economic, and social conditions in France were of course quite unlike those of prerevolutionary Russia. Yet with regard to the role of the masses in revolutionary strategy the French Communists could also adapt the Russian experience of 1917, assuring themselves that regardless of the mass support they had enjoyed before the advent of a revolutionary situation, at the decisive moment the "overwhelming majority" of the

[17] See Andrew C. Janos in Cyril E. Black and Thomas Thornton (eds.), *Communism and Revolution*, p. 35.
[18] *Lenin: Selected Works*, p. 572.

population would achieve revolutionary consciousness through their personal experience.

The *grand tournant* in the movement during the period 1934–38, which transformed the Party from an incipient sect into a mass movement whose size had become a new problem in the formulation of revolutionary plans, also produced a fundamental change in the Party's attitude toward the masses. From that point onward, a dominant though not exclusive preoccupation with increasing its *immediate* electoral and mobilization followership became basic not only to the minimum program, which could be sacrified if necessary, but also to the maximum program: revolution. Although at the time few realized the permanence of this departure from the Bolshevik model and the consequences that would ultimately arise from it, the extent to which the movement's increase in size had altered the revolutionary strategy from the original Russian example became apparent as the postwar epoch developed.

This transformation of revolutionary strategy during the 1950s and 1960s was discussed in chapter 8, but at this point it is necessary to speak briefly once again of the adoption of the doctrine of a "peaceful transition to socialism" insofar as it concerns the question of the masses and the role of tribune.

Essentially, the notion of a peaceful transition to socialism does not revise the Leninist reformulation of the revolutionary sequence. The political revolution is still to precede the economic and social revolution, and the role of the Communist Party is still vital to the success of the enterprise. The crucial doctrinal innovation is that the political revolution is now said to be obtainable by peaceful methods, built around electoral victory and parliamentary legislation. Furthermore, implementation of the economic and social transformation to follow is also said to be possible by peaceful means, despite the still-cited assertion that the "ruling class never gives up its power willingly." The ultimate key to both aspects of the revolution remains "the masses," but the doctrine of peaceful revolution introduces a subtle yet significant reformulation of the role the masses are to play.

Whereas in the 1917 revolution the Bolsheviks received their mass support only after the revolution had begun, the doctrine of peaceful, electoral revolution presupposes tremendous mass support for the

Party in order for the revolutionary situation to arise, that is, for the Communist Party and its allies to be elected to power. The Popular Front and Tripartite experiences were of great significance to the new Communist strategy of revolution in this regard because they were concrete evidence that under certain conditions the French public would accept a government with Communist participation. Yet, neither in the Popular Front nor in the Tripartite coalition did the Communists operate with a goal of immediate revolution, or to be more precise, of beginning "the transition to socialism."

In order to be successful "the next time," when socialism will be presumably a short-term rather than a long-range goal, the new Communist strategy hinges on the possibility of fomenting huge outpourings of mass support to such an extent that the Communist-socialist coalition will be rendered invincible at the same time that the PCF itself is voted into a position of leadership within the alliance. Moreover, to permit the coalition to carry out its program, it will be necessary (so goes the doctrine) to prevent the capitalist class from returning to power by force, and in this as well, the role of the masses is asserted to be "decisive." The essence of the role assigned the masses in the new Communist strategy of revolution is shown in the following extracts from Waldeck Rochet's report to the 18th Congress and the Political Resolution of the 16th Congress:

Our Party begins . . . with the fundamental idea according to which it is the movement of the masses which decides everything. . . . [The] elections are only an intermediate stage . . . In our epoch, in a country such as France, the possibilities are growing of reaching socialism along a peaceful road, by preventing the *grande bourgeoisie* from having recourse to civil war. . . . In all cases, it is the extensiveness of the movement of the masses that will be decisive in order to prevent the exploiters from waging civil war against the people.[19]

---

[19] PCF-18, pp. 75 and 569; PCF-16, p. 574. The use of mass demonstrations by the Allende coalition in Chile is an instructive example in this regard, as was the counter-demonstration tactic of the Christian Democrats as a device to attach the Popular Unity government. The "Housewives' March" against food shortages and inflation, and the August 1972 strike of most of the country's 150,000 shopkeepers (the largest antigovernment protest by private business) were merely the most significant of numerous examples. In the shopkeepers' strike, the government charged it was "illegal," "politically motivated," and threatened government takeovers. The merchants replied strongly

One may easily conclude that such millenarian theorizing is but the purest nonsense, demonstrating at once the puerility of contemporary Marxist-Leninist doctrine (or at least the Soviet brand) and the futility of present Communist revolutionary strategies. This, however, would be a conclusion both overly hasty and facile. On the one hand, it is unwarranted to conclude that the theory of peaceful revolution is absolutely impracticable, unless one adopts the position that the term is a self-contradiction. On the other hand, to denigrate the degree to which Communist leadership continues to think seriously in millenarian categories would probably be a gross error, for while success in the role of tribune has underlain the mass strength, and thus the political influence, of the French Communist movement in the Third, Fourth, and Fifth Republics, such an achievement is for the Communist mentality by definition only a success of the second degree. In sum, the justification of taking such pains to retain its nonrevolutionary support by acting in a nonrevolutionary manner can be found in the future use to which this mass base is to be put. By choosing the tribune role, the French Communists have made a gamble, hoping to gather enough electoral support to win the ultimate prize and offering their *raison d'être* as collateral. The odds are long, but they would seem to reflect more the difficult position of any revolutionary organization in a modern Western society than an inherent foolishness in the wager.

The likely future of the PCF's electoral and mobilization clienteles may take two forms. On the one hand, it is very possible that a successful union of the Left parties around a common program of government would result in a expansion of the Leftist vote as a whole, although it appears unlikely that the PCF itself would benefit as much as the Socialist Party. Of the potential "switchers" available to a Left coalition, most would likely refuse to vote Communist.[20] On the other hand, the possibility of a decline in electoral strength if a Left government is not realized in the near future must be discussed taking account

with a threat of unlimited strike, and the government was constrained to back down.

[20] Once again, the Chilean experience is instructive: in the 1970 general elections, won by Allende, the Socialist Party obtained 300,000 votes and the Communist Party 100,000. Note that the March 1973 election in France showed a similar tendency. The PS regained most of the distance separating it electorally from the PCF.

of the fact that neither domestic isolation nor international dislocations have resulted in a broad electoral disavowal of the PCF in the past. The problem of a possible decline, therefore, is essentially the problem of relating economic and social modernization and the Communist vote.

S. M. Lipset, who has investigated the possibility of a positive relation between economic growth and political democracy, has concluded the following about the future of communism in France and Italy:

> It is doubtful that structural changes alone will result in the decline of a mass Communist Party. . . . The Communist sector of the electorate will join the democratic political game in the foreseeable future only if their party, as a party, does it.[21]

At present, there exist only the beginnings of a documented answer to this question. One of the most recent and empirical investigations was carried out under the direction of François Goguel, considering the vote in selected general elections in nine departments from 1928 to 1968. Goguel notes:

> The most striking aspect of the evolution . . . of the electoral strength of the Communist Party . . . is found in the fact that, up to and including the vote of January 2, 1956, this strength had been considerably greater in those cantons whose economic, demographic and social evolution from 1954 to 1962 can be termed progressive, but that, after 1956, it was no longer the same: the percentages of votes expressed in favor of communism were practically identical in the two categories of cantons in 1967, and in 1968 the percentage in cantons undergoing a regressive change was greater by 1.5 than that in cantons undergoing a progressive change.[22]

Considering the situation *in toto*, Goguel writes that his research

> seems to confirm clearly the fact that regressive economic and demographic change, where the existence of a Right-wing political tradition does not compensate the effects, constitutes a factor favorable to the electoral penetration of communism; while, on the contrary, even where a Left-wing political tradition exists, progressive (social) change constitutes a factor unfavorable to the development of the grasp of the Communist Party on the electorate.[23]

---

[21] Lipset, *Revolution and Counterrevolution*, p. 237.
[22] *Modernisation économique et comportement politique*, p. 13.   [23] *Ibid.*, p. 83.

These conclusions, while potentially of great interest, are as yet only, as Goguel himself is quick to admit, working hypotheses. Nonetheless, if valid, they tend to support a point of view based on the logic of politics itself: if the common goal of political parties is to win power, and if the fundamental desire of their supporters is to have their interest served, a party that fails to do both cannot long flourish without extraordinary circumstances invalidating normal expectations. The thaw in the Cold War during the 1960s has, after nearly forty years of exceptional situations, left the PCF alone with its followers, so to speak. Given a relatively successful pursuance of peaceful coexistence internationally, one suspects this logic of routine political aspirations will play increasingly more heavily on the French Communist future.

Chapter Eleven

THE PCF AS A PARTY OF GOVERNMENT

Local Power

Local government in France, although at last in the incipient stages of long-discussed structural and functional reforms, still re-
tains for the most part a pattern characteristic of both the Third and
Fourth Republics. The great majority of the slightly less than 38,000
French municipalities are quite tiny and rural (35,000 contain less
than 2,000 inhabitants), and Philip Williams's description of these
remains one of the safest generalizations about French politics:

Most French towns have been ruled for years by a center coalition, usually
including and often led by the Socialists. Instead of a bitter conflict about the
content of a joint program—all the harder to agree on because it affirms principles which are unlikely to be realized—there is a common record of civic
achievement to defend. Instead of a sordid squabble about the choice of candidates, there is a recognized leader, the existing mayor, often with a team (of
incumbent municipal councilors) used to working together.[1]

In a recent study of the political character of local politics, Mark Kesselman explained the reasons for broad mixed coalitions at this level:

The major reason for balancing all political opinions on the municipal council
is . . . to exclude political divisions from the commune. It is hoped that differences about municipal affairs will not destroy the facade of local unity.
Moreover, while it is expected that national political conflicts may cause divisions at the local level, the aim is to prevent local conflicts over national issues
from disrupting the commune.[2]

In sum, the success of a typical French mayor is to paper over differences in his commune, the result of which is to produce what Kes-

---

[1] In "Party, Presidency and Parish Pump," *Parliamentary Affairs* 18 (Summer 1965):
261, as cited in Mark Kesselman, *The Ambiguous Consensus*, p. 120.

[2] Kesselman, *Consensus*, p. 126.

selman has aptly termed an "ambiguous consensus." The motivation for this desire is to be found in the conception of the community held by the mayor: he would like to imitate Rousseau's legislator, acting upon the general will of a unified and harmonious community. Since no such general will exists, however, the mayor is able, through broad coalitions and relative inaction, to achieve only a facade of consensus, and this is the fundamental ambiguity of quiescent local politics in France.[3]

While true of most small towns and a considerable number of large cities as well, such a description obviously does not fit the Communist conception of municipal power. The PCF generally constitutes an exception to the practice of consensus-building on the local level. If there are two slates of candidates in a commune, it is normally a safe bet that one is a broad coalition and the other a list of the PCF and its allies.[4] In addition, to the extent feasible, the Party seeks to run its municipalities in an openly partisan manner, according to the role assigned local victories in the strategy of eventual revolutionary change. In 1971, the PCF governed alone or in coalition in approximately 1,100 municipalities and the 787 Communist mayors administered about 5 million people, or about 10 percent of the total population. The PCF directed 45 cities of 30,000 or greater population after the 1971 municipal elections (the Socialist Party had 40; the UDR had 30). The major Communist municipal strength and prime focus in local elections are the large urban areas, in particular the famous "red belt" in the east suburbs of Paris and some major cities in the industrial north (The largest PCF municipality is Le Havre, with a population of 208,000. Next are Nîmes, with 120,000, and St. Denis, in the Paris suburbs, with 100,000).

A strong Communist presence in such areas is consonant with and confirms Brian Chapman's judgment that, "In general, national politics is most prominent in the large urban communes where industrial and social life encourages the formation of cohesive groups, and favors the party machine rather than the individual politicians." [5] The Communist Party attempts to make of municipal elections, as it does of elections at all levels, a referendum on national and even international politics, a policy designed to imbue the electorate with the idea that

[3] *Ibid.*, pp. 158–59.   [4] *Ibid.*, pp. 120 and 126.
[5] Chapman, *Introduction to French Local Government*, p. 38.

meaningful political change is impossible in the final analysis except on the global scale characteristic of the Marxist mentality. Thus for example, in a list of points in a typical Communist municipal electoral program one might find a demand for better housing directly preceding a demand for international disarmament, the latter itself preceding a demand for "democracy." Whereas the UDR and other parties do not generally play up the political character of local votes, the PCF line has always been that "Municipal elections are political elections." [6]

What is the political significance of local power in the French Communist perspective? How does the fact of being in power at the municipal level fit into the overall PCF strategy? Is municipal power in any sense "revolutionary"?

Part of the French socialist heritage of the 1880s and 1890s was a current of thought known as "possibilist" socialism. At a time when the other wings of the socialist movement, the Allemanists, Blanquists, Guesdists, and Proudhonists, were all antiparliament and advocates of a rapid and cataclysmic break with the old order, the possibilists, led by Brousse and Malon, developed a notion of peaceful revolution based on what they termed the "theory of the public services." The basic idea of this theory was that by gradually assuming control of vital public services (mail, education, transportation, etc.), the state would come to direct increasingly larger parts of the economic structure and that all large private property in the means of production would be eventually abolished in this way. For the possibilists, the task of the socialist movement was therefore to infiltrate progressively into the state apparatus from the local to the national level in order to speed and eventually to control this evolutionary process. As Brousse put it, the socialists would gradually make "a conquest of the municipalities, of the Chamber of Deputies, and, in the end, of the government . . . You see how simple it is." [7]

Having rejected such a conception from the beginning the French

[6] In the 1971 elections, the UDR leaders once again denied that the local ballot had much political significance—until the results showed an impressive victory for the Gaullists in Paris, after which they said the Paris victory was "of great political significance!" The Communists were quick to pick up the contradiction, and attempted to use it to their advantage by pointing to their own gains in the provinces.

[7] See Michelle Perrot and Annie Kriegel, *Le socialisme français et le pouvoir*, pp. 30–34; the citation is found on p. 33.

Communists nonetheless give a significant emphasis to local government, their attitude being broadly circumscribed in this brief statement by Jacques Duclos: "While it is true that the march to socialism cannot be envisaged in the form of a progressive conquest of municipalities, it is no less true that mass action in the domain of municipal work, as in other domains, will contribute to opening the path upon which our country will move to socialism." [8] Thus, the idea of a revolution being born out of a gradual infiltration of municipal governments is dismissed out of hand. The importance of municipal governments to the Communists is rather their role in broadening and solidfying the relation of the Party and the mass of the population. As the actual governors of a community, capable of producing political outputs more visibly than elsewhere, the Communists are able to serve this role in three ways: by answering to the bread-and-butter interests of their clientele (within the limits dictated by the prerogatives of French local government—see below), by making full use of a privileged channel of political communication, and by creating a network of solid Party bastions for use in both an offensive and defensive strategy, depending upon the exigencies of the moment.[9] In other words, Communist local governments are important supports of the generalized roles of tribune and countercommunity as described above. In utilizing control of municipal government as a weapon in the service of larger political goals, the French Communist Party demands a very different kind of relationship between its elected officials and the Party than is found in any other local governmental administration. Whereas on the whole local officials tend toward *apolitisme* both in practice and in rhetoric [10]—which implies a distinct lack of control of local government by national party structures—the Communist conception of municipal action is exactly opposite. The Communist municipal councilor and mayor, like the Communist deputy and every other elected official, is in theory entirely subordinate

8 "Les municipalités au service des masses laborieuses," Report to the 14th Congress, 1956, p. 107.

9 François Platone, "L'implantation municipale du Parti communiste français dans la Seine et sa conception de l'administration communale," unpublished thesis, (Paris, 1967), 163 pp.

10 On the "rhetoric of *apolitisme*" in local politics, see the lively and pertinent chapter in Kesselman, *Consensus*, pp. 136–40.

to the Party: He is expected to consider himselt Communist before mayor, a militant before an elected official. As Duclos put it:

From the moment of its foundation our Party . . . sought deliberately to break with reformist conceptions by struggling to make triumphant the Leninist principle of subordination of the parliamentary group to the Central Committee. This . . . must also be the rule . . . for cantonal officials, placed under the direction of [Party] federations, and for municipal officials, placed under the direction of sections or cells.[11]

Even in an organization as strictly centralized as the Communist Party, of course, it is impossible to put such a conception into practice everywhere and at all times. In regions where the Party as a whole is weak, for example, Communist municipal councilors are sometimes to be found on the apolitical mixed lists common to French small-town politics. This may also be true often in rural regions, where continuous contact with upper Party echelons is difficult and where personal ties are likely to be an effective counterweight to Party allegiance. In these types of cases, which overlap to a great extent, the Party policy is simply to have candidates in as many localities as possible and to make whatever propaganda possible out of the position won.[12]

During periods of exclusion and isolation from the rest of the polity, usually accompanied by internal questioning of the Party line and its leadership, close control of Communist local officials in even the mass urban bastions has become problematic. This kind of situation arose in the 1950s, for example, after the leadership crises of 1949–53 and the moral and intellectual crisis that gripped the Party during the Stalin succession and after the 20th CPSU Congress. Duclos remarked at the time that, "In the course of recent years, a certain

[11] Duclos, "Les municipalités," p. 101. In the only in-depth study of a Communist municipality, J.-P. Hoss comments on his interviews with local communist officials: "Constantly the officials pass from the Party perspective to the local administrative perspective, and the converse. For those who work in the town hall, the [deputy-mayor] is 'comrade' before he is [deputy-mayor], and it is his authority within the Party that counts, and not the rest, the exterior." *Communes en banlieue, Argenteuil et Bezons*, p. 83. Unfortunately, the study by Hoss makes little attempt to be comparative.

[12] With about 460,000 municipal councilors in the 38,000 communes, the Communists would have to find well over 100,000 more members if they wanted to present a candidate for each possible seat! As it is, the PCF elected 36,517 councilors in 1945 (*L'année politique*, 1947, p. 364); 24,206 in 1953 (*ibid.*, 1959, p. 33); 19,535 in 1965 (*Le Monde*, April 23, 1971, p. 10); and 23,242 in 1971 (*ibid.*).

climate of irresponsibility has been created in the administration of the activity of Communist municipalities." [13]

A third situation in which the Party will play down both its personal responsibility for the municipality and the "class" content of its administration occurs during periods when the policy of unity of action with socialists and Radicals leads to Communist participation in a coalition municipal council. This was true during the Popular Front, during the Tripartite period, and for the 1965 and 1971 elections, in which, despite having fought the election with separate lists (the PCF wanted common lists at the first ballot; the socialists and Radicals generally refused), the Left parties combined to elect a mayor (normally a Communist or a socialist, depending on which party had won the most seats) and to run a coalition municipality. This Communist action, which sometimes leads them to vote for "comrades" who had earlier been sworn enemies (such as Guy Mollet at Arras and Augustin Laurent at Lille), must be understood in terms of the general strategy of a parliamentary transition to socialism, and as such it is likely to be more permanent than were the local coalitions of 1935 and 1945.

Given these exceptions, the normal Communist administration, above all in the "red belt" bastions, is a conscious attempt to politicize local government and to subordinate local officials to Party discipline. This is done to the extent that the establishment of priorities in the spending of municipal funds is done within the context of the Party rather than the government: "the establishment of the municipal budget is a political act of the greatest importance. It cannot, therefore, be the affair of only the mayor and the specialists; it is also, and above all, the affair of the organizations of the Party." [14]

The Communist conception of municipal government, and for that matter government on all levels, is thus aggressively opposed to the "technocratic" spirit characteristic of much of the Fifth Republic's concern with reform of French administrative practices.

The Gaullist attempt to create an administrative corps composed of politically disinterested technicians concerned only with making the most efficient use of resources according to a set of goals given by the government, is anathema to the Communist project, whose success

[13] Duclos, "Les municipalités, p. 101.
[14] *Ibid.*, p. 96. See also Platone, "L'implantation municipale," p. 97.

would imply a priori a restructuring of the basic goals themselves. Thus, for example, the PCF has consistently fought the "tutelage" conception of local governmental administration institutionalized in the system of prefects. Party programs have invariably proposed abolition of the prefectoral corps, which acts as lieutenant for the national ministries and in whom decisionmaking power is vested rather than in the elected departmental General Councils. The Communists offer instead a plan for transferring the prefect's powers to the General Councils and their presidents. In the meantime, they have attempted to avoid insofar as possible letting their municipalities become dependent on the services of the prefect. One of the most innovative measures in this regard was the creation a few years ago of a party-affiliated computer and data-processing company, which some thirty PCF municipal administrations have called upon instead of turning to the prefectoral facilities.[15]

Another aspect of the political character of Communist municipal administration is the method of choosing Party candidates themselves. Theoretically "chosen" by the rank and file, candidates are in fact selected at high Party organizational levels. In designating a candidate, the Party's first criterion is that the person be a committed militant, who may then be given technical training to prepare him for a specific task. The Communist municipal councilor may contribute to the formulation of the Party plan for a municipality, but does so in the context of the Party and as a Party militant above all; in his governmental post, he is expected to consider himself as one who carries out the Party line. Moreover his electoral victory itself is viewed in Party terms. The Communist conception is that the electorate mandates the Party rather than the individual; therefore the successful candidate is responsible in the first instance to the Party and not the voters.[16]

---

[15] Moreover, the Party even establishes commercial construction companies (grouped in the CIFCO) and architectural planning firms (the two most important being the ORGECO and the BERIM) to work with their municipalities. The local governments save money and the Party avoids dealing with "capitalist" enterprises. (See Laurens and Pfister, *Les nouveaux communistes*, pp. 154–55.)

[16] Hoss writes of the Communist mayors of Argenteuil and Bezons: "Both, they said, accepted the job of mayor not as a great honor, but . . . because they considered it a way to serve the population, that is to say the workers, that is to say the Party" (*Communes*, p. 77). Although there is little evidence to contradict the classic pattern of subor-

Recent theorizing in political science has underlined the key role of the various forms of communication between masses and elites in the creation and retention of power within the polity in general. In effect, any political movement denied access to mass communication would be almost automatically shut out of the contest for power, whether it were of a peaceful or violent nature. The 35 Communist municipalities of the Paris suburbs, in which the Party administers the local affairs of approximately 1.5 million people, are excellent examples of the way in which a given political organization is able to employ the various channels of communication to perpetuate its control of the area. Some of these communes, among them the archtypical PCF municipality of Ivry in the southeast suburbs, in 1971 were well into their fifth continuous decade of Communist government.[17] Even in the municipal elections of 1959, held soon after the tremendous Gaullist victory and PCF defeat in the 1958 referendum and general elections, the "red belt" held strong for the Party.[18]

The types of communication available to a Communist mayor and municipal council are many. First of all, an attempt is made to link the normal communications of a local government expressly to the Communist Party where possible. When the municipality sponsors annual vacations for old people or skiing for young children, for example, the publicity is put out in a way such that "the Party of the people" and the local government benefactor are identified as one. When a new school or old people's home is constructed, it is made to seem a conquest ripped away from the *haute bourgeoisie* through tenacious Communist action; the national government and the prefect (who may have provided part of the funds) are left in the background.[19] For example, with regard to the construction of a lycée at

dination of the Communist local elected official to the Section Secretary and the Party hierarchy in general, research in progress indicates conflict and resentment as a not unusual consequence. See Denis Lacorne, "The Functioning of a Strategy of Left-Wing Unity at the Municipal Level: A Study of Four French Departments," a paper presented to the Conference on French and Italian Communism, October 1972.

[17] Paul Thibaud, "Le communisme municipal," *Esprit*, October 1966, p. 414.

[18] Nonetheless in the referendum of 1958 some PCF municipalities, such as Argenteuil (56%–44%) voted yes. In the 1962 referendum on the mode of presidential election, Argenteuil returned to the fold (59%–41%). Hoss, *Communes*, pp. 57–58.

[19] This naturally encourages the latter's instinctive tendency to disadvantage the Communist municipalities.

Argenteuil, the Communist mayor said: "It was necessary to tear the funds away [from the government], and it is thanks to the combined effort of the [Communist] deputy, of the parents' associations and of the municipality that such a result was obtained." [20] Where a project has been completed without help from the central administration, it is not unusual to see signs announcing expressly that it was "built with no financial participation by the State," or that "One Mirage IV is worth twenty-five swimming pools of the kind we would like at Argenteuil." [21] Moreover, although prohibited by Article 52 of the Communal Administrative Code, a Communist-controlled municipal council will sometimes issue political statements, ranging from a general call for international peace to endorsement of a local strike. [22]

Another type of politicization of the local government communication channels occurs in the contact between the elected officials and the people directly. In his study of the Communist vote in France and Italy, Hadley Cantril described the tactics of local Communist officials as they emerged from interviews with residents:

Their methods are like those of Tammany Hall. The communists did a good job of keeping closely in touch with the people, finding out what their needs are, pointing the blame at the government, and indicating how [they] dedicate themselves to the personal and local problems that they know are harassing the people in their districts. [23]

It is in the context of performing the routine duties of a municipal government and in helping people to solve the minor problems of daily life for which they might find it necessary to go to the town hall that the Party seizes an everpresent opportunity to associate itself with the efficient management of local affairs. The Communists attempt to present themselves as the most serious and responsible local officials, compared to whom the rest are political satraps, *des notables*, or simple incompetents. Moreover, the typical Communist local official is *un gars du quartier*, someone who has lived in the area for a number of years if not all his life, who has long been an activist, and who is well-acquainted with the problems of the locality. Finally, it is in the "red

[20] Hoss, *Communes*, p. 98.   [21] *Ibid.*, p. 99.
[22] Platone, "L'implantation municipale," pp. 94–95.
[23] Hadley Cantril, *The Politics of Despair*, pp. 85–86.

belt" that the Party press reaches its densest readership. Over 50 percent of the copies of the daily *L'Humanité* (circulation: 175,000–200,000) and over 60 percent of those of *L'Humanité Dimanche* (circulation: 450,000–500,000) are sold in the Paris region. Still further, of twenty-five local weekly Communist papers distributed throughout France, seventeen are located in the Paris suburbs, for example *La Renaissance* in the Argenteuil-Bezons area.[24]

This propaganda saturation of the Communist municipalities combined with the historic inclination of the suburban Paris working class to vote for an extreme Left-wing party [25] creates a political bastion almost impervious to attack from the outside and of strategic value in terms of an aggressive policy. It is in these bastions that the Party can mobilize the largest number of militants in the least amount of time, with the aid not only of those who have direct relations with the Party but also those who participate in a neighborhood committee, such as a sports club or a tenants' association. The Communist municipal officials attempt to keep in close contact with these local secondary groups, giving them an opportunity at least to express their views to the local administration. Of course, Party militants most often play an active and perhaps dominant role in the neighborhood committees, but the organization of such a network of secondary political groups, and consultations among its members, nevertheless permit the Communists to claim that their municipalities are the most closely linked to the masses and are thus the most democratic.[26]

The PCF practices what it calls a "class" policy of local administration. Basically, this means that a Communist-governed municipality attempts to provide the maximum amount of services to the people at minimum cost (free if possible) and to direct its action at the most disadvantaged groups in society. For example, a typical Communist

[24] Thibaud, "Communisme munipal," pp. 413–14, and Hoss, *Communes*, p. 20.

[25] The "red belt" was SFIO before the PCF won it over progressively during 1920–45.

[26] In a Communist local bastion, political opposition is rather impotent, and thus the Party can go out of its way to be "fair" even providing material aid to help the opposition to survive. In Bezons, for example, in 1965 the Communists ran unopposed. (Hoss, *Communes*, p. 59.) For a useful study of the most famous Italian case, see Robert H. Evans, *Coexistence: Communism and its Practice in Bologna, 1945–1965* (Notre Dame, Ind.: U. of Notre Dame Press, 1967), 225 pp.

policy not usually practiced by other local administrations is to pay the 20 percent of medical and hospital bills not covered by regular Social Security reimbursements, thus providing completely free medical care for those whose need is demonstrated on the basis of a verification by the municipal social services commission.[27] Moreover, medical services in Communist municipalities are often quite good: the Medical-Social Center in Argenteuil is efficient and inexpensive. In fact, each year 8,000 people from the neighboring Gaullist municipality of Colombes use its services—a matter of no little embarrassment to the UDR.[28] Old people and needy families receive particular attention, often in the form of packages of goods or even outright gifts of money to tide them over a difficult period. Communist municipalities were also the first to inaugurate year-round local sports programs and inexpensive ski vacations for young people.

This "class-oriented" policy of local administration is complemented by a financial policy based on the classic slogan "Make the rich pay!" Such an approach to revenue-seeking obliges the PCF municipalities to work on the basis of a selective revenue policy, one using direct taxes as much as possible, because indirect taxes are harder to control. Furthermore, the major indirect tax in local finances is a sales tax, which is more likely to cut into the budget of the poor than the rich. The major direct tax open to the local government is the *centime*, a tax upon real estate, developed property, the professions, and businesses. The rate of the *centime* is fixed by the municipality, within a given range established by the national government.[29] The PCF policy is to make maximum use of direct taxes, and to apply the *centime* tax with a distinction between large and small property owners in order to emburden the "large capitalists" for the benefit of the workers.[30]

Although partially successful in practicing a "class-oriented" fiscal policy, the Communist municipalities cannot avoid being placed in a difficult situation because of the extent to which they are dependent

[27] Hoss, *Communes*, pp. 31–32.   [28] *Ibid.*, p. 32.

[29] Kesselman, *Consensus*, p. 182.

[30] See, for example, "Comment est appliquée à Ivry la taxe sur les locaux industriels pour atteindre les capitalistes au bénéfice des chomeurs," *L'Humanité*, April 12, 1935, p. 4 cited in Platone, p. 107.

on the national government. Normally, about two-thirds of local government revenues are used to meet current expenditures, and it is rare that a municipality is able to find money for new projects within its own resources. Moreover, while local governments are legally permitted to borrow from private banks, in fact over three-quarters of loans to French communes originate in one source, the *Caisse des Dépôts et Consignations*, which is the government savings bank. The other important source of money for new projects also comes from the national government, in the form of grants-in-aid, or *subventions*.[31] It will surprise no one to learn that the Communist municipalities have been normally disadvantaged in the disbursement of national monies. Thus, while they have been able to keep up a flow of day-to-day welfare services more extensive than in non-Communist municipalities, their ability to construct new low-cost housing, roads, or public buildings has been considerably less successful.[32] The state is also able to limit the ability of Communist local governments to manipulate the tax burden onto the "capitalists." For example, a law exists permitting a municipal council to raise the *centime* tax to four times its normal level, with the sole precaution that this action be approved by the Minister of the Interior. When the PCF municipality at Argenteuil sought to raise this tax to the limit, the Minister rejected the proposal.[33]

Communist criticism of suggestions for local government reform follows this pattern. As opposed to those who see the major problem as one of regrouping the small rural communes into a sizable unit and

[31] On the above and for a more general description of local government finances, see Kesselman, *Consensus*, pp. 181–84.

[32] A comparison between two suburban Paris municipalities, one Communist and the other independent, for the period 1958–62 showed that the PCF-controlled government spent much more on education, leisure activities, and cultural affairs, while the independent municipality had a decisive advantage in building new roads. (See Jean-Claude Ducros, "Politique et finances locales," *Analyse et prévision*, July–August 1966). See also the budget for Argenteuil and Bezons (Hoss, *Communes*, pp. 108–15.)

While the above comparison holds true for the solid Communists areas, the Gaullist national government has nevertheless done a great amount of construction and urbanization in municipalities it hopes to win or whose electoral composition it hopes to change through consolidation with other communes. A good example of this is the Paris suburb of Nanterre, the present location of the new Hauts-de-Seine prefecture and Nanterre University, and the future location of the Education Ministry.

[33] Hoss, *Communes*, p. 122.

the urban communes into coherent and more efficient municipal *agglomérations*, they charge that the problem is not essentially one of structures but of resources. The Party would like to have more government money and to be able to use it autonomously, free from the anti-Communist prejudices of the prefects and the national ministries.[34] They oppose the reorganization of the communes as well, being rightly suspicious that one of the goals of any such restructuring would be to dilute the Communist bastions by merging them with more "bourgeois" municipalities. The present government bill on fusion of local governments would give the prefect authority to do this by decree, and the Communist proposal of eliminating the entire prefect corps and devolving his powers on the President of the Departmental Councils is aimed both at the question of fusion and the demand for greater local autonomy in general.[35]

In sum, the Communist position in French local government is difficult when seen in the long term. PCF municipal governments have often raised direct taxes quite high to meet their commitment to emphasizing a broad program of immediate social welfare measures.[36] In doing so, they have driven out some of the large employers in the "red belt" industrial areas around Paris, in effect giving impetus to the government's decentralization program (which the latter implements through financial incentives and a refusal to grant construction permits). While this is in a sense "getting rid of the capitalists," such a policy may not long be appreciated by people who are looking for jobs.[37]

---

[34] Despite this, Communist mayors realize it is in their immediate interest not to antagonize the prefect, and past relations have often been quite cooperative, if less than cordial. Also Communist mayors find it in their interest to cooperate in the Association of French Mayors and the Union of Mayors of the Seine, both of which seek greater local political and financial autonomy, as does the Party.

[35] A useful semi-official report on the reorganization of communal governments is "Libertés, fusions et regroupements des communes," *La documentation française*, June 14, 1972, Nos. 3899–3900, 51 pp. The Communist Party admits the ultimate desirability of reorganizing but seeks to avoid it until the Left is in power. Thus, the communist senators abstained on a bill proposing that the power of decision be given to the Departmental Councils instead of the prefects. (See *Le Monde*, June 18, 1971, p. 12.)

[36] At Argenteuil and Bezons, 50 percent of the direct municipal tax revenues are paid by a few dozen large firms. Hoss, *Communes*, p. 122.

[37] A point made in Kriegel, *Communistes français*, p. 242.

And once again, the PCF's inability to admit or to seek structural reforms within the present framework, for fear of prejudicing the Communist revolutionary claims, implies two dichotomous futures: unless the Party leadership opts into the established order in some unforeseeable manner, the contradiction must some day be resolved either in "revolution" (even in the diluted and still changing sense assigned the term since the beginning of de-Stalinization), or in the decline of Communist municipal strength. For example, the contrast between the amount of construction and reconstruction presently going on in a now-Gaullist municipality such as Chelles (in the eastern Paris suburbs) and a Communist bastion such as St. Denis or Champigny is quite striking.[38] Sooner or later a continuation of the present situation would probably lead even a highly committed electorate to reconsider its interests. This is all the more probable in that much of the basis of local Communist strength, and above all in the "red belt," rests not so much on the Party as on the CGT. In order to retain this CGT-oriented support, the PCF municipal governments must, as Georges Marchais has said, "put more butter on the workers' bread." And while a narrow definition of "butter" may have sufficed during the lean years after the war, the present economic progress seems to have stimulated popular demands for the sort of public works that isolated and underfinanced Communist local governments cannot provide alone.

In the immediate and even medium-term perspective, on the other hand, the "red belt" and other urban Communist municipalities appear to be retaining their vigor and political discipline, despite their integration into the supradepartmental Paris Region. In the 1969 referendum, which de Gaulle lost nationally by 53.2 to 46.8 percent of the vote, the Communist municipalities in general voted 60 to 70 percent against, with the classic "red belt" bastions of Ivry and Gennevilliers producing 73 and 75 percent *non* respectively.[39]

[38] Before it elected a Gaullist coalition led by Guy Rabourdin (who until 1973 was also the deputy), Chelles elected the traditional broad-based coalition. Besides the very active efforts of Rabourdin, government interest in Chelles was stimulated by the possibility of capturing it permanently, despite a large group of Communist-voting railroad workers, who had settled there after the war. Paradoxically (or perhaps typically), in the midst of the renovation of the city, Rabourdin was defeated in the March 1973 legislative elections by a Communist Left unity candidate.

[39] *L'Humanité*, April 28, 1969, p. 1.

The future of Communist local governments is thus uncertain, for it will in all probability develop with the national pattern, which is itself uncertain. While it is true the fortress-like character of these municipal enclaves within the bourgeois order is likely to become diluted over the years, rejection of the one-party concept and a serious policy of long-term alliance with the socialists may give rise to a new pattern of local Communist activity consonant with the doctrine of a peaceful transition to socialism and all the other transformations of traditional Communist attitudes implied therein.

The PCF and National Government: Spoils System or "Noyautage"?

As is evident in many places in this study, a fundamental questioning of the single-party model of postrevolutionary society seems to characterize the PCF's present strategic perspective. The change is not yet complete, however, and may not be completed, at least in doctrine. In any case, any discussion of the governmental role of the French Communists would be grossly inadequate if one did not underline more forcefully the element of *noyautage* or "packing" the ministries, which occurred under Communist ministers during their participation in the Provisional Government. The experience of 1944–47 remains the only evidence of how the French Communists have acted in the government.

Essentially, packing the ministries meant utilizing the methods of purge, political nepotism, and the creation of a parallel chain of authority—the classic techniques of implementing the one-party model from inside a structure and without physical violence—to produce an administrative hierarchy dominated by Communists or Communist allies. Should events have turned "favorably" in 1945 or 1946 the "purified" ministries would surely have been part of a dual power tactic; as things turned out, of course, rather than developing into a crucial aspect of a revolutionary takeover of power, the packed Communist ministries were taken from the Party's control in May 1947, and repurged thereafter. Nonetheless, this episode was to be of lasting importance for two reasons: first, it demonstrated the French Communists would attempt to implement the theory of a single legitimate political force wherever possible; second, it created additional motivation for the exclusion and isolation of the Communists from government once *le grand schisme* had become irreversible.

The Communists attempted to use their leverage in the cabinet to infiltrate and control the reconstruction of industries falling under the jurisdiction of their ministers. Whereas the Party leadership had been only lukewarm to the nationalizations in the 1943 program of the *Conseil National de la Résistance*, after the Liberation the Communists supported nationalizations on the basis of a highly centralized structure, "since the administrative boards would be under the supervision of Communist-dominated economic ministries." [40]

In the coal industry, for example, the administrative board of the central structure was composed of eighteen members—six representatives each of the workers, the government, and the consumers. The employee representatives, named by the CGT, were for the most part Communists, as were the government representatives, named by Marcel Paul, the Communist Minister of Industrial Production. Given one or two Communist consumer representatives, the central organ of decision was easily manipulated by the Party. [41] In the aircraft industry, the large Gnome-et-Rhône Company had been nationalized, falling under the jurisdiction of the Air Force Minister, Charles Tillon. Tillon appointed Marcel Weil, a Communist, as Director General of the company, and from this position Weil was able to pack the entire administration of the enterprise with Party militants. Moreover, Communists were also given preference in employment. Often, job openings in the aircraft industry were advertised only in *L'Humanité*, *Franc-Tireur*, *Paris-Liberté*, *and Ce Soir*—all Communist sympathizer papers. This led to a situation in which a large majority of the working force in the aircraft factories was either Communist or dependent on the Party for job security. And even after Weil was replaced, Communist labor inspectors in the plants often refused to sanction dismissals, thus retarding the anti-Communist purge after 1947. [42]

---

[40] Rieber, *Stalin and the French Communist Party*, p. 289. Rieber also notes the example of the proposal by Marcel Paul for the nationalization of gas and electricity. (Assemblée Nationale Constituante, *J. O. Débats*, March 27, 1946, 1st session, pp. 1108–1109. Hereinafter cited as *J. O.*)

[41] See *ibid.*, p. 289.   [42] See *ibid.*, pp. 290–91.

The simple device of packing an administrative apparatus sometimes proved inadequate to Communist intentions, however. In such cases, other methods were used, one of the most interesting of which was that undertaken in the Ministry of Reconstruction and Urbanization (MRU), under the direction of the Communist François Billoux, from January 23 to November 22, 1946.[43]

Control of the functioning of the MRU, as in other ministries, was the task of a Department of General Inspection (DGI), one of four departments of the central administration as it was reorganized under Billoux. Within the DGI, two sorts of inspectors were created: administrative inspectors and technical controllers. Wary that this corps of inspectors, inherited largely from the previous (non-Communist) ministry headed by Dautry, was too "technocratic" in character, Billoux proceeded to create a parallel group of controllers, to be known as Workers' Representatives in Reconstruction (WRR). The ministerial decree creating them appeared in the *Journal Officiel* in June 1946.[44]

The WRR, who were to come almost entirely from the CGT, would have the function of "bringing to the Minister of Reconstruction all useful remarks and suggestions as well as the constant support of syndicalist organizations of workers adhering to the CGT."[45] In reality, the powers of the WRR were to be very extensive, all of the demands of the CGT having been honored in this regard.[46] They were to be present at all meetings of the department heads, to be informed of all work programs, and to be capable of making investigations of work programs as well as verifying the production of materials, the state of inventories, etc. Moreover, they were to be part of negotiations on ministerial contracts and to be members of the Departmental Reconstruction Committees. In brief, they were to have all

[43] The following is based on an unpublished thesis by François Pommerolle, "Etude de la gestion communiste du Ministère de la Reconstruction et de l'Urbanisme," Nanterre University, Paris, 1969, 177 pp., multigr. Pommerolle had access to the archives of Billoux's *Chef de Cabinet* (3 vols., 744 pp.), as well as reports of meetings, letters, statistics and other documents. See also the not very revealing book by Billoux himself, *Quand nous étions ministres* (Paris: Editions sociales, 1972) 190 pp.

[44] *J. O.*, June 12, 1946, pp. 5163–64.

[45] From the ministerial decree, cited in Pommerolle, "gestion communiste," p. 117.

[46] Pommerolle, based on archives of the Chef de cabinet, p. 122*n*.

the functions of the regular administrative and technical inspectors, with the reservation that, unlike the latter, they lacked the authority to order direct sanctions. A hint that they might eventually be given more direct powers not mentioned in the ministerial decree was given by Billoux in an interview with the newspaper *L'Aube* on March 8, 1946: "The WRR will have as their essential task to send the Minister each month a confidential and detailed report on the activity of the organization and the morality of the civil servants." Billoux asked of these "political commissars . . . all their support, given that he finds it impossible to rely on the civil servants of the Ministry [whose] moral and technical capacity leaves something to be desired." [47]

After being Minister of Reconstruction for ten months in the governments of Gouin and Bidault, Billoux was replaced in the government of Léon Blum, which, as noted above, was entirely an SFIO cabinet. In the Ramadier government formed on January 22, 1947, Billoux was named Minister of National Defense; his old post at Reconstruction was given to another Communist, Charles Tillon. Shortly thereafter, the Communist ministers were evicted, thus terminating the WRR experiment as well, at least insofar as the PCF interest was concerned.

The purge, packing, and parallel structure aspects of French Communist ministries in the Provisional Government were an implementation of classic Communist tactics whose motivation may be traced in the end to the development of the one-party doctrine as the characteristic form of Marxist-Leninist regimes. At the same time, attempts to pack ministries were carried out by the MRP and SFIO as well during the Provisional Government period, but the latter are comparable to the PCF methods neither in actual scope nor in the strategic significance attached to them. The Communists may legitimately deny that their use of ministerial prerogatives constituted a violation of legal norms. Nonetheless, no one denies that their ultimate objectives were implicit in the example they sought to approach, and all interested in the future of French politics wonder to what extent the Provisional Government experience is relevant to contemporary events.

[47] Cited in *ibid.*, p. 118.

Chapter Twelve

THE CONTRADICTIONS
OF FRENCH COMMUNISM

The evocative, decadent, and "bourgeois" prose of the nine-teenth-century literary historian Hippolyte Taine has often been admired, although his status as a historian has been seriously undermined since he wrote. In terms of the interests of modern social science, Edmund Wilson has pointed out with apt imagery how Taine's very broad scope and his effort at generalization left him an unknowing prey to one of the most common shortcomings of the generalist seeking to treat a large subject systematically and with conceptual rigor: "Taine feeds history into a machine which automatically sorts out the phenomena, so that all the examples of one kind of thing turn up in one section or chapter and all the examples of another kind in another, and the things which do not easily lend themselves to Taine's large and simple generalizations do not turn up at all. The thesis is the prime consideration, and he will allow only a moderate variety in the phenomena that go to fill it in." [1]

Of course, any generalization about history or society is inevitably an oversimplification, although the simplest and most elegant formulas are often the most provocative and even the most fruitful in terms of what the German historians used to call *Verstehen*. The theoretical conception of French Communism presented so far in this book has thus unavoidably oversimplified matters somewhat too much and has given the impression of much greater clarity and separation among the four major "faces" of the PCF than is actually the case. The purpose of the present chapter is to ameliorate this oversimplification as much as possible, by attempting to draw the major interconnections and

[1] *To the Finland Station*, p. 47.

overlaps between the political roles of the French Communist movement.

Yet this is not by any means a disclaimer of the previous four chapters: each of them does indeed analyze an identifiable object, recognizable, presumably, by any observer. On the other hand, analysis, the opposite of synthesis, is a poor tool for rendering the dynamic relations between the parts of a whole. The plurality of the role structure of a communist movement in opposition has been too little underscored in previous writing, and it has been therefore important in the present work first to emphasize the simultaneous existence of the four "faces" of French Communism before drawing the composite visage which is the goal of the following pages.

How, then, do the four "faces" of French communism relate to each other? Where are they supportive and where are they in opposition? What are the overlaps and what are the independencies? What are, as a Marxist would ask, the "contradictions" of French Communism?

To begin with, let us summarize the ideal-type model, the "useful fiction," with which the French Communist movement has been characterized in the preceeding four chapters.[2] In Figure 1, the four "faces" and the two nodal points of strategy are rendered schematically. The model of Figure 1 is, to be sure, both static and atemporal: It ignores both the problem of change on a theoretical level, and actual history. To begin its refinement, it will help to briefly recapitulate the development of French Communism as presented in this study.

Marx and Engels were fond of asserting that their own "scientific" socialism differed from "utopian" socialism in that whereas the latter merely speculated upon the possible, the former was founded on the actual. One of the most important consequences of this concern with approaching the transition from the present to the future society in a realistic manner was to meditate upon the length of time, and the intermediate actions and transformations, necessary to ready bourgeois society for the passage to socialist society. However, to admit that revolution was not immediately and at any time possible was equivalent to saying that the bourgeois regime was in this sense justified by History until the conditions for revolution had ripened. In combining

---

[2] The term is H. Stuart Hughes's evocative translation of Max Weber's concept of the "ideal type" (*Consciousness and Society*, [New York: Alfred A Knopf, 1958], p. 65).

Figure 1.

The four faces of French Communism

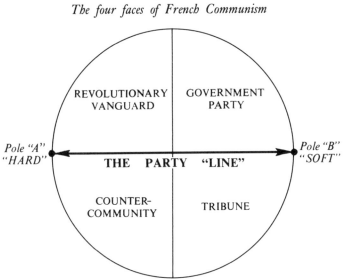

REVOLUTIONARY | GOVERNMENT
VANGUARD | PARTY

Pole "A"
"HARD"   **THE   PARTY   "LINE"**   *Pole "B"*
"SOFT"

COUNTER-
COMMUNITY | TRIBUNE

the two ideas of the necessity of further development of the established order and a necessary and inevitable proletarian revolution at some indeterminate future date, Marxist doctrine from the beginning was thus characterized by a dual and ambivalent attitude toward the established prerevolutionary situation: the task of the Marxists was both to assure the "success" of bourgeois society (to prevent retrogression) and to revolutionize it.

The writings of Marx and Engels said very little about the practical conduct of a revolutionary movement however. It was the German Social Democrats and, later and most importantly, Lenin and the other Bolshevik leaders (in particular Trotsky) who bequeathed the practice of a dual hard-soft, maximum-minimum strategic outlook and the broad arsenal of tactics later elaborated by all the Communist parties created after the Russian Revolution. The Leninist organization of revolutionary work, in another sense, can be expressed as the triumph of the notion of "consciousness" over "spontaneity," of a conscious stalking of the revolutionary situation rather than the *surprise divine* envisioned by those who believed a broad social evolution, a spontaneous and unpredictable popular uprising, or a general strike would in itself somehow effect a revolutionary change. In effect, the Leninist legacy was to justify conscious tactical maneuvering for "partial gains" and "partial collaborative actions" while simultaneously, and above all, striving to succeed at the maximum, revolutionary pole of Communist activity. This produced a Communist movement practicing such an ambivalent tactical combination of hard and soft tendencies that its political activity and presence, when viewed globally and without reference to ultimate intentions, was rendered to a greater or lesser extent (depending on the situation) ambiguous in relation to the established regime. The success of the Bolshevik Party was a proof that up to the time of the revolutionary situation itself a communist party need not "choose" either the option of "economism" or that of "revolution," and that an ambivalent long-term strategy was workable given the proper conditions and proper leadership. Furthermore, the Russian Revolution and the creation of Soviet society firmed up the dual perspective of the later non-Russian communist parties by providing an actual model of the "dictatorship of the proletariat" with which their own supposedly prerevolutionary societies could be juxtaposed.

By 1924, after four years of uncertainty the French Communist Party began its process of bolshevization. At this point the Soviet model had already developed into a one-party dictatorship, although perhaps this had not been foreseen. The bolshevization of French communism took a decade to complete, and the process was decisively influenced by the Soviet evolution during this time so that from the moment of its consolidation as a Bolshevik-style party, the PCF operated with the pre- and postrevolutionary perspective that one may accurately, if clumsily, term Marxism-Leninism-Stalinism. The Party has never moved beyond its prerevolutionary perspective, which has produced a dual and ambiguous relationship between the French Communist movement and its environment—a relationship whose fundamental ambiguity is incomparably deeper and more complex than that of the Russian Bolshevik Party and the pre-1917 regime because of the vast differences in conditions. The French Communists have acted to participate in the regime, and even to protect it when it has been threatened with a less advantageous set of institutions; they have also simultaneously sought to use this participation as a base for the transformation to a revolutionary situation. The PCF's participation in coalitions, however helpful to its partners or reform-oriented in the context (e.g. 1934–38, 1944–47), could not be accepted entirely at face value. To the Communists such alliances were potentially a way to move toward a situation in which the question of coalition with noncommunist forces had become moot. The distinction is fundamental: Communist *intentions* with regard to the established order have been unequivocal; the *effect* of Communist relations with the established order has been persistently ambiguous. The assertion of ambiguity is based upon an analysis of behavior, not intentions.

Having been bolshevized into Stalinist modes of thought and behavior between 1924 and 1934, the French Communists have since then almost always taken the cause of the international movement as the ultimate guide to the choice of their own goals and tactics. And serving the cause of "proletarian internationalism" has been translated above all as serving the foreign policy interest of the Soviet Union. The French Communist leaders have long equated Soviet interests with those of the worldwide revolution. Thus the *grands tournants* in French Communist history have unfailingly reflected changes in Soviet policy and attitudes. The post-1956 transformation has been the most unusual: Since then the PCF has developed the possibilities of the "peaceful transition to socialism" doctrine—which had been initiated by the CPSU—largely on its own, and has even stood fast in disagreements with the Soviet Party on a few important occasions. Thus one concludes the direct CPSU influence on the PCF leadership is now at its least since the period of bolshevization. This is the basis of what might be called the "nationalization" of French Communism. Still, it remains unclear whether the de-Stalinization of French Communism implies complete autonomy, particularly in the limiting case of a possible renewed East-West split and a new Soviet foreign policy posture. Moreover, in terms of the French Communist postrevolutionary perspective, after the launch of anti-Stalinism in 1956 the earlier proposal, built around the installation of a one-party system based on the Soviet example, or, at least the one-party-dominant system of the East European communist regimes, was revised in fundamentally important respects, in particular between 1959 and 1964 (See chapter 8).

In Table 8 the major ambivalent manifestations in the relationship of the French Communist movement and the established order are separated.

Part One of this study analyzed how the dual and ambivalent strategic perspective of the French Communist Party has worked out in practice.

During the early years of French Communism, before the Popular Front initiative of 1934, the most important effort was spent in bolshevizing the organization and its leadership. Inherent in this process, the "reformists," Trotskyites, and anarchists were purged, at the same time as the party organization was reconstructed according to the principles of democratic centralism as practiced in the Soviet Party. The emergence of Maurice Thorez as the dominant party leader after 1930 symbolized both completion of the bolshevization and commitment of the PCF to Soviet leadership of the "world revolution." In terms of tactics, during the first years of its existence the lack of leadership and organizational coherence made Party action weak and ineffective. Attempts to practice united front alliance tactics with the socialists, at the leadership level as well as at the mass level, failed more or less completely. The introduction of class against class tactics in 1928, a foreign policy corresponding to the hardening of Stalin's domestic policy at the same time, was likewise a failure, although by pursuing them through 1933 the French Communists proved the dubious virtue that their self-subordination to the Comintern was solid, despite catastrophic damage to their own national concerns.

The Popular Front tactic was capable of success because it was introduced at a time when Soviet foreign policy initiatives coincided with the interest of potential PCF allies, in particular the SFIO and the left wing of the Radical Party. That this was to be a fundamental condition of Communist "reintegration" into French politics was to be verified at each important turning point afterward. At the same time, however, practice of the collaborative aspect of Leninist-style strategy, to the extent of joining the governmental majority and calling for an end to the general strike of June 1936, raised the question for the first time of whether or not the PCF had given up its fundamental opposition to bourgeois capitalism and its revolutionary intentions. Although the answer was not to be given definitively until 1939, several Communist actions during the period of the Front indicated that

Table 8: The Role Structure of French Communism: Ambivalence as the Basis of Communist Opposition in a Liberal or "Bourgeois" Democracy

	The Dual Perspective	
	Partial Collaboration in the Established Order (Pole "B")	*Fundamental Opposition: Preparation for Revolutionary Action (Pole "A")*
Roles	The Party of Government The Tribune	The Revolutionary Vanguard The Countercommunity
Doctrinal Justification (The Dual Legitimacies)	Bourgeois democracy is justified (i.e. "historically necessary") until revolution is possible. Immediate reforms are possible and desirable. Retrograde movement in the class struggle (e.g. fascism) is avoided by support of the established regime.	A socialist revolution is inevitable. This revolution will be made by the working classes, whose (sole?) authentic guide is the Communist Party. The communist works to promote a revolutionary situation and for the demise of the established order.
Strategic Orientation (The Dual Program)	*The Minimum Program:* a) Political reforms. The extension of liberal democracy organizes the working classes and gives the revolutionary elements greater legal political power. b) Economic and social reforms: Labor union and parliamentary activity create the best life possible for the working class in a nonsocialist state.	*The Maximum Program:* a) Despite success in the minimum program, the working class and the Party must be prevented from being integrated with the established order. b) The existing situation must always be pushed toward a revolutionary situation by directing events along the "French road to socialism."
Possible Tactics: (The "Zigzag").	a) *The United Front:* alliance among parties, unions, ancillaries. ("unity of action"; "common program") b) Participation in elections, in parliament, in government. c) Seeking social and economic reforms.	a) *The United Front:* infiltrate and absorb allies ("organic unity"). Enlargement of the countercommunity. b) Participation in "proletarian internationalism." c) Prepare eventual revolutionary action.

while the tactical emphasis was temporarily on collaboration, the Party was preserving its revolutionary outlook. Among these were the "ministry of the masses," the attempt to unify the SFIO and syndicalist movements under Communist hegemony (an explicit manifestation of the monist mentality), and the doctrinal presentation of the Popular Front as a possible step towards a "republic of soviets."

French Communist support of the Nazi-Soviet Pact after August 1939 confirmed undeniably that the PCF leadership was still capable of radical initiatives and had not led the Party toward conciliation with the established order in the manner of the Social Democrats of the Second International. Whereas the SFIO had rallied to the national government at the outbreak of war in 1914, the PCF, in deference to Stalin's pact of nonintervention with Hitler, and despite a vicious hatred of Nazi Germany, adopted a pose of neutrality as its country was invaded and occupied. The entire Communist organization was declared illegal and forced underground in September 1939. The ensuing decimation of the Party confirmed that the decision to support the Soviet Union had been an almost suicidal gesture.

The Nazi attack on the Soviet Union in June 1941 permitted the PCF to begin its second successful practice of alliance tactics. First in the Resistance movements and then in the Gaullist and Tripartite provisional governments, the French Communists proved to be effective partners in driving out the Germans and in commencing the reconstruction of France. Although persistently denied the degree of governmental power they demanded, the Communists nonetheless decided to play an important role in the rapid increase in production of coal, steel, and other strategic resources, as well as insuring that no strikes occurred to disrupt the reconstruction. Furthermore, they participated in the reestablishment of parliamentary democracy in France, ratifying a compromise constitution when their own proposal had been rejected. These actions were guided by the interest of the new Soviet bloc, which was that France avoid becoming dependent on American economic and military aid, thereby falling under American political influence. With the possibility of revolution "objectively" denied them by the presence of American and British troops on French soil and the Yalta arrangement, support of Soviet foreign policy, whose interest in an independent France coincided with the policies of both the Gaullist and metropolitan Resistance movements, was once again the key to understanding PCF behavior.

At the same time, Communist participation in the Liberation and Tripartite governments had again raised the question of whether or not the Party had given up its potential for radical action. As during the Popular Front, secondary trends within the dominant tactic of alliance provided evidence that such was not the case. As in 1935–37, the PCF leadership attempted a merger with the SFIO on the basis of Leninist principles, and not surprisingly the SFIO again refused. Also in repetition of the Popular Front era, the communist and socialist factions in the labor movement were once again unified, and whereas the events of 1939 had interrupted the infiltration of the CGT organization, by 1946 the Communists had won control of the entire hierarchy. Despite its failure to absorb the SFIO, the PCF had since 1935 become the larger party (in fact the largest in France), and this and its takeover of the CGT were both successes directed to the Soviet example. In the end, however, another divergence of Soviet and French interests—in the shape of the Cold War—required an unambiguous reassertion of French Communist alienation from the established order, once exclusion from the Ramadier government and its consequences forced the choice upon them.

After a six-year period of successful alliance with other groups, the Communists were excluded from the French government in May 1947. By accepting the "Zhdanov line" and the Cominform establishement in September 1947, they reaffirmed that the years of alliance had not weakened their conception of revolutionary action, which, in a nonrevolutionary situation, meant allegiance to Stalinist "proletarian internationalism" above the national state when the two interests collided. At first pushed out of the Tripartite alliance against its wishes, the Party thereafter accepted its exile as an acceptable price for doctrinal fidelity.

General de Gaulle's assumption of power in 1958 helped the Communists to flee their ghetto in two ways. First, his authoritarian governmental style and his Algerian policy alienated the Center and Center-Left by 1961–62. Secondly, his foreign policy of independence from the two Superpowers, combined with a certain thawing in the international Cold War, once again brought Soviet and French foreign policy interests close enough together that alliances became a possibility for the French Communists.

The continuing pattern of alliances on the French Left, begun with informal and unwritten agreements in 1962, reflects the contemporary evolution in both national and international politics in such a way that in many instances the precedents of 1934–38 and 1944–47 appear to be outdated.

Electoral cooperation in the form of mutual withdrawals has remained the least difficult type of common action among Communists, socialists, and some Center groups. This was also true during the Popular Front, when elections opposed Left and Right coalitions as they now oppose the Gaullist majority and a Popular Front-style opposition. During Tripartism, characterized by a miniscule opposition and three governing parties competing with each other for dominance, electoral coalitions were of course a moot point.

The question of "organic unity" or merger among the parties and trade unions has not been raised seriously since the post-1962 thaw for two reasons. First, the relative weakness of the Socialist Party and the CFDT prohibits any present thought of reunification on the part of the socialists, and there is in any case no sign that they would eventually wish to reunify with the Communists: In this sense, the Tours schism is likely never to be repaired. It could only perhaps be "surpassed." A second reason for the lack of any talk of merger is the Communist adoption of the multiparty thesis, which would in effect legitimate the socialist claim to a share of power in the postrevolutionary society. This is also perhaps the harbinger of a change in the classic Communist tactic of infiltrating and sooner or later absorbing its opposition, although it is still too soon to know whether the Communist impulsion to ubiquitous control has been primarily a result of the one-party doctrine, of a tendency for "democratic centralism" to expand more or less "by nature," or of simple militant fervor.[3]

Strangely enough, it is the question of governing together, which was answered affirmatively both in 1936–38 (Blum asked the Communists to participate, even though they at first declined) and in 1944–47,

---

[3] The various Communist participations in non-Communist governments, and in particular the important precedent in Chile, may be proof enough that a tendency toward monopoly is not an *uncontrollable* function of the structure of a Leninist-style party.

that posed the greatest obstacle to a renewed alliance between the PCF and the Socialist Party. The reason is that both parties agree the next Left government will seek to be a "revolutionary" government, unlike the Popular Front and Tripartite governments, in the sense that it will attempt to begin a socialist transition. Despite persistent Communist entreaties to write a common program of government, the socialists held off until June 1972. They first sought greater Communist modifications of the Soviet model, greater proofs of sincerity on the part of the PCF leadership, and time to rebuild their own movement.

By signing the Common Program of June 27, 1972, the Socialist Party and the dissident left-wing Radicals have in effect announced that they are prepared to risk a coalition government in the event of an electoral victory by the present opposition.

In sum, a study of the history of French communism reveals a zigzag pattern of tactical action consistent with the radically dual and ambivalent structure of Leninist strategic thought.[4]

The 1934–38 Popular Front tactic was not a repudiation of the increasingly sectarian attitudes of 1924–34, just as the period of exile from 1939 to 1941 was not an invalidation of alliance tactics. Likewise, the Cold War attitudes of 1947–62 were not a contradiction of wartime alliances, just as the third period of coalitions since 1962 does not deny the "correctness" of the Cold War line. In the Communist mentality, these *grands tournants* were "necessary" responses to a given set of circumstances, none of which changed the fundamental reform-revolution, mini-maxi perspective that guides "correct" Marxist-Leninist behavior. In Jacques Fauvet's words, "For most other parties, opportunism takes the place of doctrine. But they do not have the same need to justify themselves. For them, politics is after all nothing but the art of the possible, whereas for the Communists it is the science of the necessary."[5] The nature of Communist opposition in French politics has thus been consistently ambivalent, emphasizing either collaboration or fundamental opposition at any given time, but never yet resolving the "dialectical" tension of its si-

[4] I do not mean, of course, that Lenin would have adopted the same balance of collaboration and sectarian militancy. (This question is obviously unanswerable.)
[5] Jacques Fauvet, *Histoire du Parti communiste français*, 2:363.

multaneously "within" and "without" mentality and the dual poles of strategy, which one day will supposedly reach a revolutionary synthesis, the "unity of theory and practice" in the "transition to socialism." [6]

Moreover, because the actual practice of Communist opposition remains ambiguous and its intentions unrealized, all discussions of the loyalty or disloyalty of the Communist Party are doomed to inconclusiveness. This is, in terms of the vanguard role, the essence of the phenomenon today.[7]

Figure 2 diagrams the history of French communism dynamically within the terms of the two-pole, four-role model.

Although in the diagram Pole "A" (hard) is represented on the left and Pole "B" (soft) on the right, this is not meant to indicate that the tactics pursued toward one or the other pole are necessarily "Left" or "Right" in the classic political usage. For example, it is at least a matter of serious doubt as to whether support of the Nazi-Soviet Pact was a "Left" action or whether the "peaceful transition to socialism" is a "Right" tactic. Rather the sense to be given the polar directions is that of sectarianism and a radical exterior position as opposed to coalition and reintegration with the polity.

Moreover, even tactics tending toward the same direction have been no more than broadly similar. Let us take, for example, the three "hard" tactics of class against class, support of the Nazi-Soviet Pact, and the Zdhanov line. The class against class line was almost a fanatical gesture in the case of the French Party, an aggressive defiance by a millenarian sect of the reality of political forces in France, more a proof of radical credentials than of revolutionary guile. The PCF

[6] In terms of the logic of functional analysis, one might express the conception presented here in the following, highly abbreviated way: the consequence, or homeostatic variable, which the French Communists have sought to maintain is their ambivalent position in the established order of society, therein to preserve the potential to fundamentally transform that society. The structure which functions to preserve homeostasis is the elaborate four-role presence with an axis upon the two-pole continuum of strategy. The structure must resist tensions tending to destroy homeostasis, these being, *grosso modo*, the tendencies toward on the one hand complete exclusion, isolation or destruction, and on the other hand, complete integration and co-optation.

[7] Thus, one finds it impossible to credit such polemics as "A Communist party has no moral right to exist in a democracy." Benjamin Lippincott, *Democracy's Dilemma* (New York: Ronald, 1965), p. 181.

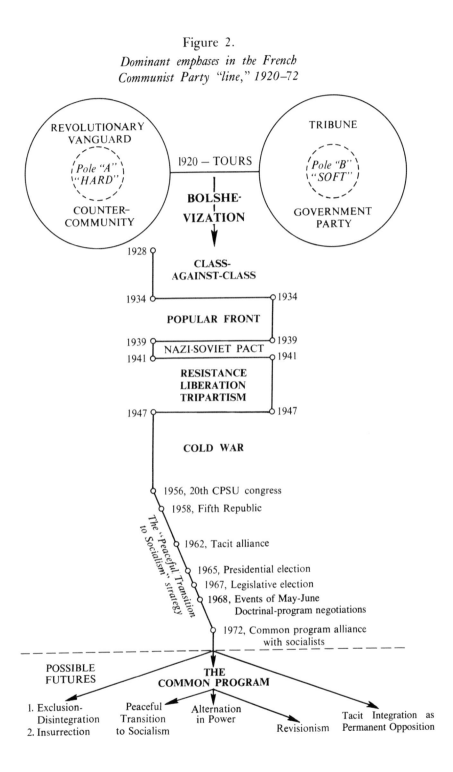

Figure 2.

*Dominant emphases in the French
Communist Party "line," 1920–72*

380   *The "Faces" of Communism in France*

excluded, a priori, all significant potential allies and furthermore proceeded to vilify them to an extent such that the movement relegated itself to sectarian isolation and political weakness. On the other hand, PCF support of the Nazi-Soviet Pact, while once again placing the French Communists far outside the established order, did so quite unwillingly. The PCF adopted this line to follow the Soviet Party, but at the same time it sought to remain within the bounds of coalition politics (even to return to take part in the government itself!), wooing allies as far to the right as the conservatives with its proposal for a "French Front." The Cold War tactic, finally, again represented only a partial reanimation of earlier hard-line postures. Once again, the key to PCF policy was the direction of Soviet policy, but this time neither did the French Communists seek completely to avoid potential allies, as in 1928–33 nor were they faced with the problems of clandestine existence and a war. Calculating their own tactics within the situation of "two blocs," the PCF and the other West European parties chose to play only a very secondary and partially diversionary, partially offensive role: they were to provide enough agitation to prevent their governments from opposing the consolidation and expansion of the Soviet bloc, as well as to do whatever possible to hinder the formation of the Atlantic bloc. Besides this, given the inhospitable situation in Western Europe, only identification with the Soviet world and its doctrinal debates and purges recalled their role in a "world revolution."

The differences in the three "soft" tactics of Popular Front, Tripartism, and the joint governmental program are in their larger aspects more obvious. From a policy of "support without participation" to defend "bourgeois" democracy, the French Communists moved to a policy of governmental participation to reestablish that same democracy, and now, finally, to a policy of governmental alliance of socialist forces which, unlike its two predecessor coalitions, is expressly undertaken to "open the road to socialism." [8] Beyond this essential dif-

[8] Although the judgment of Annie Kriegel is somewhat overstated, she summarizes the direction of the previous section in her assertion that within each broad alliance tactic in the history of French communism it is necessary to "distinguish an infinity of positions extending from the most radically exterior to intertwinement and interpenetration, each of them marked by the dominant ambiguity of both hostility and cooperation." *Les communistes français*, p. 250 and *passim*.

ference in tactical objective, other very important changes in the French Communists' attitudes toward alliance should also be noted: an acceptance to debate and to partly reformulate (e.g. the multiparty doctrine), though not thus far in essence, the ultimate goal of a "necessary" and "inevitable" political hegemony or monopoly; a consequent reluctance to raise the question of reunification ("organic unity") and the problem of internal takeover implied therein; the willingness to criticize in public certain "regrettable" features of the Soviet experience, at least "as they relate to the French case," and finally, the willingness to be explicit and to compromise in a program for the "transition stage" to the future society. To the present point, however, this "nationalization" or "repatriotization" of French communism has not yet signified a decommunization of the movement.

In Part Two of our analysis we have examined the ambivalence of French Communism in another way, by examining the quadrapartite role structure or "faces" of the movement taken as a whole. In three Republics the Party has played four dominant roles: government party, tribune, countercommunity, and revolutionary vanguard (see Figure 1).

It is part of the uniqueness of communist parties in general that they are able to act such a plurality of contrary roles simultaneously, for while the four faces of French Communism might be mutually consistent "after the revolution," in the past context of French politics their coexistence has implied a consistent tension, a "dialectical" framework at cross-purposes with itself, and an ambivalent pattern of self-manifestation wholly reflective of the fundamentally dual nature of Marxism-Leninism as opposition to a "bourgeois" order.

Were the contradictions all there in the beginning? The fundamental contradiction, the existence of a revolutionary party in a nonrevolutionary situation, was of course part of the creation of French communism, but neither all the roles nor the various overlaps and contradictions between them existed at the time of bolshevization.[9] Nor has the form of the original contradiction remained the same.

---

[9] The "contradiction" of being a revolutionary party (at least self-avowed) in a nonrevolutionary situation has been obviously not peculiar to Communist parties. It is true, in more or less exaggerated form, of all revolutionary parties who have not opted more or less entirely for one of the two strategic poles. The extent to which Communist par-

Essentially, the Janus-like quality of the PCF role structure is expressed in the tensions between the roles of *government party* and *tribune* on the one hand, and the roles of *countercommunity* and *revolutionary vanguard* on the other.

In its role of government party, whether on a national, regional, or local level, the French Communist movement has practiced the minimalist aspect of Leninist strategy to an extreme. It is here that the PCF has been most integrated into the established political structure and legitimacy, and thus most drawn toward the Second International's pattern of compromise with the bourgeois capitalist society it had proposed to revolutionize.

Although cabinet participation was not viewed by the Communists (in contrast to the social democrats) as a question of principle, the PCF leaders were extremely reluctant to undertake a role in *national* government when this first became possible in 1936; it was not, for example, a role the movement "needed" (after all, why *four* major roles instead of three, five, etc.? There is no "inherent" requirement). Participation was in a sense an admission of defeat, even if only temporary, which the Communist mentality must have found difficult to digest. The decision to support the Blum government but not to participate with ministers (i.e. to force the social democrats to support the biggest doctrinal crisis themselves) was largely an attempt to avoid this aspect of coalition tactics as long as possible. The Comintern's mention of a possible road to socialism out of the Popular Front in 1935–37 briefly excited doctrinal hopes at the time, and when the Soviet interest obliged the PCF to participate in the de Gaulle government a decade later, the result was the equally brief "national road to socialism" perspective of Thorez's November 1946 interview in the *London Times*.

Despite the integrative content of the PCF role as government party, it is probably in its role of tribune that the French Communist movement has penetrated most deeply into the socioeconomic vitals of

---

ties attempt to employ "consciousness" at the expense of "spontaneity" (i.e. *plan* the revolutionary struggle and attempt to manipulate the birth of a revolutionary situation) differentiates them in the depth of this inner tension from other revolutionary parties, often less emphatic about their own importance and inclined to be less rigorous in their activities.

French society, it has forged links with a bewildering variety of groups, social strata, and classes, so that while originally based on a concept introduced from a foreign environment, one is today scarcely able to imagine France without a powerful Communist movement acting in all the normal outlets for political organization characteristic of liberal regimes. Although not so linked to the rest of society as the Italian Communist movement, the French Communist movement is certainly remarkable in the extent and diversification of its activities in comparison with parties in France generally.

While the roles of government party and tribune are thus *primarily* a manifestation of the "soft" pole of Communist behavior, in a dialectical sense they nonetheless serve to reinforce the Communist demands for fundamental change. Communist local governments, for example, through their immediate provision of social welfare and by emphasizing the political and financial limits that inhibit a better life, may be able to convince many to retain or to adhere to the Communist critique of the regime and perhaps even the Communist community. In parliament, where only a series of unfavorable electoral laws has prevented the PCF from seeing its control of approximately one-fifth of the electorate translated into a proportional share of seats in governmental assemblies, Communist orators are further able to underline the gaps between the theory and the practice of the existing order.[10] Moreover, because public opinion polls show that the French people consider the PCF to be the party most representative of the disadvantaged and of the working class, its parliamentary or syndicalist demands as tribune—even though not conceded by the ruling majority—nonetheless fulfill the Communist purpose, which is to demonstrate that "bourgeois" democracy can never be fully realized. Alfred de Grazia has rightly asserted that representation is "the foremost structural problem of democracy,"[11] and while the Marxist-Leninist explanation of the deficiencies of French democracy is specious, both the injustices of present society and the underrepresentation of the Communist Party in proportion to its electoral strength

---

[10] This deprivation is in another way a blessing in disguise, as it has no doubt lessened pressure toward accommodation with the Gaullist revision of the institutions.

[11] *International Encyclopedia of the Social Sciences* (1967), s.v. "representation," vol. 13, p. 464.

appear in the public eye to verify the conclusion if not the premises. Finally, however, in order to make this point, the PCF is motivated to increase as much as possible the number of those who support its tribune role. Such an increase simply ties it closer to the existing social structure by rendering the Communists spokesmen for an incredible string of "bread and butter" demands, many of which are not only nonrevolutionary but plainly conservative or reactionary.

It is almost self-evident to add that the roles of government party and of tribune reinforce each other. In a sense, the Communist proposal for the future is to make the present "tribune" into the future "government," both before the revolution, in a Left-wing coalition, and during the revolution, when both roles will combine with the vanguard role.

For approximately four decades the tendency of these two roles to assimilate the Communist movement permanently within the established order has been opposed by the roles of countercommunity and revolutionary vanguard. The countercommunity institutionalizes fundamental opposition within a structured and resilient prefiguration of the future society, while the revolutionary vanguard provides the theoretical and doctrinal (i.e. intellectual and emotional) nourishment that permits the Communists to retain a millenarian perspective.

The formation of a French Communist countercommunity and its solidification in the years after the *grand schisme* of 1947 was functional in the same sense as Stalin's lowering of an "Iron Curtain" over Eastern Europe at the same time. In both cases, isolation from "outside" influence permitted the consolidation of a distinctively Stalinist system. Yet while it is true, as Isaac Deutscher has written, that this "isolation was in fact essential to the political and cultural climate of Stalinist Russia," and that "To maintain the 'iron curtain' became Stalin's major economic and political interest," [12] in France the situation was different in that the isolation of communism from the rest of the nation was sought first of all by non-Communists. The Third Force and the Fourth Republic were of course very weak at this time, and it can be argued there was no other way to deal with the Communist movement and still preserve the Republic, particularly in that

---

[12] *Stalin*, pp. 540, 543 ff.

after General de Gaulle had deprived the new institutions of a charismatic focus by resigning in January 1946, he compounded his weakening of the new regime by creating the RPF in 1947.

In any case, by thus constructing a domestic "containment" policy, the non-Communist forces in France were influential in consolidating the Communist movement as a countercommunity, which, from the PCF point of view, was to help enormously in preserving the radical and external character of the movement as a whole.[13]

The importance of this act of preservation was quite simple: to preserve at the same time the role of revolutionary vanguard, or, putting it more precisely in terms of a nonrevolutionary situation, to preserve in the French Communist movement a mentality apt to seize or assume power in a revolutionary situation. The role of revolutionary vanguard is the focus of the four-role schema: it anchors the other roles and is in turn reinforced by them.

The Vanguard Clientele

At the outset of this study, it was noted that we would be little concerned with analysis of the social bases of French Communism, or, in other words, of its various clienteles. Nonetheless, it is important here to add several comments on the vanguard clientele and its relations with the rest of the Communist constituencies, in particular those of the tribune role.

In one sense, the revolutionary constituency is self-evident: those who accept the demands of this role positively—those who believe the PCF is the authentic leader in the inevitable socialist transformation—

---

[13] We have a confirmation of the importance of isolation in constructing solidity and resilience into a communist community in the following report on North Vietnamese society by Joseph Kraft. Commenting on the "closed" and "directed" quality of North Vietnamese life, and particularly the isolation of the foreign (especially Western) population from the North Vietnamese themselves, Kraft wrote: "I do not conclude from this that North Vietnam is a state seething with discontent. . . . On the contrary, the capacity to cut off contacts so thoroughly gives me the opposite impression. . . . The character of Communism in North Vietnam . . . is one of the reasons it has been so hard for the United States to beat the men from Hanoi or to make peace with them." "Hanoi Report—I," *International Herald Tribune*, July 18, 1972, pp. 1–2.

can be identified more or less with the Communist countercommunity, whose membership, depending on criteria of some arbi-
trariness, may be placed at between 300,000 and 400,000. On the
other hand, however, one may refer also to a group of individuals who
accept the PCF's vanguard pretensions, but who oppose the role. For
in order that the vanguard role be validated, it is not necessary that
one approve, but only that one accept its existence.

In terms of somehow measuring this group of individuals who see
the PCF as a revolutionary party but disagree with its goals, methods,
or both, our major statistic comes from opinion polls.

In February 1968, a SOFRES poll posed the following statement:
"If the situation appeared favorable to it, the Communist Party would
be ready to make a revolution in order to take power." In response, 27
percent of the sample agreed with the statement, 36 percent disagreed
and 37 percent expressed no opinion.[14] In December 1969, one year
after the "events of May" and the Soviet-led invasion of Czechoslovakia, the same statement brought the following response: 47 percent
agreed, 34 percent disagreed, and 19 percent were without opinion.[15]
Finally, in July 1971, in response to the statement that the PCF is a
"Party which wants a revolution," the breakdown was 31 percent in
agreement, 51 percent in disagreement and 18 percent without opinion.[16] Thus, allowing for the variation in response resulting from reactions to the extraordinary events of 1968, it appears that approximately one-third of adult Frenchmen generally believe the
revolutionary pretension of the French Communists, whether or not
they look upon it favorably. In times of crisis—for example,
1968—the percentage appears to rise sharply. (It will be interesting to
pose the same question again as the PCF moves closer to a return to
government: Will public opinion perceive this as a crisis or a normal
situation? Will a correlation appear between the decreasing distance
between the Communist party and the seat of power, even in its electoral form, and a sharply rising number of distrustful and fear-
oriented responses?) On the other hand, and varying with the situation also, a proportion somewhat or even considerably larger than this
appears to preceive the PCF's vanguard pretension as wishful and illusory.

[14] See Lancelot and Weill, in Bon et al., *Le communisme en France*, p. 289.
[15] SOFRES, 1969, p. 26.   [16] *Ibid.*, 1971, p. 4.

If one combines the positive and the negative evaluations of the vanguard pretension (leaving aside those who do not accept it or who express no opinion), those who see the Party in this role appear to exceed its electorate. Moreover, outside the Communist community itself, those who most frequently perceive the PCF as revolutionary appear to be those most hostile to it. Those who may be categorized within the tribune role constituency do not nearly so often consider the party to be revolutionary.[17] This, of course, bears out the ambivalent relationship of the PCF with its tribune clientele, which has been one of the recurring themes of this study. Finally, the youngest age group (21–24 years old) most frequently sees the PCF as revolutionary, a belief that declines quite sharply with age. Given the general skepticism of the *gauchistes* toward the PCF's revolutionary claims, I am inclined to identify the 37 percent who see the Party as revolutionary as an agreement of enemies, consisting of those young people strongly favorable and those strongly opposed to the Communist movement.

The fact that those more or less neutral to the PCF tend to reject its revolutionary pretensions or, more often, not to express an opinion on the matter may be of great significance politically. In the February 1968 SOFRES survey the following response was obtained: If a Communist regime were established in France, people like you would a) stand to gain, 19 percent; b) stand to lose, 26 percent; c) neither, 42 percent; d) no opinion, 14 percent.[18] In May 1971 a SOFRES poll found that toward the possibility of a Left government in 1973, 51 percent of the respondents felt that it would change nothing, 20 percent felt their situation would change for the better, 12 percent for the worse, and 17 percent expressed no opinion.[19] Finally, in July 1972 again 51 percent of the sample said a Left government would change nothing, while 20 percent said their personal situation would be changed positively, 14 percent foresaw a negative change, and 15 percent expressed no opinion.[20]

[17] The SOFRES 1968 poll shows that 36 percent of those "very hostile" to the PCF and 45 percent of those "rather hostile" express the opinion that the PCF still desires a revolution, as opposed to the mean of 27 percent. On the other hand, only 20 percent of those "neutral or indifferent," 24 percent of those "rather favorable" and 20 percent of those "very favorable" to the PCF see it as revolutionary (p. 289).

[18] SOFRES. 1968, p. 265.   [19] Cited in *L'Express*, May 24–30, 1971, p. 79.

[20] A SOFRES poll cited in *Le Figaro*, July 21, 1972, 4.

Before the electoral campaign of 1973 a majority of the French thus seemed to be relatively unconcerned or unmindful of the program promises of the Communist-socialist coalition, even while they seemed quite closely aware of the "communist problem" in terms of political and civil liberties. For many reasons French public opinion in the past has often been permeated with an attitude of *plus ça change, plus c'est la même chose*. This approach to public affairs, sometimes ironic, sometimes cynical, has often born unexpected fruits.

Some Unexpected Contradictions and Further Research

While the opposition between the roles of vanguard and counter-community on the one hand and the roles of tribune and government party on the other hand appear historically as the essential contradiction in the evolution of the relation between the French Communist movement and the French regime, the depth of the tensions that can be found between each pair of broadly compatible roles is unexpected.

If one considers first the roles of government party and tribune, one will note that during the periods when the PCF was a government party at the national level it was difficult to avoid tensions as the Party simultaneously supported or participated in a cabinet and presented grievances—for reform and for revolution—against the regime and the society. During the Léon Blum government of 1936–37, which had no Communist ministers and which was the first break from sectarian communism in France, difficulties in maneuvering the "Ministry of the Masses" were minimal in this regard; moreover, the division of labor between the party and its syndicalist and mass ancillaries further minimized role conflict at this time. During the Provisional Government, however, in which the Minister of Labor was a Communist, the attempt to play both ends against the middle became increasingly problematic, all the more so in that the CGT was now increasingly dominated by its Communist membership, as contrasted with the situation in 1936. The politically motivated refusal by the CGT leadership to strike against the government provoked increasing discontentment among the rank and file, and it was no accident that in the spring of 1947 the Communist Party chose to make a stand on the question of wage-price relations rather than foreign policy: in this case, vigorous resumption of the tribune role was correlated with increasing difficulties in Communist action within the government. Finally, the contemporary Communist strategy, implemented in the Common Program tactic, has brought to the fore once again the possible contradictions between the roles of government party and tribune. In particular, the low profile adopted by the CGT during the 1973 electoral campaign, in order to nurture the idea that the Communists are against extremism and disorder, was a behavior that incited bitter charges of "selling out" to the PCF governmental pretensions. One of the leaders of the CFDT, Fredo Krumnov, expressed a common "left-wing" criticism by arguing that the CGT attitude was the most "demobilizing possible. . . . [For example], when a particular enterprise was shut down, we saw comrades from the PCF or the CGT explain to the people that it would suffice to vote for the Commom Program for the problem to be resolved. The struggles for retirement benefits and wages were also slowed with the following argument: . . . 'Don't worry about it, all that will be taken care of as soon as the election is over.' " [21] In theoretical terms, one can say the goal of the post-1956 peaceful revolution strategy—to consolidate the vanguard and government party roles—has posed a problem of credibility the French Communist Party may not survive.

The contradiction between the vanguard role and the Communist countercommunity role has been more constantly vigorous and more often remarked in various ways than the above set of tensions. In *What Is To Be Done?*, Lenin argued that a true revolutionary party "must be comprised first and foremost of people whose profession is that of revolutionists." One can say that the bolshevization of French communism between 1924 and 1934 rendered this description increasingly characteristic of the pre-Popular Front PCF, and in *Fils du peuple* Maurice Thorez was able to write without irony of his co-optation into the hierarchy that "I became a *permanent* of the Party, a 'professional revolutionary.' " [22] But the two-stage rebirth of French communism as a mass movement—during the Popular Front and at the Lib-

[21] From an interview in *Le nouvel observateur*, March 19, 1973, p. 38.
[22] 1949 edition, p. 45.

eration—rendered it impossible to speak of the PCF as an organization primarily composed of professional revolutionaries.

Earlier we have considered the argument that the day-to-day existence of the PCF as a mass party, and in a broader sense its "community" life as a whole, has compromised irrevocably the vanguard pretensions of the movement. Some conclusions have been suggested on the basis of what we know at the present time. Essentially these conclusions are to suspend judgment. We do not know enough, and of the data we do have much is controversial because of conceptual and methodological complications. In this regard, if the model of the French Communist movement presented in this chapter is fruitful, in addition to permitting the classification of existing data to offer a general explanation, it should indicate further areas of research here and with regard to the other "faces" of communism in France as well.

The present broad changes in the French and European Left indicates that the approach to study of the Communist vanguard role taken in this work—the analysis of doctrine, strategy, tactics, and program—should be continued, and that the French Communist Party is not at a dead end strategically in terms of provoking radical change. Yet, it seems apparent that such an approach can be only one aspect of a broader investigation. One possible alternative would be the study of the PCF leadership psychology in the top stratum. But although this may be possible at some future date, such is not presently the case. With regard to study of the psychology of opposition communist parties, Sidney Tarrow has emphasized the importance of studying the attachments of the local and regional levels of the Italian Communist movement with its surroundings, remarking that "It is precisely where the party's organization is most efficient . . . that the party itself is most saturated by the bourgeois culture in which it operates. . . . In the absence of . . . the party structure that once insured its revolutionary élan—a structure of horizontally isolated party cells—the PCI is a mass party that is *of* Italian society as well as *in* Italian society."[23] It is evident that the nature of the PCF since the Popular Front and of the PCI since the end of World War II does not invite a search for such a structure, at least in any form approaching

[23] "Economic Development and the Transformation of the Italian Party System," *Comparative Politics* 1, no. 2 (January 1969): 182.

that of the pre-1917 Russian Bolshevik Party. Moreover, it is not certain that the lack of such a structure cannot be compensated for, or, more importantly, that the structure was more significant than the psychology of a few individuals in the top leadership in the actual revolutionary situation. Nonetheless, empirical studies of the counter-community, of the degree and kinds of contact between the PCF, its ancillary organizations, and noncommunist society, should be of great importance in understanding and evaluating more deeply the present and future radical capacities of the Communist movement in France and the state of the contradiction between vanguard behavior and community behavior. Furthermore, it would be useful to study in particular the development of Communist-socialist links at all levels, for this particular set of ties will have a powerful effect on the limits of French Communist strategy.

The tensions outlined between the tribune role and the government role suggest several lines of research as well. On the one hand, studies investigating the similarities and differences in appeal of the PCF, the CGT, and selected local, regional, and national ancillary organizations would be important, especially in attempting to detail what may be a growing difficulty for the CGT to maintain its postwar role conception and orientation as the Communist Party moves closer to a return to government. The effect of intersyndical cooperation on the PCF-CGT link (and a comparison with the Italian case, in which such cooperation is more advanced) would be another important variable to integrate into the analysis. One would also hope to have studies of attempts to coordinate syndical activities on an international level, as this new phenomenon, created partially from the problems of dealing with multinational corporations and European integration, will undoubtedly pose new difficulties for both the PCF and the PCI.

Finally, it would be of great interest to be able to define with greater empirical clarity the various aspects of the tribune role, and in particular to investigate possible correlations with socioeconomic change and political development, in order to suggest answers to the questions of whether and in what form the tribune role may or may not survive Communist entrance into the government. In a recent article focusing on the hypothesis of the "protest" vote, Thomas Greene has rejected three different versions of it after a close statistical analy-

sis of survey data from several countries with relatively important nonruling Communist parties. Greene found that in general Communist voters do not want simply to vote for the party farthest to the Left, and are not the most disadvantaged electors, either materially or psychologically (i.e. they do not feel themselves.the most alienated). Greene also found that a large Communist vote is not essentially a product of a temporary and particularly difficult stage in modernization.[24] He suggests further that what was called the protest vote, a negative action, is motivated rather by a complex of positive attitudes which he terms a "radical-humanist syndrome," a variable he defines briefly and somewhat ambiguously. Although Greene's rejections of the above versions of the "protest" vote hypothesis are convincing, it is not certain that the protest notion in other and perhaps more sophisticated forms may not still be of powerful explanatory value. For example, while Communist electors do not seem to want simply to vote for the party farthest to the Left (they do not shift in any significant numbers to Trotskyite or Maoist parties), they may perceive the communist party as the *most serious* and *most usefully active* party farthest to the Left; and while Communist electors are not the most personally disadvantaged, they may nonetheless want to protest the fundamental nature of society, perceived as brutally capitalist, riddled with privilege, and built on "inhuman cadences." Moreover, the protest vote need not be conceived as a purely negative action. It may also be identified as a positive affirmation of part of the total Communist activity, and therein implied in Greene's conclusion that the "the Communist voter is, above all, a voter who believes in what he understands by 'Communism' " (p. 95). In any case, however, it would be counterproductive to the interest of inquiry to insist unduly upon rehabilitating the "protest" notion. The important point would be to investigate and to explain the appeals of a nonruling Communist movement to that part of its social and electoral support which appears to be motivated not by any general acceptance of the maximum Communist proposal for a future society, but rather by what in this study has been broadly labeled the tribune role of French communism.

[24] "The Electorates of Non-Ruling Communist Parties," *Studies in Comparative Communism* 4, nos. 3, 4 (July, October 1971): 68–103.

The "National-International" Duality

The problem has long been posed of integrating the national-international "dialectic" with the other fundamental dimensions of the French Communist movement in a single conception. It is from an analysis of the PCF vanguard role that we are most conveniently and correctly led to define the place of the "national-international" duality in the conception presented thus far in this chapter.

As argued in chapter 8, conceptualizing the national-international duality in French communism is not *primarily* a matter of determining whether the Soviets or the French are determinant in taking this or that decision (although in practical political terms the Soviet authority over French Communist affairs had long been unquestioned). Rather, it is a matter first of all of comprehending the ultimate legitimacy —over all other demands on allegiance—given by the French Communists to considerations beyond the national state; that is, to the Soviet-led international movement.

The "international pole" of French communism developed first out of the revolutionary vanguard role: PCF internationalism, after the bolshevization, was understood as not a contradiction of the national goals but rather as a completion of them. The French Revolution was to be part of a single (though perhaps not unitary in time) world revolution: "The interest of the French Communists was the interest of all Communists," and vice versa. Only in the last decade or so have the French Communists come to admit a partial, though significant, divergence of interest among their brother parties.

Developing first as an integral part of the vanguard role, the international aspect impregnated each of the additional roles as they became solidified structurally and functionally. First the PCF local governments and the PCF as tribune were identified with the young Soviet regime and society (the headlines of *L'Humanité* 1924–34 can be perused with profit in this regard). Then, the "national and international responsibilities" of the CPSU were linked with the national governmental role of the PCF in 1936–38 and 1944–47. And finally, the Cold War linked the PCF countercommunity, in its final gestation phase, with Soviet society.

Ironically, it was precisely the international aspect of French Communism, which was responsible for the PCF's assumption of a role in national government and for the consolidation of the countercommunity, that rendered all the more difficult a Bolshevik-style seizure of power. Yet, at the same time as it preempted possible steps toward a French revolution, the international link of the French communist movement also anchored the position of the movement "outside" the established order of society—"within" that society, but not "of " it.

We can portray the connection of the national-international dimension to the four primary faces of French communism by rendering Figure 1, flat and two-dimensional, into Figure 3, which adds the third dimension, pairing the national roles with their major international counterparts.

One may give a few examples to illustrate the national-international linkage. The Soviet role as a world power in the international order is functionally equivalent to the PCF role of national governmental party, as both, by their partial cooperation with non-Communist partners, contribute toward the maintenance or preservation of the existing order. Until recently, the international and national roles were stressed simultaneously: for example, the Popular Front in France was paralleled by a Soviet search for alliance, as the PCF effort in the Resistance was paralleled by outright alliance between the Soviet Union, the United States, and Great Britain. Contrariwise, the Hitler-Stalin Pact, a revolutionary rather than a maintaining alliance, was paralleled by the obliteration of all PCF governmental responsibilities and its legality itself, a situation similar, though more extreme, to that which obtained during the Cold War. It is the interpermeation of the PCF governmental role and the Soviet world power role on the one hand, and the PCF vanguard and Soviet vanguard roles on the other hand, that explains why French Communists' alliance possibilities at the top have been limited to situations in which Soviet foreign policy is more or less congruent with that of potential PCF partners. Since the most difficult period of the Cold War, however, we have seen a progressive distance obtain between the previous pattern of simultaneous stress of similar roles. Whereas the Soviet Union has

Figure 3.

*The four "faces" of French Communism and the
corresponding national-international dimensions* *

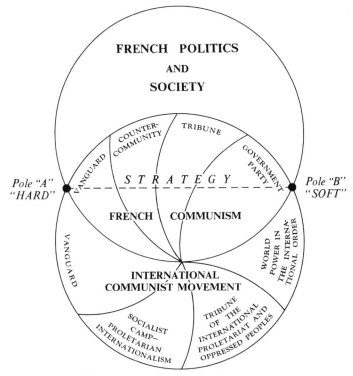

FRENCH POLITICS

AND

SOCIETY

Pole "A"
"HARD"

Pole "B"
"SOFT"

S T R A T E G Y

COUNTER-
COMMUNITY

TRIBUNE

VANGUARD

GOVERNMENT
PARTY

FRENCH COMMUNISM

VANGUARD

WORLD
POWER IN
THE INTERNA-
TIONAL ORDER

INTERNATIONAL
COMMUNIST MOVEMENT

SOCIALIST
CAMP-
PROLETARIAN
INTERNATIONALISM

TRIBUNE
OF THE
INTERNATIONAL
PROLETARIAT AND
OPPRESSED PEOPLES

* The structural presentation of this conception
was in part the suggestion of Annie Kriegel.

come increasingly to stress its world power role to the detriment of
the vanguard role on an international level, the French Communist
Party has attempted to play the vanguard role more strongly by combining it with the governmental role in the "peaceful transition to socialism" doctrine. It is this shift in the "fit" of the national and international dimensions that is manifested in such PCF-CPSU oppositions
as over the proper tactic in the French presidential elections of 1965.
And on a broader scale, the Soviets' concern with their role as a world

power rather than a revolutionary impetus has been manifested in a curiously ambiguous response to the June 1972 Common Program in France, leading to the legitimate question of whether or not, or more precisely to what degree, the Soviet Union is interested in or will support the French Communist attempt at a peaceful revolution.

The often misunderstood national-international "contradiction" in French communism did not determine all aspects of the movement from the beginning. It was first apposed and then superimposed upon the original contradiction of a Marxist revolutionary party existing in a nonrevolutionary situation, although from the bolshevization forward it imbued the French Communist hybrid with its particular form, depth, and character. Nonetheless, the national-international duality never became co-equal with, or altered the essence of, the fundamental tension, as we perceive more and more clearly, to the extent of the disassociation of the Soviet primacy in the international movement. A "nationalized" PCF, *to the extent it is able to retain a vanguard perspective*, does not relinquish either the path to, or the millenium itself; their terms are simply redefined. The question thus posed is to know to what extent the French Communist revolutionary pretension will be able to survive the present Soviet abandonment of its vanguard role on an international scale, and the routinization of the memory of its charismatic past.

May 1968: A Resolution of the Contradiction?

Let us now ask the key question with regard to the "events of May." Did the PCF sell out its revolutionary aspirations in May 1968? Did the Party finally arrive at the Rubicon only to refuse to extend the struggle to the other bank? Did the PCF strategy in May 1968 signify an end to the fundamental contradiction of a nonruling revolutionary party?

Probably not. We cannot say for certain, in one sense primarily because we cannot know or predict the intentions of the PCF leadership definitively. Nonetheless, we are able to analyze the situation, which permits at least the drawing of some negative conclusions. As Zbigniew Brzezinski has written:

The fact is that revolutions are historical rarities, and in modern times their success has generally required a combination of internal social dissolution and external military defeat. The organization of power must itself break down, the elites must be split, the socioeconomic system must malfunction, an alternative leadership must crystallize, and the more creative social forces must be, at least in significant part, convinced that a better alternative is available. Short of these conditions, reliance on revolutionary violence is likely to breed suppression, and even effectively brutal suppression.[25]

In such terms, the "events of May" did not create a revolutionary situation in France, because despite the number of individuals in the general strike, there existed no organization capable of unifying and radicalizing the largely nonradical mass demands and thereupon to channel them into revolutionary demands and action. However far the Gaullist regime had broken down—and the dissolution of the regime was probably much less a reality than is generally believed—a popularly legitimized alternative leadership did not appear. Moreover, as was demonstrated during the strike and in the general elections that followed, an alternative leadership basing itself on the Communist Party was considered by the overwhelming majority of Frenchmen an unacceptable solution to a violent crisis situation. And in any case, with regard to the technical problems of a violent seizure of power in the modern state, Edward Luttwak has concluded the following:

As the events in France of May 1968 have shown yet again, insurrection, the classic vehicle of revolution, is obsolete. The security apparatus of the modern state . . . cannot be defeated by civilian agitation, however intense and prolonged. Any attempt on the part of civilians to use direct violence with improvised means will always be neutralized by the efficiency of modern automatic weapons; a general strike, on the other hand, can temporarily swamp the system, but cannot permanently damage it, since in a modern economic setting, the civilians will run out of food and fuel well before the military, the police and allied organizations.

The modern state is therefore practically invulnerable to a direct assault. Two alternatives remain: guerilla warfare and the coup d'état.[26]

---

[25] *Between Two Ages*, p. 249.   [26] *Coup d'état: A Practical Handbook*, p. 7.

With regard to the latter alternatives, one can say that despite the nervous warnings of those who believe the French Communists have a contingency plan to fight a guerrilla war in the Massif Central (although such a plan might have existed in 1941–45), one may safely assume the PCF leadership does not today seriously consider guerrilla war as a viable means of coming to power; and despite a momentary flurry of renewed speculation in 1968, the question appears increasingly more irrelevant if not ridiculous. As for a coup d'état, unlike the 1958 situation in which the crucial sectors of the police and army were either neutral or favorable to the return of de Gaulle, armed opposition to an attempted Communist "palace coup" would be undoubtedly so great as to make this hypothesis also increasingly less worthy of mention. While some of the state security forces undoubtedly went through a crisis of allegiance to the regime in May 1968, and despite whatever Communist elements may exist in the police and army, unquestionably any attempt by the Communists to seize power by violence could not count upon a mass rally to their cause, or even neutrality. Finally, as to the possibility of a 1917-style coup d'état built upon a general uprising, the hostility of the majority of the May 1968 strikers to both the Communist Party and the CGT *and* the idea of a Communist-led revolution forces one to conclude that the PCF could hardly have realistically hoped to rally the mass of Frenchmen behind it as the Bolsheviks rallied the workers of Petrograd: unlike the Bolshevik position of October 1917, the French Communists are a known quantity.

As for the Communist leadership, quite obviously their appreciation of the possibilities of the May 1968 situation was similar. Among the myriad self-justifications, one of the least polemical and most enlightening is that of Pierre Juquin:

In May 1968, despite the hesitations, the internal struggles, and the disarray of certain subordinates, the power of State remained in the Elysée and the Matignon, and conserved solid means: a part of the top bureaucracy; army, police; international links, etc. . . . . The result of an insurrection was almost certain at that moment. It would have been crazy to undertake it . . . A civil war cannot be undertaken unless the greatest portion of citizens has accepted it at diverse levels: participation, support, favorable neutrality. . . .

[But] our decision did not result simply from a calculation of the chance to

conquer through insurrection in this circumstance. The general question of
the approach toward socialism in the France of our epoch was posed. . . . If
the popular rally is sufficient, it is possible in our epoch to raise enough force
to *dissuade* (the old regime) from beginning a civil war. . . . If the bourgeoisie
attacks us in spite of all, the workers, the democrats, legally majoritarian, will
defend themselves; that would be their ultimate recourse. But then the rebel,
the illegal one, would be the bourgeoisie and not the working class movement.
. . . At a time when the chances for socialism are serious and near, what
would have been gained by holding back this future in undertaking an insurrectional hand of poker—in blood and disavowed by the majority of Frenchmen?[27]

One does not have to accept the French Communists' political theory
to agree with them that in contemporary France a violent change of
regime, implying a violent and fundamental transformation of the
socioeconomic order, is quite unlikely. Moreover, Juquin's point concerning the legal position of a Left government in the event of violent
opposition is worth noting. One of the major concerns of the Allende
coalition in Chile was to court the Chilean military forces, exalting
their "noble role," in the words of Allende himself, and even persuad-
ing a former Army Commander in Chief to join the Popular Unity
government as Minister of the Interior. In the event of violent opposition, the instinct of the military leadership is normally to restore order
in favor of the established regime. If the courtship fails, however, the
result may be a coup d'état, even in a country such as Chile, with a
long tradition of military nonintervention in politics.

In sum, while the French Communists' reaction in May 1968
proved their unwillingness to attempt a foredoomed insurrection, it
also proved them an "objective ally" of the established order in calling
for a return to calm only "if one begins from the hypothesis that the
Communists consider their policy in terms of a single alternative:
order or subversion. The enigma is, on the contrary, less thick if one
stops asking himself what they want by reasoning in a manner which
is foreign to them. Because what they want, in fact, is to achieve
'their' order, eventually using 'their' technique of subversion." [28]
While *not* proving the PCF lacks the will to power, the events of

[27] *Le sens du réel,* pp. 94–98.
[28] Annie Kriegel, "Les communistes français, l'ordre et la subversion," *Projet* 41
(January 1972): 20.

CONCLUSION: WHAT "UNITY OF THEORY AND PRACTICE?"

In June 1972 the French Communists succeeded after more than a decade of efforts in obtaining a joint program with the French socialists. The goal of the program is avowedly to "open the road to socialism" in France. In March 1973 the Left alliance and the Common Program were defeated in the general legislative elections, although the electoral system rendered this first test of the alliance a more convincing defeat in terms of seats won than in popular support. The question of the destiny of French Communism still incites an equivocal response. Whither Bolshevism in France?

In the French Communist perspective the failure of the Left in May–June 1968 resulted above all from the lack of a joint program and of close socialist-Communist cooperation: "In turning their backs to unity . . . the socialists' leaders prevented the great movement of May–June 1968 from ending in a replacement of the Gaullist regime with a democratic regime opening the road to socialism." [1] The signature of the Common Program, moreover, gave credence to Waldeck Rochet's prediction at the 1967 Party Congress:

In reality, if the [socialist] leaders . . . hesitate to engage thmselves with the Communist Party on the basis of a common program of government . . . it is because certain among them fear . . . the Communist Party. . . . However, since there is no real change possible without the . . . Party, we do not believe they can maintain such a position indefinitely, because the situation in France is such that there is no real third road. [2]

[1] Waldeck Rochet, *L'avenir, du Parti communiste Français*, pp. 109–110.
[2] PCF–18, pp. 54–55.

The failure of Gaston Defferre in 1964–65 and in 1969, and the subsequent failure of Jean-Jacques Servan-Schreiber to accomplish what the former could not, created a context in which a magnetic leader committed to the Left strategy, François Mitterrand, was able to capture the initiative decisively within the evolving Socialist Party and within the non-Communist Left as a whole. The present success of the Mitterrand strategy among the socialists has rendered his alliance policy vis-à-vis the Communists potentially capable of effecting radical change in France in the not-too-distant future.

> The Communist Party is our natural ally. . . . I am not obliged to extend it any privilege; I am not obliged to give it preference. I observe simply that the unification of the Left involves the Communist Party. . . . And from this stems the importance which I attach to the formation of a political movement able first to equalize and then to dominate the Communist Party; and, finally, to obtain by itself and of itself a majority role. . . . One may doubt the sincerity of communist intentions, but to found a political strategy on the intentions one imputes to others makes no sense. What is important is to create the conditions which makes these others act as if they were sincere.[3]

Thus to judge by the present leadership of the two important Left parties and the actual pattern of alliance shifts and electoral results since the waning of the Cold War, French politics seems to be moving toward the consolidation of a predominantly bipolar coalition (PCF-PS-Dissident Radicals; UDR-RI-CDP) with several smaller parties on the extreme Right, the extreme Left, and the Center (notably the Republican Alliance, Democratic Center, Radical Party, PSU, *gauchiste* groups). These smaller parties face a difficult future should they attempt to remain independent of the two dominant coalitions. A catch-all party of the Center and Center-Left, a British Labour Party or SPD-style political force, appears precluded—ruled out by the historical and structural factors that have combined to produce a strong and resilient Communist movement, the perpetual bane of those who, optimistically or naively, would like to see French politics move closer to the model of two relatively non-program-oriented parties or coalitions manifesting a consensus as to the legitimate foundations of government and politics.

The Communist movement in France must be understood. After a

---

[3] Mitterrand, *Ma part de vérité*, pp. 78–79, 71–72.

half-century it has neither faded away nor become a marginal political sect. Moreover, although it has failed to achieve its ultimate goal, the fact that it occupies such a considerable portion of important political terrain in the midst of a hostile and menacing environment cannot fail to strike us as a singular accomplishment, and the broad activity and tenacity of the French Communists cannot fail to incite our astonishment, perhaps even our admiration. This continued occupation of important terrain in a Western regime is no doubt their major success.

The French Communists find themselves today at a greater distance than ever from the moment of bolshevization of the movement. But they have not yet either chosen or been forced to choose an existence other than the fundamental ambivalence inherent in the presence of a potent Communist party in a liberal regime. It is as premature to announce a definitive deradicalization of the PCF as it would be to dismiss as a tactical ruse the post-1956 evolution of the organization and its doctrine, strategy, and tactics. Perhaps the continuing transformation of the French Communist perspective should be read as a constructive and long-awaited response to the progressive destruction of a double illusion: the chimera of "democratic dictatorship" and the inevitable and "necessary" rectitude of the Communist Party line. It would be excessive to demand that the transformation of deeply ingrained concepts and behavior patterns occur with the same rapidity as a change in tactics—which would amount to a self-refutation in any case. Nonetheless, desacrilization of the Soviet experience—limited as it remains—has undeniably brought the Stalinist past of the French Communist movement increasingly closer to a mortal confrontation with the liberal humanist legacy of Marx and its filiation in the Social Democracy of Kautsky, Jaurès, and Blum. By this I do not mean that the substantive arguments are being redeveloped exactly as they were already a half-century ago, although it is surprising to note the extent to which the decades have not altered the original debate. When in 1918 Karl Kautsky first labeled the Bolshevik experience a dictatorship *over* the proletariat rather than *of* the proletariat, he launched a critique of twentieth-century left-wing Jacobinism that has now come full circle. In symbolic terms, the French Left finds itself once again at Tours.

BIBLIOGRAPHY

I. PUBLICATIONS OF THE FRENCH COMMUNIST PARTY

A. PCF Congresses

The first PCF Congress whose proceedings were published in one volume was the 13th Congress (1954). Before that, individual reports were issued in pamphlet form; at other times several reports and some accompanying documents were issued in a small volume. Only reports cited in the text are listed below. They contain the names of individual contributors if they are given. A more or less complete collection of the PCF Congresses exists at the *Institut Maurice Thorez* in Paris.

7TH CONGRESS (MARCH 1932)
Maurice Thorez: "En avant pour l'issue révolutionnaire de la crise! . . ." (171 pp.).

8TH CONGRESS (JANUARY 1936)
Compte rendu sténographique (590 pp.): report of Thorez is found pp. 75–148.

9TH CONGRESS (DECEMBER 1937)
Thorez: "La France du Front populaire et sa mission dans le monde" (96 pp.).
Jacques Duclos: "Faire l'unité!" (96 pp.).
L'action du groupe communiste au parlement: Rapport du Groupe communiste parlementaire pour le 9ème Congrès" (111 pp.).
"Deux ans d'activité au service du peuple: Rapports du Comité central pour le 9ème Congrès" (272 pp.).

10TH CONGRESS (JUNE 1945)
Thorez: "Une politique française: Renaissance, Démocratie, Unité" (64 pp.).
——: "Discours de cloture" followed by "Manifeste à la nation française" (14 pp.).
Duclos: "Vive l'unité de la classe ouvrière de France" (40 pp.).

11TH CONGRESS (JUNE 1947)
Thorez: "Au service du peuple de France" (89 pp.).
Deux années d'activité pour la renaissance économique et politique de la République française. Rapports du Comité central pour le 11ème Congrès national du Parti communiste français (400 pp.).

12TH CONGRESS (APRIL 1950)
Thorez: "La lutte pour l'indépendance nationale et la paix" (95 pp.).
"Documents du 12ème Congrès," *Cahiers du communisme* 5 (May 1950): 37–56.

13TH CONGRESS (JUNE 1954)
Special issue of *Cahiers du communisme* 6–7 (June–July 1954): 621–968.

14TH CONGRESS (JULY 1956)
Special issue of *Cahiers du communisme* 7–8 (July–August 1956) (420 pp.).

15TH CONGRESS (JUNE 1959)
Special issue of *Cahiers du communisme* 7–8 (July–August 1959) (574 pp.).
16TH CONGRESS (MAY 1961)
Special issue of *Cahiers du communisme* 6 (June 1961) (624 pp.).
17TH CONGRESS (MAY 1964)
Special issue of *Cahiers du communisme* 6–7 (June–July 1964) (573 pp.).
18TH CONGRESS (JANUARY 1967)
Special issue of *Cahiers du communisme* 2–3 (February–March 1967) (608 pp.).
19TH CONGRESS (FEBRUARY 1970)
Special issue of *Cahiers du communisme* 2–3 (February–March 1970) (594 pp.).
B. Other PCF publications cited in the text or consulted closely
——. "Les buts révolutionnaires du Parti communiste: Programme électoral du Parti"
   (Paris, 1928) 22 pp.
——. *Classe contre classe: La question française au IXe Exécutif et au VIe Congrès de l'IC* (Paris:
   Éditions Gît-le-Coeur, n.d.) 261 pp. A reprint of the 1929 edition published by the
   PCF.
——. *Histoire du Parti communiste français (Manuel)*, (Paris: Éditions sociales, 1964) 774
   pp. Written by a committee headed by Jacques Duclos and François Billoux, this is
   the "official" general Party history.
——. *Le Parti communiste français dans la Résistance* (Paris: Éditions sociales, 1967) 355 pp.
   A committee project published by the Institut Maurice Thorez, this is the "official" Party history of the Résistance.
——. *Manifeste du Parti communiste français: Pour une démocratie avancée, pour une France
   socialiste* (Paris: Éditions sociales, 1969) 79 pp. This is the general doctrinal statement of the "French road to socialism," completed by the detailed program cited
   next.
——. *Programme pour un gouvernement démocratique d'union populaire* (Paris: Éditions sociales, 1971) 251 pp. Published as this work was being completed, this is the Communist proposal for a program alliance with the non-communist Left, supposedly
   to lead to "the socialist transition"
——. *Voix du peuple au Parlement: Les 2 sénateurs et les 72 députés communistes* (Paris:
   Cahiers du Bolchevisme, supplément au no. 12, 1937) 168 pp. A collection of documents and statistics on the Communist parliamentary delegation.

*II. AUTOBIOGRAPHIES, MEMOIRS, "SELF-CRITICISMS" AND OTHER
WORKS BY FRENCH COMMUNIST AUTHORS AND DISSIDENTS*

Andrieu, René. *Les communistes et la révolution* (Paris: Union générale d'éditions, 1968)
   320 pp. Andrieu, editor of *L'Humanité*, examines in succession the past quarter-
   century, the "events of May," and the present communist conception of revolution.
(ANON.). *Histoire du Parti communiste français*, 3 vols. (Paris: Veridad et Unir) This is a
   "counter-history" of the PCF, largely anecdotal or polemical, written by an anony-
   mous group of dissidents. Although it has defects, it contains a wealth of useful information.
   1, Des origines du PCF à la guerre de 1939 (1960) 290 pp.
   2, De 1940 à la libération (1962) 315 pp.
   3, De 1945 à nos jours (1964) 319 pp.

Bonte, Florimond. *Le chemin de l'honneur* (Paris: Editions sociales, 1950) 479 pp. The wartime experiences of a leading communist.

——. *De l'ombre à la lumière* (Paris: Editions sociales, 1965) 192 pp. A partial autobiography explaining how the author became a committed communist militant, in a *Souvenirs* series published by the Party.

Dru, Jean (a collective pseudonym). *Le pari démocratique* (Paris: Julliard, 1962) 179 pp. A group of dissident communists propose a revision and liberalization of party theory and practice.

——. *De l'état socialiste*, 2 vols. (Paris: Julliard, 1965) Vol. 1: *L'expérience soviétique* (1965) 260 pp.; vol. 2: *Ici, maintenant et demain* (1968) 347 pp. The dissident communist group reflects further on the past and the future of the international and French communist movements.

Duclos, Jacques. *Mémoires*, 3 vols. (Paris: Fayard) to date covering the period 1896–1942.

    1, 1896–1934 (1968) 435 pp.

    2, 1935–39 (1969) 463 pp.

    3, 1940–42 (1970) 317 pp.

Garaudy, Roger. *Le grand tournant du socialisme* (Paris: Gallimard, 1969) 317 pp. After deciding that "it is no longer possible to keep silent," Garaudy wrote several progressively dissident works, this one the most general and the last before his exclusion in 1970. See also *Pour un modèle français du socialisme* (Paris: Gallimard, 1968) 385 pp.

——. *Toute la vérité: Mai 1968–Février 1970* (Paris: Grasset, 1970) 199 pp. Garaudy's account of events from the "events of May" to his exclusion from the Politburo at the 19th PCF Congress.

Lecoeur, Auguste. *L'autocritique attendue* (St. Cloud, France: Editions Girault, 1955) 102 pp.

Marchais, Georges. *Qu'est-ce que le Parti communiste français?* (Paris: Editions sociales, 1970) 47 pp. The first "individual" publication by the new PCF leader.

Marty, André, *L'affaire Marty* (Paris: Deux Rives, 1955) 291 pp. The author's controversial account of his ostracism in the "Marty-Tillon affair."

Rochet, Waldeck. *L'avenir du Parti communiste français* (Paris: Editions sociales, 1969) 190 pp. The last statement of the PCF leader from 1964 to 1969.

——. *Le marxisme et les chemins de l'avenir* (Paris: Editions sociales, 1966) 93 pp.

——. *Les enseignements de mai–juin 1968* (Paris: Editions sociales, 1968) 92 pp. The Party's defense of its action during the "events of May."

——. *Qu'est-ce qu'un révolutionnaire dans la France de notre temps?* (Paris: Editions sociales, 1968) 110 pp. A justification of the "necessity" of peaceful revolution in the French case.

Thorez, Maurice. *Oeuvres* (Paris: Editions sociales) 23 vols. (1950–65). Covering the period up to June 1947. Publication has been halted since 1965.

——. *Oeuvres choisies*, 3 vols. (Paris: Editions sociales). The edition of *Fils du peuple* (5th) used here appears in Volume 3.

    1, 1924–37 (1967), 471 pp.

    2, 1938–50 (1966), 565 pp.

    3, 1953–64 (1965), 589 pp.

——. *Fils du peuple* (Paris: Editions sociales, 1949) 255 pp.

Tillon, Charles. *Les FTP* (Paris: Julliard, 1962) 687 pp. Tillon's account of the FTP and the Resistance participation by the communists.

Togliatti, Palmiro. *Le Parti communiste italien* (Paris: Maspero, 1961) 173 pp. A short history of the movement and its strategy and tactics by the PCI leader until 1964.

III. WORKS ON FRENCH COMMUNISM OR RELATING TO THE PCF

Adam, Gérard. *Atlas des élections sociales en France* (Paris: A. Colin, 1964) 210 pp. Useful for its statistical and interpretive explanations of relative syndicalist strengths.

Aron, Raymond. *L'opium des intellectuels* (Paris: Calmann-Lévy, 1955). An incisive critique of the relation between Marxism and French intellectuals.

Aron, Robert. *Histoire de la libération de la France*, 2 vols. (Paris: Fayard). A standard history of the Liberation.
1 (1959), 511 pp.
2 (1959), 512 pp.

Barjonet, André. *La CGT* (Paris: Editions du Seuil, 1968) 192 pp. Somewhat schematic and polemical, but useful as a quick overview of the CGT's history. Barjonet quit the CGT and the PCF in May 1968.

——. *Le Parti communiste français* (Paris: J. Didier, 1969) 239 pp. A brief and highly polemical attack on the PCF from its left flank criticizing the Party as no longer revolutionary.

Barillon, Raymond. *La gauche française en mouvement* (Paris: Plon, 1967) 237 pp. Written by Le Monde's highly respected reporter, this is a useful quick history of the "unity" trend on the Left up through the general elections of 1967.

de Bayac, Jacques Delperrie. *Histoire du Front populaire* (Paris, Fayard, 1972) 542 pp. A useful descriptive history.

Blackmer, Donald L. M. *Unity in Diversity: Italian Communism and the Communist World* (Cambridge, Mass.: MIT Press, 1968) 434 pp. An excellent analysis of the PCI in the international movement, providing useful background to the position of the PCF.

Léon Blum, Chef du gouvernement 1936–37 (Paris: A. Colin, 1967) 440 pp. An enlightening group of analyses on the dilemma of Blum in the Popular Front.

Bodin, Louis and Jean Touchard. *Front populaire 1936* (Paris: A. Colin, 1961) 296 pp. A useful history.

Bodin, Louis. "Le Parti communiste dans le Front populaire" *Esprit* (Octobre 1966): 436–49. A provocative and informative article.

Bon, Frédéric et al., *Le communisme en France* (Paris: A. Colin, 1969) 336 pp. An extremely helpful and stimulating set of analyses on various aspects of the communist movement in France.

Brayance, Alain (pseud.). *Anatomie du Parti communiste français* (Paris: Denöel, 1952) 289 pp. A somewhat weak analysis of the PCF internal structure.

Broue, Pierre and Nicole Dorey. "Critiques de gauche et opposition révolutionnaire au Front Populaire (1936–1938)," *Le mouvement social* 54 (January–March 1966): 91–133. Some useful information on the problem of the PCF left flank.

Brower, Daniel. *The New Jacobins: The French Communist Party and the Popular Front*, (Ithaca, N.Y.: Cornell University Press, 1968) 265 pp. Although well-researched and written, this work unfortunately lacks perspective.

Cantril, Hadley. *The Politics of Despair* (New York: Basic Books, 1958) 269 pp. A classic use of the mass survey approach to throw light on the PCF electoral appeal.

Caute, David. *Communism and the French Intellectuals* (London: Andre Deutsch, 1964) 413 pp. A beautifully written and sensitive account of the relations between the PCF and French intellectuals, both within and without the Party.

Centre d'étude de la vie politique française (ed.). *L'élection présidentielle de décembre 1965* (Paris: A. Colin, 1970) 548 pp. An exhaustive look at this important election from virtually every important point of view.

Chapman, Brian. *Introduction to French Local Government* (London: Allen and Unwin, 1953) 238 pp. A standard work, still relevant.

Chapsal, Jacques. *La vie politique en France depuis 1940* (Paris: Presses universitaires de France, 1960) 618 pp. A rather schematic, wide-ranging and helpful "diagram" of French politics since the armistice of 1940.

Cobban, Alfred. *A History of Modern France* (London: Pelican Books, 1965). Vol. 3 (1871–1962) 272 pp. A standard history by one in close touch with French culture and politics.

D'Artrey, J. L. L. *Conseils généraux: Elections juillet 1925–octobre 1928* (Paris: Librairie Georges Houstens, 1929) 242 pp. Useful for its statistics but little else.

———. *Conseils généraux: Elections 18–25 octobre 1931* (Paris: Librairie Georges Roustens, 1932) 147 pp. Same remark.

———. *Elections municipales—mai 1929* (Paris: Librairie Georges Roustens, 1929) 350 pp. Same remark.

Degras, Jane. "United Front Tactics in the Comintern, 1921–1928," in David Footman (ed.), *International Communism* (London: Chatto and Windus, 1960) 149 pp., pp. 9–22. One of the few focused analyses of the subject.

Duhamel, Alain. "Le Parti communiste et l'élection présidentielle," *Revue française de science politique* 16, no. 3 (June 1966): 539–47. A quick revue of a complicated situation.

Dupeux, Georges. *Le Front populaire et les élections de juin 1936* (Paris: A. Colin, 1959) 183 pp. A useful and readable electoral study.

Duverger, Maurice. *Constitutions et documents politiques,* 5th ed. (Paris: Presses universitaires de France, 1968) 655 pp. A useful collection of documents and statistics, which should be, however, cross-checked.

———. *Political Parties* (London: Methuen, 1954) 439 pp.

Earle, Edward M. (ed.). *Modern France* (Princeton: Princeton University Press, 1951) 522 pp. A classic collection of articles on various aspects of French politics and society.

Einaudi, Mario, Jean-Marie Domenach and Aldo Garosci, *Communism in Western Europe* (New York: Cornell University Press, 1951) 239 pp. Domenach, editor of *Esprit,* wrote the section on the PCF. All the contributions reflect the Cold War atmosphere in which they were written, despite excellent information.

———. "Questions au Parti communiste," *Esprit,* October 1966. Eleven articles on various aspects of the "communist problem."

———. "Les communistes au carrefour," *Esprit,* May 1970. Five articles on the dilemma of the PCF in contemporary France.

Faucher, Jean-André. *La gauche française sous de Gaulle* (Paris: Editions Didier, 1969) 290 pp. Faucher is a Radical favorable to some kind of agreement with the PCF. His work is a mass of useful information, but there is little attempt at analysis.

Fauvet, Jacques. *Histoire du Parti communiste français,* 2 vols. (Paris: Fayard). The most complete and unbiased history of the PCF, which nonetheless suffers from a lack of focus and clarity. 1, De la guerre à la guerre, 1917–1939 (1964) 286 pp. 2, Vingt-cinq ans de drames, 1939–1965 (1965) 407 pp. (in collaboration with Alain Duhamel).

——. *La IVe République* (Paris: Fayard, 1959) 507 pp. A useful and extremely well-informed history of the years 1944–1958.

Fejtö, François. *The French Communist Party and the Crisis of International Communism* (Cambridge, Mass.: MIT Press, 1967) 225 pp. A somewhat unfocused and schematic view of a complicated problem, which nonetheless provides a wealth of data and citations.

Ferrari, Pierre, and Herbert Maisl. *Les groupes communistes aux Assemblées parlementaires italiennes (1958–1963) et françaises (1962–1967)* (Paris: Presses universitaires de France, 1969) 215 pp. A book useful for its statistical analyses, but which unfortunately does not attempt to construct the context.

Ferrat, André, *Histoire du Parti communiste français* (Paris: Editions Gît-le-Coeur, 1969) 260 pp. Former party member Ferrat's history is extremely sketchy and polemic, useful mainly for isolated bits of personal reminiscence.

Frossard, Ludovic-Oscar. *De Jaurès à Lénine, Notes et souvenirs* (Paris: Editions de la Nouvelle revue socialiste, 1930) 313 pp. An informative and self-revealing memoir by the first Secretary-General of the PCF (1921–22).

Géraud, André. "Insurrection Fades in France," *Foreign Affairs* 28, no. 1 (October 1949): 30–42. The last in a series of articles by Géraud chronicaling the fear of PCF intentions 1947–49.

Goguel, François. *Géographie des élections françaises sous la troisième et la quatrième républiques* (Paris: A. Colin, 1970) 185 pp. An updated version of the author's classic overview.

——. *Modernisation économique et comportement politique* (Paris: A. Colin, 1969) 88 pp. A helpful, if tentative, first accounting of a long-range research project that attempts to verify a link between the two halves of the subject.

——. *La politique des partis sous la IIIe République*, 3d ed. (Paris: Collection Esprit, 1958) 567 pp. This book introduces the now well-known distinction between the "party of movement" and the "party of order." This second classic by Goguel was written in a German prison camp.

——. "Les élections françaises du 2 janvier 1956," *Revue française de science politique*. Hereafter to be referred to as *RFSP* 6, no. 1 (January–March 1956): 5–17. Like the following articles, a standard of reference, based on a collaborative research effort at the Institute d'etudes politiques.

——. "Le referendum du 28 octobre et les élections des 18–25 octobre 1962," *RFSP* 13, no. 2 (June 1963): 289–314.

——. "Les élections municipales des 14 et 21 mars 1965," *RFSP* 15, no. 5 (October 1965): 911–63.

——. "L'élection présidentielle française de décembre 1965," *RFSP* 16, no. 2 (April 1966): 221–54.

——. "Les élections législatives des 5 et 12 mars 1967," *RFSP* 17, no. 3 (June 1967): 429–67.

——. "Les élections législatives des 23 et 30 juin 1968," *RFSP* 18, no. 5 (October 1968): 837–51.

Graham, Bruce D. *The French Socialists and Tripartisme, 1944–1947* (London: George Weidenfeld and Nicholson, 1965) 299 pp. Contains much useful information and some interesting conclusions regarding the SFIO, but lacks a general perspective.

Greene, Thomas H. "The Communist Parties of Italy and France: A Study in Comparative Communism," *World Politics* 21, no. 1 (October, 1968): 1–38. Focusing both on the position of the two parties in each party system and upon differences between them, the analysis is extremely useful.

Guérin, Daniel. *Front populaire, révolution manquée* (Paris: F. Maspero, 1970) 316 pp. First published in 1963, this is an extremely informative book based on a point of view to the left of the PCF: basically, Guérin argues the PCF proved itself nonrevolutionary in 1936.

Hamilton, Richard F. *Affluence and the French Worker in the Fourth Republic* (Princeton: Princeton University Press, 1967) 323 pp. Based on secondary sources, this is an often powerful and provocative analysis of political attitudes.

Hoffmann, Stanley, et al. *In Search of France* (New York: Harper and Row, 1965) 441 pp. A classic collection of essays focused on the ideas of national character and political culture.

Hoss, Jean-Pierre. *Communes en banlieue, Argenteuil et Bezons* (Paris: A. Colin, 1969) 135 pp. A highly readable if somewhat restricted analysis of two Communist municipalities.

Hurtig, Christiane. *De la SFIO au nouveau Parti socialiste* (Paris: A. Colin, 1970) 128 pp. A useful, though limited overview with statistics and documents.

Jedermann (pseud.). *La "Bolchevisation" du Parti communiste français* (Paris: F. Maspero, 1971) 118 pp. Also written by a *gauchiste*, this informative though polemical book contains some useful statistics; it also contains the standard argument about Stalinist "bureaucratization" in the PCF.

Kesselman, Mark. *The Ambiguous Consensus: A Study of Local Government in France* (New York: Knopf, 1967) 201 pp. Based primarily on keen and wide-ranging observation, this is a perceptive picture of a phenomenon difficult for foreigners to grasp.

Kriegel, Annie. *Aux origines du communisme français: 1914–1920*, 2 vols. (Paris: Mouton, 1964) 997 pp. See also the abridged version (from which the citations are taken here) (Paris: Flammarion, 1969) 442 pp. The most thorough and profound study existing.

———. *Les communistes français*, 2d ed. (Paris: Editions du Seuil, 1970) 319 pp. The closest thing to a definitive study existing on the PCF countercommunity.

———. "Les communistes français, l'ordre et la subversion," *Projet 41*, janvier 1970, pp. 20–33. A provocative argument regarding the PCF behavior in May–June, 1968.

Lancelot, Alain. *L'abstentionisme électoral en France* (Paris: Presses Universitaires de France, 1968) 290 pp. A detailed, solid analysis.

Laurens, André and Thierry Pfister. *Les nouveaux communistes* (Paris: Stock, 1973) 265 pp. A somewhat disjointed account of recent changes, by two journalists from *Le Monde*.

Lechêne, Robert. *Tambour battant: La campagne présidentielle de Jacques Duclos* (Paris: Fayard, 1969) 95 pp. An informative but hasty journalist account.

Lecoeur, Auguste. *Le Parti communiste français et la Résistance: août 1939–juin 1941* (Paris: Plon, 1968) 144 pp. An irrefutable account of the antinational attitude of the PCF during this period.

Lefranc, Georges. *Le Front populaire: 1934–38* (Paris: Presses Universitaires de France, 1968) 128 pp. A brief but accurate overview of the events.

———. *Le mouvement socialiste sous la 3ème République*, 1875–1940 (Paris: Payot, 1963) 445 pp. A standard history, extremely well-informed though sketchy in places.

——. *Le mouvement syndical sous la 3ème République* (Paris: Payot, 1967) 454 pp. Same remark as above.

——. *Le mouvement syndical de la Libération aux évènements de mai-juin 1968* (Paris: Payot, 1969) 312 pp. Same as above.

Lichtheim, George. *Marxism in Modern France* (New York: Columbia University Press, 1966) 212 pp. A highly readable analysis of the broad outlines of Marxist influence in France, limited neither historically nor thematically to Marxism's communist manifestation.

Lorwin, Val. *The French Labor Movement* (Cambridge, Mass.: Harvard University Press, 1954) 346 pp. A solid and well-informed analysis, which is dated now.

MacRae, Duncan Jr. *Parliament, Parties, and Society in France, 1946–58* (New York: St. Martin's Press, 1967) 375 pp. A comprehensive statistically oriented history, which reflects in some places a problem in its categories. Nonetheless a classic.

Macridis, Roy. "The Immobility of the French Communist Party," *Journal of Politics* 20, no. 4 (November, 1958): 613–634. An analysis basically of the PCF's slow reaction to the 20th CPSU Congress.

Magri, Lucio. "Problems of the Marxist Theory of a Revolutionary Party," *New Left Review*, March–April, 1970, pp. 96–128. A useful statement of the current controversy over the nature of a communist party by an Italian communist.

Marchand, Marie-Hélène. *Les conseillers généraux en France depuis 1945* (Paris: A. Colin, 1970) 213 pp. Useful for its statistics and qualitative information; few conclusions attempted.

Mendel, Arthur P. "Why the French Communists Stopped the Revolution," *Review of Politics* 31, no. 1 (January 1969): 3–27. A useful analysis which, however, starts from the questionable premise that May 1968 was a "revolution."

Micaud, Charles. *Communism and the French Left* (New York: Frederick Praeger, 1963) 308 pp. Unfortunately, Micaud published his work (after a gestation period of a decade) just as the PCF began to "change." Moreover, much of the book concerns the communist movement only peripherally, as it focuses upon the Third Republic and the non-communist Left.

——. "Les communistes ont changé," *Le Nouvel Observateur*, February 23, 1966. Several informative articles and essays by Maurice Duverger, Alexander Werth, etc.

Perrot, Michelle, and Annie Kriegel. *Le socialisme français et le pouvoir* (Paris: Etudes et documentation internationales, 1966) 217 pp. The first section, by Perrot, is on French socialism, 1879–1914; the second, by Kriegel, concerns the communists, 1920–1966. Useful for perspective and important doctrinal citations.

Philip, André. *Les socialistes* (Paris: Editions du Seuil, 1967) 255 pp. An informative but highly sketchy overview by an SFIO member from 1920 to 1956 when he was excluded in a disagreement with Guy Mollet over the Algerian and Suez problems.

Pickles, Dorothy. "The Communist Problem in France." *International Affairs*, April, 1952, pp. 162–70. Very much a reflection of the Cold War.

——. *French Politics: The First Years of the Fourth Republic* (London: Royal Institute of International Affairs, 1953) 302 pp. A solid, detailed analysis, once again colored by circumstances and point of view.

Pizzorno, Alessandro et al. *Le communisme en Italie* (Paris: mimeo, 1968) 254 pp. The other half of the colloquium which resulted in Bon et al., *q.v.* above. This work is extremely well informed.

Platone, François. "L'implantation municipale du Parti communiste français dans la

Seine et sa conception de l'administration communale" (unpublished thesis, Paris, 1967) 163 pp. Useful mainly for doctrinal citations.

Pommerrolle, François. "Etude de la gestion communiste du Ministère de la Reconstruction et de l'Urbanisme" (unpublished thesis, Paris, 1969) 177 pp. Much useful information in a solid study of a hitherto unworked subject.

Quillot, Roger. *La S.F.I.O. et l'exercice du pouvoir, 1944–1958* (Paris: Fayard, 1972) 837 pp. A capable history by a leading socialist, useful especially for much inside information.

Reynaud, J. D. *Les syndicats en France,* 2d ed. (Paris: Armand Colin, 1967) 292 pp. A brief and capable overview.

Revai, Joseph. "The Character of a People's Democracy," *Foreign Affairs* 28, no. 1 (October 1949): 143–53. A translation of an article by the Hungarian communist intellectual, giving the doctrinal conception of the "people's democracy," as opposed to the Soviet regime.

Rieber, Alfred J. *Stalin and the French Communist Party, 1941–1947* (New York: Columbia University Press, 1962) 395 pp. Concentrating on the period from the Liberation onward, this book is extremely well informed, but the conclusions are somewhat distorted by the author's militant anticommunist stance.

Rossi, Amilcare (pseud. of Angelo Tasca). *A Communist Party in Action* (New Haven: Yale University Press, 1949) 301 pp. A former Italian communist has written this and the following two works, which provide invaluable documentation on the PCF during the period 1939–45.

——. *Les communistes français pendant la drôle de guerre* (Paris: Les Iles d'Or, 1951) 368 pp.

——. *La guerre des papillons: Quatre ans de politique communiste, 1940–44* (Paris: Les Iles d'Or, 1954) 334 pp. plus 48 plates.

Rossi-Landi, Guy. *La drôle de guerre: La vie politique en France, 1939–40* (Paris: A. Colin, 1971) 248 pp. A helpful look at several important questions. Part Two, chapter 3 concentrates on the PCF.

SOFRES. "Attitudes des Français à l'égard du Parti communiste" (Paris, February, 1968) 59 pp.

——. "Attitudes des Français à l'égard de la CGT et du Parti communiste" (Paris, December 1969) 44 pp.

——. "Image du Parti communiste" (Paris, July 1971) 11 pp.

Sondages 28, no. 1 (1966).

Tarrow, Sidney. *Peasant Communism in Southern Italy* (New Haven: Yale University Press, 1967) 389 pp. An unusually successful study, illuminating an unusual manifestation of European Communism.

——. "Political Dualism and Italian Communism," *American Political Science Review* APSR, 61, no. 1 (March 1967): 39–53. A provocative article demonstrating two of the possible roles of a communist movement divided essentially in spatial terms (i.e. Northern and Southern Italy).

Thomson, David. *Democracy in France since 1870,* 4th ed. (New York: Oxford University Press, 1964) 346 pp. A necessary beginning source.

Tillon, Charles. *Un 'procès de Moscou' à Paris* (Paris: Editions du Seuil, 1971) 208 pp. Tillon has finally given his own account of his disgrace within the Party during the early 1950s.

Vassart, Albert and Célie. "The Moscow Origin of the French 'Popular Front,'" in Milorad M. Drachkovitch and Branko Lazitch (eds.) *The Comintern: Historical High-*

414   *Bibliography*

lights (New York: Frederick Praeger, 1966) 430 pp., pp. 234–252. Vassart was the PCF delegate to the Comintern during 1934–35; the article is a personal memoir.

Walter, Gérard, *Histoire du Parti communiste français* (Paris: A. Somogy, 1948) 392 pp. A great amount of information difficult to obtain elsewhere. An overall perspective is missing, however, and Walter has often been charged with excessive praise of Maurice Thorez and his allies.

Williams, Philip M. *Crisis and Compromise: Politics in the Fourth Republic* (New York: Doubleday, 1966) 584 pp. Williams's classic on the period.

——. *The French Parliament, 1958–1967* (London: George Allen and Unwin Ltd., 1968) 136 pp. A brief but penetrating account of a largely unworked subject.

Williams, Philip M. with David Goldley and Martin Harrison. *French Politicians and Elections, 1951–1969* (Cambridge: Cambridge University Press, 1970) 313 pp. A collection of previously published articles on particular subjects, useful mainly for the information supplied.

Wilson, Frank L. *The French Democratic Left, 1963–69: Toward a Modern Party System* (Stanford: Stanford University Press, 1971) 258 pp. An illuminating, well-researched analysis of the three attempts to unify the non-communist Left to 1969.

Wohl, Robert. *French Communism in the Making, 1914–1924* (Stanford: Stanford University Press, 1966) 532 pp. After Kriegel (q.v., above) the standard source.

Wright, Gordon. *The Reshaping of French Democracy* (New York: Reynal and Hitchcock, 1948) 277 pp. A masterly analysis of the political scene 1944–46, useful especially for the author's treatment of the drafting of the constitutional proposals.

IV. AUTOBIOGRAPHIES, PROGRAMS, MEMOIRS AND "LIVRES DE COMBAT" BY NON-COMMUNIST POLITICAL LEADERS

Blum, Léon, *A l'échelle humaine* (Paris: Gallimard, 1945) 184 pp. Written in a German prison camp and finished in December 1941, this book is basically a reflection on the faults of the Third Republic and on the decline of the French bourgeoisie, combined with a critique of the SFIO and of the PCF.

——, *L'oeuvre de Léon Blum*, 7 vols. (Paris: A. Michel, 1954–63). Vols. 4–5 cover the 1934–45 period. Vol. 5 contains among other things, *L'exercice du pouvoir*, a collection of Blum's speeches 1936–37 also published separately.

Club Jean Moulin, *Un parti pour la gauche* (Paris: Editions du Seuil, 1965) 94 pp. A statement by this influential political club on how to remake the non-communist Left and how to deal with the Communists.

Defferre, Gaston. *Un nouvel horizon* (Paris: Gallimard, 1965) 196 pp. This was Defferre's platform for his presidential bid in 1965.

(FGDS), "Programme—14 juillet 1966." The program of the Fédération de la Gauche Démocrate et Socialiste, mimeo, 61 pp.

De Gaulle, Charles. *The Complete War Memoirs of Charles de Gaulle* (New York: Simon and Schuster, 1967) 1048 pp. The dilemma posed by the Communists in de Gaulle's Provisional Government is of particular interest here, as are his general reflections on the communist movement nationally and internationally.

Jaurès, Jean. *L'armée nouvelle* (Paris: Union Générale d'éditions, 1969) 315 pp. This is a reprint of the 1915 edition, with large omissions, itself a reprint of the original 1911 edition. Besides being a proposal for a new military force, this book was a general statement of Jauressian socialism.

Mitterrand, François. *Le coup d'état permanent* (Paris: Plon, 1965) 242 pp. A polemical but often well documented attack on the Gaullist republic and especially the Gaullist claim to legitimacy. This was Mitterrand's *livre de combat* for the 1965 presidential campaign.

——. *Ma part de vérité: de la rupture à l'unité* (Paris: Fayard, 1969) 206 pp. In the form of a long interview with journalist Alain Duhamel, Mitterrand provides a general philosophical statement and an account of events on the French Left from 1965 to 1969.

Mollet, Guy. *Les chances du socialisme* (Paris: Fayard, 1968) 138 pp. A general statement by the former SFIO Secretary-General 1946–69.

Savary, Alain. *Pour le nouveau Parti socialiste* (Paris: Editions du Seuil, 1970) 185 pp. A statement by the P.S. leader 1969–71.

(SFIO) "Déclaration de principes et programme fondamental," 1962, n.p. The first is Léon Blum's statement of 1946, the second is the program adopted by the National Congress May 20, 1962.

(Parti socialiste) "Plan d'action socialiste," *Bulletin socialiste*, September 8, 1970, supp. to N. 92, 16 pp. A 10-year plan of action drawn up by the PS while Alain Savary was still Secretary-General. This plan was superseded by the PS *programme de gouvernment* made public in March 1972.

V. SOURCES ON SOVIET OR INTERNATIONAL COMMUNISM CITED IN THE TEXT

Almond, Gabriel. *The Appeals of Communism* (Princeton: Princeton University Press, 1954) 415 pp. Although still a standard source on the psychology of communism, it must nevertheless be read with attention to its biases.

Aron, Raymond. *Le grand schisme* (Paris: Gallimard, 1948) 346 pp. A very deep study of the early postwar period both domestically and internationally, despite the date of publication.

Borkenau, Franz. *European Communism* (London: Faber and Faber, Ltd., 1953). Pp. 115–229 are on the French situation. They reflect both a Cold War influence and the author's personal position, but are nonetheless very solid.

——. *World Communism* (Ann Arbor, Mich.: University of Michigan Press, 1962) 442 pp. Same remark as above.

Black, Cyril E. and Thomas P. Thornton (eds.). *Communism and Revolution* (Princeton: Princeton University Press, 1964) 467 pp. A very useful collection of articles by leading authorities.

Brzezinski, Zbigniew. *Between Two Ages: America's Role in the Technetronic Era* (New York: The Viking Press, 1970) 334 pp. Some stimulating arguments on the Soviet system included in a vigorous and insightful essay of broader scope.

Carr, E. H. *The Bolshevik Revolution, 1917–1923*, 3 vols. (London: Penguin Books, 1966), Vol. 1, 448 pp. A classic study.

Deutscher, Isaac. *The Prophet Armed: Trotsky, 1879–1923*, 3 vols. (London: Oxford University Press, 1954) 540 pp. Volume 1 of the 3-volume definitive biography.

——. *Stalin: A Political Biography* (London: Penguin Books, 1966) 648 pp. One of the standard biographies, which has the incomparable benefit of the author's perspective on the other Bolshevik leaders.

Drachkovitch, Milorad and Branko Lazitch. *The Comintern: Historical Highlights* (New York: Praeger, 1966) 430 pp. A useful collection of articles on selected aspects.

Kaplan, Morton A. "The Communist Coup in Czechoslovakia," Unpublished monograph (#5) at the Princeton Center of International Studies, 1960, 44 pp. A helpful source.

Lenin, V.I. *Selected Works* (London: Lawrence and Wishart, 1968) 798 pp.

Luttwak, Edward. *Coup d'état* (New York: Fawcett Books, 1969) 209 pp. An unusual perspective with controversial results.

Marcuse, Herbert. *Soviet Marxism: A Critical Analysis* (London: Penguin Books, 1971) 221 pp. A critique of the USSR in Marxist categories. Often turgid and vague.

Meyer, Alfred. *Marxism: The Unity of Theory and Practice* (Ann Arbor, Mich.: University of Michigan Press, 1963) 181 pp. A classic analysis, both penetrating and brilliantly written.

Monnerot, Jules. *Sociologie du communisme* (Paris: Gallimard, 1949) 511 pp. An important analysis.

Selznick, Philip. *The Organizational Weapon: A Study of Bolshevik Strategy and Tactics,* 2d ed. (Glencoe, Ill.: The Free Press, 1960) 350 pp. One of the few analyses of the functioning of a communist party which is able to capture conceptually the complexity and apparently contradictory actions which are the Bolshevik norm.

Shulman, Marshall. *Stalin's Foreign Policy Reappraised* (New York: Atheneum, 1969), 320 pp. Very useful both on the last years of Stalin's foreign policy and in particular on the PCF and the place of France within it.

Shub, David. *Lenin: A Political Biography* (London: Penguin Books, 1966) 496 pp. A standard biography in English.

VI. NEWSPAPERS, JOURNALS AND OTHER PERIODICALS

L'année politique
Annuaire de la Chambre des Députés (1945)
Annuaire de l'Assemblée Constituante (1947)
Annuaire de l'Assemblée Nationale
Bulletin Socialiste (SFIO)
Cahiers du bolchevisme (pre-WWII PCF monthly)
Cahiers du communisme (post-WWII PCF monthly)
Le combat républicain (CIR)
La documentation socialiste (internal SFIO bulletin)
L'Humanité
Journal Officiel
Le Monde
Le Nouvel Observateur
Official Register of the Conseil de la République (1947–58)
Official Register of the Sénat (1959–71)
Le Populaire (SFIO)

INDEX

Books Published Under The Auspices
Of The Research Institute On Communist
Affairs

Diversity in International Communism, Alexander Dallin, ed., in collaboration with the Russian Institute, Columbia University Press, 1963.

Political Succession in the U.S.S.R., Myron Rush, published jointly with the RAND Corporation, Columbia University Press, 1965.

Marxism in Modern France, George Lichtheim, Columbia University Press, 1966.

Power in the Kremlin, Michel Tatu, Viking Press, 1969, was first published in 1967, by Bernard Grasset under the title *Le Pouvoir en U.R.S.S.*, and also in England by William Collins Sons and Co., Ltd. in 1968.

The Soviet Bloc: Unity and Conflict, Zbigniew Brzezinski, revised and enlarged edition, Harvard University Press, 1967.

Vietnam Triangle, Donald Zagoria, Pegasus Press, 1968.

Communism in Malaysia and Singapore, Justus van der Kroef, Nijhoff Publishers, The Hague, 1968.

Radicalismo Cattolico Brasiliano, Ulisse A. Floridi, Istituto Editoriale Del Mediterraneo, 1968.

Stalin and His Generals, Seweryn Bialer, ed., Pegasus Press, 1969.

Marxism and Ethics, Eugene Kamenka, Macmillan and St. Martin's Press, 1969.

Dilemmas of Change in Soviet Politics, Zbigniew Brzezinski, ed. and contributor, Columbia University Press, 1969.

The U.S.S.R. Arms the Third World: Case Studies in Soviet Foreign Policy, Uri Ra'anan, the M.I.T. Press, 1969.

Communists and Their Law, John N. Hazard, University of Chicago Press, 1969.

Fulcrum of Asia, Bhabani Sen Gupta, Pegasus Press, 1970. (Sponsored jointly with the East Asian Institute.)

Le Conflict Sino-Sovietique et l'Europe de l'Est, Jacques Levesque, Les Presses de l'Universite de Montreal, 1970.

Between Two Ages, Zbigniew Brzezinski, Viking Press, 1970.

The Czechoslovak Experiment, Ivan Svitak, Columbia University Press, 1970.

Communist China and Latin America, 1959–1967, Cecil Johnson, Columbia University Press, 1970. (Sponsored jointly with the East Asian Institute.)

Communism and Nationalism in India: M. N. Roy and Comintern Policy in Asia, 1920–1939, John P. Haithcox, Princeton University Press, 1971.

Les Regimes politiques de l'U.R.S.S. et de l'Europe de l'Est, Michel Lesage, Presses Universitaires de France, 1971.

The Bulgarian Communist Party, 1934–1944, Nissan Oren, Columbia University Press, 1971. (Sponsored jointly with the Institute on East Central Europe.)

American Communism in Crisis, 1943–1957, Joseph Starobin, Harvard University Press, 1972.

Sila i Interesi: Vanjska Politika SAD, Radovan Vukadinovic, Centar za Kulturnu Djelatnost Omladine, Zagreb, 1972.

The Changing Party Elite in East Germany, Peter C. Ludz, The M.I.T. Press, 1972.

Jewish Nationality and Soviet Politics, Zvi Gitelman, Princeton University Press, 1972.

Mao Tse-tung and Gandhi, Jayantanuja Bandyopadhyaya, Allied Publisher, 1973.

The U.S.S.R. and the Arabs, the Ideological Dimension, Jaan Pennar, Crane, Russak, and Co. (New York) and Christopher Hurst (London), 1973.

Moskau und die Neue Linke, Klaus Mehnert, Deutsche Verlags-Anstalt, 1973.

Bukharin and the Bolshevik Revolution: A Political Biography, 1888–1938, Stephen F. Cohen, A. Knopf, 1973.

The Soviet Volunteers: Modernization and Bureaucracy in a Public Mass Organization, William E. Odom, Princeton University Press, 1973.